Before the West

How would the history of international relations in 'the East' be written if we did not always read the ending – the rise of the West and the decline of the East – into the past? What if we did not assume that Asia was just a residual category, a variant of 'not-Europe', but saw it as a space with its own particular history and sociopolitical dynamics, not defined only by encounters with European colonialism? How would our understanding of sovereignty, as well as our theories about the causes of the decline of Great Powers and international orders, change as a result? For the first time, *Before the West* offers a grand narrative of (Eur)Asia as a space connected by normatively and institutionally overlapping successive world orders originating from the Mongol Empire. It also uses that history to rethink the foundational concepts of international relations, such as order and decline.

AYŞE ZARAKOL is Professor of International Relations at the University of Cambridge and a Fellow at Emmanuel College. She is the author of *After Defeat: How the East Learned to Live with the West* (Cambridge University Press, 2011) and the editor of the prize-winning *Hierarchies in World Politics* (Cambridge University Press, 2017).

LSE INTERNATIONAL STUDIES

SERIES EDITORS

George Lawson (Lead Editor)
Department of International Relations, London School of Economics

Kirsten Ainley
Department of International Relations, London School of Economics

Ayça Çubukçu
Department of Sociology, London School of Economics

Stephen Humphreys
Department of Law, London School of Economics

This series, published in association with the Centre for International Studies at the London School of Economics, is centred on three main themes. First, the series is oriented around work that is transdisciplinary, which challenges disciplinary conventions and develops arguments that cannot be grasped within existing disciplines. It will include work combining a wide range of fields, including international relations, international law, political theory, history, sociology and ethics. Second, it comprises books that contain an overtly international or transnational dimension, but not necessarily focused simply within the discipline of International Relations. Finally, the series will publish books that use scholarly inquiry as a means of addressing pressing political concerns. Books in the series may be predominantly theoretical, or predominantly empirical, but all will say something of significance about political issues that exceed national boundaries.

Previous books in the series:

Culture and Order in World Politics Andrew Phillips and Christian Reus-Smit (eds.)

On Cultural Diversity: International Theory in a World of Difference Christian Reus-Smit

Before the West

The Rise and Fall of Eastern World Orders

AYŞE ZARAKOL
University of Cambridge

CAMBRIDGE
UNIVERSITY PRESS

CAMBRIDGE
UNIVERSITY PRESS

University Printing House, Cambridge CB2 8BS, United Kingdom

One Liberty Plaza, 20th Floor, New York, NY 10006, USA

477 Williamstown Road, Port Melbourne, VIC 3207, Australia

314–321, 3rd Floor, Plot 3, Splendor Forum, Jasola District Centre, New Delhi – 110025, India

103 Penang Road, #05–06/07, Visioncrest Commercial, Singapore 238467

Cambridge University Press is part of the University of Cambridge.

It furthers the University's mission by disseminating knowledge in the pursuit of education, learning, and research at the highest international levels of excellence.

www.cambridge.org
Information on this title: www.cambridge.org/9781108838603
DOI: 10.1017/9781108975377

© Ayşe Zarakol 2022

First published 2022

A catalogue record for this publication is available from the British Library.

ISBN 978-1-108-83860-3 Hardback
ISBN 978-1-108-97167-6 Paperback

A Cihannüma
dedicated to the memory of my father,
Cihan Zarakol (1949–2016),
who taught me to love history as if it were a puzzle.

Contents

List of Figures and Maps   *page* viii

Acknowledgements   ix

1 What Is the East?
  Theorising Sovereignty and World Orders in Asia and Eurasia   1

  Part I   Cihannüma   45

2 Making the East: Chinggisid World Orders
  The Empire of Genghis Khan and Its Successor Khanates
  (Thirteenth–Fourteenth Centuries)   47
3 Dividing the East: Post-Chinggisid World Orders
  The Timurid and the Ming (Fourteenth–Fifteenth Centuries)   89
4 Expanding the East: Post-Timurid World Orders
  The Ottomans, the Safavids and the Mughals
  (Fifteenth–Sixteenth Centuries)   124
5 How the East Made the World: Eurasia and Beyond
  Chinggisid Influences on a Globalising World
  (Sixteenth Century)   173

  Part II   Lessons of History   215

6 Rise and Fall of Eastern World Orders
  Lessons for International Relations   217
7 Uses and Abuses of Macro History in International Relations
  Am I a 'Eurasianist'?   244

Bibliography   273
Index   302

Figures and Maps

Figures

2.1 The house and empire of Genghis Khan   *page 65*
3.1 Post-Chinggisid Great Houses   105
4.1 Post-Timurid Great Houses (*Sahibkıran*)   138
5.1 A Eurasian world   207

Maps

0.1 The world empire of Genghis Khan   xiii
0.2 The Timurids and the Ming Dynasty   xiv
0.3 Post-Timurid world order   xv

Acknowledgements

Any book, especially one so long in the making, is a product of the generosity of friends and family towards the author. This is compounded in my case by the fact that I wrote this book during a particularly difficult time, partly due to reasons specific to my personal situation and partly due to the state of the world. I owe a lot of gratitude to a lot of people, many even beyond those I am able to list here by name.

Initially I had set out to write a more straightforward book challenging the conceptions of 'rising powers' operating in International Relations (IR).[1] The sudden passing of my father in 2016 made me rethink the project. My father was a lifelong (amateur) student of history. My best childhood memories involve traipsing around half-excavated archaeological sites around Turkey with him. I decided to try to write something a bit more durable in my father's memory. I was doing some research at the time for other projects around the concept of sovereignty in Islam, as well as the early modern period of the Ottoman Empire, and those readings led me to think bigger about the problem of 'rise and decline' by digging deeper into history and exploring the legacy of the Chinggisids in world politics.

A number of encounters at this early stage gave me the courage to continue down this path. At the ISA panel where I first presented my initial notions for this project, both Bob Denemark and Victoria Tinbor Hui told me I had a good idea that I should keep pursuing. Julia Costa Lopez and Benjamin de Carvalho organised some 'early sovereignty'[2] panels where I first played with some of the ideas here, and I was encouraged by the feedback from other participants,

---

[1] This research eventually led to Zarakol (2019).
[2] This eventually became Zarakol (2018a), a part of a broader forum in *International Studies Review*.

especially Iver Neumann. I met James Millward at a workshop, and his reading suggestions made the project immediately more doable. I am also grateful to Christian Reus-Smit and Andrew Phillips for both facilitating that workshop and commissioning some of my early research into the Ottomans[3] from which I got some great research ideas. Andrew also shared his own research with me. Similarly, I am thankful to Einar Wigen for sharing his work. Aslı Niyazioğlu also gave me helpful reading suggestions about *sahibkıran* and the Ottoman–Safavid–Mughal connections. Deniz Türker gave me some excellent reading suggestions about Timurid influences on art history. I emailed David Sneath, a world-leading expert on the Mongols and the anthropology of Inner Asia, to express my admiration for *The Headless State*, and he not only kindly met me but spent hours of his time discussing the Mongols and giving me suggestions.

I am of course very privileged to be at an institution like Cambridge, where I can read a best-in-its-field book like David's one week and then meet up with the author the next. That privilege extends also to my own department, POLIS. It is no small luxury to feel that one's research is understood and appreciated. I am grateful to my colleagues with whom I co-convene the IR & History Working Group: Jason Sharman, Duncan Bell and Giovanni Mantilla. During the course of writing this book, I was also lucky to supervise a great group of PhD students from whom I learned a lot (they know who they are!). I cannot thank everyone in POLIS by name, but let me also mention Devon Curtis (for making my college tasks easier), Adam Branch (for making our shared introductory IR course work so well), Brendan Simms (for involving me in discussions I would not get to otherwise), Chris Bickerton (for teaching me how to box and thus keeping me sane) and Mette Elstrup-Sangiovanni (for getting me involved in rowing, which really helped with getting over the lockdown malaise). Yi Ning Chang contributed as an undergraduate research assistant. I also want to take this opportunity to remember my colleague Aaron Rapport and his wife Joyce Heckman. They were both lost to cancer at a very young age in the summer of 2019. I think of both of them often; Joyce and Aaron's cats, Ollie and Dixie, have kept me company during writing, along with my Çörek (2000–19) and Fırça.

---

[3] Zarakol (2020a), in Phillips and Reus-Smit (2020).

Beyond POLIS, I am grateful to the historical IR community in the United Kingdom and beyond for giving my work a home. Colleagues at the LSE immediately welcomed me into their history-theory network upon my arrival in the United Kingdom in 2013. George Lawson, whose judgement I trust implicitly, has enthusiastically supported this book from the very beginning. Tarak Barkawi, Martin Bayly, Barry Buzan, Or Rosenboim, Edward Keene, James Morrison and John M. Hobson have given me helpful suggestions at different stages of the project. I am also happy to be involved in the larger Nordic research community. I would like to especially thank Halvard Leira, Benjamin de Carvalho, Ole Jacob Sending, Jens Bartelson and Rebecca Adler-Nissen, both for their friendship and for making possible, through various grants, lots of great things. Rebecca involved me in her ERC-funded project DIPLOFACE, allowing me to buy myself out from teaching for two terms. And of course, there is an even wider community of IR scholars that I feel lucky to belong to. This book has directly or indirectly benefitted from my conversations with Zeynep Gülşah Çapan, Jelena Subotic, Brent Steele, Manjeet Pardesi, Dan Nexon, David Lake, Lerna Yanık, Frederic Merand, Srdjan Vucetic, Julian Go, Hendrik Spruyt, David Kang, Ian Hurd, Maj Grasten, Jon Askonas, Stacie Goddard and Ron Krebs. I am also grateful for many other friendships in my academic community.

I presented drafts in a number of great settings. The first time was in-person at Ohio State University in early 2020, thanks to the generous invitation of Bear Braumoller, putting me on the correct course for finishing up during a pandemic. I presented a version at the LSE in March 2020 and was very encouraged by the reception there. Later drafts were presented during the course of the pandemic (usually over Zoom) at the University of Kent, the University of Chicago, the University of Oxford, the University of Queensland, the European University Institute, McGill University, the University of San Francisco, Johns Hopkins University and the University of Cambridge Central Asia Forum. I have received amazingly useful questions and feedback in all of these sessions and would like to thank the audience members. I am also grateful to the convenors of these seminars for facilitating these conversations: Karen Smith, Philip Cunliffe, Austin Carson, Duncan Snidal, Andrew Payne, Seb Kaempf, Marius Ghincea, Juliet Johnson, Nora Fisher Onar, Sebastian Schmidt and Prajakti Kalra.

I am also blown away by everyone who read and provided comments on the finished manuscript (during a global pandemic!), starting with my former PhD advisor, Michael Barnett, whose support and kindness I very much rely on still, and continuing with George Lawson, Jason Sharman, David Sneath, Aslı Niyazıoğlu, Manjeet Pardesi, Jaakko Heiskanen, Lucas de Oliviera Paes, George Gavrilis and Iver Neumann. I am more grateful than I can express for all of their suggestions. Any remaining errors are my own entirely. I am also in debt to the two anonymous reviewers at Cambridge University Press for their very helpful feedback. I am also grateful to my indexer, David Prout, and my copy editor, Wade Guyitt, for their thoughtful handling of my manuscript. I would also like to thank John Haslam: since my first book, it has been an absolute pleasure to have John as my editor at Cambridge University Press.

Finally, I would like to acknowledge a few of my non-academic friends and family members. First, I am thankful to Ed Richens, for keeping me on track during the pandemic with strength training and tolerating my research-related chatter during workouts. Heather Webb and Pierpaolo Antonello, together with Catherine and Mike Vilhauer, make us feel at home as a family in Cambridge. I am also thankful to my gang in Istanbul, who have put up with me for all these decades. Liz Amado, Pelin Arıner, İrem Çavuşoğlu, Irazca Geray, Elif Özerman, Ayşe Özler, Arzu Soysal and Aylin Ülçer: without them my life would be much more boring. Our WhatsApp chat 'Bu Cumartesi' kept me going during lockdown. Petek Salman also deserves a mention here. My aunt, Nurcan Akad, helps me worry less about what is happening back home. Aras Zarakol has been a devoted uncle to my son. And of course none of this would be possible without the support and the understanding of my husband, Dmitri Jajich, and my son, Kaya Zarakol Jajich, who – at eleven – is already an incisive interlocutor. Last but not least, my mother, Necla Zarakol, continues to inspire with her resilience: far from retiring at seventy-two, she works harder at her job than anyone. Not even being randomly jailed for five days in 2019 by what has essentially become a mafia state has broken her spirit. I admire her more than anyone I know.

Maps

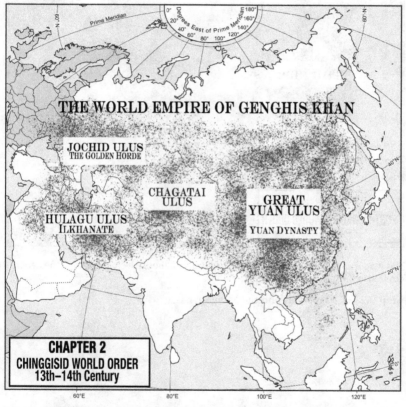

This map is an approximation of the furthest reach of these sovereigns during the period covered in the relevant chapter.

Map 0.1 The world empire of Genghis Khan

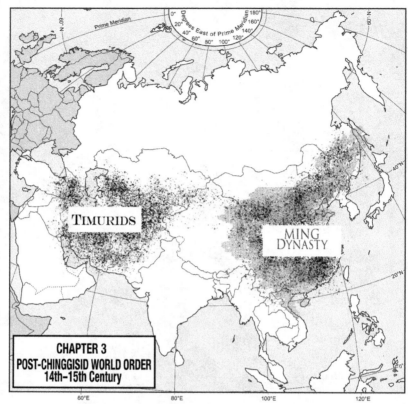

This map is an approximation of the furthest reach of these sovereigns during the period covered in the relevant chapter.

Map 0.2 The Timurids and the Ming Dynasty

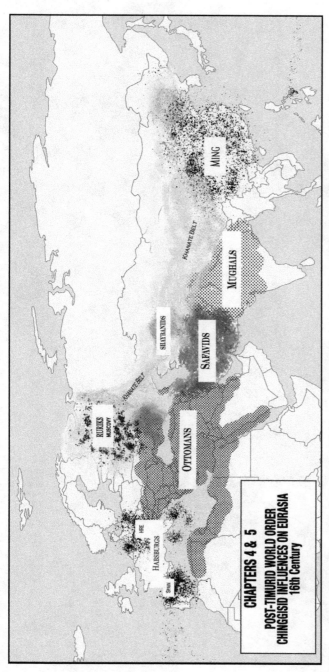

This map is an approximation of the furthest reach of these sovereigns during the period covered in the relevant chapter.

Map 0.3 Post-Timurid world order

1 | *What Is the East?*

Theorising Sovereignty and World Orders in Asia and Eurasia

Introduction

Imagine you are in one of those situations often depicted in fantasy novels where you discover a portal that will take you to another parallel universe. You step through to find a world that is in many ways very much like ours. Most of the superficial details are the same: there are roads, houses and bicycles. The technology is familiar. The sun, the clouds, the trees, they all look the same. Yet something feels different. To figure out what, you step into a bookstore and pick up a general history book to understand this world better (your old phone does not work in this universe, though you see other people using theirs). You order a bubble tea and settle in the bookstore's café. Soon you make a startling discovery. In this universe, it was not England that was the first site of the Industrial Revolution in the eighteenth century but Japan! [1] What is more, in this universe, the Third Estate Rebellion had gone nowhere in France, but the Chinese Revolution of 1794 had succeeded, fundamentally transforming the Chinese state in directions (republican, vegetarian, anti-tax) later emulated by other states in Asia and the rest of the world. To make a long story short, in this world, it had been Asia that experienced the radical lift-off in the nineteenth century that we associate in our universe with 'the West'. It is 'the East' that is considered to be the centre of gravity in this parallel universe, not Europe or the West.

You run back to the history section to understand what caused this difference. You find a lot of books dealing with 'The Rise of the East', complete with some critical authors even questioning whether the Industrial Revolution was just a historical accident that could have happened in other places – for example, England. Most others maintain, however, that it was the specific qualities of Eastern culture, going

---

[1] See Collins (1997); Goldstone (2000, 2002, 2015).

back centuries if not millennia, that had made these breakthroughs to modernity possible, so it is unthinkable for these developments to have happened in the West. Europe lags behind because it just does not have those qualities, they suggest, but it can still learn from 'the East'. Hopefully, most academic books allow, one day European countries will also catch up. Some say these days they are getting close. You do notice, however, that there are also some more disturbing books in the popular non-fiction section, books that raise disturbing questions about the innate abilities of whites or the suitability of Christian cultures for technological innovation.

What is especially odd about these debates, you observe with alarm, is that the historical facts they are working with up until that fateful turn in the eighteenth century are not that different. In terms of major events, their history looks more or less the same as ours until the mid-1700s. Yet scholars in this parallel universe have woven a completely different narrative around the same basic facts, using them to explain instead why it was Asia that was destined to rise and Europe that was to lag behind. Historically, Europe has always been politically fragmented and religiously intolerant, these books argue. European cultures have always exaggerated small cultural and religious differences to the level of major conflict and then fought for decades, if not centuries. It did not occur to European rulers to maintain standing armies until much later than the rest of the world, so each war was long and costly to fight, depriving regular people of basic sustenance, which is why there had been little in the way of political development in this region until Asian models were imported into the area. Yes, the continent was once unified as the site of a great empire – Rome – but most people think it has stagnated ever since, for more than a millennium, unfortunately.

Less Asiacentric scholars in this parallel universe allow that Europe has had its moments since Rome: there were historical periods in which it even produced great works of art and architecture. The fifteenth century was such a glorious moment of Greco-Roman revival in the south. But even such scholars have to note that, sadly, these bursts of innovation and individualism in Europe were dead ends until Asian models were imported into the region in the nineteenth century. In any case, most of these great works of European art have been destroyed in conflict, the books note, especially, in the twentieth century, by radical Christianist terrorist groups whose ideologies yearn for the so-called golden age of Christianity, the period which came after the fall of

Rome. The historical fabric of most European cities has also been destroyed due to unplanned urbanisation induced by the rapid industrialisation of European countries in the twentieth century, which was undertaken in an effort to catch up with Asia. Most European cities are now overcrowded, overbuilt and ugly. Venice, a one-time centre of attraction for travellers from around the world even in this universe, was cemented over some decades ago for the construction of a large shipping port, you find out. Even though some scholars here do suggest that the Greco-Roman revival in the Italian peninsula was equal in creativity to the Timurid Renaissance in western Asia, very few people in this universe seem to have studied or written about Florence, compared, say, to Samarkand. The titles of some recent books do suggest, however, that critiques of Asiacentrism may have opened up some space in the departments of history for that sort of thing, just as parallel critiques of Eurocentrism did in our universe.

Further perusing the 'Rise of the East' bookshelf, you notice that these books do not all agree as to when Asia took off. Some date Asian greatness back to the twelfth and thirteenth centuries. These books argue that the Empire of Genghis Khan[2] essentially seeded the entire continent for its eventual take-off by facilitating the exchange of ideas, know-how and skills across the continent. Other books, found under the heading of 'International Relations', date the emergence of the modern order back to the thirteenth century, to *Pax Mongolica*. These books underline how unusual it was for the Mongol khanates, which did not share the same religion, to exist relatively peacefully side-by-side in the fourteenth century. This was the beginning of modern international relations, they argue, when rational state interest trumped religious affiliation. Yet others point to the aforementioned Timurid Renaissance[3] in the fifteenth century as the real turning point for Asia, a period when not only Asian art flourished via new leaps of

---

[2] Even in our universe there are those who argue that the Mongol Empire made the modern world. See, for example, Weatherford (2004).

[3] There was a 'Timurid Renaissance' in our universe as well, but, apart from art historians who study it, most are unaware of this period between the end of the fourteenth and beginning of the sixteenth centuries. Some historians object to calling this period a 'renaissance' because in our universe it seems a dead end, unlike the Italian counterpart. I submit that an actual person living in the fifteenth century, if somehow given the opportunity to compare the art and science of the two, would not necessarily rank them in the way we would. For more, see, for example, Lentz and Lowry (1989). See also Chapter 4. Of course sophisticated

creativity but also astronomy and mathematical sciences, setting the stage for Asian innovations centuries later. Some scholars, however, are sceptical that sources of Asian take-off can be dated so far back. They suggest that the strong centralised states built throughout Eurasia in the sixteenth century were the real engine of Asian development. Some of these books suggest that the foundations of the modern international order were forged in the sixteenth- and seventeenth-century peace treaties between western Asian states such as the Ottomans and the Safavid, and even label the modern international order 'Zuhabian'.[4] Yet others are sceptical that this is the point of divergence, pointing out that Europe was also building relatively strong centralised states around the same time. This group of scholars are in favour of dating the divergence of the Asian and European paths to a later period, for example in the eighteenth- and nineteenth-century developments of Asian industrialisation and subsequent global military expansion.

Now let us step back through the portal, back to our universe, where, as you know, history went another way entirely. Our modern international order, which emerged in the nineteenth century,[5] has been made possible by 'the Rise of the West', and it is Europe/the West that has occupied its core seat of privilege for the last two centuries. Not only has this fact continuously shaped our politics in the present, but it has distorted our understanding of world political history and thus also our *theories* about international politics. Many have invariably read the conclusion of the story into that history. This is why I suggested that thought exercise: I want you, as the reader, to consider how the same historical facts could look very different if filtered through the lens of a different ending to the story. This does not mean the 'facts' of history are meaningless or subject to infinite interpretation but rather that the same 'facts' take on different meanings depending on the eventual outcome. Imagine you are wearing a red suit to a job interview. Your day goes well, you get the job: the red suit becomes part of your success story, something that made you stand out. Or your day goes badly, you do not get the job: the same red suit becomes part of the

---

cultural activity in Central Asia goes back even further; see, for example, Starr (2013).

[4] After the Treaty of Zuhab (or Kasr-ı Şirin) in 1639, which affirmed the Peace of Amasya of 1555.

[5] See, for example, Buzan and Lawson (2015).

narrative as to why you failed, something that made you stick out like a sore thumb. In both scenarios, you are wearing the red suit, but the story around it changes depending on how your day ends, though it is not even clear if the suit had any causal impact whatsoever. We are all susceptible to this kind of attribution error. This is why it is a good idea to approach even well-established historical narratives of causality with a degree of scepticism.

The Need for a New History of 'The East' in International Relations?

This book explores how the history of international relations in Asia and Eurasia could be written if we did not read into that history its eventual conclusion: that is, 'the Rise of the West' and 'the Decline of the East'.[6] What if we were in the parallel universe I posited earlier, where it was Asia or Eurasia or 'the East'[7] that was the desirable 'brand' in world politics rather than Europe or the West? What if liminal countries[8] such as Russia or Turkey emphasised their historical connections to Asia or the East rather than to Europe or the West? What if China was more interested in a grander narrative of Asia, instead of a Sinocentric view of East Asian regional order(s)? What if we did not read back into (Eur)Asian history the inevitable stench of 'failure' of the nineteenth century, and what if we did not assume that

---

[6] See also Phillips (2021); Sharman (2019); Spruyt (2020).

[7] Unfortunately, the terms 'Asia', 'Eurasia' and 'the East' are themselves are problematic and Eurocentric, but this cannot be avoided. The concept of 'Asia' was introduced to 'Asia' in the seventeenth century, for example *yaxiya* in the Chinese context, as brought in by Jesuit missionaries. The concept did not become widely used there until the nineteenth century. See Korhonen (1997, 2001, 2008, 2014 and so forth). The term 'Eurasia' has its own political baggage, some of which I discuss in the Epilogue. For a discussion on 'the East' as a stigmatising label, see Zarakol (2011). In the parallel universe where 'East Asia' took off, we might not be using these concepts at all but some other ones. The labels used throughout this book should be taken with these caveats and should be understood more as geographic terms used for mutual intelligibility, even when I refrain from using scare quotes. And of course had 'Asia' come to dominate globally instead of Europe, our periodisation of history would be different as well, but these are objections I will have to bracket off for this project. For more about periodisation biases, see Davis (2008); Goldstone (1998).

[8] By liminal countries I mean those who are caught in between the East and the West (though there is a plausible argument to be made that this description applies to all countries in Eurasia). For more on this, see Zarakol (2011).

Asia was just a residual category, a variant of 'not-Europe', but rather saw it as a space with its own history and sociopolitical dynamics, not defined or constructed entirely by encounters with European colonialism? What would that history look like? That is the history I aim to recover in this book, starting in the thirteenth century with the creation of the Empire of Genghis Khan and ending soon after 'the General Crisis' of the seventeenth century,[9] before European take-off.

Before the West thus provides what we do not yet have: an account of the history of Eastern 'international relations'[10] that understands actors of the past in that part of the world primarily through their relations with each other and not with Europe.[11] Though the recent turn towards global IR has raised the field's interest in the history of international relations outside of Europe, even this turn has its blind spots. As long these persist, our theorising about both the past *and* the future will suffer. Let me underline three such blind spots that the historical account in this book addresses directly.

First, in IR accounts, actors and states outside of the West are almost always only compared to the West (and rarely to each other).[12] The case for the importance of the East in world politics is often made by showing how Asian or Eurasian[13] actors were contributors to

---

[9] See, for example, Parker (2013); Parker and Smith (1997); see also Goldstone (1991). Not every region discussed in this book experienced this crisis evenly. More on this in Chapter 5.

[10] See also Brook, van Praag and Boltjes (2018), which has similar aims, but as an edited book it cannot offer a fully integrated account.

[11] The account offered here inevitably leaves many things out. For instance, its geographic focus is limited: there is not much Africa or America in it, and it also mostly leaves out south-eastern Asia and the Pacific. Because it is interested in actors with universal empire claims, it cannot cover other types of actors or political arrangements such as mercantile guild cities. Thus, it is not a exhaustive history but an alternative or supplemental one to that already existing in IR. I hope others will fill in the blanks in other ways. See also Brook, van Praag, and Boltjes (2018).

[12] See, for example, otherwise excellent books such as Phillips and Sharman (2015); Hui (2005); Park (2017). Spruyt (2020) is the exception in that it compares Sinocentric, Islamic and South East Asian political orders. This problem is not specific to IR. For example, in attempting to learn about land-grant systems across Asia, I could not find any comprehensive source that compared different Asian polities with each other, but comparisons of each arrangement with European feudalism do exist.

[13] The term 'Eurasia' essentially separates northern Asia from our imagination (as the word Middle East does for south-west Asia). In the following pages, whenever I say 'Asia' alone, it should be understood to refer to the whole

European take-off.[14] While we desperately need such accounts to underline that European development was not endogenous, they do not necessarily give us a full picture of Asian politics in history as it would have been experienced and understood by the actors of the time. To put it another way, 'how the East contributed to Western development' narratives make Asia only a supporting player in the story of the West. We also need historical accounts where the East is the *protagonist* in its own narrative. The account in this book does not assume that Asian actors' interactions with Europeans must have been the most important ones for them just because (western) Europe would eventually come to dominate the globe in the nineteenth century. Historical actors could not see into the future. They would have evaluated their interactions based on the information available to them at the time, as well their own understandings of their history which framed their world view in various ways. However, we also need to avoid the projection of modern national(ist) myths back onto the past. Though some narrative bias in favour of threads that lead to the present day is inevitable, the reader should not assume any kind of equivalence or intrinsic continuity between present-day actors and historical counterparts who bear similar names and/or have been claimed by modern nationalist histories.[15]

Second, in IR, non-Western states and peoples are frequently understood as without *international* politics or an interest in the world at large until Europeans brought them into a global order in the nineteenth century: that is, they are understood to be local actors only. It is true that in recent years, the rise of China (and 'the Rest'), as well as the growing criticism about the Eurocentrism of traditional IR theories, has increased interest in studying the history of other parts of the world from an IR perspective, especially that of East Asia. Welcome as such efforts may be, most of them also still suffer from the assumption that

---

continent. Every now and then I will say 'Asia and Eurasia' to remind the reader that I am talking about both, because I realise that present-day usage reserves Asia for East Asia alone (and sometimes the 'subcontinent').

[14] Again see, for example, otherwise excellent books such as Anievas and Nisancioglu (2015); Hobson (2004).

[15] This is not to say there is no continuity. The modern 'nation' should be thought of as a pool to which hundreds of streams have contributed; the modern nationalist project picks one of these around which to emphasise historical continuity and erases all the others. By doing so it corrupts our understanding not only of the present but also the past.

all non-European orders were only *regional* not only in practice but also in aspiration.[16] Furthermore, in studying non-European orders as regional we tend to impose on to the past today's regional divisions[17] and sometimes also today's national historiographies and myths.

The way we have introduced Chinese historical international relations into IR theorising is illustrative in this regard.[18] Studies often seem to take at face value[19] the modern idea of 'China' as 'a unique unitary cultural-political entity that, though ruled by an "emperor" (*huangdi* 皇帝), was never "imperialist"'.[20] But this only works if we accept the Chinese practice of 'writing prior (often inimical) states into the history of the current one'.[21] Moreover, the concepts we use to understand Chinese regional international relations historically are modern constructs themselves, as introduced first by European Sinologists.[22] As Milward observes, it was John King Fairbank who articulated the view of the 'historical East Asian world order that had endured from ancient times until the nineteenth century'.[23] It is from this account that we get the usual description of Chinese world view: 'The world, also known as tianxia 天下 (all under Heaven), was Sinocentric. Chinese civilization was superior to non-Chinese (barbarian) culture, its centrality validated by Confucian belief.'[24] It is also from Fairbank that we get the description of 'the tributary system': 'Chinese emperors imagined themselves sovereigns over the whole world (*tianxia*) and required foreign emissaries to acknowledge this fact. Outlying states had to express fealty to the Chinese emperor through a court visit, a kowtow and presentation of symbolic local

---

[16] Much of the recent literature on historical orders in Asia, whether English School or not, also assumes this region-ness. For exceptions see Kang (2003, 2010); Spruyt (2020) (but even these books do not deviate too far from regions as understood in our day). Focusing on the historical precursors of present-day regional dynamics is of course helpful in some ways, but this also downplays the 'international' ambitions of Eastern actors and the extent to which Asia has been interconnected through time. Pardesi (2019) makes a similar critique.

[17] Modern notions of what constitutes a 'region' can usually be traced back to nineteenth-century developments and categories.

[18] See, for example, Zhang and Buzan (2012); Buzan and Zhang (2014).

[19] Hui (2005, 2020) avoids many of these traps.   [20] Millward (2020, p. 72).

[21] Ibid.

[22] This is not to say they are completely wrong, but they need further historical scrutiny, especially if they are being presented as the antidote to the Eurocentrism of the discipline.

[23] Ibid., p. 74.   [24] Ibid.

goods (*gong* 貢 or tribute). In return, they were allowed to trade with China.'[25] It was only after losing the Opium Wars that China is supposed to have realised the reality of the larger world and gave up its traditional Sinocentric beliefs.[26] Gradually, Fairbanks' conceptual schematic emerged as *the* history of China: 'Sinocentric China, *tianxia*, the tributary system, Sinicization and the eternal nature of China as a continuous civilization-state became received wisdom; the claim that a benevolent China presided for centuries over a uniquely peaceful East Asian world order was ritually repeated without much thought and little evidence.'[27] This questionable description has now made its way into IR and foreign policy discussions. It does not receive much push-back from China, either, in that it offers a Sinocentric conception of East Asian history which can also come in handy to justify the present-day foreign policy choices of the PRC such as the 'Belt and Road Initiative'.[28]

As we will also see in Chapter 3, the reality of the 'tributary system' was much more complicated. Gifts coded as tribute by the 'Chinese'[29] court did not necessarily come from parties that considered *themselves* a part of a tributary system or shared a Sinocentric world view. More importantly, there has not been one eternal, unchanging 'Chinese' world view. Nobody would get away with claiming such a thing about Europe, so why should any other part of the world be any different? What was considered 'the world' by 'Chinese' rulers underwent profound changes during the Yuan Dynasty (Mongol rule), expanding well beyond what we call 'East Asia' today, and the subsequent Ming understanding very much reflected that expansion, especially in the early decades of the dynasty. In other words, there have been historical periods where dynasties ruling the area we now call China have been well aware of a world beyond the Sinocentric understandings of China and East Asia; they were not introduced

---

[25] Ibid., p. 75.   [26] Ibid.

[27] Ibid., p. 76. A similar reification happened to the concept of a 'millet system' in the Ottoman Empire. See Zarakol (2020b).

[28] Ibid. See also Benabdallah (2020).

[29] Even the term 'Chinese' is rather anachronistic when mapped back onto the historical periods under consideration here. To avoid this problem, I refer to specific dynasties instead of ethnicities or country names where possible in the book, but here I am deferring to lay usage.

to a broader world by Europeans for the first time in the nine-teenth century.[30]

This brings me to the bigger issue of describing all non-Western international orders as 'regional'. The implicit assumption in much of the IR literature is that only European states had the imagination of having 'international relations' beyond their region and creating 'inter-national orders' of a global scale.[31] In a sense this is true by definition because it was the Europeans who 'discovered' the Americas, and any order before the 'discovery' of the Americas was literally not global. Nations in the sense we understand them also did not exist until at least the eighteenth century, so it is misleading to speak of 'inter*national* relations' or 'inter*national* orders' before then as well (not that this stops anyone from speaking about Europe using these terms). Yet if we abstract from 'international relations' to inter-polity relations and think about 'international orders' as universalising *world* ordering arrangements, then we can be more open-minded about what sorts of 'world orders' have existed outside of Europe. This book will show that there were also Eastern actors who had aspirations – for better or worse – to create orders that spanned the world in all its multiplicity. When they thought about the world, they were not thinking just in terms of their immediate neighbourhood (however, that was under-stood) or just in terms of their co-religionists. Such actors did in fact exist in Asia/Eurasia,[32] and, as we shall see, not only did they aspire to universal sovereignty but they also came close to dominating (and thus ordering) the world – such as it existed – from the thirteenth to the seventeenth centuries. Neither the dreams nor the sins of universal world order and empire projects can be attributed solely to Western or European actors.

Third, the problem in the IR literature runs even deeper than just assuming that only Europeans created international orders and every-one else was content to sit in their regional, cultural or religious silos. Even the emergence of 'sovereignty' is considered by many to be

---

[30] See Cheng (2020), who extends this critique to the pre-Mongol period.

[31] Bull (1977) argues this explicitly. See also Bull and Watson (1984). However, there is also a long-standing acknowledgement in the English School literature that regional international orders have existed outside of Europe. See, for example, Wight (1977); Buzan and Little (2000).

[32] Perhaps elsewhere, too. By making the argument about Asia exclusively I am not implying an absence of such ambitions in other locales. See also Eaton (1993).

a solely European development. Notwithstanding an onslaught of recent criticism,[33] many IR textbooks still date both the emergence of state sovereignty and of an 'international system' to the Westphalian Peace (1648). The assumptions about where and when state sovereignty and international order emerged tend to go hand in hand, because you presumably cannot have one without the other: 'Without sovereign states being present in some guise, there can be no modern international system, and hence no meaningful study of international relations.'[34] This leads many to conclude also that sovereignty is an alien concept outside of the West and that the modern state was imported wholesale around the world via European colonialism.[35] John Hobson calls this 'the *Eurocentric big bang theory* of world politics' (emphasis in original).[36] Most explanations of sovereignty in IR assume that 'the big bang of modernity explodes within Europe in 1648, having previously unfolded through an evolutionary process that is entirely endogenous to Europe, before the sovereign state is exported to the East through imperialism and proto-globalization'.[37] The big bang theory also demarcates the East from the West, relegating it 'to a backward ghetto that endures only regressive and barbaric institutions',[38] condemned to follow in the West's shadow, while the West is inscribed with all the progressive properties.[39] Yet, as I have also argued elsewhere,[40] most European developments associated with the development of modern state sovereignty are not unique to Europe and

[33] The majority of attacks have come from scholars who disagree that anything resembling the modern sovereign state emerged from the Treaty of Westphalia. The overwhelming majority date modern sovereignty to a much later period, arguing that territoriality in the modern sense did not exist before the nineteenth century; nor did the principle of external recognition. See, for example, Reus-Smit (1999); Beualac (2000); Osiander (2001); Krasner (2001); Branch (2011); Bartelson (2018); Buzan and Lawson 2015; see also Elden (2013); Benton (2009); Croxton (1999); Kayaoğlu (2010). A related line of criticism sees the Westphalian discourse as a project of nineteenth century. See, for example, Osiander (2001); Kayaoğlu (2010); Schmidt (2011); Zarakol (2017a). What unites both the old and new origin stories, however, is their rootedness in the (western) European historical experience exclusively.
[34] Bartelson (2018, p. 510). See also Krasner (1996, p. 121).
[35] Sometimes this is assumed in a self-congratulatory way, for example in some early English School accounts. These days, however, one is more likely to encounter these claims in the more critical veins of IR literature, in postcolonial or decolonial scholarship.
[36] Hobson (2012a, p. 32); see also Hobson (2012b, 2009). [37] Ibid.
[38] Ibid., p. 33. [39] Ibid. [40] Zarakol (2021).

have their corollaries elsewhere, certainly in Asia. Put simply, Asia has its own sovereignty tradition(s) and associated world ordering projects, a repertoire of practices and ideas which first influenced and later was influenced by the European trajectory, one that deserves to be studied in its own right.[41] Let's then start with sovereignty models and work our way back to Eastern world orders.

Theorising and Comparing Sovereignty Models

Most IR definitions of sovereignty can be reduced to the components of 'supreme authority' and 'territory'.[42] For example, Krasner defines 'the Westphalian state' as 'a system of political authority based on territory and autonomy';[43] elsewhere he distinguishes between 'interdependence sovereignty ... [i.e.] the ability of states to control movement across their borders';[44] 'domestic sovereignty' which denotes the extent to which political authority can 'effectively regulate behaviour'[45]; 'Vattelian sovereignty ... [i.e.] the exclusion of external sources of authority both *de juri* and *de facto*'[46] and 'International legal sovereignty [which] refers to mutual recognition'.[47] Yet given enough degrees of abstraction, these are just different ways of answering the question 'Is there an exclusive political authority within a (unified) territory?'.

When we think about modern state sovereignty, we look for the presence of two factors at a minimum: (1) *the centralisation of political authority* – that is, the elimination of rival authority claims, external and internal, to the point that it has become both supreme and exclusive; and (2) *territoriality* – that is, the expectation that political authority is claimed over a unified and bounded territory (as opposed to people or specific symbolic sites, etc.). We could add that discussions of modern state sovereignty usually assume external recognition (3) – that is, that facts of (1) and (2) are also acknowledged by the representatives of other similarly formed entities. Our current international order is characterised by the mutual recognition of sovereign states. Once broken down into these three components, it becomes possible to trace and contrast alternative models of sovereignty in different time

---

[41] On this point, see also Neumann and Wigen (2018).   [42] Bartelson (2018).
[43] Krasner (1996, p. 115).   [44] Krasner (2001, p. 19).   [45] Ibid., p. 20.
[46] Ibid.   [47] Ibid., p. 21.

periods and geographies.[48] But before we turn to the historical discussion, let's take a moment to analyse how each feature could vary in different settings.

Sovereignty as Centralisation of (Supreme) Political Authority

The centralisation of political authority that we take for granted in the modern state sovereignty model is not a given, historically speaking. There are many periods and societies in which authority was in fact divided in a myriad number of ways; a very common pattern is to see authority divided between political versus religious actors (and institutions), with neither having supremacy. Soldiers, nobility or even companies[49] could be autonomous centres of authority, presenting alternative sources of power to political rulers. Most readers will be aware that medieval Europe was a setting of divided sovereignty, with kings, aristocrats and the church all claiming authority over regular people (and in fact often the same people). This is indeed one of the reasons IR has not shown much interest even in Europe of the pre-Westphalia period.[50] Medieval Europe lacks actors comparable to the modern state due to the divided, competing and overlapping nature of authority claims made by actors not of the same type. Competing sovereign claims is thus one alternative to centralisation. Also on that side of the spectrum is a decentralised arrangement which nevertheless functions in the absence of a clear sovereign. In fact, the Chinggisid sovereignty model of extreme centralisation that we will discuss in this section often gave way to such a decentralised arrangement when it collapsed, which is part of the reason why Inner Asia is associated with lack of order rather than extreme centralisation.[51] IR has difficulty capturing or modelling these alternative sovereignty arrangements and their relations. By comparison, the Roman or the Ancient Greek city states seem more similar as they also had centralised political authority. But so did Ancient Egypt, arguably.[52]

---

[48] On this question, see also Zarakol (2017a). Note that this is not an exercise of abstracting from the modern sovereignty model but rather one of translating alternative arrangements to a language comparable to ours.

[49] See Sharman and Phillips (2020).   [50] See, for example, Ruggie (1983).

[51] See Sneath (2007). Sneath argues that the disorderliness of the steppes is a Eurocentric misconception because aristocratic bonds still organised these societies even in the absence of a centralised state.

[52] On Egyptian notions of authority, see Assmann (2014, 2003).

Centralisation of political authority can take very different forms. We can trace increased centralisation of political authority along at least three dimensions: (A) *vertical*, wherein units with different sources of authority increasingly come under the same central authority which is elevated to the top of the hierarchy; (B) *spatial or relational*, wherein the central actor/unit increasingly commands power over peripheral actors units (periphery defined either spatially or relationally); and (C) *assimilationist*, wherein the homogenisation of the people under the control or jurisdiction of central authority increases.

In observing historical forms of political centralisation we are usually observing (A), the route to which also can take a number of different forms: (a) *fusion* – that is, when political authority centralises power by taking on other types of authority (e.g. a prophet ruler like Muhammad, or King Henry VIII becoming also the head of the Church of England);[53] or (b) *domination* – that is, when the political authority elevates itself over other authority claims which now accept its sovereignty (e.g. most modern states). Note that supreme political authority could be highly centralised because it has asserted itself over vis-à-vis competing authority claims (e.g. the church) but within itself institutionally divided for reasons of checks and balances, as is the case in most modern democracies.

Centralisation along a spatial or relational axis (B) has to do with how the centre or seat of authority relates to the peripheries of the polity. In our modern international order, this type of centralisation would take the form of, for instance, the central government of a given state removing the autonomy or privileges of a region or city, as happened with Hong Kong in 2020. This type of centralisation (as well as resistance to it) is closely associated with modern state-building processes from the nineteenth century onwards. However, if we do not think of it just in territorial or administrative categories associated with modernity, similar practices can also be observed in pre-modern eras. For example, Mehmed II razed the walls of the Galecian settlement near Constantinople after he conquered the city, thus making that settlement more dependent on his protection. There have been other

---

[53] To the extent it exists in historical periods, political centralisation tends to take the form of (A)(a), but it is a mistake to think that all monarchs in history had this type of authority. Divided sovereignty and decentralised authority is much more common than we assume (or know to look for due to the hammer/nail bias). And decentralisation does not have to be disorderly: see Sneath (2007).

historical methods of centralising peripheries: for instance, by population transfer.

Finally, centralisation of political authority can also be achieved
through increasing the homogenisation of those who are being ruled
or governed (C). The more homogenous the society, the more generally
applicable the rules made by the centre and thus the further reaching
the power of the centre. For example, the increased homogenisation of
American society in the twentieth century has decreased the power of
the states vis-à-vis the centre which is occupied by the federal government. Americans today are less attached to their particular state identities – Minnesota, Virginia etc. – in general, at least in comparison to
their historical forebears. This is one of the reasons why the power of
central political authority, that is, the federal government (as well as the
US president, further within that centre), has increased throughout the
twentieth century.

From a broader historical perspective, we can observe that homogenisation of populations clustered around various centres starts increasing with early modernity, especially in Europe but not exclusively.
Confessionalisation is a step in this direction. Nationalisation of societies from the nineteenth century onwards is a further manifestation of
this trend.[54] However, we should not simply assume that only modernity can produce social homogenisation, as it has been achieved in other
ways before. The population of Ancient Egypt, especially in the Old
and Middle Kingdoms, seems to exhibit a high degree of
homogenisation.[55] Finally, while homogenisation of society invariably
increases the power of the centre (if it exists), even a cursory survey of
history shows that not all centres are interested in promoting this type
of centralisation.

Different types of centralisation do not have to go together, even
though an average modern state exhibits relatively high degrees of
each. In fact, there are ways they can hinder each other. For example,
spatial-relational as well as assimilationist centralisations are likely
to require administrative oversight, policing, enforcement etc.
Therefore, they require the cooperation of others: civil officials,

---

[54] Different explanations have been given as to why modernity simultaneously
increased individuation while homogenising the population. Gellner (1980)
famously links it with industrial society (but also the centralised state). Elias
(2000 [1939]) also links it with the rise of the centralised state in Europe.

[55] See Assmann (2014).

judges, those who run the (interior) apparatus of coercion, religious officials etc. Even if measures are taken to keep these groups within the vertical hierarchy under the sovereign's authority, the more developed these institutions become the more likely they are to have their own leverage, pulling away from the centre's authority. That means at the very least de facto decentralisation. De facto centralisation can become institutionalised, however, if these alternative sources of authority are successful in advancing an ideology that legitimates decentralisation.

This brings me to a final observation: increases in political centralisation, along any of these axes, are almost always resisted, because they inevitably create material, political and social costs for segments of the population subjected to them. And if successfully achieved, centralisation is always susceptible to fraying. After all, as Weber famously asked, why do (or should) men obey?[56] Centralisation thus requires constant ideational legitimation. The higher the degree of centralisation, the more difficult is its legitimation (because more people must give up more things). Therefore, *if* a particular mode or narrative of legitimation works, it can become very sticky, linking sovereignty practices across changing world orders. More on that in a moment.

Sovereignty as Territoriality

The second feature of modern state sovereignty is territoriality (association of sovereignty with a unified and bounded territory), which according to most scholars[57] emerged in Europe relatively late, much later than centralised, supreme political authority. The addition of territoriality in the late eighteenth and (more so) the nineteenth centuries is what turned Europe from an order of absolutist monarchies to an order of territorial nation states (if we discard the overseas imperial holdings).[58] Thus, for comparative purposes, alternative sovereignty models can also be interrogated in terms of their level of territoriality.

Given the intimate links between territorial borders (rather than frontiers) and modern cartography,[59] there is not much point looking

---

[56] Weber (1965 [1919]).   [57] See Benton (2009); Elden (2013).
[58] See Bartelson (2009, 2018).
[59] See, for example, Branch (2013, 2011); Goettlich (2019).

for this type of territoriality in historical polities. Asian historical polities – like their European counterparts – had boundaries and frontiers rather than borders. However, we can still interrogate degrees of territoriality from the perspective of territorial unification within a bounded realm. When compared from that vantage point, we are likely to find more practices of proto-territoriality in Asia before modernity than we do in Europe. This is likely because, as we will see, political centralisation was more advanced and common in Asia before modernity, and there seems to be a correlation between increased levels of political centralisation and territoriality in the sense of unification of space.[60]

Sovereignty as External Recognition

The third feature of modern state sovereignty is its dependence on external recognition from other sovereign states.[61] Thus in looking for alternative models of sovereignty we can also ask to what degree that sovereignty hinged on 'external' recognition from other sovereigns versus 'internal' recognition from one's subjects (or citizens). Note, however, that – due to the lack of territoriality in the modern sense, especially in terms clearly demarcated borders – what counts as external versus internal is not so clear-cut with historical polities (e.g. is a competing house that enters a vassalage relationship with a more dominant dynasty to be understood as an external or internal dynamic?).

The question becomes a more illuminating one if we interrogate instead whether rulers needed to be recognised by others with competing sovereignty claims of their own to be truly sovereign. Could they rely only on recognition from their own subjects?[62] There are historical polities in which 'external' recognition of this sort was central to sovereignty claims and its domestic legitimation. In fact, the sovereignty model this book traces across the 'world orders' of Asia, what

[60] Spatial/relational centralisation would likely have the effect of increasing territoriality, but they are not the same thing.

[61] See, for example, Krasner (1999); see also Lawson and Shilliam (2009) as well as the accompanying forum in *International Politics* and the 2018 *Review of International Studies* forum on 'misrecognition' in world politics.

[62] Using a Hegelian framework, I have argued elsewhere that internal recognition tended to be much more important historically, whereas modernity greatly increased the external recognition requirement Zarakol 2018.

I call the 'Chinggisid' sovereignty model, operated very much according to such a principle. This is in fact what makes it – once identified – more legible to modern IR.

The 'Chinggisid' Sovereignty Model

With these theoretical distinctions now out of the way, we can go back to our alternative history of the East. We can indeed find many sovereignty models and practices in Asia[63] manifesting in many different ways from those of the modern state, across different time periods. Such alternative sovereignty arrangements range from mercantile guild networks to essentially ungoverned areas with complete political decentralisation.

The particular sovereignty tradition that I will be tracing in this book, however, is what I[64] call the *Chinggisid*[65] *sovereignty* model. This is not to imply a blood-based ownership of these norms by Genghis Khan's descendants but rather to point to Genghis Khan's empire as the origin of association (both in the minds of many latter-day practitioners but also in a historical-sociological sense). Not even the Chinggisids practised Chinggisid sovereignty all the time.[66] In other words, I use the term 'Chinggisid' throughout the book in a similar way as 'Westphalian' – that is, a descriptor of a loose but real historical association as well as a shorthand label for a particular cluster of deep sovereignty norms identifiable across time as being in the same family.

The Chinggisid model (or ideal type) was marked by the extreme centralisation of power and authority in the person of the Great Khan

---

[63] See also Spruyt (2020).

[64] Borrowing from relevant historiography as discussed in the historical chapters.

[65] The actual origins of the world view as it was manifested by Genghis Khan in the thirteenth century is beyond the scope of this book and is much debated among historians as well. Genghis Khan seems to have borrowed elements from Chinese dynastic notions of legitimacy but also from previous polities of the steppe going back over a millennia. On this question, see Neumann and Wigen (2018) for a discussion of the 'steppe tradition' within Eurasian empires, which they classify as an ideal typical-type different from European empires.

[66] Perhaps because the threshold for sovereignty was so high, in Inner Asia there were also many periods where there were no sovereigns, at least in the Chinggisid sense. Sneath (2007) argues, however, that aristocratic norms were strong enough in the steppes to order social arrangement even in the absence of a sovereign. He contends that what looks like no sovereign from the top down was probably not experienced as such from the bottom up.

(the supreme ruler). As with Genghis Khan, 'Chinggisid' sovereigns did not share authority with any others. They claimed lawmaking power above and beyond that of religious (and other) actors. In other words, in the Chinggisid sovereignty model we have a high degree of vertical centralisation. Genghis Khan's empire spanned across almost all of Asia and attempted to govern all sides of the continent by relatively uniform rules (at least in principle), so it exhibited, at least initially, an increased degree of spatial-relational centralisation as well, at least compared to what had existed before. By contrast, there was hardly any assimilationist centralisation, as the Chinggisids had little to no interest in homogenising the population under their control. They inevitably did in certain important ways (which is why we can trace the presence of the Chinggisid sovereignty norm in subsequent orders), but this was not by design. Their general attitude to differences in cultural and religious practices was usually one of mild curiosity. For example, the Great Khan invited representatives of different religions to debate in Karakorum for his amusement.

As for the other components of sovereignty, a notion of territoriality was not entirely absent, given the geographic distribution of the appanages among family members, but it was also not fundamental to the legitimation of Chinggisid sovereignty, except in a more general sense of having achieved an expansive reach. There are specific preoccupations with ruling over specific locations that we can also trace across time – 'China', 'Inner Asia' etc. – but these locations were not understood as territories as such but more as bestowing symbolic power. Beyond that, an expansive territorial reach was important, because the ruler's reach on earth below was to mirror the heavens above, understood in a rather literal manner.[67] Thus instead of a modern understanding of territoriality and an accompanying preoccupation with cartography, what we find in the Chinggisid model is an emphasis on territorial reach and an accompanying preoccupation with astronomy and astrology.

---

[67] 'The legitimacy of the institution of the khan comes from heaven ... Heaven ordains the khan to rule. This is his destiny ... Thus his investiture marks the union of heaven and earth under one government ... His rule is consubstantial with heaven itself. He possesses the power to bind. That is, he determines the fates of others, and he and his descendants will continue to do so as long as they continue to succeed. His rule is affirmed by heavenly signs. Reliance on heavenly signs in government implies that the khan has the power to know and to predict celestial phenomena' (Baumann 2013, p. 250).

Another fundamental element was the role 'external' recognition played in legitimising Chinggisid sovereignty. The Great Khan had to be a world conqueror. In the Chinggisid model, extreme centralisation of political authority was intimately linked with the notion of universal sovereignty. The two went together, and this is why the Chinggisid model started destabilising when conquests stopped. In such situations, the Chinggisid sovereigns experimented with hybrid forms of legitimation for as long as they could; Islam (as reflected through Persianate kingship models) proved a particularly productive companion for the modified Chinggisid model,[68] though not without its own challenges. A particular hybrid version of the Chinggisid model and Islam will be called Timurid (more on this in Chapters 3 and 4).

But before we get to that, it should be recognised that the Chinggisid model is something relatively rare in history, and its uniqueness has to do with this link it creates between extreme political centralisation and the power of lawmaking, on the one hand, and world conquest or universal sovereignty, on the other. Let me explain. Though we strongly associate lawmaking with the modern state, it is not historically the norm for sovereigns to *make* laws, especially if sovereignty is highly personalised. In the pre-modern era across the globe, laws were much more likely to be (or said to have been) received from God(s), found in sacred texts or existing societal traditions, studied and interpreted by priests, jurists, scholars. In fact, for this reason, historically religion acted as one of the primary checks on absolutism and arbitrary rule, a fact that is rarely appreciated from our modern vantage point. Of course, the power to make new laws was claimed by rulers when they could, but they would have to have a good explanation of why *they* got to make all the laws instead of listening to sacred texts or obeying existing jurisprudence. When that question came up, the answer to 'Who gave you the authority to make laws?' was almost always 'God(s)'. Lawmakers claimed to be expressing God's will. Muhammad had supreme authority because he was Allah's prophet. In such a scenario the origin of laws is still God, mediated by a person who is speaking in God's name (whose words then get written down). In principle, God remains sovereign, the prophet-ruler becomes merely the medium, even if in a de facto sense he is the supreme authority in this world.

---

[68] At least in comparison to, for instance, Confucianism. See Chapter 3.

Genghis Khan took this a step further.[69] He made himself the lawgiver[70] but did not claim to be a prophet. Nor did he claim to be merely verbalising divine laws. *He* made the law and still expected people to obey, even if they already had their own religious rules and laws.[71] Genghis Khan's *yasa* (law code) would now trump these. Such extreme centralisation of supreme authority[72] in one person requires extremely robust legitimation. The claim to have such awesome authority could only be justified by a mandate for universal sovereignty over the world, as corroborated and manifested by world conquest and world empire.

Like political centralisation, claims of universal sovereignty are not historically unique (though rarer and less varied in manifestation); many religions at least implicitly operate on such a claim.[73] What is historically much harder to find are claims to universal sovereignty that are not based on *religious* justifications; in other words, claims by what is primarily *political* authority for universal sovereignty over the entire world. It could be argued of course that what is 'religious' versus 'political' authority is not always easy to ascertain[74] and that Genghis Khan's (and his successors') claims to have the 'mandate of heaven' was a type of 'religious' claim. What makes it more of a political claim that is comparable to similar modern claims, however, is that the proof of the mandate was in the empirical sphere of this world and was not at all a matter of belief (at least in the ideal-type version of this norm).[75] A Great Khan proved he had 'heaven's mandate' for

---

[69] For an interesting comparison between Muhammad and Genghis Khan, see Khazanov (1993).

[70] There is some debate about Genghis Khan's law code (*yasa*) and whether it was an actual set of laws or a general notion of law-giving. See Morgan (1986); Biran (2007). For the purposes of the discussion here, it matters not whether these laws were written down; in fact, if they weren't that points to an even greater power in the hands of the khan.

[71] See, for example, Morgan (1986); Baumann (2013).

[72] By contrast, the appeal to God or divinity opens up the possibility for others to claim the ability to interpret the will of God and thus points to a check on centralisation. Even a prophet is likely to be constrained by their earlier reports of God's wishes and cannot easily change track. A ruler who only appeals to their own charisma for law-making is bound by nothing in principle.

[73] See Spruyt (2020) for examples.

[74] For more on this question, see Zarakol (2017a).

[75] For more on the meaning of heaven in the Mongol belief system, see Baumann (2013). This was no Christian or Muslim heaven: 'We do not find the

universal sovereignty by winning wars, by having others submitting to and recognising the khan's authority, especially those with their own sovereignty claims (i.e. other noble houses), by making laws for the whole world, and by ruling over subjects of different religions.[76] Imagine if modern state sovereignty could only be legitimated via superpower-dom and we are in the vicinity of the Chinggisid sovereignty model.

World Orders of 'The East'

Genghis Khan and the Chinggisids were thus world conquerors above anything else. That makes them also *world order*ers. For the purposes of this book, I define 'world order' as the (man-made) rules, understandings and institutions that govern (and pattern) relations between the actors of world politics. A 'world order'[77] is more deliberately created (or designed) by its various actors[78] and more reflexively maintained (or undermined) than structure.[79] Structural dynamics, by contrast, are not primarily driven by agency and include collective human processes that emerge without deliberate design, as subject to material forces beyond deliberate human agency, such as climatological or environmental pressures, macro-economic processes (e.g. of capitalism), long-term demographic

---

abstraction of heaven into a moral, everlasting realm where good prevails and evil, sin, and death are no more. Nor does the Mongols' heaven stand for common humanity, as that of the monotheistic traditions does' (Bauman 2013, p. 246). It was a natural, material, historical understanding of heaven. 'Heaven to the Mongols is amoral' (Bauman 2013, p. 248).

[76] I realise that there is a tautology here, but all legitimation ideologies are tautological. They work until they stop working.

[77] 'Goodness' or 'orderliness' cannot be part of the definition of 'order'. The meanings of those words vary by culture and therefore are either endogenous to the logic of a particular order or not the proper criteria to evaluate it. After all, what looks orderly to one may look like disorder or chaos to another.

[78] In this book, I am interested only in world orders created by world-empire-making efforts, but, as the historical chapters will demonstrate, I am not arguing that the order is coterminous with the empire itself (the former extends beyond the latter in all of the cases we are focusing on). Nor am I claiming that orders could only be made by such top-down efforts; it is theoretically possible (and there are some historical examples of this) for order to emerge bottom-up (though it is more debatable whether world orders could be generated in that manner). For another take on order, see Adler (2019).

[79] See also Go and Lawson (2017, p. 17).

trends, and technological and scientific raptures. It is possible to create order without conquest, but it is not possible for empires not to have ordering effects. No matter how brutal or 'disorderly' they are, conquests change the world, thus re*order* it.[80] Formal or informal conquests (and by extension, empires) are not just disruptions, interludes or deviations from the norm. They are irreversible *ordering* events, for better or worse, especially if conquests are sustained over long periods of time. One does not just shake off the 'yoke' of a conqueror and go back to what existed before the conquest. Even if one resists the conquest, or hates it, or resents it, one is nevertheless shaped by it; one's world is reordered as a result of having lived through conquest, submission (or resistance),[81] decline and replacement.

The story of Genghis Khan as a world conqueror *and* lawgiver lived on for centuries (as inflected by the example of Timur/Tamerlane later), legitimising a certain type of political rule throughout Asia and strengthening the hands of rulers desiring to claim centralising political authority. The empire of Genghis Khan created a political arrangement in Asia from the beginning of the thirteenth century that spanned almost the entire continent (as we define it now), from the shores of the Pacific Ocean to the Black Sea. At the end of the thirteenth century, the Mongol (or better, Chinggisid[82]) Empire broke up into four competing khanates: the Golden Horde/Jochid Khanate ('Russia'), the Ilkhanate ('Persia'), the Chagatai Khanate (Inner/Central Asia) and the Yuan Dynasty of Kubilai Khan ('China'). Over the course of the fourteenth century, these khanates eventually gave way to other ruling dynasties of Asia, some of whom were directly (e.g. the Timurids, the Mughals) or ethnolinguistically (e.g. the Ottomans, the Safavids) related to the Chinggisid ruling dynasty, and some of whom were not (e.g. the Rurik, the Ming), but all of whom exhibited degrees of

---

[80] See also Phillips (2021).

[81] All of this is also true for the modern international order as originally constituted by European empires.

[82] Calling Genghis Khan's empire Mongol, while technically true, introduces a presentist distortion into our thinking. See fn 16 of this chapter. Readers should keep in mind that this was not a 'national' designation at the time (nor was it tribal). Mongol politics were organised around powerful houses and their appanages. For more on this, see Sneath (2007), as well as Chapter 2 in this book.

influence from the earlier periods of Mongol rule in their approach to sovereignty. We can thus observe both increased degrees of political centralisation and universal empire claims in these successor polities.

This is not to claim that Genghis Khan 'invented' political centralisation around supreme authority, though as already discussed his particular take on power was relatively rare in history. Political centralisation (and resistance to it) is a transhistorical dynamic; it is not owned by any particular culture or geography. We find varying degrees of it in almost all societies because every society has centralising actors and those who would suffer from such centralisation. The manoeuvring room of would-be centralisers in any given society can be expanded, however, by both structural and material dynamics that favour centralisation and *also* normative repertoires that make it possible for centralisation to be cast as the appropriate solution to various historically contingent problems.[83] The Chinggisid model of sovereignty survived for centuries, and it was packaged along with world empire aspirations, successfully pursued by at least some political actors who managed to create relatively durable world ordering projects. We can thus identify at least three 'world orders' in Asia and Eurasia constructed by political actors implicitly or explicitly operating in the Chinggisid mould.

Along with the Chinggisid sovereignty norm, several supporting institutions associated with the Chinggisid model also diffused across Asia, as will be traced in Part I. For example, the practice of tanistry, labelled as such by Joseph Fletcher,[84] was one such institution. Tanistry is a way of handling succession that is different from the primogeniture model more common in European monarchies. In tanistry, members of the ruling house are all eligible to inherit but there is no established order of succession. Sometimes the ruler designates an heir before their own death, but even that is not necessarily obeyed. Typically, then, in the Chinggisid model, brothers and other relatives would fight each other (to the death) to claim sovereignty. Tanistry can be thought of as a way of using the succession period to select for the heir who actually

---

[83] See, for example, the promotion of increased presidential powers in the United States in response to the War on Terror.

[84] Fletcher notes he is borrowing and modifying the term as used in the Celtic tradition (Fletcher 1986, p. 17, fn 3). Tanistry is not a practice unique to the Chinggisid model (or this geography) but is nevertheless closely associated with it.

had the heaven's mandate: because only a conqueror clearly had this mandate, it follows that dynastic succession would also need legitimation via in-house 'aristocratic' competition through warfare, even against siblings and uncles. We thus find elements of this institution also in post-Chinggisid polities and world orders.

As discussed, yet another institution associated with the Chinggisid sovereignty model was scholarship around astronomy and astrology (and increasingly other occult sciences), due to the significant role 'heaven' played in securing sovereignty: 'conceiving of heaven in symmetry as the source of knowledge for governing the earth ... is tantamount to saying that they ruled others by the power of superior knowledge'.[85] The study of heavens was deeply implicated in the Chinggisid understanding of the 'world' (as the corollary of 'heaven') and thus their universal empire project. Thus we find that Chinggisid and post-Chinggisid rulers all facilitated the study of astrology and astronomy, to a greater extent than is the case with their contemporaries.[86] Such normative and institutional continuities[87] constitute one of the primary reasons why Chinggisid and post-Chinggisid[88] 'world orders' of the East are comparable to the international orders of modernity which also exhibit a degree of normative and institutional continuity around the 'Westphalian' sovereignty model.

Furthermore, by studying the Chinggisids and their successors throughout Asia and Eurasia, we learn about not just another sovereignty model that is reminiscent of the modern state model (in that it exhibits a high degree of political centralisation) that is so central to IR but also something similar to the so-called Great Powers in our order: political actors with a particular vision of *the whole world* (not just their regions), who want to order it in a particular way and, in doing so, create, modify and reproduce political, economic and social institutions in the world. I hesitate to label these Great Powers, however, as

[85] Baumann (2013, p. 252).
[86] More on this especially in Chapters 3 and 4. Other commonalities include dream and hunting symbolism.
[87] I do not mean to imply that the norms remained static over this period, but, as we will see, they exhibit a continuity nevertheless, in the same way there is some continuity between the nineteenth-century international order and our present-day one.
[88] I use this term to denote subsequent legacy orders.

this term has a particular history without correspondence to the time period we will be examining. The abstraction from individual rulers to powers in foreign policy thinking happened in Europe from the seventeenth century onwards, echoing a similar development in theorising of the state.[89] Following Sneath, the better descriptor for the House of Genghis Khan as well as others we will be studying therefore is 'Great House', and the 'world orders' we will be analysing are at a minimum orders consisting of networks and rivalries of houses who claim sovereignty over others (and their appanages by implication, with subject populations included under that heading).[90] In other words, the orders in this book are inter-house orders, rather than inter-national orders. I refer to both as 'world orders' to maintain commensurability. Some readers may be sceptical that the Chinggisids should be called a Great House if they are more familiar with the usual characterisation of the Mongols as chaotically tribal, but most historians today agree that such earlier characterisations were wrong. The Mongols were 'first and foremost, aristocrats', and Chinggisid society was very stratified; their house (with its heavenly connection) was above everyone else.[91]

Using the theoretical and conceptual framework now laid out, we can thus identify the three 'world orders' created by the Chinggisids and their successors. The time period we will cover extends from the thirteenth to the seventeenth centuries. This five-century period opens with the 'Mongol' or 'Chinggisid' world order as created by Genghis Khan and members of his house (thirteenth to fourteenth centuries), followed by the 'post-Chinggisid' would-be world order(s) of the Timurids and the early Ming (fourteenth to fifteenth centuries), and, finally, a globalising world with its core position occupied by three post-Timurid (and therefore, Chinggisid) empires and their order(s) (fifteenth to seventeenth centuries), the order of *sahibkıran* (millennial sovereigns). My main argument is that, in each of these periods, the world[92] was dominated and ordered by Great Houses who justified their sovereignty along Chinggisid lines.

[89] See Keene (2013), also Bartelson (1995).
[90] Sneath (2007). I offer this definition to underline the fact that states or empires in this period are different from the modern states and nineteenth-century empires IR is more accustomed to studying. However, the notion of 'house' should not be read to indicate that these were primitive political arrangements.
[91] Baumann (2013, pp. 250–1). See also Sneath (2007).
[92] Of course there were areas beyond their domination, but that is true of even modern 'great powers'.

Part I of this book thus recovers these three 'world orders' of the East, all linked to each other because they were created by 'houses' with a common understanding of sovereignty and what constitutes greatness. 'Greatness' was manifested above all else by having your house be helmed by a world conqueror. Thus, the historical narrative[93] in each chapter will inevitably focus on particular individual rulers who made such claims (and tried to order the world accordingly), to an extent that may seem jarring to our modern eyes. Note however, that this focus on particular chosen individuals (from Great Houses) and their ruler 'charisma',[94] as demonstrated by world conquest, was itself an institution of the Chinggisid and post-Chinggisid orders and, in fact, a source of tension over time, as Chinggisid-style polities inevitably tended to become more bureaucratised and alternative institutions of authority and sources of legitimacy emerged.

Let me now give a brief overview of each of the 'world orders' that will be explored in Part I of this book, before turning to the issue of what IR can gain from this recovered history, which is the subject of Part II.

An Alternative History of the East (Part I)

First was the 'world order' created by Genghis Khan (and his house) in the thirteenth century, which will be explored at length in Chapter 2. If there is indeed an 'East' that is distinct from the 'West',[95] one of the points of separation can be placed here. After all, Genghis Khan's empire was primarily an 'Asian' one, spanning the distance from the Pacific Ocean in the east to the Mediterranean in the west. Actors of

[93] In constructing this historical narrative, my approach could be said to fall under the broad contours of the Global Historical Sociology research agenda, as developed by Go and Lawson (2017). See also Lawson (2019). Even when speaking of particular places and actors, I assume they are connected to and shaped by their relations to the broader world.

[94] Throughout the book, I am using the word 'charisma' somewhat colloquially, but there are implied links here to the Weberian concept of 'charismatic authority'. See, for example, Derman (2011), Caabbuag (2016). Despite some overlaps, Chinggisid sovereignty is not the same thing as charismatic authority as Weber imagined it, however. It could perhaps be argued that the former is an attempt to institutionalise the latter.

[95] The problem is not so much in having various categories such as East and West but automatically imputing normative value to such categories. Even worse is treating such normative hierarchies in an essentialist manner.

(and within) this order interacted with the Indian subcontinent to their south and the European/Mediterranean regional orders to their west (and influenced developments therein and vice versa), but for the most part, polities in those regions were not incorporated into this order and retained their own logics of power, legitimation, warfare etc. In this 'Asian' order, people living in the geographies that we now call 'Russia', 'China', 'Iran' and 'Central Asia' – basically most of continental Asia – shared the same sovereign for the first time and then were ruled/dominated by dynasties (the Golden Horde/Jochid, the Yuan, the Ilkhanate and the Chagatai) that directly inherited Chinggisid norms – that is, ambitions of universal sovereignty and dynastic legitimacy based on world conquest, as well as high degrees of political centralisation around the supreme authority of the Great Khan.[96] They were also significantly connected to each other through overland and naval routes that spanned the entire continent, as well as the Indian Ocean.

While the existence of such trade routes – the so-called silk roads[97] – predated the Chinggisid Empire, the Mongols strengthened these connections through institutions such as the postal (*yam*) system and homogenised the points of contact throughout by their omnipresence in the major spheres of influence within the continent. Famous explorers of the fourteenth century – for example, Marco Polo or Ibn Battuta – could thus make their way from Europe or North Africa to China with relative ease, causing hardly any more commotion than some curiosity among hosts (who must have been accustomed to travellers along these routes) and facing not much more than some demand for updated information about cities and rulers encountered along the way. Yet others travelled in the opposite direction, from China to west Asia, and started new lives in Europe or what is now called Iran, under new rulers. A mostly forgotten aspect of this order (at least in IR) is the facilitation of epistemic exchange of all sorts, most notably between 'Iran' and 'China': bureaucrats, scientists, artists, craftsmen, engineers could be born on one side of Asia and finish their careers on the opposite side, with profound implications for the artistic, cultural and scientific standards of both societies. The best (but

---

[96] I do not imply this was the only legacy. There were many other influences, material and political. See, for example, Anievas and Nisancioglu (2015); Neumann and Wigen (2018) for an overview.

[97] For a history, start with Frankopan (2016) and Millward (2013). See also Abu-Lughod (1989).

not only) example of this cultural exchange is the fundamental transformation of Islamic art under Chinese influences. This process is sometimes called the 'Chinggisid Exchange' by historians of the empire[98] and is similar to the Columbian exchange in terms of its world historical impact.

After holding most of Asia under the same sovereign for more than half a century – which would be no small feat even today, let alone in the thirteenth century – the world empire/khanate ruled by the Great House of Genghis Khan fragmented into the four aforementioned smaller khanates, each based in territories originally given to different branches of Genghis Khan's descendants to govern. Once autonomous, these rival khanates went through a period of intense fighting to reclaim the mantle of world sovereignty but settled into a 'balance-of-power'-type equilibrium in early fourteenth century. However, various structural pressures – especially the spread of the Black Death from the East (or Central Asia) to the West at the turn of the fourteenth century – spelled the end of that arrangement as well. All but one of the khanates fell apart. The Golden Horde continued to rule the north-western steppes of Asia (present day Russia), but the Chagatai Khanate and the Ilkhanate disintegrated, eventually giving way to the Timurid empire originating from Transoxiana, and the Yuan were replaced by the Ming Dynasty.

The second world order we will look at, in Chapter 3, was less uniform compared to the previous one created by the world empire of Genghis Khan and its successor khanates, but it was still recognisably influenced by Chinggisid norms of universal sovereignty. This was the world order created in the last third of the fourteenth century by the rivalry among two would-be successors to the Great House of Genghis Khan: the Great Houses of Timur (Tamerlane) and Zhu Yuanzhang (Hongwu) – that is, the (early) Ming Dynasty. Though one explicitly emphasised their Chinggisid lineage and the other had come to power repudiating the Chinggisid dynasty before it (Yuan), Chapter 3 will demonstrate that early rulers on both sides were demonstrably operating in ways influenced by Chinggisid sovereignty norms. This is relatively easy to show in the case of Timur, who deliberately fashioned himself after Genghis Khan and died on the way of attempting to conquer 'China', but it can also be demonstrated that, on the Ming

[98] See, for example, May (2012).

side, the preoccupation of Hongwu and Yongle emperors with world recognition was *also* driven by the same legacy. As noted in the previous section, there has been a welcome resurgence[99] of interest in studying the historical international relations of 'China' in recent years, but the degree to which the early Ming were shaped by both their Yuan (Chinggisid) predecessors and their Central Asian rivals[100] in their pursuit of external recognition (a modified form of universal sovereignty by conquest) is often overlooked in IR, which erroneously imagines Inner Asia to be as peripheral to world politics in history as it has been in the twentieth century. Nothing could be further from the truth. Even the Ming 'treasure voyages' should be understood first in this context of inter-Asian competition.

Timur failed to conquer China and eventually the two sides settled into something like mutual recognition.[101] Connecting these two Great Houses was a whole continent of lesser houses, some with their own Chinggisid-style world empire aspirations, others operating at a minimum with a mutual understanding of the same Chinggisid legacy (including, for instance, the Joseon Dynasty in Korea). Furthermore, it was not only the shared Chinggisid understandings that connected the continent but also a relatively robust network of trade, as Chapter 3 will discuss. In other words, there were material connections as well. It could be objected that direct contact between these two Great Houses on the two sides of Asia was infrequent and therefore not enough to constitute a world order. To that I would counter: there is a certain resemblance between the world order of the Timurids and the Ming in the late fourteenth and early fifteenth centuries, and the way they related to each other, and the previous order of the Chinggisid khanates, on the one hand, and, on the other, the world order created by the rivalry of the United States and the USSR after the Second World War and the way they related to the previous order of European Great Powers. In both orders, one pole downplayed or even ostensibly rejected the legacy of the former world order whereas the other

[99] See, for example, Musgrave and Nexon (2018); Kang (2010); Spruyt (2020).
[100] The Yuan retreated to Inner Asia and continued to make claims to be Great Khans; the early Ming were motivated above all else to delegitimise these claims. See Chapter 3.
[101] IR arguments that characterise Ming relations with everyone as being hierarchical based on the fact that the Ming coded every gift as tributes overlook the fact that the Timurid and the Ming rulers related to each other (perhaps begrudgingly) as equals. See Chapter 3.

embraced it, but both sides were products of a shared historical experience and therefore had a lot in common in how they saw the world. The two dynasties competed with each other symbolically even when they did not interact, and in so doing they reinforced the normative fabric of the fourteenth- and fifteenth-century world order in Asia.

Not unlike the Cold War order, the Timurid–Ming world order was not around for very long, however. Another period of structural crisis – this time having to do with shortage of money, a 'bullion famine' – hit Eurasia in the middle of the fifteenth century, to the detriment of dynasties especially in west Asia. The Timurids lost control over their territories. The Chinggisid influences on the Ming faded, and neo-Confucianism took over. Bureaucrats and officials increasingly constrained the power and authority of the Ming rulers, checking centralisation. The Ming realm turned increasingly isolationist.[102] The 'bipolar' world order of the Timurid and the Ming Great Houses thus fragmented before it had the opportunity to congeal into something more institutionalised, and the trade networks connecting the two were disrupted (if briefly, from a world historical perspective).

But the Chinggisid sovereignty norm lived on, intersecting with local traditions. The Ming still had to contend with Mongol warriors on their frontiers, motivated by these same notions; in the north-west, Muscovy was still trying to shake off the 'Tatar Yoke' of the Golden Horde. The various peoples of Inner Asia mostly operated with Chinggisid sovereignty norms still, even if the expectations around centralisation and world empire remained only aspirational. The next truly fertile ground for world-ordering projects based on Chinggisid sovereignty and universal norms turned out to be the south-western corner of Asia, however: areas that were dominated by or were within the reach of the Timurid empire/khanate in the fifteenth century. Chinggisid sovereignty norms, as inflected via the Timurids, merged with existing Persian notions of kingship, millennial expectations, astrology and other occult sciences, as well as folk practices of Islam within this region. This fusion gave rise to at least three Great Houses with some of the more ambitious universal sovereignty claims in history: the Ottomans, the Safavids and the Mughals, discussed in Chapter 4.

---

[102] Even if not quite to the extent it has been made to be. More on this in Chapter 3.

These three Great Houses together claimed sovereignty over more than a third of the human population of the world in the sixteenth century, and they also controlled the core of the world economy. What they had in common was more than religion, was more than Islam. What they shared was rather a particular sovereignty model: a type of sacred kingship, a fused form of vertical political centralisation achieved by the unification of political and religious authority in the same person, made possible by the Chinggisid-Timurid legacies they inherited. The Ottoman, Safavid and Mughal claim to greatness was based on the claim of particular rulers from these houses to be *sahibkıran*,[103] universal sovereigns marked by signs from the heavens, living in the end of days, delivering on millennial expectations. Universal sovereignty projects of these would-be world empires were once again supported by the study of astrology and other occult sciences. In the sixteenth century, it was the post-Timurid 'millennial sovereigns' who ordered an increasingly globalising world.

The idea that there was a sixteenth-century world order originating from Eurasia as centred on the Ottomans, the Safavids and the Mughals goes against received wisdom in IR, which sees *only* the promise of subsequent European global hegemony in that century. It is undeniable that the sixteenth century was also a period of growth and expansion for Europe (especially Spain), but Europe was growing from a position of greater deprivation compared to Asia. If we do not read the ending of the story back into the historical narrative, in the sixteenth century it was still not at all obvious that European actors would come to dominate the world. Almost all histories of this period within IR treat the Habsburgs' Eastern relations as relatively insignificant, but that is also a projection of the standards of a later time to the sixteenth century. Especially in the first two-thirds of the sixteenth century, the main rival of the Habsburgs were the Ottomans, who were themselves engaged in a simultaneous rivalry with the Safavids, from whose orbit the Mughals were trying to break from. Other European houses had aspirations, to be sure, but their time in the sun had not really come yet, and they initially had to rely on Eastern alliances as well as trade with Asia to get on an upward trajectory.

All of this is to say that we must scrap the traditional narrative lurking in the background of the Westphalian origin myth of IR[104] – that

---

[103] See also Spruyt (2020).   [104] See de Carvalho, Leira, and Hobson (2011).

is, the narrative of an ascendant European order in the sixteenth century with non-European hangers-on such as the Ottomans on its periphery (or the Russians). The real picture is just the opposite: the sixteenth-century world had a core of post-Timurid empires in (south-)west Asia animated by a millennial competition focused on universal sovereignty, and European actors such as the Habsburgs were trying to challenge the dominance of *that* core (while other European players linked into it through trade networks and other alliances). Chapter 5 thus broadens our visions from west Asia to all of Eurasia, first showing the ways in which the European regional order linked *into* the post-Timurid imperial space dominated by the Ottomans, the Safavids and the Mughals, rather than the other way around. It then turns its gaze back to Eurasia and Asia, catching up with Muscovy to the north, Uzbeks and other khanates to the north-east and the Ming to the east, discussing the ways these polities were also still shaped by their Chinggisid legacies as well as the modes in which they interacted with the post-Timurid core of the sixteenth-century globalising order. The ascendance of Muscovy – and the trajectory of Russian state formation[105] – must also be understood in the context of the legacy of Chinggisid and post-Chinggisid world orders, as well as Russian aspirations to rival its southern and eastern competitors who contributed to these orders. In sum, in the sixteenth century we had a globalising *Eurasian* order, whose dominant norms emanated from the Chinggisid–Timurid model, rather a European one (or just a European one).

The world-ordering projects of the post-Timurid empires of the sixteenth century as described earlier (and in more detail in Chapters 4 and 5) were stopped in their tracks, however, by the developments between the late sixteenth and mid-seventeenth centuries, a politically tumultuous period throughout Eurasia, labelled by some historians as 'the Seventeenth-Century General Crisis'.[106] This was a period of prolonged rebellions, civil wars and demographic decline throughout the northern hemisphere. Historians have given different explanations as to what ushered in this period of upheaval, with some suggesting financial causes (e.g. the global repercussions of

[105] For a different take on the same legacy, see Neumann and Wigen (2018).
[106] See, for example, Trevor-Roper (2001); Hobsbawm (1954). Originally this crisis was understood to be a European one, but now it is seen as a global crisis. See also Goldstone (1991).

the Spanish 'price revolution' due to silver from the New World) and others demographic ones.[107] Others now link the chaos of this period to the Little Ice Age.[108] Interestingly enough, the end of *each* world order we will discuss in Part I is similarly punctuated by periods at least some historians have identified as times of structural crises. As already alluded to, the decay of the Chinggisid world order coincides with the westward spread of the plague, and similarly, the fragmentation of the post-Chinggisid world order coincides with what is sometimes called 'the fifteenth-century crisis': another period of abnormal cooling in Eurasia, marked this time by a coin *shortage* as well as political upheaval, especially in west Asia.[109] But the 'Seventeenth-Century General Crisis' is the most prolonged period of upheaval we will encounter within the timeframe of this book, lasting the better part of that century.

This was turning point for the East because, while aspects of the Chinggisid sovereignty norms survived the seventeenth century and motivated particular rulers (e.g. Nader Shah of Persia [r. 1736–47]), no new 'world orders' organised around those norms were successfully created after the seventeenth century. A global perception set in during the nineteenth century that Asia had been irreversibly declining for centuries, even though most Asian and Eurasian states had materially recovered from the 'Seventeenth-Century General Crisis' and had, in some cases, even gone on to territorially expand in the eighteenth century. These two developments – the loss of 'world orders' originating in the East, on the one hand, and the perception of decline despite continued durability of Eastern states, on the other – are linked. This brings me to the subject of theoretical payoffs IR will get from recovering the history of 'world orders' in the East, which will be the focus of Part II of this book.

Lessons from Asian and Eurasian World Orders (Part II)

Learning about 'world orders' of the East has a number of significant implications for our theorisation and understanding of world politics today. Chapter 6 will revisit these lessons with the benefit of the full

[107] See, for example, de Vries (2009).
[108] See, for example, Parker and Smith (1997); Parker (2013).
[109] See, for example, Atwell (2002). More on this in Chapter 3.

historical account, to draw out their implications for contemporary debates on US decline and 'power transition', as well as the future of our international order, but let me offer a preview of some of the main arguments as I conclude this first chapter.

Because IR has focused almost exclusively on European/Western history, it has not problematised 'Westphalian' sovereignty until recently. This has given the discipline some serious blind spots. For example, it is not unusual to encounter assumptions in IR that 'sovereignty' itself is an invention of the West, exported or imposed violently upon the rest of the world. In fact, the term 'sovereignty' is often used without any qualifiers and implicitly understood to mean only modern state sovereignty. This book shows that operating with such a narrow conception of sovereignty limits our understanding of the world. If sovereignty is analytically defined in a way that can accommodate variations across time and space, the myth of European uniqueness is immediately undermined. And we do not even have to travel very far from what is assumed to be unique to see versions of it elsewhere and in other time periods. Political centralisation[110] – an essential component of modern state sovereignty – can be easily found before modernity and outside of Europe (and in fact much more easily outside Europe). This has wide-ranging – if long overdue – implications for IR's global understanding of state development. The historical account offered in this book demonstrates that we need to pay much more attention to the link between different forms of sovereignty and the type of 'international relations' they produce.

Broadening our understanding of sovereignty is not just useful for our theorisation of sovereignty and order; it also properly opens up aspects of periods and geographies heretofore thought incommensurable with IR theorising. This will have many theoretical yields, but in this book – as indicated by the title[111] – I am particularly interested in rethinking the notions of 'rise' and 'decline'. The alternative history of

---

[110] This does not mean that political forms that deviate greatly from sovereignty as we understand it today are unworthy of scrutiny. IR should certainly spend much more time thinking about decentralised and deterritorialised forms of sovereignty.

[111] I am of course aware that the 'rise and fall' template is problematic to begin with, so there is a degree to which the title of the book is tongue-in-cheek. But for reasons to be explained in more detail in Chapters 6 and 7 (Epilogue), it is not enough to just reject such narratives; they need to be engaged with directly and, if possible, replaced with alternatives.

Asian and Eurasian 'world orders' presented in *Before the West* clearly challenge existing conceptualisations of 'rise' and 'decline' from an IR history derived almost exclusively from a Eurocentric timeline.

To begin with, IR has focused on the 'rise' and 'decline' of Great Powers at the expense of other, broader understandings of decline. As a result, in traditional IR accounts the social order and the deep norms that give meaning to the behaviour of primary actors (e.g. Great Powers) are taken for granted. In other words, the 'rules' that make possible the rise of particular actors are assumed to be given, fixed and ahistorical. Definitions of Great Power also tend to be ahistorical. In IR, structural, material conditions that shape world politics, including climate, are also taken just as background and assumed to be more or less unchanging.[112] The taken-for-grantedness of the world has led IR theorists to assume that they can study Great Power behaviour as mostly constituted of agency against an unchanging, timeless setting of anarchy.

The historical account offered in Part I of *Before the West*, by contrast, shifts our focus from the agency of Great Powers to the rise and decline of 'world orders', as well the deep norms that organise and allow for (or preclude) degrees of continuity between those 'world orders'. The historical account offered here suggests that we should not conflate the material decline of specific actors (or houses or states) with the decline of the 'world orders' they help create. It is possible for polities to remain relatively prosperous but nevertheless appear to have declined if the social fabric which gives meaning to their actions has frayed. 'Greatness' is never self-evident; nor is it just about material power and domination. It is also about manifesting certain symbolic markers, the meaning of which can only be culturally determined and thus must be intersubjectively shared. 'Decline' is thus partly about not displaying the correct symbolic markers or displaying the markers of greatness from a previous social order as another is coming into being. Thus neither 'rise' nor 'decline' can be studied as being solely endogenously determined.

The Asian and Eurasian polities which are the focus of this book invariably reached a point in their political trajectory where the Chinggisid sovereignty model had to be abandoned or modified, because external conquest – the primary source of its legitimation – could

---

[112] In IR we tend to assume climate change is a problem of recent vintage.

not be infinitely sustained. The modification of the Chinggisid model usually took the form of increasing emphasis on alternative sources of legitimation – such as religion (e.g. Islam) – and a move away from more personalised (or 'absolutist') forms of rule. The increased bureaucratisation necessitated by the demands of running world empires and the eventual need to find alternative modes of legitimation both decreased the concentration of power in the hands of the sovereign in the long run. In almost all of the cases discussed in this book, such changes, whether introduced gradually or rapidly, were perceived as decline, at least by some contemporary observers, especially because they ran counter to the established modes of legitimation along Chinggisid lines. Hence, we find many examples of 'declinist' discourse in the cases scrutinised in this book. These were internal (or 'domestic') debates on 'decline'. However, such debates also had external (or 'international') dimensions. The dissemination of the Chinggisid sovereignty norms throughout Asia and Eurasia had been a product of 'international' or 'world order' dynamics in the first place. Second, the legitimation of the Chinggisid sovereignty model depended greatly on exogenous dynamics, as explained.

Before the West thus suggests that 'rise and decline' – defined for the purposes of this book as a (gradual or rapid) increase in or erosion of influence to shape outcomes – are better understood as another 'level of analysis' type of problem in IR. We need to separate our theorising about 'decline' at the level of *actors* (i.e. Great Power, Great House) or hegemonic decline (and their eventual replacement by other similar actors) from the decline of *orders* (i.e. decline of a 'world order' and its eventual replacement by another order). In the historical account in this book, we find both types of decline – of Great Houses and also of 'world orders' – but the two dynamics are not always coupled. And underwriting all of it is a larger story of the 'Decline of the East', a normative structural (or ecumenical)[113] shift that happens as 'world orders' cease to originate from Asia and Eurasia.

This brings me to another theoretical contribution of this book. The analytical framework proposed here – when coupled with the historical reconstruction of Asian and Eurasian 'world orders' – makes it possible to give one answer to what I consider the real puzzle of 'Eastern decline'. The real puzzle of 'Eastern decline' is not the one it was

---

[113] More on this in Chapter 6.

assumed to be for the last century. We no longer wonder why the East has been declining for centuries because we know it has not been, at least in a material sense. In recent decades, new historiographies of various Eurasian and Asian polities (China, the Ottoman Empire, etc.) have unequivocally shown us that the material decline of states in these geographies do not extend back centuries.[114] The long-standing presumption of the irreversible decline of the East, shared by *both* nineteenth- and twentieth-century European accounts *and* local nationalist narratives critical of the ancien régimes in each context is wrong. We can be reasonably confident about that now. 'The East' was not sitting idly by while Europeans came up with innovation after innovation for centuries or even millennia.[115] That is all retrospective projection of presentist biases back onto historical dynamics.

However, such compelling revisionist challenges to the 'decline of the East' account have raised a new set of questions. The real puzzle is this: if the material gap between Europe and Asia (or Eurasia) before (the second half of) the nineteenth century has thus been retroactively exaggerated, why did 'Eastern' elites so easily fold ontologically in (especially the second half of) the nineteenth century when faced with narratives of European civilisational superiority? To put another way, why were they so easily stigmatised[116] by Western actors? Why did they internalise the Western civilisational schema which found them inferior, even as they challenged their own countries' particular placement within that schema? Why did this process unfold so rapidly and so evenly (all things considered) throughout Asia and Eurasia, given the varying material strengths of the actors in the East as well as the

---

[114] This general argument about lack of material decline in Asia until the nineteenth century is most closely associated with what is called the 'California School'. See, for example, Goldstone (1991, 2000, 2002, 2008, 2015); Pomeranz (2001); Hobson (2004, 2020); Frank (1998); Wong (2000) etc. (For a critical take on the California School, see Vries [2010]). In IR, parallel arguments to the California School can be found, for example, in Buzan and Lawson (2015); Sharman (2019) (in addition of course to Hobson's work).

[115] Admittedly, the strongest versions of such stigmatising narratives of stagnation were often generated locally. For an example focused on the Turkish case, see Çapan and Zarakol (2019). See also Zarakol (2011); Hobson and Sharman (2005).

[116] For more on stigmatisation, see Zarakol (2011, 2014). In using this word, I am operating with Goffman's (1963) understanding of stigma, which is distinct from discrimination or shaming and requires a certain degree of buy-in from the recipient.

differing degrees of trauma in their interactions with European colonialism? These questions are especially vexing if we accept the standard
IR account of Asia being made whole as late as the second half of the
nineteenth century, only via incorporation into an increasingly expansive international order created by European Great Powers.

The historical reconstruction of Asian and Eurasian 'world orders'
offered in Part I points to some possible answers. I will return to this
puzzle in Chapter 6 and Chapter 7 (the Epilogue), but, to put it briefly,
the reasons why Eastern elites were vulnerable to stigmatisation by
Europeans in the nineteenth century were several-fold. First, despite the
fact that Asian and Eurasian states had recovered from their various
crises by the eighteenth century, something was lost as a result of
seventeenth-century upheavals. This is the period during which the
last would-be 'world order' centred in the East had fragmented, with
existing overland networks which had carried people, goods and ideas
for centuries severely disrupted. The result, even after material recovery, was increased regionalisation throughout the continent. This is not
to say that there were no would-be Great Houses left in the East with
universalist ambitions after the seventeenth century, but none came
close to reproducing the scale of the previous world-ordering projects
discussed in this book. After the seventeenth century, the centre of
gravity shifted. By the early eighteenth century, it was no longer located
in the East, though it was not yet located in the West either.

By the nineteenth century, the then dominant actors of the
previously *regional* order of Europe had started reconnecting the
various fragments of this lost social ecumene of Asia and Eurasia,
as they did the other parts of the world. But all of these new
connections now went through bilateral relations with Europe
(e.g. Iran and China were now connected to each other through
the British Empire), so 'Asia' never fully recovered the degree of
social, political or economic coherence it had exhibited in previous
periods. More troublingly, the ramping up of nationalisation projects as demanded by the emerging international order of this
period increased the amnesia about shared elements of continental
history due to the artificial imposition of what were then cutting-
edge notions of ethnicity, nation, race, tribe and civilisation.[117]

---

[117] Heiskanen (2020).

Furthermore, we could even speculate – though it is not possible to demonstrate this within the scope of this book – that by the nineteenth century there may have been a sense of social loss throughout most of the continent, a lingering echo in collective memory of what once had been there. The Epilogue (Chapter 7) gets into some of these issues.

Attempts to create nationalised histories rendered Asian and Eurasian states of the nineteenth century vulnerable both domestically and internationally.[118] Domestic vulnerability stemmed from the fact that the cultural diversity of populations in Asia rendered such projects much more difficult to pull off in the East (at least in comparison to Europe). As we will see in Chapter 5, European actors in the sixteenth century were on average more fanatical about religion and less tolerant of any other kind of difference than their Asian contemporaries, and this turned out to be an 'advantage', so to speak, in later dynamics of nationalisation. Both geographies experienced confessionalisation in this period (i.e. centralisation as homogenisation; axis C),[119] but in Europe the realms increasingly confessionalised in the sixteenth and seventeenth centuries were both smaller to begin with and less culturally heterogeneous (at least compared to Asia). Homogenisation measures were also more drastic; that is, the expulsion of Moriscos and so on. European empire building happened late(-ish) and was mostly overseas, so it did not hinder these efforts. By contrast, Asian and Eurasian houses already controlled vast (and relatively continuous territorial) realms in the sixteenth century, with extremely heterogenous populations. Thus, increased centralisation/confessionalisation in Asia in the sixteenth century never quite produced the degree of homogenisation in ruled societies that it did in Europe, though Asian polities had centralised much earlier along the (A) axis (i.e. the establishment of political authority as supreme over alternatives). What ended up happening instead was the increase in the homogeneity of the core segment of society more closely associated with the ruling house (e.g. the

---

[118] For more on this, see, for example, Çapan and Zarakol (2019); Zarakol (2010, 2011, 2014).
[119] See the earlier centralisation discussion.

Sunnis in the Ottoman Empire). To make a rather complicated story short, this meant that many Asian empires entered the nineteenth century more culturally heterogeneous (within continuous territories) than their European counterparts. This is partly what rendered nationalisation projects difficult (and later violent), siphoning off energies that might have been better spent creating Asian solidarities.[120]

Asian and Eurasian states were also vulnerable internationally. Studies of stigmatisation dynamics have shown us that it is very difficult, if not impossible, for individual actors to resist such group narratives of normative superiority if they cannot advance alternative group narratives about their own norms.[121] By the nineteenth century, groupness was hard to come by in Asia: the fact was that 'the East', much more connected from the thirteenth to the seventeenth centuries, had become increasingly regionalised from the seventeenth century onwards. Those regions were now becoming increasingly nationalised in the nineteenth century, further emphasising their distinctness rather than their commonalities. All of these dynamics rendered the behaviour of Eastern actors and polities 'anomic' at exactly the time when they were dealing with a group narrative of civilisational superiority emanating from Europe.[122] By the nineteenth century, European states, though still in competition with each other, were operating as a 'society' when dealing with other regions of the world[123] and pushing a narrative of group superiority about European (white) civilisation. In the nineteenth century, because there no longer existed a shared social, normative community in the East, Eastern elites could not successfully advance such a counter-narrative, though some did try, as I discuss in the Epilogue.

At the same time, the ghosts of past 'world orders' of the East were present enough for these polities to be tainted by association with each

---

[120] This is not to say there were no attempts to create such solidarities, but, as the Epilogue also discusses, such efforts came too late.

[121] See Zarakol (2011), chapter 2.

[122] For more on attributions of anomie to outsiders and why groupness is an advantage in social hierarchies, see Zarakol (2011); see also Elias and Scotson (1994).

[123] See also Keene (2002).

other in the face of European advancement. This residue hurt in another way as well. Many Asian and Eurasian states – for instance, the Ottoman Empire and China – had their own traditional historiographies and literatures discussing problems of decline. Unsurprisingly, these decline literatures had their heyday in the sixteenth and seventeenth centuries, coinciding with the period of decline and fragmentation of the post-Timurid 'world order' and the 'Seventeenth-Century General Crisis'. Even though there had been subsequent recovery (and even expansion) in Asia and Eurasia in the eighteenth century as referred to previously, these 'Eastern' decline narratives found new life in the nineteenth century, repurposed through their encounter with the European narratives about the inferiority and the stagnation of the East.[124] The externally imposed narrative of civilisational hierarchies (of the nineteenth century) and the internal narratives of decline (from the sixteenth and seventeenth centuries) seemed to be corroborating each other across the ages, especially because not much attention was paid to the intervening period but also because something had been lost in the way of the social fabric of 'the East'. The result was an amplification of the concept of Eastern decline from the nineteenth century onwards and its rereading back into history, even to previous periods where it did not apply.

Before the West ends with an Epilogue (Chapter 7), 'Uses and Abuses of Macro-History? Am I a "Eurasianist"?'. The Epilogue reflects on the benefits and the pitfalls of developing such an alternative macro-history and deals with the epistemological, methodological and normative questions my approach brings up. It does so by walking the reader through the intellectual biographies of three Eastern and three Western authors who have attempted to write about Asia and Eurasia at the turn of the nineteenth and in the first half of the twentieth centuries, while our current order was taking its current shape. Through them we learn what makes macro-history appealing and also be found wanting, as well as the ways in which our own positionality as scholars, citizens, immigrants etc. may distort or enhance our approach to such projects. The book thus ends with a defence of macro-history, especially to study

---

[124] Notwithstanding the fact that Spain/the Habsburgs had their own 'decline' literature from the same seventeenth-century period.

regions outside of the West. In the uncertain future we are headed to, we need better and more connected histories of 'the East' in IR through the lens of global historical sociology; that is, 'a relational approach recognizes that all places – even seemingly "local" or "national" ones – are constituted and reconstituted by their complex relations to other places'.[125] I hope *Before the West*, though inevitably incomplete, is a step in that direction.

[125] Go and Lawson (2017, p. 24).

PART I

Cihannüma

2 | Making the East: Chinggisid World Orders

The Empire of Genghis Khan and Its Successor Khanates (Thirteenth–Fourteenth Centuries)

Heere bigynneth the Squieres Tale.
At Sarray, in the land of Tartarye,
Ther dwelte a kyng that werreyed Russye,
Thurgh which ther dyde many a doughty man.
Which in his tyme was of so greet renoun,
That ther was nowher in no regioun
So excellent a lord in alle thyng.
Hym lakked noght that longeth to a kyng;
And of the secte, of which that he was born,
He kepte his lay, to which that he was sworn;
And therto he was hardy, wys, and riche,
And pitous, and just, and everemoore yliche,
Sooth of his word, benigne, and honurable,
Of his corage as any centre stable,
Yong, fressh, strong, and in armes desirous
As any bacheler of al his hous.
A fair persone he was, and fortunat,
And kepte alwey so wel roial estat
That ther was nowher swich another man.
This noble kyng, this Tarte Cambyuskan
From Geoffrey Chaucer's *The Canterbury Tales* (1387–1400)

Introduction

In 1325, a young man called Ibn Battuta set out on the road, embarking on a travelling career that would span most of his life, and one that would eventually take him very far from his hometown of Tangier in

North Africa.[1] Battuta (1304–69) moved around for the next thirty years, to locations ranging from North Africa to the Arabian Peninsula to Anatolia and the plains of Volga and from there to Central, South and South East Asia and to the Indian subcontinent, as well as to 'China' and later also Spain, Mali and Timbuktu, with brief to extended stays in each location. He was welcomed in most places he visited and usually made his living as an Islamic jurist. Sometimes he was given generous gifts or allowances by his hosts, who were eager to receive news from places he had visited and welcomed his advice on world matters. We know all of this because, after Ibn Battuta retired back to his hometown, he produced an account of his journeys – *A Gift to Those Who Contemplate the Wonders of Cities and the Marvels of Travelling* – which has survived to this day and is a rather fascinating read, a genuine precursor to the travel blogs and Instagram accounts of our day.

Still, Ibn Battuta is less known to the general public than is his Venetian counterpart, Marco Polo (1254–1324), who made a similar journey some decades before Battuta, travelling from Venice to Bolghar and eventually moving via Central Asia on to Dadu/Khanbaliq (Beijing), the seat of Kubilai Khan, who was the fifth Great Khan of the Mongol Empire and also the founder of the Yuan Dynasty in China. Marco Polo, whose travel account was called *The Travels of Marco Polo*, is of course a larger-than-life figure in the European historical imagination, providing seemingly endless fodder for popular historical fiction. People thus can have the impression that he was the only person to traverse Eurasia. Marco Polo's continuing popularity is partially underwritten by the long-standing – and still not entirely discredited – Eurocentrist trope that Europeans were naturally curious about the world and adventurous enough to discover so much of it, while non-Europeans were essentially parochial and disinterested in travel. This trope was used to explain why Europe took over so much of the world while Asia declined, yet it is easily proven false by Ibn Battuta, whose

---

[1] The word *Cihannüma*, which gives Part I its title, is a compound word, pronounced as 'Jehan-noumah'. *Cihan* means 'the universe' or 'the world'; *numa* is the thing that makes it visible. A *cihannüma* is a tower or a room from which you can see everything (i.e. a panopticon but without the negative connotation); among other things, it was also the name of a universal geography book prepared by Katip Çelebi between 1648 and 1657.

travels were even more extensive, adventurous and immersed than Marco Polo's.

Nor was Ibn Battuta the only 'non-Western'[2] person to engage in such a journey. In terms of being eclipsed by Marco Polo in the popular imagination, Battuta shares a similar fate with a number of known Asian travellers of that period. For example, towards the end of the thirteenth century, Rabban Bar Sauma (1220–94) and Rabban Markos (1245–1317), two Nestorian monks of Öngüd origin from Khitai/ 'China', set out from Dadu/Khanbaliq (Beijing) for a pilgrimage to Jerusalem. Their journey was derailed due to various conflicts, and they ended up seeking refuge in Baghdad, which was then under the control of the Ilkhanate Khan Arghun, a nephew of Kubilai Khan. While there, Rabban Markos was elected Patriarch of the Church of the East. Rabban Bar Sauma, on the other hand, was sent on a mission to Europe to conduct alliance talks with the Franks. He travelled via Trebizond and Constantinople to Rome, Genoa, and later Paris and Bordeaux. Like Ibn Battuta and Marco Polo, Bar Sauma also dictated an account of his travels towards the end of his life. And even before the monks, we have the example of Isa Kelemechi, who started his career as an astronomer in the court of Kubilai Khan and later travelled to the Ilkhanate, only to be sent on a diplomatic mission to Rome to seek the support of the Pope in the Mongol campaign against the Mamluks in Egypt.

When we start filling out the space around the popular image of Marco Polo as bravely going where no man had ever gone before[3] with examples of other travellers who travelled all the way from China to Europe, or from Morocco all the way to China, the world of the thirteenth and fourteenth centuries surprises us. It is a world that is much more connected than we would expect, with well-established

---

[2] I use the term anachronistically (and somewhat ironically) here because such distinctions did not exist back in the thirteenth century. Arguably Ibn Battuta was as Western as Marco Polo, given that he came from an area that was geographically the west of the Italian peninsula, and also given the fact that the Mediterranean coast of North Africa had long been part of the same ecumene as the Mediterranean coast of Europe. Alternatively, one could argue, given Venice's interconnectivity with 'the East', that Marco Polo was not truly of 'the West'.

[3] Some even question whether Marco Polo went all the way to China because he did not mention the Great Wall. But this is based on a misreading of Chinese history. The wall was constructed on Polo's route later. See May (2012).

overland and naval routes.[4] This is, simultaneously, a banal observation to make, because people are almost as familiar with the 'Silk Road' as they are with 'Marco Polo', and yet it is still one that has to be made because the image of Marco Polo traversing this distance for the first time ever persists in the popular imagination. Nothing could be further from the truth: in the thirteenth and early fourteenth centuries, thanks to the Mongols, Eurasia was *more* connected than it had ever been – and would be for some centuries to come.[5]

The 'Silk Road' was not a Mongol invention,[6] but the 'Mongol *World* Empire'[7] secured its traditional routes, and helped facilitate the establishment of new ones. These routes survived the dissolution of the empire into four khanates, even when they were fighting each other.[8] Another connection was the *yam* system of postal stations[9] spanning the length of the empire, which highly impressed Marco Polo and other observers.[10] Each station was backed by one thousand households who maintained the postal horses, tended to the couriers and patrolled the main routes nearby.[11] In order to use the *yam*, one needed to have a *gerege*, a passport of sorts that indicated the privileges of the traveller.[12] Thanks to these networks and roads, bureaucrats, couriers, merchants and clergymen (i.e. a lot of people) moved great distances across Asia with relative ease. In fact, we must assume that, however exceptional travellers such as Ibn Battuta and Marco Polo may have been, for every Ibn Battuta who gave an account of his travels, there must have been many others who did not or who did but whose memory did not survive. It is extremely unlikely that the figures known to us from their travel accounts were the only people who travelled from one end of the known world to the other. There would have been other travellers – many more in fact – who did not travel the whole way but still traversed parts of this world, carrying

[4] May notes: 'I can think of no period other than perhaps the past 200 years in which the world was more interconnected' (2012, p. 7).
[5] May (2012, p. 8).   [6] See Frankopan (2016); Millward (2013).
[7] Italics added. Labelled as such by John Andrew Boyle, as cited by May (2012, p. 7).
[8] Shim (2014); see also May (2012, pp. 117, 123); Biran (2007, p. 77).
[9] Likely borrowed from Khitans in north China, precursors. See Morgan (1982). Note, however, that Morgan later revised his views on how much the Mongols borrowed.
[10] May (2012, pp. 124–5).   [11] May (2012, p. 117); Shim (2014).
[12] May (2012, p. 120).

with them not only material goods (today even the most dismissive accounts of the Chinggisid Empire concede the role of *Pax Mongolica* in facilitating Eurasian trade) but also knowledge, information and technique.[13]

In the thirteenth and fourteenth centuries, we thus had a world in 'the East' where (at least some people) who lived on one side of Asia were quite aware of those who lived on the other (or beyond), and vice versa.[14] That this was the case for Europeans has been well-documented: for centuries after, the travels of Marco Polo were the main source of knowledge for Europeans about East Asia. Christopher Columbus carried a copy of Marco Polo's book on his voyage to find the land of the 'Great Khan'.[15] There are references to the Mongols in the European art from the period, from the *Canterbury Tales*[16] to Italian church frescoes,[17] and no doubt more would have been (and could still be) found if there had been more curiosity about such references in modern times.[18] However, such European notions of Asia are not what I am referring to when I say this was a connected world. Europe was very much on the periphery of this world order, and European artists still took notice; imagine, then, how much knowledge was shared within that world order itself.

There are many fascinating things about Ibn Battuta's travel memoirs, but reading them one is struck above all by the fact that he travels with the greatest of ease, with the kind of entitlement to being treated well that in our time is available only to holders of Western passports. Even allowing for the fact that Ibn Battuta's encounters could have been somewhat sanitised for the consumption of the reader (though clearly not entirely, as he does recount a couple of incidents of robbery and brushes with death), the most remarkable thing about Battuta's travels is how *unremarkable* his hosts find him. In return, Battuta also

---

[13] For instance, the counterweight trebuchet was introduced to East Asia (from Europe and the Middle East) by the Mongols, as discussed in May (2011, pp. 137–8).

[14] May (2012, p. 8); Abu-Lughod (1991).   [15] May (2012, p. 129).

[16] See the epigraph to this chapter.

[17] See, for example, Dunlop (2015; 2018); see also Mack (2001); Prazniak (2010).

[18] As Dunlop notes: 'There has been almost no study of one of the most enormous and consequential geopolitical shifts, the uniting of much of the Eurasian landmass under the four linked states of the thirteenth-century and fourteenth-century Mongol Empire ... For European art history, the impact has been essentially unexplored' (2018).

takes everything he experiences very much in stride. This is not to say
that he is ignored or treated with disrespect: to the contrary, he is a man
of some standing almost wherever he goes due to his background in
Islamic jurisprudence, which also is a source of income for him during
his travels.

Two things are noteworthy here. First, Ibn Battuta's social capital
transfers easily throughout 'Asia': he is treated more or less the same
wherever he goes, with access to the highest echelons of power in
almost each political setting he encounters. Second, there is no indica-
tion that his arrival is a surprise for any of his hosts, nor do they ever
express any confusion as to who he is or what he looks like or about his
place of origin. Instead, they use him as a source of information to get
updates on places that they have clearly heard of and thought about
before.[19] And Ibn Battuta, for his part, also knows where to go and
how to get there, and he always seems to have a decent understanding
of the local conditions and the political dynamics of the next place he is
going to visit. He is also very rarely judgemental of the things he
witnesses during his travels. All of this strongly creates a picture of
not only a very well-connected world, in which Ibn Battuta (like Polo) is
simply taking advantage of well-established routes, relationships and
networks, but also one sharing an ontological fabric. In the critical IR
literature, much is made of first colonial encounters,[20] of the 'othering'
that accompanied European[21] expansion into other parts of the world,
but none of that is present in what we find in Ibn Battuta's account (nor
Marco Polo's) for that matter. In other words, the fourteenth century
does not seem to be a time of first encounters at all; the world Ibn
Battuta was moving in was thick with intersubjective understandings as
well as established trade routes and goods coveted throughout Asia.

The other examples of travellers mentioned here also support this
observation. Is it not striking that a person in the thirteenth century
could start their career as a monk in 'China' and end up a Patriarch in

[19] For example, '[The Sultan of Birgi (in Asia Minor)] enquired of me about myself
     and my coming, and then questioned me about al-Hijaz, Egypt, Syria, al-Yaman,
     the two Iraqs, and the lands of the Persians'; 'Bayalun, the daughter of the king
     of Constantinople the Great [and wife of Özbeg Khan of the Golden Horde] . . .
     asked about us and our journey hither and the distance of our native lands'.
[20] For example, Todorov (1999).
[21] It is also debatable whether first encounters of Europeans *always* ended up in
     'othering' – we may be projecting dynamics of a later period back onto the first
     European explorers.

Baghdad? Or that someone from 'China' could be sent on a diplomatic mission to Europe, after first rising through the ranks in 'Persia'? This type of geographic-cultural mobility is still rare today, and it is precisely one that many take pride in our global liberal order for having provided (at least before COVID-19). I grew up in Istanbul, Turkey, moved to the United States at the age of seventeen and ended up in Cambridge, United Kingdom, some fifteen or so years later. My ability to adjust to these new settings and succeed in them was facilitated by the high levels of exposure I had growing up to American and British cultures. People like me are not exactly a novelty in our time, but we are still a global minority, notwithstanding the fact that global capitalism has made it easier than ever to move around (at least for certain demographic segments) and to integrate into new settings. How could something similar have been possible in the thirteenth or fourteenth century in Asia, a continent that is imagined in IR to have been a disconnected – at best a regionalised – space prior to the global expansion of the European states system?

The answer is straightforward: there were 'world orders' in Asia and Eurasia before the arrival of Europeans. Europe and Asia have been interconnected[22] 'since the dawn of time', to use a turn of phrase popular with students. However, if there is one event that made the continent of Asia a space with its own generalisable dynamics (rather than just a variety of 'not-Europe', as IR often assumes), that event is located in the thirteenth century. Asia was first made whole, for better or worse, by a man called Genghis Khan and his followers. The empire that Genghis Khan created not only connected the different corners of 'Asia' but profoundly transformed them economically, socially and especially politically, to the extent that we can speak about not only a Chinggisid 'world order' in Asia but post-Chinggisid ones as well.

This chapter traces the historical narrative from the emergence of the empire (1206–[94]) of Genghis Khan (r. 1206–27) to its four successor dynasties: the Yuan Dynasty in eastern Asia or 'China' (1271–1368); the Chagatai Khanate (1225–1340) in 'Central Asia'; the Ilkhanate (1256–1383) in western Asia (or the 'Middle East'); and the Golden Horde (1240–1502) in northern Asia, the region occupied by Russia

---

[22] The non-Wallerstein branch of the world systems school has been making this point for decades. See, for example, Frank (1998); Frank and Gills (1996); Denemark (1999); Abu-Lughod (1989).

today. We will see that the Chinggisid Empire not only had
a considerable material impact on Asia but also significantly changed
the ideational landscape. The Islamic/Persian and Chinese worlds had
contact before Genghis Khan, but the Chinggisid Empire increased the
density of the connections between the two sides of Asia by actively
transferring intelligentsia, artisans and scientists from one side of the
continent to the other. Even more significant for our purposes, however, was the transmission of a particular norm of Chinggisid sovereignty as detailed in Chapter 1, an understanding of the khan as the
centralised, supreme political authority above all, the awesome power
of whom was legitimised through world domination and universal
empire.

What Is 'Asia'?

What, if anything, makes Asia *Asia*?[23] Some might argue that it was the
shared colonial experience and trauma of the nineteenth century that
made the continent into an ontological category, but such accounts put
too much power in European colonialism in creating the world we live
in (and are thus Eurocentric in their own way). Furthermore, 'shared
colonial experience' as an explanation of constituting Asia as
a continent falls short analytically. Gesturing to European colonialism
does not distinguish Asia enough from other regions of the world with
similar experiences, leaving us to puzzle over those shared patterns
which are unique to Asia. Furthermore, there are too many parallel
historical-sociological developments throughout the continent which
predate experiences with European colonialism. With a few exceptions,
European colonialism was not experienced severely in Asia until the
nineteenth century; therefore it cannot be the cause of commonalities
that predate this period. There are also regions of Asia that were never
fully or formally colonised, regions which nevertheless exhibit similarities with the regions that were.

All of this points to this continent as having existed as a coherent
space of its own, with its own shared history, long before Europeans
came on the scene in a noticeable way. Indeed, the various corners of
'Asia' have long been connected through trade and sometimes through

---

[23] As noted in Chapter 1, in this book Asia includes Eurasia and the Middle East.
See Chapter 1, fn 17.

conflict as well. Most readers would have heard about Alexander the Great's campaign into the Indus Valley (present-day Pakistan), following the Gordian knot prophecy about the conquest of Asia. Accounts of these campaigns by Alexander's contemporaries imply a degree of familiarity that suggests that even this was not 'first contact'. Other memorable contacts between the two sides of the continent include the Battle of Talas in 751, when the nascent Abbasid Caliphate, in alliance with the Yarlung Dynasty (Tibet), stopped the expansion of the Tang Dynasty (China) into Transoxiana. Furthermore, the spread of goods and of ideas (especially in the realm of religion) suggests a high degree of conductivity throughout the continent. Islam arrived in China relatively soon after its emergence, for instance. Thus we could say 'Asia' always existed in some sense; it did not need to be imagined by Europeans.

Some may object here that transcontinental contacts in Asia were not very durable, especially when compared to the shared historical experiences that constitute 'Europe' as a unique category. But the concept of 'Europe' does not stand up to similar scrutiny either. To the extent that the self-evident nature of 'Europe' is justified in IR discussions, it is by reference to two things: the common legacy of the Roman Empire and of Christendom.[24] The notion of Christendom constituting Europe as a self-evident order is at odds with the conflict-intensive history of the region, however, and is also at odds with the historical record. The Roman Empire justification also involves some hand-waving, because the Roman Empire covered (North) Africa and 'the Middle East' but not the northern parts of Europe.[25] If shared imperial legacy goes a long way in constituting a particular geography as an ontologically defensible 'region' and/or category, 'Asia' also has a similar legacy.

By that standard, in the thirteenth century, Asia was certainly made whole as a continent by the empire of Genghis Khan, which united eastern Asia ('China' today), central Asia (the region from Transoxiana to 'Mongolia' today), north-western Asia ('Russia' today) and

---

[24] The English School is one of the few places where this discussion is even raised; see, for example, Bull and Watson (1984).

[25] In fact, it makes much more sense to think of Europe plus Mediterranean plus MENA as a coherent order. This is also similar to Marshall G. S. Hodgson's thinking as explained in *The Venture of Islam* (1977). See also Phillips (2016). All of this is to say that such justifications, though they seem reasonable from a distance, do not map neatly to the category of 'Europe' as it exists today.

south-western Asia ('Iran' and 'the Middle East' today). Not many students of world politics realise that 'Iran' and 'China' were under the authority of the same sovereign for much of the thirteenth century and were ruled (along with much of the rest of Asia, including 'Russia') by dynasties that were very much influenced by the sovereignty norms of the Chinggisid Empire for the next century as well (and in some cases even further beyond).[26] Even in parts of Eurasia that did not come under the direct control of the Chinggisids (e.g. Japan, the Indian subcontinent, North Africa and, yes, Europe), first the expansion of this empire and later its presence was transformative. The thirteenth and fourteenth centuries in Asia belong very much to the Chinggisid Empire (and its successor khanates).

In recent years, there has been some interest in IR in the Mongols in particular and steppe polities in general. The importance of Mongol conquests to European history has been highlighted, especially in terms of their impact on the transmission of goods from Asia to Europe. For example, Buzan and Little devote a section to nomadic empires and their interest in facilitating trade relations.[27] More recently, Anievas and Nişancıoğlu observe that 'such was the reach of Inner Asian nomadic empires that their legacy could be found to the north in the Muscovy Empire, to the south in the Mughal Empire, to the west in the Safavid and Seljuk Empires, and to the east in the Yuan and Manchu Dynasties'.[28] Yet Anievas and Nişancıoğlu are primarily interested in the role the Mongols played in the 'rise of the West' by putting Europe and China in direct contact for the first time,[29] and they go on to argue that Europe was the main beneficiary of the transfer of goods, technologies and knowledge via this connection. The Black Death, which is supposed to have spread to Europe from Asia via these same routes,[30] is also considered a contributing factor in Europe's eventual rise, having drastically changing the demographics there and undermined feudalism.[31] A related literature explores alternative routes to state formation, most notably of the nomadic kind or that of the

---

[26] Historians have long noted the transformative effects of the Chinggisid Empire on successor states. See May (2011, p. 8) for an overview. For a more recent take, see Favereau (2021).

[27] Buzan and Little (2000, pp. 183–9).

[28] Anievas and Nişancıoğlu (2015, p. 71).

[29] Anievas and Nişancıoğlu (2015, p. 70).

[30] Schamiloglu (2017a); Pamuk (2007).

[31] Anievas and Nişancıoğlu (2015); May (2011).

steppe.[32] These scholars take an almost Khaldunian[33] perspective to argue that the differentiating logics of nomadic polities and their legacies in existing states bear closer scrutiny. Adopting an approach rooted in an uneven and combined development framework, Matin argues nomadic geopolitical pressures on agrarian society were central to pre-modern state formation in Iran.[34] Most recently, Neumann and Wigen[35] have argued that the steppe tradition, which goes back thousands of years, is crucial to the emergence of complex polities, giving rise to steppe empires which then hybridised with sedentary societies on the peripheries of the steppe. They traced how steppe-nomadic traditions were incorporated into Russian and Ottoman state-making approaches and pointed to the durability of these practices.

In this chapter and those that follow, I build on this recent IR scholarship (in addition to state-of-the-art scholarship from Mongol Studies). However, for reasons explained in Chapter 1 of this book, this chapter is focusing on the Chinggisid Empire not because of its steppe origins, nor because of its facilitation of trade during *Pax Mongolica* or the contributions the Mongols made to the European historical trajectory. Rather, this book focuses on the Chinggisid Empire and its successors as historical equivalents of our modern Great Powers and 'world order' builders – and as world historical actors in their own right. The Chinggisid Empire played a fundamental role in creating Asia as a political space of its own right by acting as a unifying sovereign over much of Asia and transmitting deep sovereignty norms along with material goods throughout the continent. Its main legacy is thus the creation of an Asian 'world order' in the thirteenth and fourteenth centuries, a universalising ambition which would shape the region for centuries to come.

Prior to the conquests of Genghis Khan, political power was fragmented throughout Asia: 'in the steppe, China, and the Muslim world, there was no one central authority but rather multiple, competing dynasties'.[36] Even 'China', a region more familiar with centralised political authority than most, was divided into three kingdoms: the

---

[32] See Matin (2007); Pijl (2007); Kang (2010); Neumann and Wigen (2013); MacKay et al. (2014); MacKay (2016); Hall (2018).

[33] Ibn Khaldun (1332–1406) was a near-contemporary of Ibn Battuta, from the same general region. He posited a cyclical theory of nomadic conquest to sedentary civilisation to decay. See, for example, Dale (2006); Irwin (1997).

[34] Matin (2007).   [35] Neumann and Wigen (2018).   [36] Biran (2007, p. 26).

Song Dynasty in the south, the Jin Dynasty in the north and the Xi Xia Dynasty in the north-west. Furthermore, compared to what was to come under the Yuan, these prior dynasties were much more willing to diffuse power and authority even within the territories they held: the Song, for instance, balanced power between military and civilian officials, as well as administrative units, though power was technically centralised in the emperor.[37] In the west of Asia, the Abbasid Caliphate technically reigned supreme over Muslim lands, but by the twelfth century it had all but lost any power beyond its symbolic claims. Political power was in the hands of various dynasties whose authority was shared with not only the caliph but also the *ulama* (Islamic jurists).[38]

In other words, in the early part of the millennium, not only was political power fragmented throughout Asia among many competing dynasties, but political power also did not equal sovereign power in the sense we understand it today. Kings did not have supreme authority yet; their authority was undermined or checked by various other claimants, such as the *ulama*, the caliph, the soldiers,[39] the literati etc. The later association of Asian polities with Oriental despotism[40] has also distorted views of historical antecedents and created the impression that centralised rule was always very pronounced in Asia, which is entirely misleading, as we will see in the next chapters as well. While it is fair to say that the rule of the Seljuk Dynasty (ruling over Asia Minor and much of the present-day Middle East) or the Song Dynasty (in the southern part of present-day China) in the twelfth century were more centralised than many of their European counterparts, these polities nevertheless were also characterised by a certain extent of power-sharing between the nominal ruler, warriors, religious authorities and/or local landlords (or some combination thereof). The picture in Asia on the eve of Mongol conquest, then, was one of political fragmentation, a high number of competing polities and dynasties with weak central authority, especially as compared to what would come next.

---

[37] The Song Dynasty is considered to be a relatively 'liberal' period in Chinese history. See, for example, Deng (2020); Xiaonan and Lamouroux (2005).

[38] See, for example, Crone (2004); Crone and Hinds (2003).

[39] For example, the first Song emperor, Zhao Kuangyin (Taizu), had to confront the armies which had become regular king-makers.

[40] See also Zarakol (2017a).

Chinggisid Conquests: A Timeline

The transformative effect of the conquests of Genghis Khan should be clearer against this fragmented political landscape of Asia on the eve of the thirteenth century. Genghis Khan not only politically unified most of Asia;[41] he also changed the conception of sovereignty throughout the continent by disseminating, through his own example, the norm of the political ruler as the exclusive supreme authority, legitimised by world domination. This section thus gives a brief history of the conquests as led by Genghis Khan and his immediate descendants (i.e. the Great House of the Chinggisids). The timeline is important because Genghis Khan and his conquests became a template for sovereign aspirations for centuries to come. The section after the timeline will scrutinise the features of the world order created by these conquests.

The Rise of (Temujin) Genghis Khan (r. 1206–1227)

The rise of Temüjin (later Chinggis/Genghis Khan) (1162–1227, r. 1206–27) from what is claimed to be the most humble beginnings to become one of the most powerful men in world history is fascinating.[42] What we know about the life of Genghis Khan comes primarily from *The Secret History of the Mongols* (SHM), written soon after his death in 1227.[43] This text is noteworthy both for what it relates and for what it emphasises in the life of Temüjin. Temüjin was born (c. 1162) into a politically fragmented landscape: what was noted earlier about Asia in general was true especially of Inner/Central Asia, with the various houses of Tatars, the Kereyids, the Naiman, the Merkids, the Onggud, the Qonggirad and so on, all competing for resources.[44] These groups are usually called 'tribes' in the literature, but, as noted in Chapter 1, this book follows David Sneath's

---

[41] Note that in Japan, which never came under direct Chinggisid rule, the de facto shared authority dynamic between the imperial court and the military leaders (*shogun*) lasted well into early modernity.

[42] See Weatherford (2004) for a popular and very readable account of Genghis Khan's life story. For my recounting of this narrative, I have relied mostly on Biran, May and Sneath, who are in general agreement about the chronology of events.

[43] There are other texts from the period, for example Altan Debter or works by Rashid al-Din, Juwayni etc.

[44] May (2012, p. 27).

characterisation of this political space as competing aristocratic 'houses'.[45] At the time, Mongols were dispersed as a group as a result of their recent defeats by the Tatars; they did not have a khan.[46]

Much is made of the fact in the SHM of Temüjin's very difficult beginnings, and his 'origin story' is significant because it becomes part of his latter-day individual charisma as a ruler. The story of having to fight one's way to sovereignty, and having to fight against kin and friends on that path, in addition to outsiders faced in conquest, is part of the normative package that is passed down and disseminated by Genghis Khan and his empire. As we will see in the next chapter, post-Chinggisid successor houses often either have tanistry as an institution or tolerate tanistry-adjacent practices within their world order.[47] Genghis Khan's well-known life story could have further legitimised and popularised this pre-existing practice as an institutionalised simulation of what Genghis achieved.

Temüjin's father Yesügei – who was a leader of some standing among the Mongols[48] – was poisoned when Temüjin was a child, and his mother, after being cast aside by Yesügei's followers, could barely feed her children. By the time he was a teenager, Temüjin had started improving the situation of his family[49] by standing up to threats and making alliances with the more powerful families. Temüjin also killed his older half-brother, Bekhter, who was entitled to marry Temüjin's mother. Around this time, his wife, Börte, was kidnapped. Temüjin managed to save her[50] and accepted the child – Jochi – (likely) born out of this kidnapping episode as his own.[51] Temüjin's continued military successes gained him an enthusiastic following from his kinsmen (while

---

[45] Sneath (2007) argues that the notion of a pastoral, egalitarian society conjured up by the notions of nomadic tribes are a myth and that steppe societies (including the Mongols) were highly stratified, with very clear distinctions between noble houses and commoners, and in fact this is what allowed these societies to function relatively well even in periods of great decentralisation (p. 5).

[46] May (2017, p. 28).

[47] See, for example, Fletcher (1979, 1986). Fletcher was the first to write on this practice as a norm in Asia with shared origins.

[48] He was the grandson of Kabul Khan, the ruler of the Khamag Mongols. See Sneath (2007).

[49] May (2012, pp. 29–30).

[50] Sneath (2007) notes that Temüjin was already powerful (and connected) enough at this point to raise a military unit described as *tümen* (ten-thousand).

[51] Biran (2007, p. 35).

also straining some of his erstwhile alliances), and in 1185 or 1186 he was enthroned as khan by the Borjigin Mongols (his father's people).[52]

Initially, Temüjin dealt with only 'internal' rivals to power. In 1187, he was defeated by Jamuqa, a former ally,[53] but managed to escape and convince others to defect.[54] For a few years after that Temüjin was absent from the scene. By 1196, however, he was fighting the Tatars with the encouragement of the Jin (a major regional power dynasty located in what is now northern China).[55] At this time, Temüjin was still fighting alongside his patron, Toghril or Ong Khan of the Kereyids.[56] In the meantime, Jamuqa organised his own coalition of lesser houses, who declared him Gür-khan (universal khan),[57] presenting a major challenge to Temüjin. In 1201, Jamuqa was defeated by Ong Khan and Temüjin.[58] In 1202, Temüjin also defeated the Tatars, ordering all male Tatars (of nobility) above two feet in height to be executed.[59] However, soon after this victory Temüjin had a falling out with Ong Khan, who was persuaded by his own son (and possibly Jamuqa) that Temüjin had become a threat to his own authority. Ong Khan decided to assassinate Temüjin, who was saved from this fate at the last moment by two loyalists who warned him.[60] Temüjin barely escaped with his life, and the few people who stuck with him in this dark period swore a loyalty oath (by drinking from the water of Baljuna), which later became a very important pedigree of legitimacy for their descendants.[61]

As Neumann and Wigen also note, in the steppe tradition, bonds were not ethnic or by kinship but based on loyalty oaths.[62] Temüjin's loyalists at this point were not necessarily Mongol but 'an extremely heterogeneous group: Khitans from northern China, Tanguts, Muslim traders from Central Asia, and perhaps also Indians ... Kereyid and Naiman'.[63] Temüjin avenged this betrayal in 1203 – Ong Khan was defeated and killed – and he then turned his attention to the Naiman, defeating them soon after and incorporated parts of their khanate to his

---

[52] May (2012, p. 32); Biran (2007, p. 35).
[53] In fact Jamuqa had been Temüjin's *anda* (they had sworn oaths to each other).
[54] Biran (2007, p. 36); May (2012, p. 32). Both suggest that Temüjin may have spent the missing years in Jin territory, possibly even as their captive.
[55] Ibid.   [56] Ibid.   [57] Biran (2007, p. 36); May (2012, p. 33).
[58] Biran (2007, p. 37); May (2012, p. 33).   [59] Ibid.
[60] Biran (2007, pp. 37–8); May (2012, pp. 34–5).   [61] Ibid.
[62] Neumann and Wigen (2018); see their concluding chapter for an overview.
[63] Biran (2007, p. 38).

own army. In 1205, Jamuqa was betrayed by his own forces. Temüjin executed both Jamuqa and his betrayers.[64] By 1206, Temüjin had eliminated all of his internal rivals to power. A *qurultai* (a grand assembly of nobles)[65] was called, and Temüjin was elected as the leader of all Mongol tribes: 'Genghis Khan'.[66] At this *qurultai*, Genghis Khan also reorganised the military and officially proclaimed (or re-proclaimed) the Khamag Mongol Ulus (United Mongol People).[67]

Expansion to the East (Northern 'China')

Genghis Khan then turned his attention to neighbouring territories. He first swallowed the disparate groups to the north into his forces.[68] Then he turned east. By 1211, he had subjugated the Tangut Xi Xia Dynasty (located in outer Mongolia and northern China), who agreed to pay tribute and end their allegiance with the Jin.[69] A number of dynasties submitted without war, especially along the western flanks of Mongolia: in 1209, the Uighur ruler declared his allegiance, and in 1211, Arslan Khan, the leader of the Qarluqs, became the first Muslim ruler to join Genghis Khan, followed by the Almaliq.[70] In 1211, Genghis Khan waged a campaign against the Jurchen Jin in northern China. At this point the Mongols were still technically the vassals of the Jin. The campaign was successful and concluded with an arrangement for the Jin to pay tribute to Genghis. The Jin however moved their capital soon after, which the Mongols saw as a violation of their agreement. In response, in 1214, Genghis laid siege to the traditional

---

[64] Biran (2007, pp. 38–39); May (2012, p. 35). May notes that Jamuqa was executed by suffocation because of the taboo against shedding aristocratic blood.
[65] Not unlike the prince-electors of the Holy Roman Empire.
[66] Some argue that Genghis/Chinggis means 'firm' or 'fierce' (see, e.g., Biran [2007, p. 39]), but there is no consensus. In this book, I use the more common spelling of Genghis to refer to the man (Temüjin) and Chinggisid to refer to the house and sovereignty model.
[67] May (2012, p. 36); later this would be replaced by Yeke Mongol Ulus (Great Mongol People). Ulus is often translated as nation or people (following its modern usage), but Sneath (2007) notes that, at the time, Khamag Mongol Ulus is more likely to have been the name of *the dynastic realm*. Furthermore, it is probable that Kabul Khan, Temüjin's great-grandfather, had proclaimed this sovereignty first and therefore that Temüjin was reunifying what had fragmented. See also Munkh-Erdene (2011); Atwood (2015).
[68] May (2012, p. 37).   [69] May (2012, p. 38); Biran (2007, p. 48).
[70] Biran 2007, p. 49; May (2012, p. 39).

capital of the Jin, Zhongdu (in modern-day Beijing). By 1215, the Mongols had entered Zhongdu. Once again Genghis gave an opportunity to the conquered to join his army: the Khitans changed sides from the Jurchen to the Mongols.[71]

Expansion to the West (Transoxiana to the Caucasus)

Having successfully conquered northern 'China', Genghis turned westward, easily conquering territories and peoples under the rule of the Qara Khitai (Western Liao, a Sinicised empire near Kashgar). The population, majority Muslim, were not happy with their ruler, Güchülüg, a Christian married to a Buddhist princess, who was forcing them to convert. They welcomed Genghis.[72] The next rival in Genghis Khan's sights was Sultan Muhammad, ruler of the Khawarazm Dynasty located in present-day Central Asia and a major player controlling trade routes between eastern and western Asia. In 1219, the Mongol army waged its campaign against Khwarazm, taking its major cities – Utrar, Bukhara and Samarkand – one by one by 1220. The Khwarazm Shah escaped to an island on the Caspian Sea where he died a year or two later.[73] The Mongol forces chasing after him moved into the Caucasus and Crimea, defeating the local population there first and later in 1223 the Kipchaks and the Russians across the steppe. However, the threat from the Khwarazm Dynasty was not yet over: Muhammad Sultan's son, Jalal al-Din Khwarazm Shah, now challenged the Mongol forces. He would not be defeated until 1231, necessitating continued Mongol presence in western Asia even after Genghis had returned to Mongolia in 1225.[74]

The End of Genghis Khan and the Rise of His Great House

Genghis Khan died in 1227. By that time, his realm extended from present-day Iran, the Caucasus, Crimea and parts of Russia in the west and to northern China in the east. In other words, Genghis Khan, in addition to eliminating local rivals among the steppe dynasties of Inner Asia, conquered the major eastern Islamic dynasties in Central Asia

---

[71] Biran 2007, p. 50; May (2012, p. 39).
[72] May (2012, p. 40); Biran (2007, p. 53).
[73] May (2012, pp. 41–2); Biran (2007, p. 54). [74] Biran (2007, pp. 55–61).

(but not yet those in the 'Middle East' of our day) and the major Sinic dynasties in northern China (but not yet the Song Dynasty). He had four sons – Jochi, Chagatai, Ögödei and Tolui – who had been given different parts of the growing empire as their appanages. Genghis Khan's Great House would build on his conquests to broaden the frontiers of the empire even further (see Figure 2.1).

Ögödei Khan (r. 1229–1241) and the European Campaign

After Genghis Khan's death, his third son Ögödei took the title of Great Khan in 1229. Ögödei was instrumental in establishing or cementing many of the institutions of the empire. He also established a new capital – Qara Qorum – in the Orkhon Valley.[75] Ögödei's conquests focused on China and Europe: in 1234, the remnants of the Jin Dynasty in northern China were eliminated, and a campaign from 1236 to 1241 moved Mongol forces through what is now southern Russia and Ukraine all the way to present-day Germany via Hungary.[76] The Pontic steppes were controlled at the time by Turkic Cumans and the Bulghars on the Volga River, neither of whom could successfully resist the Mongols.[77] The cities of Rus did not fare any better: all the southern and northern cities fell or swore fealty, Kiev and Novgorod included.[78] Mongol forces also conquered the Georgian and Armenian kingdoms in 1239. In 1241, a Mongol regiment moved into 'Poland' and defeated a 'combined army of Poles, Germans and Teutonic Knights, a military order that emerged out of the Crusades in 1193'.[79] In the meantime, a larger segment of Mongol forces invaded 'Hungary' and defeated King Bela IV, who 'was considered by many to possess the finest cavalry in Europe'.[80]

After this string of victories, the Mongols quickly departed from Europe, a withdrawal which has puzzled many historians but is likely attributable to Ögödei's death in 1241 and the desire of the commanders of the western regiments to participate in the succession struggle. In recent years, a climatological explanation has also been posited for this hasty withdrawal. Büntgen and di Cosmo suggest that tree ring evidence indicates 'warm and dry summers from 1238–1241, followed by

---

[75] Biran (2007, p. 49). The Orkhon Valley figures in origin myths of Turkic peoples and is the site of the earliest Turkic runes.
[76] Biran (2007, p. 78).   [77] May (2012, p. 47).   [78] Ibid.   [79] Ibid.
[80] Ibid., p. 48.

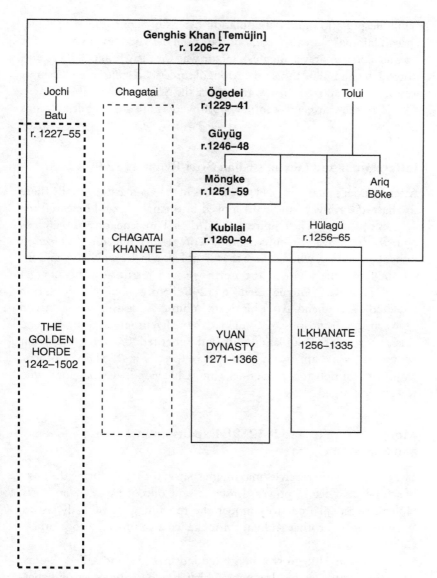

Figure 2.1 The house and empire of Genghis Khan

cold and wet conditions in early-1242' and that 'marshy terrain across the Hungarian plain most likely reduced pastureland and decreased mobility, as well as the military effectiveness of the Mongol cavalry, while despoliation and depopulation ostensibly contributed to wide-spread famine'.[81] In any case, Europe at the time was no great prize for Asian rulers: whatever the push factor was for the Mongols, there was not much of a pull. At this time Mongol forces had conquered Kashmir and had also started their war against the Song Dynasty in southern China. In the thirteenth century, both were more significant holdings than Europe.

Interregnum and Güyüg's Khan Brief Reign (r. 1246–1248)

After Ögödei's death in 1241, the forces in the Caucasus (initially there to chase the Khwarazm Shah) moved into Anatolia and defeated the Seljuks of Rum.[82] The empire was ruled by Töregene, one of Ögödei's widows, for a five-year interregnum. Töregene engineered the election of her son Güyüg, who became the Great Khan in 1246. Güyüg and his cousin Batu, the khan of the north-western territories, did not get along. However, Güyüg died in 1248 before their confrontation could come to a head. After his death, a bitter succession battle ensued between the grandsons of Genghis Khan. Eventually, Möngke, who was the son of Tolui and who had inherited the territories near Mongolia as his appanage, emerged victorious in 1251 over others, namely the supporters of Ögödei's and Chaggatai's descendants, who were then purged.[83]

Möngke Khan (r. 1251–1259); Expansion into Persia and Southern China

The empire would reach its maximum span across Asia during the reign of Möngke. Once in power, Möngke sent one of his own brothers, Hülegü, west in order to conquer the remaining Muslim dynasties. With his other brother Kubilai, Möngke led a campaign into southern China.

In the west, Hülegü stormed Baghdad in 1258 and killed the last Abbasid Caliph, a development which has had long-lasting reper-cussions for Muslims. Hülegü then conquered Aleppo and Damascus, but his forces were defeated by the Mamluk Dynasty

---

[81] Büntgen and Di Cosmo (2016, p. 1).
[82] May (2012, p. 50); Biran (2007, p. 78).   [83] Biran (2007, p. 80).

of Egypt.[84] Because Mongols were rarely defeated in this period, much is made of the fact of their humiliation at the Battle of Ayn Jalut (in modern-day Israel), which has gained increased historical significance in modern Islamic historiography. However, the Mamluk Dynasty themselves were in some ways a product of the Mongol conquests. The Ayyubid Dynasty[85] had traditionally used *mamluk* (i.e. military slaves) to run their reign, which spanned Egypt and the Levant. By the mid-thirteenth century, most of the *mamluk* corps consisted of Turkic peoples, who had been forced into slavery as a result of the Mongol invasions of the Kipchak (now Russian) steppe. These *mamluk* soldiers executed a coup in 1250 but kept a minor Ayyubid prince on the throne for legitimacy. After their victory at Ayn Jalut, the Mamluks became the official ruling house of Ayyubid lands.[86]

In the east, Möngke planned to attack the Song from the south, as the Mongol forces had not been able to penetrate the northern fortifications. The attack properly began in 1257. In the next two years, the Mongols captured a number of Song cities, but Möngke died during the campaign, sometime in 1259, forcing Kubilai to return to the Mongol steppe.[87] Upon reaching Qaraqorum, Kubilai discovered that his brother Ariq Böke, who had been left to rule in Mongolia during Möngke's campaign against the Song, had held a *qurultai* (assembly of nobles), which had named Ariq Böke the next Great Khan. Möngke refused to recognise Ariq Böke, and in this he was supported by his brother Hülegü, the commander of the western forces. Kubilai convened his own *qurultai* in 1260, which named him the Great Khan instead. The result, unsurprisingly, was a civil war that lasted for the next four years (the Toluid Civil War). Kubilai emerged victorious, but the war caused the destruction of the capital, Qaraqorum, and hastened the dissolution of the empire by cementing the autonomy of the empire's various administrative divisions.[88]

---

[84] Biran (2007, p. 79); May (2011, pp. 53–4).

[85] May (2011, p. 82). The Ayyubid dynasty was founded by Saladdin Ayyubi, the famed defender of the Holy Lands against the Crusades. The tradition of using slave soldiers was not specific to the Ayyubids but was a practice shared by most Muslim polities of the time. See also Crone (1980).

[86] May (2012, p. 82). For more on the relations between Mamluks and the Chinggisids, see Halperin (2000a); Dekkiche (2016); Amitai-Preiss (1996).

[87] May (2012, pp. 56–7); Biran (2007, p. 78).   [88] May (2012, pp. 59–60).

Division of the Empire

The division of the empire among various members of the Chinggisid house had in fact been there from the beginning: Genghis Khan had given the territories he conquered to his four sons as appanages (*ulus*[89]).[90] The dynastic branches that controlled these territories have taken on different designations, based mostly on the particularly historiography of their successor states (e.g. the 'Golden Horde' in Russia but the 'Yuan Dynasty' in China), but at the time they functioned more or less the same, and the appropriate designation for each of them in English is 'house'. Descendants of Genghis Khan's sons came to represent dynastic lineages in each region, which were called khanates, but remembered under different designations depending on the historiography of the region.

The Jochid Khanate ('Golden Horde') ('Russia')

North-western Asia (i.e. the Pontic-Caspian steppe), to the west of the river Irtysch, had been given to Jochi, the eldest son, who died before Genghis Khan, and thus was inherited by Jochi's sons: Batu Khan, who controlled the Blue Horde; and Orda Khan, who controlled the White Horde.[91] This appanage would eventually take the form of the Golden Horde[92] (or Jochid) Khanate, ruling over 'the Russian principalities, Eastern Europe to Hungary, Khwarazm, the Kipchak steppe, and Siberia eastward to the Irtysh river'.[93] The European conquests already

[89]   As also noted in fn 67, the word *ulus* is often translated 'nation' because that is what it means today, but in the thirteenth century it would have meant domain, patrimony or appanage. Sneath (2007, pp. 31, 63).

[90]   Sneath (2007, p. 31); Biran (2007, p. 68). Initially this division was likely to be more for administrative ease.

[91]   Colours were often used to indicate direction in the Turko-Mongol world (e.g. black meant north, white represented west, blue meant east, gold the centre and red the south) but could also mean other things. See May (2016). For example, blue (*kök* or *gök*) implied connection with the sky and Tenggri (heaven). Incidentally this is why we associate Chinese porcelain with blue and white, a pattern developed during the Yuan Dynasty. Gold (altan) implied imperial claims.

[92]   The Golden Horde (Altan Orda) designation was sometimes used to refer to the Blue Horde and the White Horde acting together but was adapted by Russian historians in the seventeenth century to refer to all of Mongol forces of this period. May (2011, p. 76).

[93]   May (2012, p. 81).

discussed were mostly undertaken by the forces of Batu.[94] After Batu's death in 1256, Berke replaced him and renewed the campaigns against Lithuania and Poland. During the Toluid Civil War, Berke tried to play it both ways. While he eventually recognised Kubilai as the Great Khan, his sympathies probably lay with Ariq Böke because of his religious and personal conflict with Hülegü, the ruler of south-western Asian territories (later the Ilkhanate) and a close ally of Kubilai. Berke had converted to Islam so was not happy about Hülegü's destruction of Baghdad and his execution of the Abbasid Caliph. Finally, Hülegü's campaigns threatened the claims of the Jochid line to control all of western Asia.[95] The Jochid Khanate of Berke and the Ilkhanate of Hülegü would soon be embroiled in war.

The Chagatai Khanate ('Central Asia')

The second son of Genghis Khan, Chagatai, had been given Transoxiana (between the Amu Darya and Syr Darya rivers) and Turkestan.[96] The third son, Ögödei, as we saw, had become the Great Khan after Genghis Khan, and he controlled the area between Transoxiana and Mongolia.[97] The fourth son, Tolui, was given the Mongol homeland as his appanage.[98] As discussed, after Güyüg's death, the line of Tolui executed a coup of sorts to install Möngke as the Great Khan instead of another heir from the Ögödeid line and purged both the Ögödeids and the Chagataids from positions of power.[99] As a result, the territory under the control of these purged lines became the site of a bitter power struggle between the various great-grandchildren of Genghis Khan. Eventually an agreement was reached in *qurultai* that issued the Talas Covenant, dividing the Chagatai Khanate between Kaidu and Baraq khans.[100] But this area would not be unified until Timur came on the scene (Chapter 3).

The Ilkhanate ('Iran'/'Middle East')

The third khanate was the Ilkhanate, centred in the present-day Middle East over a territory carved by Hülegü's campaigns. Hülegü recognised

---

[94] Sneath (2007, p. 32).   [95] May (2012, p. 69); Biran (2007, p. 80).
[96] Sneath (2007, p. 31); Biran (2007, p. 81).   [97] Sneath (2007, p. 31).
[98] Ibid.   [99] May (2012, pp. 52–3).   [100] Ibid., pp. 71–5.

Kubilai as the Great Khan and thus used the title Ilkhan ('subordinate Khan'). The Ilkhanate extended over 'Iran, Azerbaijan, Georgia, Armenia, Anatolia, and Iraq – territories which Kubilai assigned to Hülegü in return for the latter's support of Qubilai's [Kubilai's] cause against their brother Arigh Böqe'.[101] In Anatolia, the Seljuks of Rum became vassals of the Ilkhanate,[102] and most of the petty kingdoms (*beylik*) who replaced them continued this arrangement. The Ilkhanate faced many threats in its initial years, as they were fighting the Jochid Khanate to their north, who quickly developed a staunch alliance with the Mamluks to their west, with a Byzantine Empire acting as a conduit between the two allies. The Jochid Khanate's meddling in the Chagatai Khanate's affairs turned the eastern flank of the Ilkhanate into a threat as well. In 1295, the then ruler of the Ilkhanate, Ghazan Khan, converted to Islam, making the Ilkhanate the first officially Muslim Mongol khanate.[103]

The Yuan Khanate (Dynasty) ('China')

Finally, we have the Yuan Dynasty in China, which is the fourth khanate to emerge from the Chinggisid Empire. Having been named the Great Khan after the Toluid Civil War, Kubilai moved the capital of the empire from Qaraqorum (which had been destroyed) to China, building a winter capital – Khanbalikh – in Daidu (Beijing) and a summer capital in Shangdu (Xanadu). He completed the conquest of the Song Dynasty by 1276, by using naval forces as well as technologies transferred from the Middle East, such as the counterweight trebuchet, to overcome Chinese fortifications.[104] He also exerted Chinggisid hegemony over the dynasties in (modern-day) Korea, Vietnam and Myanmar and attempted to conquer Japan as well, only to be thwarted by a typhoon. He also sent a large fleet to Java, but the campaign was not successful.[105]

Kubilai ruled over northern and southern China (conquered in 1276–9), Manchuria, Mongolia, parts of eastern Turkestan, and

---

[101] Biran (2007, p. 80); May (2012, pp. 67–70).   [102] Arjomand (2016, p. 6).
[103] May (2012, pp. 68–70). Berke of the Jochid Khanate had converted earlier, but his successor, Möngke-Temür, was not Muslim. The Golden Horde became a Muslim house in the fourteenth century.
[104] May (2012, p. 62).   [105] Sneath (2007, p. 32).

Tibet.[106] Though technically the Great Khan, Kubilai faced serious legitimacy challenges from the other khanates, especially the Chagataid, made worse by the increasingly Sinicised manner of his rule: 'He [became], in effect, the senior member and nominal overlord of a royal family that ruled relatively independent khanates in Russia, Persia, Turkestan, and northern China.'[107] This pattern would continue with Kubilai's successors. Hence, most historians date the dissolution of the empire to 1259, the year of Möngke's death, even though the khanates made peace with each other by the beginning of the fourteenth century. The Chinggisid Empire continued to exist in principle until the end of Yuan Dynasty in 1368. However, as we will see in the next chapter, even after the Ming took over China, the Yuan line in Inner Asia continued to claim the title 'Great Khan'.[108]

Fragmentation of the Chinggisid World Order

The four khanates kept the Chinggisid world order going even after the fragmentation of the empire. In terms of institutions of the order or its operating norms, very little changed from the period of unified empire to the balance-of-power arrangement of the khanates, at least initially.

The 'multipolar' arrangement of the four khanates across Asia lasted about three quarters of a century. The Ilkhanate was the first to fall, fragmenting after the 1335 death of Abu Sa'id (and his sons) due to the plague. The Yuan Dynasty was the next to go in 1368, overthrown by the Ming. Despite the fact that Chinggsisid rule in both the Middle East and China was shorter lived than elsewhere (about a century each), its influence was monumental in both regions, as the next chapters will trace. The Yuan rule profoundly transformed notions of sovereignty in China. There is no way to make sense of the behaviours of the early Ming emperors, especially Hongwu and Yongle, without understanding the legacy of the Yuan. The Ilkhanate (in Iran) jumpstarted a fusion

---

[106] Biran (2007, p. 80). In Tibet, Kubilai 'made an alliance with the Tibetan Phagspa Lama, who identified Kubilai with figures in the Buddhist pantheon in return for the emperor's support for the religion (Rossabi 1988, p. 144)'. Sneath (2007, p. 33).

[107] Sneath (2007, p. 32).

[108] Toghan Temür, the last Yuan emperor, escaped to Mongolia, and his descendant continued their rule there as the Northern Yuan until they were conquered in the middle of the seventeenth century by the Later Jin/Manchu (who would go on to establish the Qing Dynasty in 'China').

between Persian traditions of statecraft and justifications of kingship and Islam and Chinggisid notions of world sovereignty,[109] the effects of which would be felt for centuries to come, as we will discuss in Chapters 3, 4 and 5. The Ilkhanate also expanded the Persianate ecumene into Anatolia as well as west Asia, with Persian bureaucrats serving rulers from anywhere in West Anatolia to Xorasan.[110]

It is harder to date the beginning and the end of the Chagatai Khanate, which was a fragmented entity for most of its existence. In 1331, the Chagatai ruler Tarmashirin encouraged the conversion of his subjects to Islam and met considerable resistance. Out of the fragmentation of the Chagatai Khanate there emerged in the western territory a new aspirant to the Chinggisid mantle: Timur (Tamerlane), who increasingly consolidated his power from 1370 onwards. Timur (r. 1370–1405) was not of Chinggisid lineage; not that he let that fact stop him. He married a Chinggsid princess and ruled through puppet Chinggisid khans to bolster his legitimacy. He was a great conqueror who came close to restoring the Chinggisid Empire through his successful campaign in Central Asia, the Middle East as well as the Pontic Steppes. Though he very much wanted to, he did not manage to reconquer China. We will return to him and the Great House of the Timurids in the next chapter.

The Jochid Khanate (the Golden Horde) was the most durable of the khanates. The Rus principalities were an integral part of the Jochid Khanate, but the Jochid branch – unlike their relatives in 'China' or 'the Middle East' – did not adapt to local expectations. They did not Russify or convert to Orthodox Christianity, perhaps reflecting their dismissive views of the area. Instead, as discussed, the khanate converted to Islam during the reign of Uzbek Khan (1313–41). While the Jochid line, unlike the Ilkhanate, survived the Black Death, it was considerably weakened as a result. This allowed Muscovy, the principal tax collector for the Mongols, to grow its power over the other Russian cities relatively unchecked and, eventually, to defeat Mongol forces at the battle of Kulikove Pole in 1381. However, the Golden Horde made a comeback under Toqtamish (1377–95), an ally of Timur. Toqtamish sacked Muscovy[111] but soon after Toqtamish and Timur had a falling out. Eventually Timur emerged victorious, sacking Sarai and New Sarai, the capital cities of the Golden Horde. Afterwards, the Golden

[109] Arjomand (2016, pp. 3–4).   [110] Ibid., p. 7.   [111] May (2012, pp. 78–80).

Horde fragmented, though it technically lasted until 1502. We will return to Muscovy in Chapter 5.

Understanding the Chinggisid World Order

If we date its beginning to the election of Genghis Khan as the Great Khan in the 1206 *qurultai* and its dissolution to Möngke's death in 1259, the Mongol Empire – or better yet, the empire of the Great House of Genghis – lasted for about half a century. From 1260 to the middle of the fourteenth century, most of Asia was still under the direct rule of the Chinggisid family, though now divided into smaller autonomous khanates: Jochid (Golden Horde), Ilkhanate, Chagatai and Yuan. For about half a century, the khanates constantly warred with each other, but then they reconciled, and the first half of the fourteenth century was relatively peaceful throughout Asia, a period also known as *Pax Mongolica*. Then the Black Death arrived.[112] By the end of the fourteenth century, Ilkhanate (Persia) and Yuan (China) were gone, the Chagatai Khanate had given birth to the Timurid Empire, and the Golden Horde was limping into the next century.

We are thus talking about a time period of direct Chinggisid domination throughout Asia that extends at least a century and half and is in fact closer to two centuries. The period of United States hegemony is shorter. Yet few would claim that the influence of the United States on the international order has been fleeting. Why would we believe so about the empires of the Chinggisids? Once we start looking, tallying their influence even on the arts of 'Asia' alone becomes a significant undertaking. Islamic Art as we know today – with its heavily East Asian influences – would simply not exist without the Chinggisid exchange, but that is just one example. The main task of this book is to trace their influence on the political institutions and norms of the East across subsequent centuries.

The Political Structure of the Chinggisid Polity

Recently, a spate of books – including a few in IR[113] – have drawn attention to the contributions of the Chinggisid Empire to world

---

[112] For the effects of the plague on the khanates, see Schamiloglu (2017a, 2017b). See also Fancy and Green (2021).

[113] See fn 32.

history, but – as explained in the Introduction (Chapter 1) – I am much more interested in their sovereignty model, which I consider to be the basis of the Chinggisid world order and what makes it possible to talk about degrees of continuity between the Chinggisid world order and the post-Chinggisid ones we will discuss in the next chapters.

Chapter 1 has already set out the Chinggisid sovereignty model as an ideal type. Let's now turn to the historical story of how this ideal type manifested in the empire of Genghis Khan and the Chinggisid khanates. To properly understand the basis of Chinggisid sovereignty as it was realised then, we have to first dispel a number of long-standing myths about the Mongols' lack of political organisation and the supposedly chaotic way they conducted their political affairs. Most accounts,[114] even some of the more recent ones, describe the Mongols as a 'tribal' society, which can create the impression that this was an entity that lacked sophisticated political organisation. Mongols are also described as an example of 'stateless' or 'pre-state' steppe societies, which solidifies the impression that they were a primitive people whose military victories could be attributed to their savagery in battle. The word 'horde' in fact has precisely that meaning in English: 'A wandering troop or gang; especially, a clan or tribe of a nomadic people migrating from place to place for the sake of pasturage, plunder, etc.; a predatory multitude.'[115] Ironically, the origin word of 'horde' – *orda*[116] in Mongol – denotes an institution, something in between a military unit and a palace entourage. Genghis Khan's *orda* was the opposite of disorganised.[117]

As Sneath argues powerfully in *The Headless State*, the application of the word 'tribe' to Central Asia has confused matters much more than it has clarified them: 'Well into the late twentieth century, the

---

[114] See, for example, Golden (2000); Lee (2016); Rossabi (1998).

[115] This common definition is from Wiktionary: https://en.wiktionary.org/wiki/horde/.

[116] This institution was not unique to the Mongols: 'A central feature of Kitan society was the ordo, an institution that appears in many Inner Asian languages and remained fundamental to steppe polities throughout the Mongol period. The ordo was the palace or court of a ruler. "Each ruler had his own ordo which functioned as a bodyguard in peacetime and elite corps in war. The number of warrior households attached to a single ordo might be as high as 15,000" (Franke 1990, 404).' Sneath (2007, pp. 117).

[117] 'It is hard to think of a less appropriate use of a term meaning the palace of a great ruling house, such as the Golden Ordo of Batu Khan, the vast and disciplined headquarters of a small empire.' Sneath (2007, p. 117).

dominant view in both Western and Soviet anthropology was to regard tribes as "survivals" of earlier stages of political evolution, a view that continues to inform many state bureaucracies.'[118] The colonial order of the nineteenth and early twentieth century distinguished between 'civilizations [which] were governed by monarchs and aristocrats and more primitive "tribal" societies ... ruled by chiefs'.[119] Although an evolutionary model was later mapped onto this classification allowing for the possibility of 'tribal kinship societies' to eventually evolve into statehood, the descriptor was never used for European history: 'Each one of the hundred or so petty rulers of seventh-century Ireland was termed a king, for example, despite the fact that they governed a few thousand people at best. The hereditary ruler of the Bemba, however, governing some 140,000 aristocrats and commoners, was termed a "paramount chief".'[120] Some scholars were drawn to the tribal kinship model because they thought it allowed for more equality.[121] Our notions about 'tribes' in Central Asia has even influenced our translations of primary texts, where these words have been inserted against a number of words with entirely different connotations in historical context.[122] Eventually this got in the way of any comparative study, rendering societies described thusly as existing outside of time and unlike any political formation which has ever existed in Europe. Historical evidence, when viewed with fresh eyes, suggests that, far from being an egalitarian kinship society, the Mongols (as well as other nomadic societies described as 'tribal') were highly stratified: 'what little evidence we have on political alliances suggests shifting pragmatic alliances between powerful nobles with little or no respect for genealogical proximity, the most bitter warfare often breaking out between

---

[118] Ibid., p. 42.

[119] Ibid., p. 43. This scheme evolved over time – earlier British imperial ideology had recognised aristocratic orders in other settings. See also Cannadine (2002).

[120] Ibid., p. 45. [121] Ibid., p. 53.

[122] 'There is no single term that corresponds to the way that the word "tribe" has been inserted in the translations of the Secret History. Instead, a series of different words – irgen (people, subjects), ulus (polity, realm, patrimony, appanage), and aimag (division, group) – have been translated as "tribe" in places in the text when the unit concerned is believed to be tribal. Similarly, there are two terms, obog (family, lineage, line) and yasu (bone, descent, lineage), commonly translated as "clan" depending on the context, and often the term "clan" has simply been inserted next to any group noun that the translator believes to be a clan.' Ibid., p. 62.

close aristocratic relatives'.[123] In reality, Mongol society was not egalitarian, nor was it disorganised: it was hierarchical and capable of the greatest degree of political centralisation (though it did not always manifest it).

If the Mongols were not a disorganised, decentralised kinship 'tribe', what were they? Sneath suggests that 'house society' is a better descriptor than 'tribal': 'this makes it easier to conceptualize a society in which ancient aristocratic descent groups existed alongside commoner families who may not have traced descent back more than a couple of generations'.[124] The Mongols inherited many of the institutions they used from other steppe polities that had existed before them (which also have been mis-characterised by Eurocentric [or Sinocentric] historiographies), such as the Xiognu, Uighur or Kitan.[125] One of these institutions was a military aristocracy. The actual number of 'Mongols' were relatively small: 'Most Mongol armies numbered in the tens of thousands, the majority of whom were often drawn from subject allies such as Tatars, Kitans, and Turks.' They were controlled by 'noble Mongol families such as the Chinggisid "white bone" houses that continued to rule the Kazakhs until tsarist times'.[126] By contrast, 'the Mongol commoners often found themselves entirely impoverished by the process of conquest, so that some ended up having to sell their wives and children into slavery to meet the military and other obligations owed to their lords'.[127] In other words, both the rulers and the military forces were drawn from noble houses, with commoners simply filling the ranks in battle, faring hardly better than livestock. Mongol commoners did not get better treatment than any other commoner just because they had any 'ethnic' ties to the ruling families. By contrast, 'the power of these noble houses was more enduring than any of the states that they dominated',[128] resurfacing in different historical time periods and geographies over and over again, as we will also see in the next chapters. The durability of these Great Houses was facilitated by a far-flung marriage network across Asia and intersubjective notions of desired pedigree and legitimacy.

---

[123] Ibid., p. 61.   [124] Ibid., p. 112.

[125] For a historical overview of Inner Asian states and empires, as well as their administrative hierarchies, see Rogers (2012). In IR, see Neumann and Wigen (2018); Neumann and Wigen (2013) for an overview of the history of steppe traditions.

[126] Sneath (2007, p. 165).   [127] Ibid.   [128] Ibid.

This is why it is also erroneous to translate Genghis Khan's designation of his followers as Yeke Mongol Ulus as 'Great Mongol Nation'. *Ulus* now means 'nation', but in the thirteenth century it meant 'complex of herds, grazing grounds and peoples granted to a Mongol prince; used especially of the larger territorial units held by Chinggis Khan's sons and his descendants'.[129] The Mongol *Ulus* was a collection of ruling families who had sworn loyalty to Genghis Khan and their commoner subjects (including subjects whose masters had been executed by Genghis Khan and who had been subsequently redistributed). The commoners did not keep genealogical records, and they had different origin myths from the nobles.[130] It was not until the late nineteenth and early twentieth centuries that the aristocratic conceptualisation of Mongol history was nationalised to include the commoners[131] in the area we call Mongolia today.

To sum up, until modernity, Asia was dominated by house societies: a network of powerful noble houses, each with its own territorial sphere of influence, with claims to anything living on those territories, including people. This is not particularly different from European history.[132] Genghis Khan introduced to this setting an extremely high degree of political centralisation (along vertical lines, by subordinating all competing forms of authority to himself). In this, Genghis Khan was innovative, but not radically so: he had received some of his ideas from other steppe polities (some of which were also Sinicised) via these aristocratic networks (across both space and time). He also was not just a humble child who rose to great power through sheer grit, but someone with the appropriate family lineage for the task. He gained his 'Mandate from Heaven' through military victories, but, in the world of the thirteenth century, you had to have a certain pedigree to even go for the mandate.

Genghis Khan, as the Great Khan, ruled through a highly centralised authority as implemented via a hierarchical network model of aristocratic houses, with houses of his own sons at the top of the pyramid, each with their own *ulus*/appanage (i.e. a territory and people they governed). The Chinggisids displaced, subsumed or eliminated many other houses with ordering aspirations when they became *the* Great

---

[129] Jackson (2018, p. 367), as cited by Sneath (2007, p. 168).
[130] Sneath (2007, p. 171).   [131] Ibid., p. 173.
[132] But what sets it apart in the thirteenth century are the *world* ordering ambitions of the Chinggisid.

House, but others resurfaced later on (as we will see in the next chapter). In other words, when the power of the Chinggisids fragmented (e.g. in the Chagatai Khanate), it did not revert to commoners but became contested between aristocratic lineages with plausible claims to the throne and who understood basic institutions of this order (and passed down its norms). This allowed considerable continuity between periods of centralisation and decentralisation.

Genghis Khan's Centralising Model

One of Genghis Khan's most noted accomplishments was the reorganisation of Mongol forces: 'the whole manpower of Mongolia was reorganized into decimal-based military units of 10, 100, 1000 and 10,000'.[133] This way of organising the military forces had a long history in Central Asia, dating back to the Xiongu, if not before. Genghis Khan is credited for using it along non-tribal lines for the first time,[134] but the main change he seems to have introduced was to give leadership roles to his *nöker*[135] and to redistribute manpower among them. The power to confer rank certainly suggests increased centralisation of authority. Above the military was his imperial guard of 10,000 men, 'responsible for the Khan's personal security ... well-being ... writing his decrees and recording his deeds. In addition, the guard had police functions'.[136] The imperial guard essentially became the administrative bureaucracy of the empire.

The second major innovation was the promulgation of *Yasa*, a set of governing laws long believed to have emerged out of the 1206 *qurultai* that recognised Genghis Khan as the great khan. In Mongol studies there is considerable debate as to whether there was actually a *Yasa* that was laid down in the 1206 *qurultai*.[137] Whether there was a written-down legal code or not, what is not disputed is that the ultimate lawmaking power was attributed to and claimed by Genghis Khan. He instituted very specific regulations about 'the duties and rights of

---

[133] Biran (2007, p. 41).
[134] Ibid. There is some debate about this – see Atwood (2015).
[135] 'A *nöker* was an individual who chose to attach himself to a leader of his own choice despite the lack of any kinship between the two' (Ibid., p. 10). The institution of *nöker* has been traced all the way down to Mughal India. See Kolff (1990) (as well as Chapter 4).
[136] Biran (2007, p. 42).
[137] For the debates on the *yasa*, see also Morgan (1986); Munkh-Erdene (2011).

commanders and soldiers ... rules regarding military training ... the basics of penal law'.[138] He was 'therefore was not only the enforcer, but also the giver of law',[139] and he would be portrayed as such for many generations to come; in the next chapters, we will be tracing this particular legacy all the way to the sixteenth century. In other words, in collective memory, Genghis Khan became the lawgiver par excellence.

Genghis Khan thus established 'a juridical authority meant to enforce the new order and supervise its administration'; the chief judge was 'asked to register his decisions – and Chinggis' legal decrees – in a blue register, thereby creating a body of precedents for future use'.[140] These regulations built upon antecedents from Mongol customary law (*töre*) but were portrayed even by critical contemporaries such as Juwayn-i as being 'at least partly invented by Chinggis "from the page of his own mind without the toil of pursuing records or the trouble of confirming with tradition"'.[141] This claim to a type of authority by the ruler to make laws from scratch unchecked by tradition or religion (as well as the demographic group that traditionally was held to have the authority to decide on the correct interpretation) was a major 'innovation'[142] for the thirteenth century that would have repercussions for the sedentary polities conquered by the Mongols, as most of them at that point had developed complicated social or bureaucratic systems that diffused or checked the power of the rulers.

The legitimacy of this awesome power was underwritten by the heavenly mandate held by Genghis, a ruling claim which he extended from the steppes over the entire world. Though not always so universally applied, the notion of a heavenly mandate was a well-established concept in the Turco-Mongol tradition.[143] Heaven (Tenggri) in the Mongol tradition is not the Christian or the Muslim heaven that one goes to in the afterlife as a reward. In the Mongol conception, heaven governed life and especially ordained the khan to rule by giving him protection and charisma: 'his investiture [as Khan] marks the union of heaven and earth under one government ... He possesses the power to bind. That is, he determines the

---

[138] Biran (2007, p. 43). [139] Ibid. [140] Ibid., p. 44. [141] Ibid., p. 43.

[142] As noted, authority was very much fragmented and shared throughout Eurasia in this period. The idea that political authority must reign supreme over others would come to spread in the next centuries. The development of this notion is well-studied in the European context, but, as this and next chapters will demonstrate, if this idea has a place of birth, it is in Inner Asia.

[143] See, for example, Fletcher (1986); Sneath (2007, p. 111).

fates of others, and he and his descendants will continue to do so as long as they continue to do so as long as they continue to succeed.'[144] The importance of 'aristocracy' was thus reflected in this heavenly ontology: 'In their heavenly origin the Mongols were, first and foremost, aristocrats ... Known as the Golden Clan (Altan Uruq), it is the substance of gold that sets them apart ... as being heavenly originated.'[145] In principle, the khan was the chosen leader among a group of aristocratic leaders thus destined to rule. He was chosen by heaven first, but the choice of heaven was affirmed by signs of military victory and then affirmed at the *qurultai* by others who had the heavenly right to affirm such signs (i.e. the other leaders and the shaman).

Speaking of the shaman, soon after the 1206 *qurultai* Genghis Khan removed the shaman from office because the latter undermined his rule.[146] Instead of instituting another shaman, however, he claimed his own direct connection to Tenggri (heaven): 'by eliminating the noted shaman Chinggis Khan asserted not only the primacy of imperial power over that of the priests ... but also his close and personal relation to heaven'.[147] In such a set-up, there was no one who could challenge the authority of the Great Khan. As noted in the first chapter, the Chinggisid interest in heavenly sciences (e.g. astronomy, astrology, math) also stemmed from this particular understanding of heaven. It had bestowed a mandate on Genghis Khan and his descendants to rule the world, so they knew its mind, so to speak. We can draw a direct line from such Chinggisid practices to the millennial sovereigns and the sacred kings of the sixteenth century, to be discussed in Chapters 4 and 5. Finally, when it came to the practice of religion by subjects, Genghis Khan (and his descendants) was not particularly interventionist. The khan was above it all.[148]

The Legacy of Genghis Khan as a World Conqueror

To sum up, the Chinggisid sovereignty model as advanced by the empire of Genghis Khan was a 'much more centralized, political-military system'[149] with its own bureaucracy, with power centralised around a ruler whose authority rested on the fact that was chosen from

---

[144] Baumann (2013, p. 250).   [145] Ibid., p. 251.
[146] It should be noted that Mongol scholars debate how official Teb Tenggri's position was to begin with. See Atwood (2004b).
[147] Biran (2007, p. 45).   [148] See, for example, Atwood (2004a).
[149] Biran (2007, p. 41).

a group of people destined to rule over others, who claimed a heavenly mandate to rule over the world, as proven by victories over both internal rivals and external enemies. Lineage was thus important but was not enough by itself. This sovereign claimed the authority not just to enforce laws but also to promulgate them, and, as long as he was successful as a world conqueror, he did not answer to anybody once the *qurultai* affirmed him: in theory, no religious authority or civil servant could check his power. In the Chinggisid model, the sovereign was the top of a very clear hierarchy.

We can observe two significant things about this sovereignty model, with implications for IR. First, it is a vision of a *world order*, based on universal aspirations which qualify the Chinggisid Empire as a Great Power equivalent in the thirteenth century, or as a Great House as discussed earlier. Whether this vision evolved over time to justify the conquests or whether it drove them is an interesting academic question, but the fundamental point is that it was there, and it justified Chinggisid rule over almost all of Asia (or the known world at the time). Genghis Khan and his followers thus *ordered* the world (both within and outside their territories) according to this vision, and they were quite successful at it for nearly two centuries, with legacies that lasted well beyond that.

Second, the Chinggisid sovereignty norm favoured rulers who built and ordered worlds much more than rulers who maintained existing institutions. This is because so much of the legitimation for sovereignty was driven by conquest. The tanistry principle for succession was a clever way of getting around this problem (at least for a while) by essentially forcing claimants to the throne to fight each to prove their heavenly mandate. However, the tanistry institution had the downside of creating long periods of interregnum. Furthermore, once the khan was in power, he still had to keep conquering. Conquest could not go on forever, so the Chinggisids and their heirs who operated with a version of this norm always ended up being the victim of their own success. We will see this same pattern keep repeating in the post-Chinggisid orders.

For the Chinggisid family specifically, the claim of universal rule for any khan was much harder to maintain once the empire broke up into four de facto autonomous khanates. If there are four khans, the implication is that there is not a 'Great Khan'. The fact that no khanate could impose its will on the others by reconquering them and therefore had to settle into a balance-of-power arrangement of sorts created a fundamental hypocrisy in the sovereignty claims of the Chinggisid rulers in these khanates. The inability to maintain legitimacy within the Chinggisid normative ecumene may be why the khans all eventually converted to the religion of (some of) their subjects: Islam in the case of the Ilkhanate, the Golden Horde and the Chagatai Khanate, and Buddhism in the case of the Yuan.[150] The first combination would eventually turn out to be very potent, especially in south-western Asia, as the next chapters will show. There was a universalizing strain within Islam that made a suitable bedfellow for the world empire legitimation model of the Chinggisids, and the resulting fusion turned out to be very significant for its world historical impact:

Globalisation, in short, was first prosecuted under the radically ecumenical Mongol banner – precisely through its marriage to the reigning universalist culture of the era, which had long since synthesised the Hellenic, Semitic, Persian and Indic patrimonies of late antiquity: Islam. With the fusion in western Asia of the first world religion with the first world empire, 'mixing of cultures', a principle forcefully championed by both, became the template for a new dispensation in human intellectual, cultural and economic history – the early modern.[151]

But all of that was yet to come (and is the subject of Chapters 4 and 5). The initial marriage of Islam and the Chinggisid model did not help save the Ilkhanate or the Chagatai. But if the plague is to blame,[152] perhaps nothing could.

Legacy of the Chinggisid World Order in Asia and Beyond

The next chapters in Part I will be tracing the legacy of the Chinggisid 'world order' in Asia, Eurasia and beyond. Though the Chinggisid Empire covered almost all of Asia, its organisation was not primarily territorial.[153] As discussed previously, it makes much more sense to

---

[150] Based on these conversions, it could be argued that the Chinggisid universal sovereignty model of legitimacy through world conquest had its own expiration date built into it. Modern observers should not be so sure, however, that this is a flaw unique to this particular sovereignty norm. More on that in Chapter 6.

[151] Melvin-Koushki (2016, p. 148).   [152] Fancy and Green (2021).

[153] As noted in Chapter 1, there is a degree of territoriality to how the appanages were divided among the branches of the family.

think of this world order as made up of aristocratic networks of Great Houses and smaller houses. At the origin of this world order was the Great Khan, Genghis Khan, with an undeniable claim to heaven's mandate, empirically verified in the fact he did conquer the world. As universal sovereign, he provided the primary political ordering principles of this world order: the division of territories under the control of his house (Korea to Hungary at its peak) into appanages under the control of his sons and grandsons. As also discussed previously, these divisions became a more formalised division of the world in the second half of the thirteenth century, with branches of the Genghis Khan family constituting the new Great Houses: the Jochid (the Golden Horde) Khanate, the Ilkhanate, the Chagatai Khanate and the Yuan (Dynasty) Khanate. After a period of fighting, these four khanates settled into something resembling a balance-of-power arrangement in the fourteenth century. We can trace the legacy of this fourfold division of primary actors of the Chinggisid world order even to this day in how we perceive the different regions of Asia: Russia/Eurasia, the Middle East, Central Asia and China/East Asia.

The houses of Genghis Khan and his descendants were not the only political actors in this system. The secondary actors of this world order could be grouped into three categories. In the first category are the numerous lesser houses throughout (Eur)Asia that were in vassalage relationships with either the Great Khan or one of the khanates. Some of these lesser houses were Mongol or Turkic and thus were likely to share the ontology of the Chinggisid core even before they entered into vassalage relationships (e.g. the Ottomans in Anatolia); yet others were shaped by the experience of vassalage (e.g. the Goryeo Dynasty in Korea). Some of these lesser houses/dynasties would come to shape the next world orders, as we will see in the following chapters.

In the second category we have semi-peripheral actors that were not formally part of the Chinggisid order but nevertheless were transformed by its existence for various reasons: because they were under Chinggisid invasion for a period, or because they faced an ongoing threat from Chinggisid forces, or because they took in 'refugees' from regions that were conquered. The Mamluks in Egypt, various kingdoms in eastern Europe or the Delhi Sultanate would be examples of such actors. As discussed, the Mamluk Sultanate was in some ways created by the Chinggisid world order: *mamluks* were escapees from the northern steppes into Egypt. Though the Chinggisids never managed to conquer the Indian subcontinent, the Delhi Sultanate especially was also transformed by their presence to the north, because it also took in many refugees. In any case, many of the dynasties active in the Indian subcontinent in this period had Turkic origins, so this area, though a separate regional order in its own way, was not entirely disconnected from the ecumene of the Chinggisid world order either.

Finally, in the third category we have peripheral actors who never came under direct Chinggisid rule or faced an immediate threat from it but who nevertheless benefitted from the ideational and commercial networks created by *Pax Mongolica* in direct and indirect ways and were thus drawn to participate in this order from outside:[154] our two travellers from the introduction of this chapter, Marco Polo and Ibn Battuta, hailed from regions that fit this profile, southern Europe and Muslim north-west Africa. In another example of this sort, the Byzantine Dynasty was linked to the Genghis Khan via marriage: Byzantine princesses married into both the Golden Horde and the Ilkhanate ruling houses.[155] Even the Mamluks, sworn enemies, asked for a Chinggisid princess bride in their diplomatic negotiations: 'Tulunbay Khatun who arrived in Egypt in 1320'.[156] Such was the sovereign charisma of the House of Genghis throughout Asia.

A primary legacy of the Chinggisid world order on these sets of actors as described above was to facilitate political centralisation almost everywhere that had come under direct Chinggisid sovereignty. Centralisation was encouraged throughout (Eur)Asia both by the dissemination of Chinggisid norms of universal sovereignty and by the fact that the Chinggisid conquests eliminated some of the competing houses throughout Asia, thus making it easier for those houses remaining (or newly constituted, as the case may be) to centralise authority (often by invoking the Chinggisid model as justification) after the fragmentation of the Chinggisid world order. This may be one of the reasons why political centralisation around a supreme authority in Asia predates European experiments of the same. Furthermore, as explained

---

[154] See also Di Cosmo (2010).

[155] For example, the Chora Church in Istanbul (now the Kariye mosque) has an engraved date in Arabic numbers: ١٨١١ or 6811, which corresponds to the year 1302/3 in the Byzantine calendar. The inscription commemorates the wedding of a Byzantine princess to the Ilkhante Khan Ghazan. Zachariadou (2013). Ibn Battuta's travel memoirs also detail his encounter with a Byzantine princess who was married to the khan of the Golden Horde.

[156] Moin (2012, p. 32).

in Chapter 1, many of the institutions associated with Chinggisid sovereignty norms, from tanistry to military organisation models to sovereign investment in astronomy/astrology, were reproduced throughout Asia (and beyond) across the next centuries, as the following chapters will trace.

The second political consequence of the Chinggisid world order was to create a connected political, economic and social space throughout (Eur)Asia, thus making 'the East' (or 'an East'). Not only did the primary actors[157] of the Chinggisid world order bolster the existing Silk Road routes by repairing roads and bridges (and maritime trade), but they also facilitated the travel of persons and information through the *yam*, the mounted postal courier system referred to in the introduction to this chapter, which connected the far-flung corners of the empire: 'they provided horses, fodder and couriers for authorized travelers, who were able to cover about 350–400 km a day. The system enabled the Qa'an [Khan] to transmit his orders efficiently and acquire information from the far reaches of the empire, in addition to securing the routes for ambassadors and merchants.'[158] The Chinggisid sovereigns also promoted literacy and record-keeping and issued their edicts in a number of languages. Even more significantly, in order to run this world, they transferred many people from one side of Asia to the other, bringing artisans to Mongolia, Chinese physicians to Persia, Persian craftsmen to China etc. The existence of postal system and the trade routes, as well as the centralised planning of the empire to move people around as needed, facilitated an exchange of goods and know-how throughout Eurasia to an extent that had never been achieved before (and would not be again for a long time, if ever).[159] This is what makes it possible to speak of a shared (if now forgotten) ecumene of Eurasia and a Chinggisid world order, the legacy of which we will be tracing in the following chapters.

What Caused the Fragmentation of the Chinggisid World Order?

Genghis Khan created a world empire – thus a Great House (or a 'Super House' even) – which fragmented into four khanates, two of which

---

[157] Chinggisid nobility invested in trade.   [158] Biran (2007, p. 76).
[159] See also Allsen (2001, 2004, 2019).

collapsed (Ilkhanate, Chagatai) and one of which became more peripheral (the Golden Horde). This is a relatively straightforward story of
imperial rise and decline, even if it has not been studied nearly as much
as Rome.[160] But there is more to the story if we look at the level of order
rather than Great House.

As discussed, within the Chinggisid model of sovereignty there could
only be one 'Great Khan', as manifested especially in the person of
Genghis Khan as a world conqueror. After the Toluid Civil War
(1260), however, the 'Great Khan' existed only in name. Kubilai,
who had fought his way to this title, became in practice one of four
khans roughly equivalent in power (Great Khan/Yuan; Ilkhan; the
Khan of the Golden Horde; the Chagataid Khan) and was no longer
able to dominate the others. The dilution of the 'Great Khan' institution pointed to the normative contradictions in the sovereignty model
underwriting the basis of that world order, contradictions which would
come to haunt all post-Chinggisid Great Houses which aimed to legitimate their sovereignty using the same logic, as we will see the next
chapters.

The primary legitimation of Chinggisid sovereignty, world domination (or universal empire), was not sustainable to chase in the long run
for practical reasons. As discussed, once the Chinggisid Empire fragmented into four khanates, their choices were either to continue fighting with each other and other rival polities in order to demonstrate
the continuing presence of world domination aspirations or to settle
into a 'balance-of-power' arrangement. In the fourteenth century,
the second, more practical choice won, perhaps because no khanate
could prevail over the others but also because the settlement allowed
for more trade, which had been fundamental to the economy of the
unified empire. What was practical from an economic and political
perspective for the maintenance of the 'world order', however, also
undermined the legitimacy of each khanate. The existence of multiple
khans contradicted the very basis of a Chinggisid khan's claim to
universal sovereignty. In the Chinggisid sovereignty model, a khan
had to be a world conqueror – this is how the proof of the mandate
of heaven manifested in one person. What we would call a 'balance-of-
power' arrangement does not make sense in a world order organised by
world empire norms. Attempts to find alternative methods of

---

[160] See, for example, Morgan (2009).

legitimation (e.g. through religious conversion and religious symbolism) undermined the normative fabric and the existing understandings of the Chinggisid world order, causing its fragmentation.

Finally, structural pressures also played a role in bringing about the fragmentation of this order. Today we understand disease as something within our control, subject to human agency, but pre-modern pandemics are better thought of as structural pressures that people would have to endure. The traditional account of the Black Death centres the narrative on the fourteenth century and on European experiences. By contrast, Fancy and Green have recently argued that the plague reached west Asia in the thirteenth century; they show that a number of contemporary observers of the fall of Baghdad in 1258 also recorded a plague-like disease.[161] They conclude that the plague may have been endemic in the Chinggisid order, especially in the West. No major episodes were recorded, however, during the period of *Pax Mangolica*. We encounter it again in the fourteenth century, in the demise of the Ilkhanate. As noted, some historians believe that the Black Death brought the end of the Ilkhanate by claiming the life of the last Ilkhan khan, as well as his heirs, while inflicting significant damage on the surviving elements of the Chinggisid khanates. Fancy and Green suggest that a reservoir of the plague had survived in west Asia from the thirteenth century and in the fourteenth century may have spread eastward in Asia from the Ilkhanate/Golden Horde rather than only westward towards Europe as it is traditionally believed.[162] If we thus do not think of the plague as something that only affected European history, we are able to see the implications of the fourteenth-century flare-up on the Chinggisid world order.

Some historians think the fourteenth century may qualify as a 'General Crisis' period even beyond the Black Death, however.[163] It was in the fourteenth century that the 'Medieval Warm Period'[164]

---

[161] Fancy and Green (2021). See also Buell (2012) (on China and the plague).
[162] Fancy and Green (2021), especially 175–6.
[163] Parker and Smith (1997, p. 6). See also Tuchman (2011).
[164] The Medieval Warm Period is generally held to have lasted in the northern hemisphere from the mid-tenth century until the mid-thirteenth century. There is an argument within Mongol studies that the rise of the Chinggisid Empire was facilitated by a change in climatological and environmental conditions of the steppes in the thirteenth century. The steppes are supposed to have gotten wetter, with more grass for the grazing of the Mongol horses. See, for example, Pinke et al. (2017); Pederson et al. (2014); Putnam et al. (2016).

ended and 'the Little Ice Age'[165] began. There was famine and pestilence throughout Eurasia,[166] likely linked to climate change conditions. There were also monetary fluctuations[167] and banking crises.[168] It was not only the Chinggisid world order that fragmented in this period (with three of the four khanates replaced): much of the rest of Eurasia also witnessed wars, revolts and dynastic changes (e.g. the Hundred Years War in Europe; the fall of Goryeo in Korea; the fall of the Kamakura Shogunate in Japan, etc.).[169] This could all be a coincidence (after all, if you zoom out enough any period has its share of collective troubles), but there is enough evidence to consider the role of structural pressures in decaying the Chinggisid world order. I will return to the balance of the explanation in Chapter 6. For our purposes at the moment, the main takeaway is that the Chinggisid sovereignty model (i.e. the deep norms underwriting the Chinggisid world order) survived the decline of the house of Genghis as well as the associated world order. Whatever caused the decline of the Chinggisid world order, neither the Chinggisid pedigree itself nor the type of sovereignty Genghis Khan modelled had lost its appeal in Asia. Their example would continue to motivate other would-be Great Houses for many more centuries, as we will see in the next chapters.

---

[165] We will discuss the Little Ice Age in Chapter 5.

[166] The Great European Famine of 1314–22 was the worst such disaster in European history, killing 10–15 per cent of the population. Soon after the Great Bovine Pestilence hit (and seems to have spread to Europe from East Asia), killing more than half of the animal population. See Slavin (2012, p. 1239). And after that, the Black Death arrived.

[167] Atwell (1990, p. 661). One explanation is that existing institutions were not well-equipped to deal with food scarcity caused by crop failures and bovine mortality.

[168] Major Florentine banks went bankrupt.   [169] Atwell (1990, p. 661).

3 | Dividing the East: Post-Chinggisid World Orders

The Timurid and the Ming (Fourteenth–Fifteenth Centuries)

Look 'round thee now on Samarcand! –
  Is not she queen of Earth? her pride
Above all cities? in her hand
  Their destinies? in all beside
Of glory which the world hath known
Stands she not nobly and alone?
Falling – her veriest stepping-stone
Shall form the pedestal of a throne –
And who her sovereign? Timour – he
  Whom the astonished people saw
Striding o'er empires haughtily
  A diadem'd outlaw –

From Edgar Allen Poe's 'Tamerlane' (1827)

The Sage Lord personally leads,
One million troops,
Already arrived in Weilu,
The Heavenly Encampment arrayed.
Within the encampment is territory,
All is Weilu [cowed]
Beyond Heaven, no country
Does not submit to the Ming.
Pennants for a thousand miles,
The broad ocean of clouds.
Swords and halberds of the Nine Skies,
Snow peaks pure.
Surpassing wisdom and brilliant strategies,
All are marvelous.
We gather to sweep away the stench of mutton,
And bring about peace.

An official's poem about Zhu Di/the Yongle Emperor (1422)[1]

---

[1] Robinson (2019, pp. 70–1).

Introduction

The Chinggisid world order sketched out in the previous chapter declined in the fourteenth century, but the Chinggisid sovereignty model survived. Asia continued to be populated by (would-be) Great Houses who either saw themselves as direct heirs to the Chinggisid or wanted to live up to the Chinggisid as a shared measure of greatness. These successor houses chased a universal empire, sometimes for decades, sometimes longer, and invoked, reproduced and modified the Chinggisid sovereignty model in doing so, creating 'world orders' as part of their quest. This particular normative (and practical) heritage therefore links the continent throughout time and space, not in a functional sense but almost as an invisible ecumenical fabric. The 'world orders' these post-Chinggisid Great Houses created (or attempted to create) were normatively more varied and more heterogeneous. This is partly because even the most successful of these houses never reached the territorial span of Genghis Khan's empire. As a result, they always had to coexist with rival houses with similar universal ambitions and thus had to find other justifications for their sovereignty, resulting in orders that were normatively hybridised, even more so than was the case for the four Mongol khanates discussed in the previous chapter. However, these rival (would-be) 'world orders' also interlocked and interacted with each other, gradually expanding the spatial reach of the Chinggisid ecumene as they did so.

This chapter will look at the 'world order' that nearly replaced the Chinggisid order in Asia in the following century, a post-Chinggisid order that was almost created (or the interlocking orders that were created) by the twin – bear with me – successor Great Houses of Timur and the Ming. The Timurids are generally ignored in historical IR. By contrast, with the rise of China, there has been an increased interest in the Ming Dynasty in IR in recent years, especially their tributary system, which is seen by some as evidence that Chinese foreign policy was more likely to be dictated by hierarchy rather than by competition.[2] Apart from the fact that IR discussions about the Ming tributary system sometimes attribute a coherence to this arrangement that did not exist – an attribution much criticised by historians of

[2] For IR takes on Chinese history, hierarchy and the tribute system, see, for example, Kang (2003, 2010a, 2010b); Buzan (2010); Goh (2008); MacKay (2018); Park (2017); Musgrave and Nexon (2018); Wang (2012).

China – they are misleading because they ignore the larger context in which Ming ambitions were forged.

This fourteenth-century Asian world order can be called a 'post-Chinggisid' world order, because there were many continuities between the Chinggisid world order and this one. Perhaps the following comparison will help the reader: the nineteenth- and twentieth-century international orders were different in many ways, but there was a degree of continuity within their operating norms, for example in the notion of Great Powers. Imagine Europe as a tree: the United States and the USSR were its branches, and after the Second World War it was the tree trunk that had hollowed out (yet still held up), while the branches were still as powerful or even more so.

In a similar manner, the decline of the Chinggisid order rendered what was symbolically, politically and economically central to that order – that is, Inner Asia – weaker, and power was diffused to what used to be the more peripheral areas within the Chinggisid order, to east and west Asia. The centre of gravity of the Chinggisid world order was originally in Inner Asia: Genghis Khan had originated from Mongolia; until much later, the capital of the empire (Qaraqorum) was based there; the *qurultai* for electing the new khans had to be held in Mongolia for both political and symbolic reasons, despite the great logistical costs of the potential khans having to travel there from various corners of (Eur)Asia; and the main trade routes, as well as the postal *yam* system connecting the empire, went through Inner Asia. After 'China' was conquered by the Chinggisids, however, power (or sovereignty) could no longer stay centred in Inner Asia. It divided under China's symbolic, economic and political gravitational pull. Some of the sovereign power in the Chinggisid order thus shifted eastward to China in the later period, with the titular Great Khans, starting with Kubilai, settling into rule there. Inner Asia still retained its symbolic power for bestowing sovereign legitimacy within the Mongol order.

When the Chinggisid order fragmented, what rose in its place replicated this pattern of dual loci of power. The immediate heirs to the Great House of Genghis Khan thus rose from the two regions where power had been held in the previous world order: the Ming Dynasty in China and the Timurids in (the west part of) Inner Asia. The Timurids took over the Chagatai Khanate and the Ilkhanate in west Asia (in Transoxiana), and the Ming replaced the Yuan in China/East Asia, but they were far from being the only heirs to the Chinggisid legacy in Asia.

The Golden Horde still continued to rule the northern Eurasian steppes, and the Yuan had survived in a manner as well, by relocating back to Inner Asia. Inner Asia continued to be a place wherein Chinggisid notions of world sovereignty were very much part of the normative fabric. In fact, such was the case throughout the continent: 'The Chinggisid family ... retained its unique charisma and remained ... Eurasia's premier family. Historical memory of the empire also survived, serving as both a model (positive and negative) and a shared reference point for courts from Seoul to Samarkand.'[3] This was true even for areas that had not fallen under the direct sovereign control of the Chinggisid khanates.

In the late fourteenth century, Asia included many smaller houses[4] beyond those directly descended from the Chinggisids, but even the world views of such houses were still thoroughly shaped by the Chinggisid world order of the previous two centuries. To give a few examples: after the fragmentation of the Chinggisid Empire, the Ilkhanate continued to rule the area of modern-day Iran and also controlled Anatolia. Their primary vassal in Anatolia was the Seljuk of Rum, but the small regional polities that replaced the Seljuks after their collapse – such as the house of Osman (the Ottomans) – had established similar relationships with the Ilkhanate. The Golden Horde further north had even more power over the Duchy of Muscovy, which collected tax from other cities of the Rus on behalf of the Golden Horde.[5] In South Asia, the Chinggisid Empire had established domination over the territories to the north of the Indian subcontinent (e.g. Kashmir) but had never defeated the Sultanate of Delhi and therefore had never penetrated the subcontinent, though, as was the case with the Mamluk Sultanate, the Sultanate of Delhi had been entirely transformed during the Chinggisid world order, both due to its interactions with the Mongol forces and as a result of the influx of refugees from the north. Finally, in the east, vassalage relations of the Chinggisid empire and the khanates had extended to Korea as well as to South East Asia. Islands – Japan, Java – had remained out of reach, but there had been considerable Mongol naval presence (as well as interest

[3] Robinson (2019, p. 15).
[4] Some of these small houses became the great houses of future world orders. We will catch up with a few of them in Chapters 4 and 5.
[5] We will pick up this thread again in Chapter 5.

in naval trade routes). The (early) Timurids and (early) Ming were the rising Great Houses of a post-Chinggisid Asia in every way.

As we will see in this chapter, both the Timurids and the (early) Ming chased a universal empire in the post-Chinggisid mould, and together they nearly managed to reconstitute the political coherence of Asia before developments in the fifteenth century turned both dynasties' gazes regional. A reminder first, however: by attributing to their world sovereignty ambitions a Chinggisid lineage, I do not mean to be understood as implying that only the Chinggisid produced such a vision of world domination. As readers will be familiar with from European history, universal empire projects have been historically justified by other referents as well: Alexander the Great, Rome and so on.[6] Nor do I mean to argue that it is just this normative legacy alone that activates in various ruling houses such ambitions. The quest for universal empire/world sovereignty by any given political actor is likely produced by material structural conditions as well as various contingent factors such as leader personality, but, as we will see in this chapter and the next, the availability of the notion in a cultural repertoire is important as well, sometimes crucially so.

Dividing Asia: The Ming and the Timurid

Some readers may question the labelling of the Ming Dynasty[7] as a successor to the Chinggisid order (or their pairing with the Timurids as a twin dynasty). After all, the Ming Dynasty was officially founded by Zhu Yuanzhang (also known as Hongwu Emperor, r. 1368–98), a peasant with no ethnic ties to the Yuan Dynasty or the Mongols, in general (he was Han Chinese), who had ridden the waves of the Red Turban rebellion to power. The dynasty he founded ruled until 1644, when it was replaced by the Qing Dynasty (also of Inner Asian origins). The Ming rule restored some traditional practices (such as the examination system for bureaucrats) which had been abandoned during the Yuan period. Furthermore, despite early signs of foreign policy ambition, especially in their second century, the Ming had officially become isolationist (and thus were very much in contravention of Chinggisid

---

[6] On this question, see Pollock (2005). I am grateful to Manjeet Pardesi for the suggestion.

[7] To read generally about the Ming, see Mote and Twitchett (1988); Twitchett and Mote (1998).

norms of sovereign legitimacy by that point). There is thus a temptation to understand the Yuan period as an aberration and the Ming as the restoration of a 'proper' Chinese dynasty, but – as we will see – this is a mistaken reading of history.

In contrast to Zhu Yuanzhang, not only was Timur (also known as Tamerlane or Gürkani, r. 1370–1405), the founder of the Timurid Dynasty, ethnolinguistically Turco-Mongol, originating from what had been the realm of the Chagatai Khanate, but he fashioned himself explicitly after the image of Genghis Khan, even to the extent of claiming kinship in order to legitimise his rule.[8] Timur also faced a more fragmented political landscape than did Zhu Yuanzhang, as centralised political order in Central/West Asia had broken down at an earlier moment in the fourteenth century.[9] In a manner reminiscent of Genghis Khan, Timur first united the feuding houses and then went to conquer neighbouring regions. In the case of the Timurid Dynasty, the Chinggisid lineage is therefore much more visible. It was also emphasised in the very ambitious and successful military campaign Timur waged throughout western and southern Asia, from the northern steppes ruled by the Golden Horde to the Ottomans in Asia Minor to the Delhi Sultanate in northern India.[10] Timur's plans to attack the Ming Dynasty territories in the east were foiled by his death on the way to China in 1405. The dynasty that he founded ruled various bits of the territory he conquered for about another century, with increasingly weakening power in the second half of the fifteenth century.

Despite these differences, thinking of these two dynasties together in the context of the late fourteenth and early fifteenth centuries unearths a number of similarities and helps us to see that this was a period in which another potential world order was in formation, still animated by Chinggisid notions of sovereignty and world empire. Both houses retained Chinggisid-style aspirations to rule the world, at least initially.[11] This particular world order did not quite congeal as a continent-wide order due to the structural developments of the

---

[8] Lentz and Lowry (1989, p. 27). He also claimed he was a descendant of Ali. Ibid., p. 28.
[9] See the Ilkhanate/Chagatai Khanate discussion in the previous chapter.
[10] On Timur's military campaigns, see Manz (1998, pp. 5–6). In fighting the Golden Horde, he faced against and defeated Toktamish, who had a better Chinggisid pedigree.
[11] On this point, see also Kauz (2015, p. 253).

mid-fourteenth century, but, at least as far as the one generation who lived at the turn of the fourteenth century was concerned,[12] it was very present. Neither the early Ming nor the Timurids could help being shaped by their shared Chinggisid legacy; it was the extent to which they emphasised and made visible that legacy that varied, based on local conditions and expectations. Historians[13] of the Ming Dynasty increasingly recognise the way the polity had been radically transformed by the Yuan period, and, whatever its claims, the Ming Dynasty did not signal a return to the old customs: 'The charismatic Mongol khan having become a routine Chinese emperor, the potential nonetheless lingered for the Chinese emperor to claim the charisma of a Mongol khan, and to act without regard for the constitutional constraints of emperorship. A few Ming emperors, most notably the first (Hongwu) and third (Yongle) would do just that.'[14] Viewed from this perspective, there are many parallels between the (early) Ming and the Timurid dynasties.

Founders: Timur versus Hongwu (Late Fourteenth Century)

Zhu Yuanzhang (i.e. the Hongwu Emperor, r. 1368–98) and Amir Timur (r. 1370–1405) were near-contemporaries in the late fourteenth century. They ruled for almost the same decades, and their houses almost went to war with each other, spared from that fate only by Timur's death on the way to China. Both are remembered as brutal rulers, and both came to power by reconsolidating an increasingly fragmented political space in the wake of the eroding power of the Chinggisid world order. We tend to think of 'China' as a self-evident entity[15] and therefore tend not to think of dynastic takeovers in Chinese history (especially by ethnically Han dynasties) as conquest, but if conquest is measured from where one starts to where one's projected power reaches by the end of one's reign, the Hongwu Emperor and Timur are comparable – if not exactly equal – conquerors.[16] Moreover, both came from relatively humble

---

[12] Some would argue this is about as long as the life cycle of the Liberal International Order.

[13] See, for example, Brook (2010, 2019); Brook, van Praag and Boltjes (2018); Robinson (2012, 2019, 2020).

[14] Brook (2010, p. 79).   [15] See also Milward (2020), as discussed in Chapter 1.

[16] And they both fell short of their goal.

beginnings, and both were 'self-made' rulers who had not inherited their rule.

The model of Genghis Khan and his world conquests as a basis for sovereignty loomed large in both men's imaginations, even though it is much easier to demonstrate this in the case of Timur. In order to legitimate his world sovereign ambitions, Timur married a Chingissid princess (taking the title *güregen* – son-in-law) and ruled through a Chagataid puppet khan (hence his own title was only *amir* – commander).[17] By doing so he laid claim to the realm of the entire Chinggisid empire.[18] He also fashioned himself 'a Turkic *ghazi* championing the cause of Islam' and supported 'Sufis to ensure access to their sacral power'.[19] Building from the fragments of the Ilkhanate and the Chagatai Khanate, Timur thus drew from the hybrid wells of legitimation: the Persianate kingship ideal of the 'Just Ruler' (*khosrow-e adel*),[20] Islamic notions of *ghaza* (a type of holy war), Sufism[21] and Chinggisid charisma. He was building on the khanate experiment of hybrid legitimation of sovereignty. These experiments were matched by symbolic displays. For example, Timur gave his universalist sovereignty 'claims material expression by inaugurating a new style of monumental architecture that combines mausoleum, *madrasa* (residential college) and Sufi lodge (*khanaqah*) within a single, massive complex, bodying forth his personal sanctity and Islamic transcendence'.[22] He also invoked other symbols of world recognition. For example, a series of wall paintings in Timur's garden palaces depicted 'his battles and sieges and his conversation with kings, amirs, lords, wise men, magnates, and sultans offering homage to him and bringing gifts to him from every side and his hunting-nets and ambushes and battles in India, Dasht, and Persia and how he gained victory and how his enemy was scattered and driven to flight'.[23] As we

---

[17] Melvin-Koushki (2018a, p. 357).
[18] Robinson (2020, p. 366); Manz (1988, 1998, 1999).
[19] Melvin-Koushki (2018a, p. 357).   [20] Arjomand (2016, p. 7).
[21] The Persianate model of kingship had changed under 'the paradoxical impact of Sufi world renunciation'. Kings were coming to be seen as real Sufi disciples. Arjomand (2016, p. 8). At the same time, Sufi orders were absorbing local saint cults and Sufi leadership was becoming hereditary. Moin (2012, p. 33). For more on this, see Chapter 4.
[22] Melvin-Koushki (2018a, p. 357).
[23] Lentz and Lowry (1989, p. 33 [as depicted by Ibn Arasnshah]). Note the similarities to depictions of the early Ming tributary system.

will see in this chapter, Zhu Yuanzhang was constructing a comparable model of recognition at the same time.[24] But let's start first with Timur.

Timurid Modification of Chinggisid Sovereignty: Sahibkıran

The most important manifestation of Timur's emulation of the Chinggisid model of universal empire was his claim of the title of *sahibkıran* (Lord of Conjunction),[25] which, as we will see in Chapter 4, would go to play a very significant role in the post-Timurid world order. The title itself was not new, with origins in Islamic/Arabic astrology, and it had been used increasingly from the thirteenth century onwards in relation to Ilkhanate but also Seljuk and Mamluk rulers.[26] The conjunction in this title is that of Saturn and Jupiter, believed to mark auspicious events and born leaders: Alexander the Great, Genghis Khan and Prophet Muhammad were all supposed to have been marked by it as world conquerors.[27] However, Timur made this title his own: it 'became so pivotal to his imperial-sacral persona – both supra-Chingizid and supra-Islamic – that its invocation thereafter came to signify adherence to the specific-ally Timurid model of kingship'.[28] As the Timurid polity settled, a number of quasi-sciences – astrology, lettrism, geomancy – also sprung up around the study of conjunction titles, further justifying the imperial project.[29] *Zafarnama* (*Book of Conquest*), a popular his-tory of Timur's victories completed before 1436,[30] made the case that Timur's glory was 'inscribed in the text of the Qur'an and mathematic-ally encoded in the cosmos itself',[31] in addition to being driven by planetary conjunctions.

This title of *sahibkıran* can be thought of as a Timurid solution to the tension between the Chinggisid universal sovereignty tradition and Islamic political tradition, as alluded to in the previous chapter. Chapter 4 will discuss this in even more detail, but suffice it to say that Islam, while having its universal vision, had developed by the ninth century (at least within the Sunni tradition) a practice of divided sovereignty: Muslim kings were not supposed have absolute power; they could not make laws (the *ulama* [jurists] did by 'interpreting'

---

[24] Brook (2010, p. 93).   [25] Melvin-Koushki (2018a, p. 357).
[26] Ibid., p. 358.   [27] Moin (2012, p. 26).   [28] Ibid.   [29] Ibid.
[30] Ibid., p. 359.   [31] Ibid., pp. 358–9.

sharia [Islamic law]); and the universal claim of the religion symbolically rested with the caliph. But the last caliph had been killed when
Chinggisid forces, under the control of Hülegü, sacked Baghdad in
1258. And the Chinggisid (and post-Chinggisid) rulers claimed, in
contravention of Islamic tradition, to be lawgivers themselves. How
to reconcile their claim to supreme authority with the Islamic tradition
would not have been immediately obvious, even if, as discussed, three
of the four khanates had ended up converting to Islam in the previous
century.

The famous scholar Ibn Khaldun[32] was residing in Damascus in
1401 when Timur arrived with his army and wanted to meet him:
'When given the chance to speak, Ibn Khaldun told Timur that he
had been waiting for this moment for thirty or forty years.'[33] Ibn
Khaldun had done his research and flattered Timur accordingly:

he called Timur a Lord of Conjunction whose rise to the mastery of the world
was signaled by a 'conjunction of the two superior planets'; a leader awaited
by the most learned men of the age, by Sufis, astrologers, and physicians, by
preachers and metaphysicians, by Muslims and Jews, in Muslim North
Africa and in Christian Spain; a man who would inaugurate a new era,
possibly the last one before the end of time; a man who was potentially the
awaited messiah descended from the prophetic line.[34]

Note a number of things about the description of this title: first, it was
a messianic category. It involved millenarian beliefs in the arrival of
a saviour. Millenarian beliefs were also very common throughout Asia
and Eurasia in this period; they were widely shared by people of all
faiths. This should not be particularly surprising given all the wars,
plagues and other crises alluded to in the narrative thus far. We may
even be tempted to observe that it is not unusual for people to turn to
such belief systems when life is nasty, brutish and short. As such, it was
a category that had cross-cultural and interfaith appeal. Astrology has
this ability to travel across different cultures even in the present day. We
have also discussed in previous chapter the affinity between the
Chinngisid sovereignty model and the study of the heavens (astronomy
or astrology) as a legitimating institution. However, it is also important
to realise that astrology then was not the astrology we know today: it

---

[32] For more on Ibn Khaldun and his present-day influence, see, for example, Dale
(2006); Kalpakian (2008); Fromherz (2011); Irwin (2019).
[33] Moin (2012, p. 27).   [34] Ibid., p. 28.

'was at the time a "global" science, with texts, methods, and results shared across the Christian and Islamic worlds'.[35] It was an 'intellectually demanding ... part of the educated person's knowledge of the world and the cosmos'.[36] Consider also that determining who was entitled to the *sahibkıran* title was very political; after all, this is how sovereignty was supposed to be bestowed. This makes conjunction astrology in that era something akin to the political science of our day: the study of sovereigns, including who/what they are, how they should rule/govern etc.

To make such determinations, conjunction astrology 'used the cyclical motion of the celestial spheres and the periodic alignment or "conjunction" of the planets to divide historical time into meaningful eras'.[37] Especially important were the conjunctions of Saturn and Jupiter, which 'recurred every twenty, 240, or 960 years, depending upon how they were calculated, and were called "small," "medium," and "great"'.[38] Even Ibn Khaldun himself linked great conjunctions to great events 'such as a change in royal authority (*mulk*) or dynasties (*dawla*), or a transfer of royal authority from one people to another'.[39] As noted, conjunction astrology had its forebears in ancient Iranian, Greek, Indian and Jewish traditions.[40] Prophet Muhammad was believed to be a Lord of Conjunction so marked, signalling 'the end of the Persian-Zoroastrian dispensation and the beginning of the Arab-Islamic one'.[41] The worry now was about 'when the era of Muslim ... supremacy would end'.[42] Astrologers proposed 960 years after the conjunction that signified its birth.

Put another way, millennial sovereignty as associated with conjunction astrology brought the Chinggisid and Islamic traditions together in a fashion: the Turco-Mongol interest in the heavens meets the Islamic millennium, both pointing to the *sahibkıran*. The title thus helped preserve Chinngisid-style sovereignty without losing Islamic legitimacy. The idea that Timur was supposedly marked by the heavens in this

---

[35] Ibid., p. 29.   [36] Ibid.

[37] Ibid. Conjunction astrology was a mixture of ancient Iranian, Indian and Greek traditions but was also significant within Jewish and Islamic ontologies. For discussions of the role of astrology and other occult sciences within the Persianate world, see also Melvin-Koushki (2016, 2018a, 2018b, 2018c, 2019a, 2019b).

[38] I note for the reader here that these two planets conjuncted again on 21 December 2020, the closest they have come since 1623.

[39] Ibid., p. 30.   [40] Ibid., p. 29.   [41] Ibid., p. 30.   [42] Ibid.

manner also explained his meteoric rise to power from relatively humble beginnings (not unlike Genghis Khan). Publicly, however, Timur did not accept the title Lord of Conjunction. He also maintained the fiction that he was merely a general (*amir*) until he died, the 'real' king being a Chinggisid.[43] In Chapter 4, we will see this Timurid version of Chinggisid sovereignty taking full force in the sixteenth century.

In fact, it was after his death in 1405 that this title of *sahibkıran* really became associated with Timur. This is because Timur, in building his sovereign charisma, was drawing not only from the Chinggisid legacy but also from a specific style of Sufism. In this period, Sufi orders had become very important in the social landscape of this region.[44] As a result, we increasingly see a hybridisation between sacred and political orders and rulers (as would be manifested to a greater degree in the Safavids). Timur 'enjoyed a cult-like following among a group of his soldiers who treated him as their spiritual guide. These soldiers had a bond with Timur much like that of a Sufi devotee's to his pir or master. In their eyes, he was already a qutb (axis mundi) around whom the world revolved and a qibla (focus) upon whose image they would meditate.'[45] Sufi leaders were turned into saints after their deaths,[46] and a similar thing seems to have happened to Timur, with his kingship gaining a sacred aura after he died,[47] despite his successor Shah Rukh turning more towards Islam for sovereign legitimacy.

Over time, the myth of Timur was connected both to Genghis Khan and Ali, the son-in-law of Prophet Muhammad and the Fourth Caliph and, for many, the second-most revered figure in Islam. This was accomplished through tracing Timur's ancestry to Genghis Khan's mythical ancestor princess Alanquva, who in Mongol mythology was believed to have conceived a child from a light which visited her and took the shape of a man.[48] Some decades after Timur's death, the story became that it was a descendant of Ali who visited Alanquva. Timur was also linked to Alexander the Great. All of these figures were also considered Lords of Conjunction and great warriors.[49] The supplementation of the Chinggisid charisma with other figures, especially that of Ali, points to the fact that the Chinggisid ecumene was fusing with regional lores and adapting to changing times: 'The existing Mongol order was receding. Its symbol was Chinggis Khan. Another Islamic

43 Ibid., p. 31. 44 Ibid., p. 34. 45 Ibid., p. 34. 46 Ibid., p. 35. 47 Ibid.
48 Ibid., p. 38. 49 Ibid., p. 39.

order was arising. Its symbol was Ali. The sacred myth that could explain this grand change in world affairs was the rise of a messianic figure who would inaugurate the new era. Timur inhabited this myth and performed it with relish.'[50] And while the empire he founded would fray in half a century, the Timurid take on Chinggisid sovereignty model would go on to find yet another life in another world order.

Early Ming as Chinggisid Sovereigns: Hongwu as Khan

Turning back to 'China', Zhu Yuanzhang (the Hongwu Emperor) was also operating with the sovereignty models and institutions inherited from the previous period of Chinggisid rule. He perhaps did not go as far as Timur in reproducing the Chinggisid sovereignty model (or modifying it in a way that ensured its survival), but the Chinggisid legacy is nevertheless visible in how the realm was governed during his reign as well as that of his successor, Yongle. His Yuan predecessors had claimed to rule *the world* as the Great Khan, so now there was an expectation that Hongwu must also or seem small in comparison: 'Hongwu needed ratification that Heaven had transfered the mandate to rule from Kubilai's house to his own ... As Kubilai had done, Hongwu looked to the rulers of maritime Asia to confirm that he occupied the apex of the world.'[51] No surprise, then, that he both welcomed from and sent envoys to Vietnam, Japan, Korea, Java (Indonesia), Yunnan and the east coast of the Indian subcontinent, seeking recognition and tribute.[52] Yet by focusing solely on the maritime activity of the early Ming (due to assumed European parallels), we sometimes miss the full picture of what the early Ming ontology entailed.

Hongwu also distributed aristocratic titles, not only to Ming subjects who had distinguished themselves in service but also 'to men clearly beyond dynastic borders like the king of Japan, Choson [Joseon], and Annam (Dai Viet) and personnel from the even more distant Timurid and Moghul polities of Central Asia', despite the fact that doing so was financially burdensome.[53] By doing so, the early Ming throne aimed to

---

[50] Ibid., p. 54.   [51] Brook (2019, p. 83).   [52] Robinson (2019, p. 9).
[53] Ibid., p. 10.

create a hierarchy within east Eurasia atop which sat the Ming. There are good reasons to believe that in seeking this recognition Hongwu (and Yongle after him) were competing not just with the memory of the Great Khan but also various houses in Inner Asia which had a claim to this pedigree, including the Yuan Dynasty which had withdrawn back into the steppe after losing the capital Daidu (Beijing): 'Put simply, the Great Yuan was the Great Ming's foundational and formative rival.'[54] Hongwu could not claim the pedigree of being related to Genghis but instead emphasised victory over his descendants, while seeking the allegiances of Mongol nobles who could claim direct kinship. Hongwu and his successors also engaged in symbolic displays intended to convince an external audience steeped in Chinggisid norms (e.g. martial spectacles involving mounted archers).[55]

There was also a link again to astronomy and the study of heavens. There is some evidence to suggest that in the early years of the Ming Dynasty 'Islamic astronomers' continued to be present at the Bureau of Astronomy, as they had been in Yuan times. Some of these astronomers could have even come from the Timurid realm, from Samarkand (a centre for the study of heavens, as we will see): 'in 1383 Zhu Yuanzhang ordered two Hanlin members (Li Chong and Wu Bozong) to work with two Muslims summoned from the "Western Regions" (*xiyu*, i.e. Central Asia), Mahamu and the "great Muslim teacher Sheikh Ma" (*Huihui da shi Ma sha yi hei*), to translate [an Islamic] book [about calendar making] into Chinese'.[56] The story is difficult to verify because it comes from a seventeenth-century family history, but it is rather plausible given everything else we know. It is a verifiable fact that Chinese Muslims continued to venerate Hongwu for centuries after, believing their ancestors to have come to China at his explicit invitation, often to serve him: for example, 'Chinese Muslim scholar Wu Yiye recently related how the Wu family arrived in China from Samarqand in the fourteenth century to serve as astronomers in Ming Taizu's court.'[57] Hongwu and Yongle's patronage of Islam was not limited to astronomers either; they encouraged Muslim merchants and gave permission to build and renovate mosques.[58] All of this is very unusual if viewed from the usual Sinocentric view of Ming history, but

---

[54] Robinson (2019, p. 15).   [55] Robinson (2020, p. 5).
[56] Ben-Dor Benite (2008, p. 282).   [57] Ibid., p. 283.   [58] Ibid., p. 287.

it makes complete sense if we think of the early Ming as a post-Chinggisid house, similar to the Timurids.

The fates of these dynasties throughout the fifteenth century are also more similar than what we might assume if we study each in isolation. Both Hongwu and Timur favoured successors – specific grandchildren – who did not get to rule. Timur's favoured grandson Pir Muhammad could not even assume command. Other grandsons also vied for Timur's throne, controlling their own territories: for example, Khalil Sultan briefly ruled over Samarkand (r. 1405–9) and Iskandar[59] Sultan (r. 1409–14) briefly ruled over Shiraz and Isfahan. The latter is noteworthy because his ideological experiments took the Timurid model of kingship a step further by claiming 'saint-philosopher-king status' and sponsored 'astronomers, astrologers and various other occultists'.[60] In a preface he 'wrote for a comprehensive Persian manual of mathematical astronomy (*'ilm-i hay'at*), *Jami'-i sultani* ("The Sultanic Compendium"), possibly his own work ... [Iskandar] provides an overview of his personal intellectual and spiritual development as proof of his status as Perfect Man (*insan-i kamil*) and universal ruler, emperor of realms both seen and unseen'.[61] As evidence of this universal sovereignty, Iskandar also claimed 'a total mastery of "all the traditional and rational sciences in both fundamental principles and applications" ... including theology, philosophy, and Sufism'.[62] Eventually Iskandar lost out to his uncle, Shah Rukh (r. 1405–47), who was more conservative in these claims, but the mode of legitimation he advanced lived on. Shah Rukh's son Ulug Beg, who essentially was Shah Rukh's co-ruler as the governor of Samarkand (r. 1409–40), established the world's leading observatory there with similar motivations.[63]

Just like Timur's would-be sovereign grandsons Khalil and Iskandar, Hongwu's grandson Emperor Jianwen was also killed by his uncle Zhu Di after a four-year rebellion which devastated the countryside. Zhu Di – with support from Mongols among his men – mounted the throne as Emperor Yongle (r. 1402–24, also known as Chengzu). As we have seen in the previous chapter, this type of violent competition over the throne – tanistry – was institutionalised in the Chinggisid world order,

---

[59] Note also that this is the Arabic version of the name Alexander.
[60] Melvin-Koushki (2018a, p. 360).   [61] Ibid., p. 361.   [62] Ibid., p. 361.
[63] Ibid., p. 361.

with victory demonstrating heaven's favour of the ruler more clearly than any other symbol of legitimacy. What is of course unusual is seeing it in the Chinese context: post–Yuan Dynasty, 'conduct (such as tanistry) that had once been regarded as incompatible with Chinese traditions became, if never quite openly, a Chinese norm'.[64] Admittedly, Yongle still had to cover up what he had done by altering court records, but that does not change the fact that he did it and those around him accepted what he had done.

Consolidating Greatness: Yongle and Shah Rukh (Early Fifteenth Century)

Emperor Yongle followed in his father's footsteps in engaging in an ambitious international campaign for recognition and competing for the legacy of the Great Khans of the Chinggisid world order (see Figure 3.1). He engaged in ambitious military campaigns in which he personally took to the field:[65] 'He fought repeatedly on the steppe against military forces of the Yuan court, often deploying Mongol personnel whose allegiance he had either inherited or won in his own name.'[66] His decision to lead the armies himself was both unprecedented in pre-Yuan dynastic history and controversial in the Ming court, and it can only be understood by factoring in the influence of the steppe ecumene in shaping Yongle as he was growing up. Furthermore, in his communications with various rulers in Inner Asia, Yongle 'sought to persuade audiences at home and abroad that Mongol sovereigns after 1368 were not emperors, that their reigns did not constitute a continuation of the Great Yuan, and that the Ming dynasty held exclusive possession of Heaven's Mandate'.[67] In other words, Yongle seemed extremely preoccupied with the 'external' recognition of his sovereignty, as acquired by military strength or diplomacy.

Remember that in the Chinggisid model the main proof of heaven's mandate is conquest – that is, the projection of power over external territory and having that projection be recognised in return. The early Ming emperors' foreign policy should be understood in that context, even if they were deviating from it in form. Yongle sent instructions, for

---

[64] Brook (2010, p. 76).   [65] Robinson (2019, p. 37).   [66] Ibid., p. 27.
[67] Ibid., p. 34.

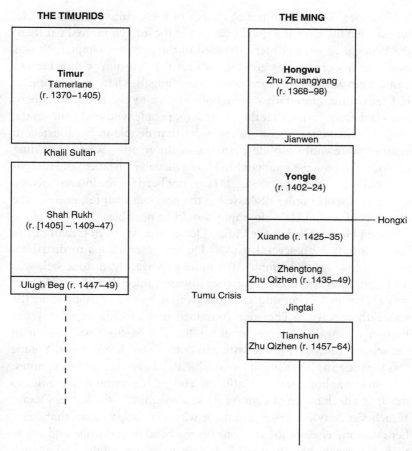

Figure 3.1 Post-Chinggisid Great Houses

instance, that all foreigners were now allowed to send tribute.[68] When the tributes did not live up to his expectations, he started sending eunuchs as envoys around the continent. Yin Qing, a palace eunuch, was sent in 1403 to Malacca (present-day Malaysia), securing tribute from King Parameswara.[69] Also in 1403, Yongle ordered the construction of 137 ocean-going ships; later he ordered the construction of

---

[68] Brook (2019, p. 86). Hongwu had restricted commercial relations with foreigners. See also Rossabi (2014b, p. 207).
[69] Brook (2019, p. 87).

1,180 more. The person put in charge of these ships was Zheng He, whose own life story is a good example of the interconnected nature of the Chinggisid world order discussed in the previous chapter: 'It was said that his great-great-great grandfather, a Muslim with a Persian name from Khwarezm, surrendered to Chinggis Khan in Bokhara … His father and grandfather were both known by the honorific title of Ma Hazhe, signifying that they were *haji*, people who had gone on the Hajj pilgrimage to Mecca – a reminder that people in the fourteenth century were more mobile than we might realise. When the Ming invaded Yunnan, the younger Ma Hazhe died in resistance, and his ten-year-old son … was captured.'[70] Had it not been for the interconnected Chinggisid world order discussed in the previous chapter, none of the elements of Zheng He's biography would be possible.

Zheng He travelled to the Indian Ocean (the 'Western Ocean', from his perspective) on several trips.[71] He had instructions to distribute presents to kings and temples. But more importantly, a stone stele was 'to be set up to attest their reverence toward Imperial rule'.[72] This stele was set up in Ceylon and later discovered by the Portuguese in the sixteenth century.[73] The stele contained text in Chinese, Tamil and Persian (in Arabic script), invoking Buddha in the first, Vishnu in the second and Islam in the latter. In both Tamil and Persian, Yongle was identified as 'the King of Great China'.[74] However, as Brook notes: 'The stele was not a demonstration of Yongle's devotion to all deities so much as a declaration of Chinese presence within … the Indian Ocean. Whichever deity you revered, Yongle was now the patron of that deity. Let everyone else see the dragons on the head of the stone and know that his reach was universal. No other ruler could claim such authority.'[75] Note, however, that the practice of erecting stele or stone monuments was not a Ming invention and in fact may have been another way in which the example of the Yuan weighed heavy on the minds of the early Ming. The Chinggisids commonly erected stele as well,[76] and this was a well-established practice in Inner Asia

[70] Ibid., p. 89.
[71] The Yuan under Kubilai Khan had also sent envoys to this region.
[72] Ibid., p. 91.
[73] Ibid., p. 92. In the twentieth century it was rediscovered by an English engineer.
[74] Ibid., pp. 95–6.   [75] Ibid., p. 97.
[76] In fact, Yongle encountered and destroyed one such stele in one of his campaigns. Robinson (2019, pp. 71–2).

well before even Genghis Khan.[77] As they marched through Asia, Timurid armies also marked their presence with stone monuments: surviving examples have been found in modern-day Turkey, Afghanistan and Kazakhstan.[78]

The Ming stele project was not limited to maritime voyages either. Similar steles were erected in Inner Asia to project Ming authority: one in (present-day) Mongolia read: 'When this sword is once put to use . . . the feudal lords return to their former obedience, and the whole world submits. This is the sword of the Son of Heaven.'[79] The stele were a way of claiming universal rule and world recognition for one's sovereignty. Furthermore, Yongle frequently 'named and renamed important natural landmarks on the steppe, including springs, rivers and monuments'.[80] Yongle also 'remained abreast of developments in places like Hami, Besh-Baliq and Samarkand'.[81] In return, Inner Asian rulers expected Ming emperors to get involved in their disputes and, perhaps, back them up against the Timurids.[82] Zheng He was not the only major envoy sent by Yongle to foreign lands: Chen Cheng (1365–1457), who travelled to Herat (the Timurid capital) in 1414, was on arguably an even more important mission.[83] Chen Cheng's mission to Herat has received no attention from IR (or really anyone but specialist historians) because it does not capture our imagination in the same way as the sea-faring missions of Zheng He, which seem to anticipate and parallel European voyages.[84] However, from a fifteenth-century perspective, Chen Cheng's mission to Herat would have arguably been more significant geopolitically (visiting the principal rival) and economically (visiting the city controlling the 'Silk Road' trade on its other end). Yongle wrote to Shah Rukh 'affirming his rule's universal nature'.[85] Indeed, there were numerous other missions to Inner Asia during the reign of Yongle.[86] And he also received envoys from there. Overall, these diplomatic efforts – whether maritime or overland – were a success, at least from Yongle's perspective of getting

[77] Ibid., p. 73.   [78] Lentz and Lowry (1989, p. 25).
[79] Robinson (2019, p. 52).   [80] Ibid., p. 50.   [81] Ibid., p. 35.   [82] Ibid.
[83] On Chen Cheng's mission see, for example, Kauz (2015); Rossabi (2014a, 2014c); Hecker (1993).
[84] For another explanation of the purpose of these voyages, see Musgrave and Nexon (2018). That argument (focusing on legitimacy) is complimentary to the one here even if it does not discuss the simultaneous overland missions.
[85] Robinson (2019, p. 44).   [86] Rossabi (2014c, p. 110).

'universal recognition of his legitimacy as ruler of the Ming Great State'.[87]

It is well worth remembering that Ming overtures and military campaigns in Inner Asia had other audiences beyond Inner Asia as well. A number of other Asian dynasties[88] were also shaped by the Chinggisid ecumene and were therefore likely to be confused by Ming versus Mongol sovereignty claims. For example, the forefathers of King T'aejeong (r. 1400–18) – who had founded the Joseon dynasty in Korea after a bloody coup – 'had served for generations in Ssangsong Comandery, a key outpost of Mongol military and administrative control in north-east Korea during the preceding Koryo period'.[89] Emperor Yongle did not take T'aejeong's allegiance for granted, so pressed him into selling tens of thousands of horses. There were constant reports that the Joseon may aid the Mongols. The Ming court worried about this potential alliance well into the fifteenth century.[90] Perhaps ironically, Yongle used Mongol troops to project power in East Asia as well, deploying them 'to fight all the way from the northern edge of the Mongolian steppe to the subtropical region of Great Viet', which he had annexed.[91] He was a Great Khan in all but name.

Turning back to west Asia, Timur's eventual successor Shah Rukh (r. 1405–47) was no Yongle – one wonders here what Iskandar could have been – but at least initially he continued some of Timur's campaigns and universal sovereignty ambitions. Shah Rukh used the Genghis Khan connection to legitimise his rule, but he also played up his connection to the Ilkhanate in particular, adopting the title of *padishah-i Islam*. He also adopted 'an explicitly messianic title: *mujaddid* ("renewer")', a title which had been reserved for a scholarly authority in the pre-Mongol era.[92]

Just as Yongle's sovereignty claims were fashioned by the east (Eur) Asian milieu he operated in, so were Shah Rukh's by his own west (Eur) Asian setting. The Timurids' main competitors here were the Turcoman Aq Qoyunlu ('with white sheep') – and to a lesser extent

[87] Brook (2019, p. 85). Here Brook suggests that Yongle sorely needed the external recognition of his sovereigty secured by these missions precisely because he had ascended to the throne by killing his nephew. Different aspects of the Chinggisid sovereignty model presume each other.
[88] For Vietnam, see, for example, Buell (2009); Anderson (2014).
[89] Robinson (2019, p. 41).   [90] Ibid., p. 43.   [91] Ibid., p. 86.
[92] Melvin-Koushki (2018a, p. 361).

the Qara Qoyunlu ('with black sheep') – houses in present-day Turkey/
northern Iran, as well as the Mamluks in Cairo, who the readers will
recall from the previous chapter enjoyed the distinction of having
fought off the Chinggisid. The Ottomans were still reconsolidating in
Western Anatolia and the Balkans after their defeat by Timur's armies
in 1402, the subsequent capture of Sultan Bayezid by Timur and the
interregnum that ensued afterwards (1402–13). In other words,
Timur's military successes meant that Shah Rukh and Timurids were
similarly positioned vis-à-vis west Eurasian rulers with similar sovereignty aspirations as Yongle and the Ming were to Inner Asian rulers
competing for claims to Chinggisid charisma.

In the early part of Shah Rukh's reign, the Ottoman and Aq Qoyunlu
rulers paid homage to him. The Timurid rulers also received embassies
from the Mamluk Sultanate.[93] The occultists who helped Timurid
rulers concoct narratives of heaven's favour within the Islamic millennial milieu travelled between all of these seats of power, so there was
even more circulation of personnel between the competing houses in
west Asia than there was in East Asia (but there the Mongol nobles
went back and forth as well). Between these houses, the aforementioned fusion of Chinggisid, Persianate, Sufi, Ghazi – occult legitimating ideologies, which the Ilkhanate had first initiated in the region and
Timur had further elevated – started taking other creative forms. It is
also important to remember that (leaving the Mamluks aside) all of
these houses shared a common courtly language in Persian,[94] and all
shared (including the Mamluks) Turco-Mongol ethnicity (and thus
could also speak Turkish). We will see the effects of this intellectual
circulation in the next chapter.

Timurids competed with the Mamluk Sultanate especially within the
field of religious supremacy. Increasingly Islam played a bigger role in
Shah Rukh's sovereignty claims (as Confucianism did for the Ming),
repeating the pattern we saw in the previous chapter with regards to the
inability of the Mongol style of sovereignty legitimation by world
conquest to reproduce itself in settled forms of governance. In the
early fifteenth century, the Mamluks were the other main Muslim
power in west Asia, having fended off Mongol campaigns of
Chinggisids in the thirteenth century and having withstood Timur as
well in the fourteenth. As the major Muslim dynasty in the region, the

---

[93] Dekkiche (2014).   [94] Arjomand (2016, p. 10).

Mamluks had been claiming exclusive right to send the *kiswah* ('the veil the supreme representative of the Muslim community sent every year on the occasion of the pilgrimage to cover the Kaʿbah'[95]) to Mecca since 1263. In 1424, Shah Rukh challenged this claim. A number of embassies between the two rulers had to do with finding a resolution to this dispute (ten letters of correspondence have survived in Cairo). After his initial efforts were rebuffed, Shah Rukh turned to threats and asserted his claim over the Mamluk Sultanate, ordering the Mamluk Sultan Barsbay 'to mention his name both at the Friday khutbah [sermon] and on the coins'.[96] Relations became more friendly after Barsbay's death; his successor Jaqmaq worked out a compromise in 1444 in which Shah Rukh was allowed to bestow the inner *kiswah* on the Kaʿbah.

There are reasons to speculate that, at least initially, Shah Rukh's power projection ambitions were of a similar scale to Yongle's. Neither ruler challenged the other openly, however, notwithstanding the fact their had almost fought each other. Yongle and Shah Rukh exchanged twenty embassies, not counting the usual caravan trade between the two economies. There is even evidence that Yongle and Shah Rukh related to each other as equals, which is unusual from the perspective of Chinese historiography. As late as 1432, the Ming Emperor Xuande (r. 1425–35) asked Shah Rukh to protect his merchants. Shah Rukh also had suzerain claims over the Delhi Sultanate as well as Calicut (which was one of the locations Yongle had also sent envoys to) and exchanged embassies with them.

Fragmentation of the Post-Chinggisid World Order

The preceding discussion demonstrates that, from the last quarter of the fourteenth century until the middle of the fifteenth century, the Timurids and the early Ming were the Great Houses of the post-Chinggisid world order. This order was held together materially with trade networks spanning Asia but more importantly ideationally by Chinggisid sovereignty norms which motivated the ambitions of competing houses and drove them to chase universal recognition. In the middle of the fifteenth century, this order fell apart, and only one of its poles – the Timurids – generated a replacement order that operated

[95] Dekkiche (2014–5, p. 252).   [96] Ibid.

with sovereignty norms that could be traced back to the Chinggisid world order. That will be the focus of the next chapter, but let us first scrutinise what caused this world order to decay mid-century.

Reasons for Ming Retrenchment

One of the main reasons this post-Chinggisid world order was short lived is the well-known turn of the Ming towards isolationism. But the reasons why that turn happened may be more complicated than documented in IR thus far.

Yongle's successor was the Xuande emperor (r. 1425–35), and it is to his time that many date the first inward turn of the Ming. Xuande authorised only one more maritime voyage. The early Ming missions already discussed had been expensive, especially the seafaring ones. The early Ming court had also engaged inconsiderable infrastructure expenses domestically, such as the construction of the new capital (Beijing) and the refurbishing of the Grand Canal network. Thus it is likely that financial considerations played a role in Xuande's reluctance to authorise more missions. However, another major factor seems to have been opposition by (some) senior civil officials to this 'Mongol' style of foreign policy. As we will see, the political developments of the fifteenth century gave this sceptical, isolationist camp the upper hand. Many senior civil officials of the Ming Dynasty did not feel at home in steppe politics, finding 'the steppe alien and disconcerting'.[97] Yongle's 'firsthand knowledge of the geography, history, languages, and people of the steppe marked him as a universal ruler whose sovereignty exceeded his ministers' limited, bookish learning.'[98] Yongle often needled his officials along these lines. Still, the officials did their part, doing their best to justify the steppe campaigns and the argument that the Ming now held heaven's mandate. But they also voiced criticism at times, usually as couched in historical analogy: for example, 'the senior court minister Hu Guang ... trenchantly criticized the generals of the early Han dynasty who persuaded the sovereigns to indulge in ill-considered military action in the steppe'.[99] They also sometimes obfuscated about the resources available for such campaigns.[100] In sum, among the senior officials, there was a strain sceptical about the steppe

---

[97] Robinson (2019, p. 75).   [98] Ibid., p. 59.   [99] Ibid., p. 74.
[100] Ibid., p. 75.

from the beginning, either because they thought it was an alien experience or because they feared competition from the Mongol elites in the
realm (who could become their rivals as advisors to the emperor).[101]

The inward turn of the Ming is even more closely associated with the
trauma of the 'Tumu incident' of 1449, when Zhu Qizhen/Emperor
Zhengtong (r. 1435–49; 1457–64 as Emperor Tianshun) fell hostage to
the Mongols, whose price hike for horses Zhengtong ostensibly
decided to punish with a military campaign.[102] He was released
a year later, but another emperor had been enthroned in his absence,
and Zhu Qizhen was not returned to power until 1457. As critical as
this incident seems to have been in giving the anti-steppe lobby the
upper hand in Ming politics, it also demonstrates the continuing influence of Chinggisid notions of sovereignty on the Ming well into the
fifteenth century. The official Ming historiography[103] after the incident
(in the *Ming Veritable Records*) judged this campaign a foolish excursion undertaken on a whim, but historians now question whether this
could have been true, given that the campaign involved a 200,000-
strong army which had to be fed and clothed.[104]

It is also important to underline that the Ming were still accepting
tributes at this point, grudgingly at times because delegations were
expensive to host and posed security concerns.[105] That reluctance
notwithstanding, the idea that the Ming had disconnected from west
Asia altogether at this juncture is not borne out by the historical record.
There is even evidence that 'tributes'[106] came from as far as western
Asia throughout the fifteenth century: there is 'the record of a certain
kingdom which is called Lumi 魯迷 in Chinese texts and which figured
as the most important "tributary state" during the later Ming dynasty,
after the fundamental city Samarqand. Lumi is most probably
a transcription of Rūm, a label for the Ottoman Empire in this period,
and the appearance of its embassies at the Ming court is another
testimony to the enduring importance of the Silk Road as an Asian

---

[101] Rossabi (2014d, p. 83).   [102] Rossabi (2014c, p. 130).
[103] This official historiography (as echoed down to modern times) also causes IR
accounts to completely overlook what a fundamental role Inner/west Asia
played in Chinese history, as well the (early) Ming conceptions of world order
and sovereignty.
[104] Robinson (2019, p. 136).   [105] Ibid., p. 159.
[106] I am putting scare quotes around this term because, whether intended as tribute
or not, things were coded as tribute by the Ming. As far as the Timurid (or other
Inner Asian houses) were concerned, this was trade. Rossabi (2014b).

thoroughfare.'[107] This trade kept the Ming involved in Inner Asian affairs (even if at arms length) and forced them to compete in a way with a number of lesser houses who were still operating with Chinggisid ambitions. The first one of these were the Choros of the Oirats (another branch of the Mongols), who were heavily involved in this Central Asian route, following the trade-friendly tradition of the Chinggisid order discussed in the previous chapter: 'As the Oirats expanded their control over key trade and transportation nodes like Hami, they sought out Muslims from Hami, Turpan, and Samarkand to supervise trade with neighboring states, much as Chinggis and his successors had previously done with Uighur and Persian speaking Muslims.'[108]

The leader of the Oirots, Mahmud, had 'requested and received investiture from the Ming court, which invested him as "Obedient and Pacified King"' in 1409.[109] However, first Mahmud and then his son Toghan were not satisfied with this status quo, amassing followers using Chinggisid symbolism. Toghan also found a proper Chinggisid heir from the Kubilaid (Yuan) line – Toqto'a Buqa – to install as a puppet 'Great Khan'.[110] Toghan died in 1439, but Toqto'a Buqa's presence continued to concern the Ming court, as he was issuing edicts to previous subjects of Kubilai, such as the Joseon ruler King Sejong (r. 1419–50) in Korea, claiming sovereignty over him.[111] The Ming court countered such claims by reminding Sejong that Toqto'a-Buqa was a figurehead and requesting 'Sejong to "continue to be steadfast in his sincerity"' to Zhu Qizhen'[112] (Zhentong). In the meantime, Toghan's son Esen was also making similar appeals to Jurchens. A more plausible interpretation of the Tumu incident thus places Ming concerns about the steppe in the context of rising houses with Chinggisid pedigree.

The important thing to underline here is that if Inner Asia was so inconsequential as our projections of modern-day hierarchies back into the period make it out to be, the Ming court could easily have ignored these challenges. Yet the emperor felt obligated to issue several letters countering the claims of Toqto'a-Buqa and the Oirats,[113] in addition to

---

[107] Kauz (2015, p. 254), citing Watanabe (1975, pp. 308–9, 312–13). Also see Rossabi (2014b, p. 210). Rum is a version of Rome (later Byzantine Empire; the association continued into the Ottoman period).
[108] Robinson (2019, p. 158).   [109] Ibid., p. 139.   [110] Ibid., p. 140.
[111] Ibid., p. 142.   [112] Ibid., p. 144.   [113] Ibid.

the military excursion. For all these reasons, Zhu Qizhen's ill-fated
campaign which led to his kidnapping probably had a lot more going
on than simply fixing horse prices. In fact, when Esen learned that Zhu
Qizhen had been taken captive, he remarked that it was heaven that
had delivered the Ming emperor to his hands,[114] thus suggesting (in line
with the Chinggisid template) that heaven's favour had now passed to
him. The new emperor Zhu Qiyu (Jingtai), who had replaced Zhu
Qizhen, scrambled to reassure the Joseon court that no good would
come out of following the Yuan claims and pressured King Sejong to
deliver men and horses. The merchants involved in the Ming–Inner
Asian trade played an important role in the negotiations that led to Zhu
Qizhen's release.[115] In fact, growing Ming isolationism after the 'Tumu
incident' notwithstanding, long-distance trade between the Ming and
west Asia did not considerably slow down until the late sixteenth
century; there is evidence that it even grew in the fifteenth century.[116]
Still, the 'Tumu incident' of 1449 is a convenient historical landmark
for separating the two versions of the Ming Dynasty.

   'Ming Dynasty 1.0' (1368–1449) wanted to order the world. It acted
like a Great House in the mould of the house of Genghis Khan. 'Ming
Dynasty 2.0' (1449–1644) was mostly isolationist; it was content with
controlling its own territory and keeping foreigners out. There are
materialist explanations for this turn that I will discuss, but it is also
true that 'in Zhu Qizhen's humilating capture and the ensuing political
chaos, the civil officials had finally found an irrefutable case against
a style of rulership prominent through the first half of the fifteenth
century that they themselves had found objectionable, but had been
unwilling to attack openly'.[117] By the time of Emperor Hongzhi
(r. 1487–1505), who is associated with a Ming 'silver age', isolationism
had become official policy, justified in Confucian principles of distin-
guishing between *hua* and *yi* (those of China and not of China).[118] As
alluded to earlier, this policy of isolationism, even in this period, was
more preached than practiced. Hongzhi and his successor Zhengde
(r. 1506–21) continued to receive tributes and host foreigners in their
court, but they – especially Zhengde – were heavily criticised for this
practice which was seen as a sign of poor leadership.[119] So something

---

[114] Ibid., p. 146.   [115] Ibid.   [116] Rossabi (2014b, p. 209).
[117] Robinson (2019, p. 161).
[118] Foreigners already in China were allowed to stay.
[119] Robinson (2019, p. 204).

had shifted in terms of sovereign legitimating strategies. External recognition – what Yongle desperately needed to justify his highly centralised sovereign claim – was now something that undermined respect for the emperor.

It could be argued that Ming's withdrawal from the steppe – whatever the underlying cause – further undermined the legacy of Chinggisid norms and institutions in China, just as the competition with the other houses of Inner Asia had kept them alive in the early Ming period. Initially, 'the Ming founder, Zhu Yuanzhang [Hongwu], [had] articulated an identity for himself and his dynasty through explicit contrasts with the ruling house of the Great Yuan. His descendants in the fifteenth century similarly defined themselves by reference to fellow Eurasian rulers ... who shared overlapping ideas about rulership, its expression, and its obligations.'[120] It seems that framework increasingly lost its relevance for the Ming from the middle of the fifteenth century, perhaps due to the fact that the anti-steppe bureaucracy gained the upper hand, as already discussed. If so, this shift would support the argument that Chinggisid-style sovereignty is difficult to sustain in the long run. Later in this chapter, in the section about the early Ming and the Timurids, I will also discuss some possible structural pressures that may have been helped along this ideological shift in the Ming.

Timurid Decline

Turning back to the house of Timur, one could argue that *its* power as a Great House *also* lasted just about as long as 'Ming Dynasty 1.0'. Shah Rukh's immediate successor was his son Ulugh Beg (r. 1447–9). As noted previously, during much of Shah Rukh's reign Ulugh Begh had been almost a co-ruler as the governor of Samarqand. And while Shah Rukh's court increasingly emphasised Islam, Ulug Begh was a ruler very much in the Chinggisid mould: 'In the eyes of many of his contemporaries Ulugh Beg was remembered as an ardent upholder of Turco-Mongol traditions. In Samarqand he appointed a Chingizid shadow khan in whose name he issued yarliqhs. Like Timur he emphasized his link with imperial Mongol charisma by calling himself karagan, a title not borne by Shahrukh or his other sons.'[121] He also made scientific contributions as an astronomer. However, his solo reign was

---

[120] Ibid., p. 199.   [121] Lentz and Lowry (1989, p. 96).

very brief. Other noteworthy rulers are Abu Sa'id Mirza (r. 1459–69), grandfather of Babur (founder of the Mughal dynasty), who briefly reunited Timurid territories, and Husayn Bayqara (r. 1469–1506), who facilitated an artistic renaissance in Herat during his reign (around the same time as Hongzhi's silver age in China);[122] but the rulers after Shah Rukh/Ulugh Beg had much more limited control over territory beyond the cities in which they resided.

After Bayqara's death in 1506, Timurid territories definitively fell under the control of the Uzbeks. The Timurid Dynasty of the fifteenth century, especially the last half, is thus better remembered for its contributions to the development of arts and science than for its conquering might. This is not exactly the same thing as Ming isolationism from the second half of the fourteenth century onward, but the practical and normative consequences for power projection are comparable. We will pick up the thread of the Timurids in the next chapter with the Mughals, their direct successors.

Were the Early Ming and the Timurids in a 'World Order' in Asia?

To sum up thus far, what we have in the Timurids and the Ming Dynasty are two comparable rising Great Houses (powers) in the late fourteenth and early fifteenth centuries, on two sides of Asia, both of which inherited from the Chinggisid world order a sovereignty model and an ambition about projecting their power over the world. In other words, both the Timurids and the early Ming legitimised their rule at least initially through Chinggisid sovereignty norms of conquest and external recognition. The sovereignty and suzerainty claims of these Great Houses even overlapped in parts of Inner Asia and the Indian subcontinent. There was a chance that they might have fought each other openly, but they did not, settling into a diplomatic relationship of relative equals in the first quarter of the fifteenth century. As they settled, the Chinggisid logic of sovereignty legitimation by world conquest and recognition gradually gave way (though not entirely) to other normative logics available to each realm: Islam in the case of the Timurids, Confucianism in the case of the Ming.

[122] 'The three and a half decades of Husayn Bayqara's rule in Herat are often referred to as the Timurid renaissance .... It was, indeed, a period redolent of pre–World War I Vienna in its combination of artistic and literary achievement and simultaneous political decay' (Dale 1998, p. 44).

Furthermore, in the first half of the fifteenth century, the two sides of Asia continued to be intensely connected via overland trade routes.[123] This trade directed silver supply to the east[124] and Ming goods to the west, to the great benefit to Timurid and Islamic art and architecture. One could argue that the exchange was beneficial for both cultures, as both the Timurid and early Ming are considered high points in art history.[125] We could even argue that, due to their artistic and scientific advances, both dynasties thus retained their 'soft power' (in modern IR jargon) appeal even after they had given up their conquering and dominating ways. Starting from the second half of the fifteenth century, however, both dynasties were 'replaced'; the power house of Timur declined and eventually got surpassed by other houses; and the house of Ming evolved into something very different from what Hongwu and Yongle had initially created.

However, it bears noting that, despite the simultaneous diminishing of Great Houses on the two sides of the continent from the mid-fifteenth century, relations between the two sides of Asia never ceased. Even though diplomatic envoys were most frequent during the corresponding reigns of Shah Rukh and Yongle, Samarkand 'dispatched one official embassy every two or three years throughout the fifteenth century'[126] to the Ming. Shiraz and Isfahan, all controlled by the Timurids, also sent 'tribute' missions to the Ming with some regularity.[127] Throughout the fifteenth century, merchants brought back Ming wares to Timurid territory and other parts of west Asia: 'Ulugh-Beg is said to have amassed such a large collection of Ming blue-and-white wares in his capital at Samarqand that he even constructed a special "Porcelain House" (Chinikhana) in which to store and display it.'[128] Various Ming goods were distributed from Samarkand further west as well. A European observer travelling with a Mamluk embassy to Samarkand observed: 'The goods that are imported to [Samarqand] from Cathay indeed are the richest and most precious of all those

---

[123] Naval routes from the Chinggisid period were probably also still operational (at least on a more regional basis), but it is harder to find information on those.

[124] Atwell (2002, p. 90).

[125] 'Like the quattrocento in Italy, the long Timurid century was to be considered a golden age of high culture throughout the Persianate world and primary reference point for matters intellectual, religious, and aesthetic' (Fleischer 1986, p. 141). See also Melvin-Koushki (2018a, p. 357).

[126] Rossabi (2014b, p. 209).   [127] See also Lentz and Lowry (1989, p. 106).

[128] Atwell (2002, p. 88); Lentz and Lowry (1989, p. 229).

brought thither from foreign parts, for the craftsmen of Cathay are reputed to be the most skillful by far beyond those of any other nation.'[129] Ming porcelain as well as textiles were thus coveted also further west, for instance, by the Ottomans or Europeans. Ming textiles were so available in the markets of Cairo and Alexandria that they caused the decline of the Egyptian textile industry.[130] This also had a profound influence in the arts and crafts of western Asia, including that of the Timurids:

> Earlier under Mongol hegemony a number of Chinese elements had been assimilated into Iranian art. In the early fifteenth century traditional Chinese motifs – dragons, *qilin* (mythical Chinese beasts), lions, phoenixes, ducks, and cranes, along with stylized clouds, rocks and vegetation – were reintroduced with new vigor into the Timurid vocabulary. In Timurid works from the period, however, these subjects carry none of the traditional Chinese symbolism and reflect instead Islamic techniques and conceptions.[131]

As in the previous chapter, then, artistic influences offer one of the best measures of the interconnectedness of 'Asia' in the fifteenth century. We will see in the next section that Timurid art, as thus influenced by the Ming, itself went onto influence Timurid successor polities such as the Ottomans, the Safavids and the Mughals. I think it is fair to say that Islamic art would have evolved very differently without the 'Chinese' (or East Asian) influences as disseminated first by the Chinggisids (via the Ilkhanate) and later the Timurids, and of course that fact has implications well beyond Islamic art as well.

The preceding discussion thus should have made clear that there *was* a post-Chinggisid world order in Asia, and both the Timurids and the Ming 1.0 initially came close to reproducing the 'Chinggisid' model of universal empire in a power equilibrium that modern IR theory would label 'bipolarity'. And at least for the first half century of their existence, these dynasties disseminated a 'Chinggisid' type of sovereignty norms[132] based on external recognition by the world within their

---

[129] Atwell (2002, p. 89). See also Clavijo (1928, pp. 288–9); see also Fletcher (1968, pp. 209–10); Adshead (1988, pp. 195–6); Lentz and Lowry (1989, pp. 216–32); Rossabi (1983).

[130] Atwell (2002, p. 89). See also Lopez, Miskimin, and Udovitch (1970, p. 126). See also Fletcher (1968); Rossabi (1975, pp. 23–32); Rossabi (1998, p. 250).

[131] Lentz and Lowry (1989, p. 108).

[132] Along with other norms more specific to their regional and dynastic normative lineage, of course.

(often overlapping) spheres of influence.[133] They eventually settled into some type of economic interdependence and also developed diplomatic ties. Furthermore, there were a number of other smaller houses throughout Asia that had also inherited aspects of their world view from the Chinggisid world order of the previous century. The Jochid Khanate (the Golden Horde) still survived in the northern steppes. There were also numerous Turco-Mongol dynasties scattered throughout Asia, from Asia Minor to the Indian subcontinent, who were operating at least partly within a Chinggisid ecumene. Finally, there were other houses in Eurasia besides the Ming who, though not ethnically Turco-Mongo, were nevertheless influenced by the legacy of Chinggisid subjugation. The Rurik Dynasty in Muscovy is a good example.[134] A case could be made for the early Joseon Dynasty in Korea as well.[135] All of this is to say, this was an Asia in which seemingly distant dynasties on the various corners of the continent nevertheless shared a lot about how they understood the world and were much more connected economically and even diplomatically than is usually assumed.

Loosening of Ties and 'the Fifteenth-Century Crisis'

As the Ming charted a course away from the legacy of the Yuan towards Neo-Confucianism, and as the Timurids diminished in military might and turned more towards Islam, it does become harder to speak of a coherent normative order as constituted by these two Great Houses and their secondaries. The fact that these turns on both sides of Asia emerged roughly around the same time could point to a possible shared (or systemic) cause for the decay of the post-Chinggisid order. Interestingly, there are indeed some plausible structural explanations for why the external reach of both the Timurids and Ming Dynasty 1.0 diminished in the middle of the fifteenth century.

---

[133] There are examples of this in modern history – for example, European states competing with each other at the turn of the nineteenth and early twentieth centuries but nevertheless each spreading (slightly modified notions of) nationalism as justification for sovereignty to colonies.

[134] We will return to Muscovy in Chapter 5.

[135] See, for example, the First Strife of Princes (1398), reminiscent of the tanistry norm. See also the previous discussion regarding Yongle.

This is not to say that there are not localised explanations for either turn. For instance, in the case of the Timurids, Shah Rukh is sometimes 'disparaged for his perceived deficiencies as a leader', even as he is exalted as 'a man of great piety'.[136] We also know that Shah Rukh replaced Chinggisid law (*yasa*, as discussed in the previous chapter) with Islamic sharia, because he wrote a letter to Yongle explaining that he had done so.[137] In other words, it is possible to blame the Timurids' anti-'Mongol' turn on Shah Rukh and his pious ways, making this seem as an ideological decision by the dynasty to disavow the expansiveness of the Chinggisid-style sovereignty legitimation. But we also know that Shah Rukh's son and near co-ruler Ulugh Beg kept up with the Chinggisid traditions in Samarqand, in that he used Mongol titles and issued Chinggisid-style legal edicts. So it is not clear that the dynasty had made such a conscious rejection of the Chinggisid mode of universal sovereignty ambition. Similarly, with the Ming, we do know that Xuande had authorised one maritime mission. Even if we blame the Tumu incident for the isolationist turn after Zhengtong, the fact remains that, as explained, the Tumu incident itself was the outcome of a military campaign and the Ming's not so superficial involvement with Inner Asia. When we add to this the fact that the Ming continued to accept tributes and gather military intelligence about Asia even after Tumu – even while acting as if they did not want to do so – we are left with the fact that their isolationist Confucian reawakening may have been more of a post hoc justification of the inward turn rather than the main driver of it.[138]

When we cease treating the Ming or the Timurid realms as islands with no real international connections beyond their immediate region, and instead see them as parts of both a nascent world order as described previously, it becomes apparent that both could have been similarly susceptible to systemic, continent-wide structural trends just as Great Powers still are today. There is, for instance, a climate-based explanation: starting in 1430, summers in Eurasia became much colder than they had been.[139] The reasons for this are debated, but we do know that there was a climate anomaly around the time something seemed to shift in the political order of the continent. Ming records documented

---

[136] Lentz and Lowry (1989, p. 80).   [137] Ibid., p. 80, fn 21.
[138] We will come back to this later-period Ming in Chapter 5.
[139] Atwell (2002, p. 93). Possibly because of volcanic eruptions.

droughts and famines, as well as locust plagues.[140] This situation continued for decades, which might explain at least some of the difficulty the Ming had in collecting taxes during this period and thus also the difficulty they started having in financing external missions. Considering that all of the continent was affected by the cooling temperatures, climate change may even have played some role in the Tumu incident, which started with the Oirats hiking up the price of horse tributes. In other words, material conditions may have played a role in the Ming retrenchment and their growing attachment to neo-Confucian isolationism over the expansive manner of ruling they had inherited from the Yuan (as interpreted by Hongwu and Yongle).

The Timurids were not spared from these trends either, and they suffered even more clearly because they were indeed connected to a larger system. During their rise, the Timurids had amassed wealth both from conquest and also from being one of the primary hubs for western Asian trade in Ming merchandise (along with other 'silk road' trade), as discussed previously. But even before the mid-century climate anomaly hit, there was more demand for East Asian goods in the West then vice versa, which meant that money, rather than goods, travelled east to pay for it. This was because the economies and production capacity of most certainly Europe, and to a lesser extent western Asia, were not as developed in the early fifteenth century as Ming China's. Perhaps this was due to reasons discussed in the previous chapter – e.g. the plague having hit this region in a more devastating manner in the fourteenth century – but in any case the quality and the quantity of East Asian products well surpassed west Asian ones (and most certainly those of Europe). Westerners (broadly defined here as those who hail from any place west of Inner Asia) could trade with the Ming some spices, timber, ivory, pearls, etc., but the rest had to be paid for. To make matters worse, economic contraction in the previous century meant that this money was not in great supply either, so trade volume had already hit a ceiling, before any downturn in the mid-fifteenth century.[141]

The existing shortage of silver was then further compounded in the mid-fifteenth century by 'a sharp contraction in the international supply of precious metals'.[142] Economic activity in west Eurasia (including Europe and North Africa) thus ground to a halt in the 1430s due to

---

[140] Ibid., p. 95; see also Brook (2010).   [141] Ibid.   [142] Ibid., p. 96.

a shortage of money.[143] Mints were shut down from the 1440s until the 1460s. There were silver and gold shortages in the subcontinent and South East Asia as well, due to the Ming decision to shut down its mints in 1433.[144] Whatever the underlying cause, the combination of the environmental factors and the bullion/coin shortage (1430–70) slowed intercontinental economic activity considerably, to probably its slowest trickle in two centuries. This meant that the Ming were no longer producing their coveted goods: 'no longer were large quantities of exquisite blue-and-white porcelain being produced at Jingdezhen and other manufacturing centers'.[145] But this was not just a Ming problem; the Timurids, who depended greatly on the Ming trade,[146] must have suffered greatly as a result of this contraction in trade as well. It was not until the last decades of the fifteenth century that the 'bullion famine' ended, with economic recovery following.

A structural explanation for the fragmentation of the post-Chinggisid order is made even more plausible by the fact that it was not just the Timurids who declined in this period and were eventually usurped by other houses – what we see throughout west Asia are a high number of other dynastic declines as well.[147] The Byzantine Empire collapsed as a result of the 1453 capture of Constantinople by the Ottomans. To the north, Muscovy under Ivan III (r. 1462–1502) started consolidating its power; and the Golden Horde, limping along since Timur's walloping of Toktamish in 1396, finally lost its hold over Muscovy in 1480 (Great Stand on the Ugra River). In present-day Iran, the rival Turcoman confederations Aq Qoyunlu ('with white sheep') and Kara Qoyunlu ('with black sheep') were increasingly surpassed in influence by the Sufi Order of the Safaviyya. The Delhi Sultanate was taken over by a Pashtun (Afghan) house in 1451, paving the way for Mughal takeover in the next century. We could speculate that the Ming

---

[143] Ibid.   [144] Ibid., p. 97.
[145] Ibid., 98. See also Peng (1965, p. 640); Kobata (1969, pp. 49–50); Tanaka (1977, pp. 168–70); Ch'en (1963, pp. 30–1); Wang (1991, pp. 60–3; Wang (1992, 128–9), as cited by Atwell (2002).
[146] This was not a one-sided relationship, however. Presumably, the Ming would have benefitted from having a relatively stable counterpart at the other end of the trade link – and suffered when that arrangement destabilised.
[147] Atwell (2002) argues that change due to unrest was global in this period: see, for example, the collapse of Mayan cities, the collapse of Great Zimbabwe economic network, the Onin War in Japan etc., and the collapse of English power in France etc.

dynasty survived (if by transformation) precisely because they entered the crisis in a stronger position than their western Asian dynastic counterparts.

We will return to some of these themes in Chapter 6, but first the next chapter traces how the Chinggisid sovereignty model found new life in the post-Timurid space controlled by the Ottomans, the Safavid and the Mughals in the sixteenth century.

4 | Expanding the East: Post-Timurid World Orders

The Ottomans, the Safavids and the Mughals (Fifteenth–Sixteenth Centuries)

The date is the end of the Age of Saturn and the beginning of that of the Moon; this latter is a period of great opportunity ... You are the *ṣāḥib-qirān* (World-conqueror) and the *ṣāḥib-zamān* (Master of the Age, secret sovereign of the spiritual world), that is, the *kutb-ül-aktāb* (Ar. *quṭb al-aqṭāb*) (Pole of Poles). The signs attendant on your horoscope are such as no other World-Conqueror, including Chosroes and Darius, has enjoyed. You are the *ṣāḥib-qirān* of the last age; the signs of your horoscope and the geomancy of Daniel show that until the year 1000 after the Prophet there shall be no other *ṣāḥib-qirān*. Daniel's prophecy also shows that the *ṣāḥib-qirān* of the Last Age will also be the *ṣāḥib-zamān*; while this latter identity is now an esoteric one, it will soon become manifest in you.

From Haydar the geomancer's address to Süleyman
I the Magnificent (1535)[1]

Introduction

A few years ago, I visited the David Collection museum in Copenhagen, which is home to one of the largest collections of Islamic art. This was an eye-opening experience. Growing up in Turkey, I have had the fortune of seeing amazing Ottoman artefacts on display. But these are always presented as playing an obvious and linear role in the construction of modern 'Turkish' history and identity, awakening and modernisation. National museums use Ottoman arts to weave narratives of ancien régime and ancestral bonds in service of a nationalist story. The David Collection, by contrast, is not interested in historic 'Islamic art' as a storytelling vehicle in purpose of nation-building, as these artefacts have little to do with Danish national history. Thus the museum had categorised its exhibits according to material type first: there were exhibits of calligraphy, textiles, metalwork, ceramics and so on,

---

[1] As quoted and explained by Fleischer (2018, pp. 69–70).

marked but not organised as Ottoman, Safavid or Mughal. This mode of presentation allowed me to experience the very familiar Ottoman artefacts within their proper temporal, geographical and ecumenical milieu for the very first time in my life. Stripped of the attributed national lineage, it became immediately evident, even to someone who is not trained in art history, that Ottoman artefacts belonged very much in the same universe as their Safavid and Mughal counterparts. From the nationalist-perspective Ottoman history I was exposed to growing up in Turkey, this level of visible similarity (even while allowing for local variation) was a puzzle: Turkish official historiography[2] makes (or made) much of (the late) Ottoman emulation of the West but has little to say about the East. The Safavids ('Iran') feature primarily as a military competitor in historical accounts. I doubt that the average Turkish person – let alone a Westerner – is very aware of how porous these respective geographies were, culturally, artistically, ideationally and politically, in the sixteenth century.

The reader, may, however still bristle at the notion that this is puzzling – after all, aren't these all *Islamic* polities? Why should it be puzzling that they shared artistic and architectural (and other) styles? Of course it is tempting to refer to 'Islam' as a deus ex machina explanation for all this similarity, but that assumes a static essentialism to Islam and Islamic political thinking, art and culture that simply has not been present historically. It also assumes that conversion to Islam comes with a monolithic package of preferences that dictate even artistic taste. Islam is not one thing – what is included under this label in terms of sociology, theology, culture, politics, practice and so on has varied across time and space, not infinitely so but markedly so. Thus even when the practices among different Muslim societies converge, convergence is not a given; it is an outcome that requires as much a historical-sociological explanation as any other. Muslim faith on the part of the rulers and some of the subjects does not by itself constitute an explanation of anything. To put it yet another way: if the Ottomans, the Safavids and the Mughals were simply islands onto themselves, as they are often treated within respective national historiographies or traditional IR history, interacting in meaningful ways *only* with Europeans, learning from *only* Europeans, there would not be any

---

[2] Of course Ottoman art historians are well aware of the connections. See, for example, Necipoğlu (1990).

reason for them to have so much in common. On the other hand, if 'Islam' automatically made them a certain way, then there would not be any explanation for their differences, either from each other or from previous polities of the early period of Islam (and, as we will see in this chapter, they were very different from those). Neither assumption works when scrutinised.

If we want to properly understand these 'Islamicate' empires, then, we first need to reimagine them interacting with each other. This chapter will recreate for the reader the shared 'world order' of these sixteenth-century Great Houses but without reading the subsequent primacy of Europe into sixteenth-century developments. I want to caution, however, against thinking of this 'world order' primarily as a *religious* or Islamic one.[3] As we will see, the influences that gave rise to this 'world order' were multiple and pluralist. In fact, it will become clear that the Chinggisid sovereign legacy we have been discussing in the last two chapters found yet another life (via the legacy of the Timurids) in the world-order-making ambitions of the Ottomans, the Safavids and the Mughals.[4] Islam was in the mix, of course, but its interpretation, especially in terms of political theology, had greatly changed in this period as a result of the Chinggisid/Timurid, occultist and other local influences. In attempting to transcend the nationalistic and Eurocentric accounts of the Ottomans, the Safavid and the Mughals, this chapter is not advocating in their stead an essentialist and static reading of religion or Islam as civilisation, but the very opposite. As Chapter 5 will demonstrate, thinking of the world in terms of closed religious spheres is more of a European historical tradition. While orthodox interpretations of Islam did eventually emerge in these empires, earlier on these empires were rather heterodox and pluralist in their cultural practices.

This chapter and the next will thus construct the world politics of the sixteenth century by decentring Europe and recasting west Asia as central in our understanding of that period. This is not to say that there were not exciting things happening in Europe then that later turned out to be rather important.[5] Rather the goal is to focus on

---

[3] See also Pardesi (2017) for a similar critique.
[4] Arguably the Uzbeks (1500–1747) should be included as well. I deal with the Uzbeks (Shaybanids) in the next chapter, however, when I cover the Asian connections of the post-Timurid empires.
[5] Chapter 5 brings Europe back into the narrative but from a different perspective.

other exciting things which have been forgotten or misunderstood. If we did live in that parallel universe, outlined in Chapter 1, where Eastern decline in the nineteenth century was not a foregone conclusion tainting everything that came before it, there would indeed be a compelling argument to be made in the sixteenth century, the world was centred in west Asia (or at the intersection of Europe and Asia). We would also notice that in the sixteenth century, the ideational legacies of the Chinggisid world order of the thirteenth century were still inspiring universal empire projects and that world-order-making was still originating from Asia outward (rather than the other way around).

In order to see these patterns more clearly, we now turn to what are sometimes also called the early modern gunpowder empires: the Ottomans (1281–1924), the Safavids (1501–1722), the Mughals (1526–1858). For our purposes, a better term[6] is 'Post-Timurid empires', or empires of *sahibkıran* (Lord of Conjunction), or chasers of millennial sovereignty. As we saw in Chapter 3, *sahibkıran* was an astrological designation closely attached to Timur, both signifying and justifying a Chinggisid-style sovereignty claim to universal empire. In the person of Timur, this designation combined Chinggisid elements with Islamic, Persianate and occultist elements. But the sixteenth-century *sahibkıran* empires had influences even beyond the Timurid space: 'it is only because all the potentialities contained within the universalising Mongol model were so fully actualised by Turko-Mongol Perso-Islamic societies as a single cultural continuum, from the Timurids onwards, that the Europeans were finally able to join the era of globalisation inaugurated by the Mongols in the thirteenth century'.[7] In other words, IR history as we know it is not possible without everything we have discussed thus far and will discuss in this chapter and the next.

---

[6] The term 'gunpowder empires' comes from Hodgson (1977). Most historians disagree that this was a defining feature, but the term has stuck. Depending on emphasis, historians also use the terms 'Islamicate' or 'Persianate' to capture this space. For Islamicate, see Sood (2011); for Persianate, see Babayan (2002); Arjomand (2016); Melvin-Koushki (2019b) (and Frankopan [2016] for a Persian-centric reading of history). I am not claiming 'post-Timurid' is a better term than these in a universal sense but rather for the purposes of this book (and historical IR).

[7] Melvin-Koushki (2016, p. 148).

The Sixteenth Century in Traditional IR Narratives

The sixteenth century is not entirely absent from classic IR narratives on Great Powers.[8] Here Kennedy's well-known text[9] *Rise and Fall of Great Powers* is illustrative because it seems to cover the world outside of Europe. IR readers are much more likely to be familiar with this classic text, but not with the histories of the regions mentioned and even less so with the way regional historiographies have evolved since the time Kennedy was writing. Therefore, it is worth pointing out what exactly is wrong with Kennedy's book[10] to explain why all IR texts that build on a similar historiography should be replaced by the account provided in this chapter.

Kennedy devotes an entire chapter to the sixteenth century and what he calls 'oriental empires'. Let me quote how he describes them at length, because IR as a discipline has not really updated this received wisdom in its mainstream account of the evolution of international orders, attempts at 'Global IR' notwithstanding:[11]

The first chapter sets the scene for all that follows by examining the world around 1500 and by analyzing the strengths and weaknesses of each of the 'power centers' of that time – Ming China; the Ottoman Empire and its Muslim offshoot in India, the Mogul Empire; Muscovy; Tokugawa Japan; and the cluster of states in west-central Europe. But however imposing and organized some of those oriental empires appeared by comparison with Europe, they all suffered from the consequences of having a centralized authority which insisted upon a uniformity of belief and practice, not only in official state religion but also in such areas as commercial activities and weapons development. The lack of any such supreme authority in Europe and the warlike rivalries among its various kingdoms and city-states stimulated a constant search for military improvements, which interacted fruitfully

---

[8] For example, Waltz (1979, p. 162) includes the Ottomans (at 1700) in his 'Great Powers' chart.

[9] See Cox (2001) for why this book proved popular in American decline debates of the recent decades.

[10] I do not think Kennedy is particularly worse than other (non-specialist) historians of this period. I have targeted him for criticism not only because his text is considered a classic in IR but also because his views of the world outside of Europe are often seen to be representative of 'common sense'.

[11] As discussed in Chapter 1, our idea of fixing Eurocentrism in IR is to add histories of various regions piecemeal, without challenging the macro-narrative itself.

with the newer technological and commercial advances that were also being thrown up in this competitive, entrepreneurial environment.[12]

Though he seems to capture the significance of the fact that Asian polities of this period were characterised by centralised authority to a much greater extent than European realms, the rest of Kennedy's description is mostly wrong. To begin with, 'oriental empires' are called 'power centers' rather than Great Powers by Kennedy, who reserves the term 'Great Power' for European states only. This creates the impression that Asian states were not part of any larger 'world orders' or systems. Of course, this is not a blind spot unique to Kennedy; as explained in Chapter 1, the idea that Asian states did not have international relations, and had at best regional interests, still persists in IR.

Second, Kennedy provides an odd sampling of actors if his goal was indeed to set the global scene in the sixteenth century. His section headings are 'Ming China', 'The Muslim World' (but really only the Ottomans),[13] 'Two Outsiders: Japan and Russia' and 'The European Miracle' to finish. The Habsburgs, the dominant European dynasty in the sixteenth century, do not make an appearance until the next chapter, where they are discussed from an exclusively Eurocentric perspective, with no mention of their primary rivalry with the Ottomans. Tokugawa Japan makes an appearance here despite the fact that there was no *Tokugawa* Japan at that time: the Edo/Tokugawa shogunate governed Japan from 1603 (*not* the sixteenth century) until the Meiji Restoration in 1868. The mistake is rather illustrative of how unaccustomed Great Power researchers are to lining up seemingly disparate trajectories of Asian states on the same temporal plane as Europe; only Europe is studied as a connected space. Everybody else seems to be travelling alone, endogenously driven – a literal island, in the case of Japan.

Kennedy's chapter is also laden with conceptual problems. While there was considerable economic prosperity (and trade) in both 'Japan' and 'China' in the sixteenth century, it seems more than a stretch to call either of them 'oriental *empires*' as Kennedy

---

[12] Kennedy (1988, p. xvi).

[13] The Safavids and the Mughals, whose combined subject population and wealth well exceeded those of Europe or any other region in the sixteenth century with the possible exception of Ming territory, get only a passing mention.

does.[14] For much of the sixteenth century, the Ming rulers had little interest in outward power projection:[15] hardly an empire. For much of the sixteenth century Japan was embroiled in infighting among the *daimyo* (feudal lords). And of course, one of those *daimyo*, Toyotomi Hideyoshi, did come close to unifying Japan towards the end of the sixteenth century (paving the way for the Tokugawa period) and launched an invasion of Korea (1592–8) with the intent of continuing onto Ming China, resulting in the Imjin and Chongyu conflicts. Yet, a campaign launched at the end of the century by a centralising[16] *daimyo* who had only very recently bested his rivals hardly qualifes as an 'oriental empire' that 'suffered from the consequences of having a centralized authority which insisted upon a uniformity of belief and practice, not only in official state religion but also in such areas as commercial activities and weapons development',[17] as so labelled by Kennedy.

Not that his description applies to any other Asian polity he name-checks either. It is true that the empire(s)[18] that he discusses under the heading 'Islamic World' were more centralised in the sixteenth century than was Europe. As we will see, they did undergo a limited sort of religious homogenisation at the *end* of the sixteenth century. But so did Europe in the same period and before, and more extremely:[19] insisting on 'uniformity of belief and practice' was much more a feature of the European political landscape in the fifteenth and sixteenth centuries than it was of Asia's. Kennedy seems to be projecting back onto the sixteenth century the later notion of 'Oriental Despotism' which came to be attached to Asian polities in the eighteenth century.[20] This is evident in his choice of examples. For instance, Kennedy says: 'An idiot

---

[14] Emphasis is mine; either word in this phrase can be problematised.

[15] European merchants found workarounds. See Wills (1998); Huang (1982).

[16] This is a good place to underline that this book is not claiming all centralisers are influenced by the Chinggisid models – there are some basic dynamics to the centralising logic that arise independently from emulation, found across time and space. As Chapter 1 explained, the Chinggisid model, where available in the cultural or institutional repertoire, strengthened in the hands of such centralisers.

[17] Kennedy (1988, p. xvi).

[18] He seems to have some knowledge only of the Ottomans. Also, the term 'Islamic World' is an anachronism.

[19] See, for example, the Inquisition, the St. Bartholomew's Day massacre, the expulsion of non-Christians from Spain etc.

[20] Çırakman (2001); Hobson and Sharman (2005).

sultan could paralyze the Ottoman Empire in the way that a pope or Holy Roman emperor could never do for all Europe.'[21] But there were no 'idiot sultans' in the Ottoman Empire of the sixteenth century.[22] This is a period that was dominated by rulers and viziers considered to be the most capable in Ottoman historiography. Essentially, this whole chapter is an exercise of reading into the sixteenth century the prejudice and seemingly foregone conclusions of the later centuries. Would a sixteenth-century person describe 'Russia' and 'Japan' as 'outsiders'? Outsiders to what exactly? Such a characterisation makes no sense in the sixteenth century.

Equally anachronistic – though by no means specific to Kennedy – is the idea of a 'European miracle' being self-evident in the sixteenth century. Would a sixteenth-century person, even in Europe, know that a 'European miracle' was happening? Would *we* be talking about a sixteenth-century 'European miracle' if the next two centuries had gone differently? In the sixteenth century, other parts of the world still well outshone Europe in riches, arts, crafts and even sciences. Access to the resources of Asia was still the main driver of European trade and prosperity. Imagine that a few centuries from now South America became the core region in world politics, in the way Europe/ the West has been in the last two centuries. No doubt the twenty-fourth-century scholars would then trace the roots of its future success back to our present day, to the capable and innovative individuals who populate South America today and the choices that they are making now. Would that imply that twenty-fourth-century historians can best understand our present-day order by focusing *only* on South America? That is essentially how we have been studying sixteenth-century world politics.

Rise of the Millennial Sovereigns: A Timeline

If you find yourself still resistant to the idea that the centre of gravity in the sixteenth century was in west Asia (or central Eurasia), consider this: 'By the sixteenth century, Islamicate empires had succeeded in establishing sovereignty over a full third of the human race (some 160 million

---

[21] Kennedy (1988, p. 12).
[22] Kennedy may be referring to İbrahim I, who ruled later in the seventeenth century (r. 1640–8) and is sometimes called İbrahim the Mad.

of 500 million souls), while also presiding over the greatest expansion
of Islam in history after the Arab conquest itself (of the 1.7 billion
Muslims alive in 2016, the majority are descended from people who
converted to Islam between 1300 and 1900).'[23] But these empires did
not rule over Muslims only. The Ottoman and Mughals subjects were
predominantly non-Muslims. And as discussed in the introduction to
this chapter, they were not only *Islamic* empires; they fused
Chinggisid (and Timurid) universalising traditions with Islam,
which already had universalist ambitions of its own, having 'synthesised the Hellenic, Semitic, Persian and Indic patrimonies of late
antiquity'.[24] And together, they were much wealthier than Europe
and more cosmopolitan than either Europe or the Ming. They
'comfortably controlled the globalizing Old World economy, centred
on the Indian Ocean and Silk Road'.[25] Furthermore, they were
connected by the flows of 'precious metals, military technologies,
mercenaries, and bureaucratic and intellectual elites' as well as the
circulation of ideas.[26]

The sixteenth-century ecumene of Eurasia came to be increasingly
dominated by an millenarian and apocalyptic conjuncture.[27] And this
had very interesting repercussions for how sovereignty was legitimated and practiced. Though this millenarian mood was in many ways
global, there are some reasons to argue that it was first and foremost
the post-Timurid Islamicate empires that generated this particular
zeitgeist. All three houses had world-conquering and -ordering aspirations, but in the sixteenth century this was made most visible in the
actions of the Ottomans, perhaps because they were the most established of the three and also because of their geopolitical location. The
Ottomans should be understood 'both as a subset of the new Eurasian
empires and as a hinge that connected (*pace* Sanjay Subrahmanyam
and his concept of "connected histories") the eastern and Western
parts of Eurasia'.[28] So we start with them and then turn to the
Safavids and the Mughals.

[23] Melvin-Koushki (2019b, p. 148).   [24] Ibid.
[25] Melvin-Koushki (2018a, p. 355); Casale (2010); Bonine, Amanat and Gasper
(2011).
[26] Çıpa (2017, p. 211), citing Subrahmanyam (1997).
[27] See Moin (2012); Fleischer (2008).   [28] Şahin (2013, p. 10).

Early Ottomans

Of the three houses we will be focusing on in this chapter, if the Mughals were the richest and the Safavids the most revolutionary, it was the Ottomans who were around the longest. The origins of the House of Osman date back to the thirteenth century, when they were a small frontier band in Anatolia, competing for territory with other *beyliks* (principalities) formed in the wake of the collapse of the Seljuk sultanate of Rum, which had gradually withered away under the onslaughts of the Crusades from the West and the pressures of the Mongol invasions from the East. Osman I (r. 1299–1323) was the quasi-mythical founder of the Ottoman polity. Evidence now suggests that he was 'a marcher-lord ... who most probably recognized as his sovereign Ghazan Khan (d. 1304), the Mongol ruler of the Ilkhanate centered in Western Persia' and 'was an overlord in his relationships with his alps, or knights, who had their own subservient companions'.[29] In other words, the House of Osman was very much a participant – as a small house – in the Chinggisid world order discussed in Chapter 2,[30] and it would later go on to be a participant in the Timurid sphere of influence discussed in Chapter 3.

The early Ottoman armies were very heterogeneous, 'mixing Christians with Muslims and often directed against coreligionists, [with a] focus on booty and territorial expansion rather than conversion'.[31] This is not to say the Ottomans did not use Islamic modes of legitimation. They used *ghaza*: the Islamic notion of holy conquest.[32] The *ghazi* identity of the Ottomans became more pronounced in the second half of the fourteenth century, when the House of Osman stopped acting as mercenaries and started making conquests for themselves. It was in this period they expanded into the Balkans, facing 'new opponents who were generally not prepared to accept Turkish conquest gracefully ... [having] not lived side by side with Turks for decades or centuries

---

[29] Tezcan (2010, p. 84); Arjomand (2016, p. 5). See also Peacock (2019).

[30] In fact, while the Ottomans do not feature in Ibn Battuta's memoirs discussed in that chapter, several of the Turkish houses in Anatolia (*beyliks*) that were their chief allies or rivals in their first century are mentioned.

[31] Darling (2000, p. 135).

[32] Ibid. This did not stop them from also hiring themselves out as mercenaries to various Christian kingdoms. On the lineage of the *ghaza* concept, see also Anooshahr (2014).

like the Byzantines of Anatolia'.[33] This was also when they started
having to delegate at least some authority to other frontier *beys*, 'some
of whom ... did not identify strongly as Ottomans'.[34] The *ghaza*
narratives helped the Ottomans to cast offensives against themselves
by other Muslim rulers as 'treason against the *ghaza*',[35] hurting the
fight against the infidel.[36] Nevertheless, Bayezid I (r. 1389–1402), who
used Christian vassals not only to conquer Turkish beyliks in Anatolia
but also in the failed siege of Constantinople (1394–1402), considered
'himself to be descended from Alexander the Great, the hero of
Christians and Muslims alike' and encouraged 'attempts to reconcile
Islam and Christianity'.[37] The Ottoman rulers increasingly adapted
Seljuk – and at times also Byzantine and Persianate – practices for
governance as well.

The House of Osman was able to gradually consolidate its power over
rivals, by expanding first into the Balkans and then to the Anatolian
hinterland, both by way of conquest and also through marriage alliances
with the battered remnants of the Byzantine Empire as well as other
beyliks. The good fortunes[38] of this rising house came very close to
being a footnote to a history textbook at the turn of the fifteenth century,
however, when they clashed with Timur during his westward campaign
discussed in Chapter 3. The nascent Ottoman polity was dealt almost a
death blow in 1402 in the Battle of Ankara, where the Ottoman army
was defeated by Timur's forces and the Ottoman Sultan Bayezid I
(r. 1389–1402) was taken captive (and reportedly was dragged around
Asia afterwards, as an exhibit in a cage).[39] But Timur was not interested in
sticking around in Anatolia.[40] Bayezid's sons fought each other over the
throne for the next twelve years (the Ottoman Interregnum) until after the
Battle of Çamurlu when the victorious Mehmed Çelebi crowned himself

---

[33] Darling (2011, p. 35).   [34] Ibid., p. 36.   [35] Ibid., p. 37.
[36] Ibid., p. 38. Kafadar (1995) suggests that much of the *ghaza* narrative was in fact
      constructed in later centuries.
[37] Darling (2011, pp. 41–2).
[38] These good fortunes could include the Black Death (see Chapter 2). Schamiloglu
      (2004) argues that the plague considerably weakened both the Byzantine Empire
      (forcing them to lean on the Ottomans for support) and the Ottomans' chief
      rivals among other Turkish principalities, as well as south-eastern Europe. The
      Ottomans were less affected, he argues, because they spent little time in urban
      centres.
[39] There is some debate about this. See Milwright and Baboula (2011).
[40] Manz (1998, 1999).

as Mehmed I in the capital city of Edirne (in Thrace) in 1413. This date is sometimes considered to be the second (or real) founding of the Ottoman Empire.[41] Mehmed I's son Murad II went on a conquest spree in the Balkans, and his grandson Mehmed II (the Conqueror) would go on to conquer Constantinople in 1453, ending the Byzantine Empire (in the midst of the fifteenth-century crisis). It is from this point on and until the seventeenth-century crisis that the House of Osman becomes deserving of the label of a Great House. In this period, we also see the influences of the Timurid model very clearly.

Decentralisation Tradition in Islam

Let's open a parenthesis. Many today think Islam requires political authority and religious authority to be combined; in fact, many even think this is what sharia means. This is because, when people imagine Islamic models of governance, the main examples that they have are from the era of Prophet Muhammad or from the sixteenth century (or from the Islamic Republic of Iran today). The traditional wisdom (from the eighteenth century onwards) in Western thought also held that 'Oriental Despotism' came naturally to Eastern states.[42] Thus the existence of centralised rule within the Islamic tradition seemed to require no explanation, nor did its supposedly unchanging, static nature.[43]

In reality, notwithstanding its original fusing of political and religious authority in the person of Muhammad, by the ninth century there had developed in Islamic tradition something similar to the division between state and church in medieval Europe.[44] In our parallel universe where things had turned out differently for Asia in the nineteenth century, this is a period that could have been remembered as the period where modern liberalism developed. Even in our timeline, it is sometimes called a 'Golden' Age of Islam because of the scientific and artistic advances of the period.[45] This was also a time where authority was decentralised, and political authority especially was constrained. Absolutist and/or

[41] Tezcan (2010).

[42] Çırakman (2001); Hobson and Sharman (2005). As also exemplified by Kennedy (1988) discussed previously.

[43] See, for example, Tezcan (2010). Absolutism is treated as a necessary precursor to modern state development in Europe but not in Asia.

[44] Crone and Hinds (2003).

[45] See, for example, Bennison (2014); Saliba (1995).

universalist experiments after Muhammad, especially by the
Umayyad Caliphate (eighth century), had generated their own resistance within the Sunni tradition in the form of Islamic jurists (*ulama*):
'Elite, cosmopolitan, autonomous, and highly mobile, the [jurists]
successfully appointed themselves sole gatekeepers of Islam and
Islamicate culture and primary political counterweight to caliph
and sultan alike.'[46] Therefore, in the Sunni tradition as practised
from the ninth century onwards, even pedigreed political rulers had
very limited power in terms of domestic governance.[47] They had no
lawmaking authority; it was up to the *ulama* (jurists) to interpret
(and thus make) laws according to sharia. Legislative authority thus
rested with the *ulama*.[48] In this understanding, political rule was
'something which sat on top of society, not something which was
rooted in it'.[49] In other words, Islamic kings were even weaker in
some ways than their Christian medieval counterparts. They shared
authority with both the caliph and the *ulama*. The idea of 'state
sovereignty entailing the exclusive right to determine what is and
what is not law, or even what is not an acceptable legal interpretation'[50] was thus alien to pre-Chinggisid Islamic societies.
The Mongol invasions in the thirteenth century, as discussed in
Chapter 2, destroyed this three-way caliphal-sultanic-jurispruden-
tial divided sovereignty model.[51]

Given that tradition, however, centralisation efforts by the Ottomans
(and other Islamic polities) continued to be hotly debated and heavily
resisted. Much of the Ottoman political thought literature from the fifteenth century onwards, for example, grapples with the question of
whether the sultans had the right to assert their political authority over
the religious authority of the *ulama*. There were also debates about the
centre claiming authority over the peripheries.[52] Compounding the difficulty was the fact that the House of Osman had no special Islamic pedigree
that gave them any higher religious authority than any other *ghazi*.[53] Yet
the Ottomans did manage to clearly assert their authority over the *ulama*
(and others) in the post-Timurid era.

[46] Melvin-Koushki (2018a, p. 353); Al-Azmeh (2001, p. 182).
[47] Crone and Hinds (2003, p. 109).   [48] Crone (1980, p. 88).
[49] Crone and Hinds (2003, p. 109); Crone (1980, p. 89).
[50] Burak (2013a, p. 583), citing Jackson (2018, p. xv).
[51] Melvin-Koushki (2018a, p. 354).   [52] Darling (2008).
[53] Tezcan (2010, p. 84).

Post-Timurid Centralisation of the Ottoman Empire (Fifteenth Century)

Such moves towards centralisation may not have been possible had it not been for the other modes of legitimation available to the post-Timurid[54] Muslim dynasties, especially the Chinggisid mode of sovereign legitimation as inflected via the notion of *sahibkıran* (see Figure 4.1). As we saw in Chapter 2, the Chinggisid notion of world sovereignty did not deem rulers as subservient to (or time-sharing with) religious authority: the 'Chinggisid universalist notion of sovereignty rested on the view that divine dispensation to rule the world was given to Chinggis Khan and his descendants'.[55] Genghis Khan had ruled through *yasa*, which was likely not 'a fixed written legal code' but rather 'an evolving body of individual decrees, regulations, and practices that had been instituted or sanctioned by Chinggis Khan ... a kind of unwritten "constitution"'.[56] The House of Osman likely carried similar conceptions of sovereignty as they migrated themselves in the twelfth and thirteenth centuries from Central Asia to Asia Minor. For example, dreams as a manifestation of heaven's favour were a shared element of the Turco-Mongol ecumene.[57] The well-known Ottoman foundational myth involves Osman I visiting the home of the Sufi Sheikh Edebali and, while there, dreaming of a growing tree that covers the world, which is interpreted by Edebali as divine approval of Osman's and his descendants' claim to world sovereignty.[58]

Ottoman centralisation in the fifteenth century – which ran counter to traditional Islamic practice as explained earlier – was further encouraged, however, by the example of the Timurid model, which gained even more influence after the aforementioned reconstruction of the Ottoman polity after the Interregnum (1402–13). In the post-reconstruction Ottoman historiography, the impact of this defeat (and any type of tributary relationship with the Timurids) was downplayed.

---

[54] This section deliberately emphasises the Timurid (thus Chinggisid) influences on Ottoman state-building, so it inevitably downplays (for space reasons) other traditions (sections on the Safavids and the Mughals do the same for their alternative cultural repertoires). The exact balance of influences at any given time is a question for historians to determine.

[55] Burak (2013a, p. 595).   [56] Ibid.

[57] For Mughal dreams, see Moin (2012). For Safavids, see Quinn (1996).

[58] Kafadar (1995, pp. 8–9); Imber (1987); see also Darling (2011, p. 27). There is some debate as to whether this is a latter-day attribution to Osman.

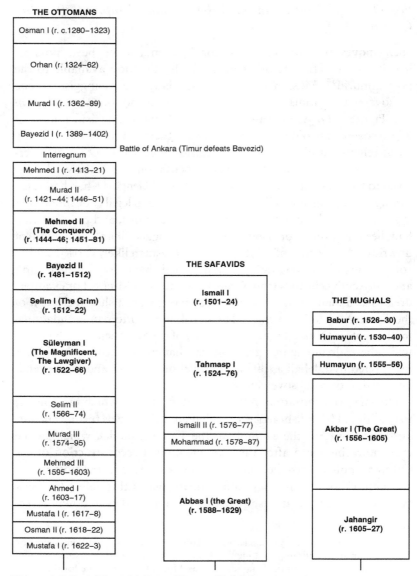

THE OTTOMANS

Osman I (r. c.1280–1323)
Orhan (r. 1324–62)
Murad I (r. 1362–89)
Bayezid I (r. 1389–1402)

Interregnum   Battle of Ankara (Timur defeats Bavezid)

Mehmed I (r. 1413–21)
Murad II (r. 1421–44; 1446–51)
Mehmed II (The Conqueror) (r. 1444–46; 1451–81)
Bayezid II (r. 1481–1512)
Selim I (The Grim) (r. 1512–22)
Süleyman I (The Magnificent, The Lawgiver) (r. 1522–66)
Selim II (r. 1566–74)
Murad III (r. 1574–95)
Mehmed III (r. 1595–1603)
Ahmed I (r. 1603–17)
Mustafa I (r. 1617–8)
Osman II (r. 1618–22)
Mustafa I (r. 1622–3)

THE SAFAVIDS

Ismail I (r. 1501–24)
Tahmasp I (r. 1524–76)
Ismaill II (r. 1576–77)
Mohammad (r. 1578–87)
Abbas I (the Great) (r. 1588–1629)

THE MUGHALS

Babur (r. 1526–30)
Humayun (r. 1530–40)
Humayun (r. 1555–56)
Akbar I (The Great) (r. 1556–1605)
Jahangir (r. 1605–27)

Figure 4.1 Post-Timurid Great Houses (*Sahibkıran*)

It seems clear, however, that Ottoman interactions with the Timurids throughout the fifteenth century were greatly influential on the former. During the decline of the Timurid Empire in the second half of the fifteenth century, various warriors, artisans and bureaucrats[59] who had been working for the Timurids were increasingly incorporated into other western Asian polities, the Ottomans foremost among them. The great influence of this influx has been especially well-studied in the realm of art history,[60] but increasingly historians are noticing influences in other spheres of life, not the least in notions of sovereignty, especially in terms of upending the conceptualisation of the proper relationship between the rulers and the *ulama*.[61] The Ottoman Dynasty increasingly used hybrid modes of legitimation, drawing from the post-Timurid well in which Islamic, Persianate, occult notions of universal/sacred kingship were swirling together, as well as the Roman tradition which they would come to inherit from the Byzantine Empire.

A significant milestone for the development of the Ottoman experiment of universal empire was the conquest of Constantinople in 1453 and, with it, the Ottoman takeover of various Byzantine institutions and practices: 'when Mehmed II finally captured Constantinople (Istanbul), ... in the eyes of many, and perhaps especially of his recent converted or still Christian subjects, he had thereby tacitly inherited the status of the Roman emperor'.[62] The promulgation of a governmental law-code (*kanunname*) as separate from jurists' law (sharia) is attributed to Mehmed II (r. 1444–6, 1451–81) after this conquest, though historians dispute this,[63] pointing out that the attribution was likely a sixteenth-century invention. In any case, the conquest indisputably enhanced the sovereign charisma of Mehmed II (the *Conqueror*). We saw how important conquest – as a manifestation of heaven's mandate – was to the Chinggisid understanding of sovereignty. The conquest of Constantinople was also foreseen within the Islamic

---

[59] For example, Mehmed II invited to Istanbul the famous poet Jami of Herat and Ulugh Beg's [Timur's grandson] astronomer Ali Kusci who lived in the court of the Aqqoyunlu ruler Uzun Hasan at Tabriz before joining the Ottoman court in 1472. See Necipoğlu (1990, p. 158).

[60] For instance, Necipoğlu (1990, p. 137) argues that Ottoman ceramic work evolved from the more 'international Timurid' style to a more recognisably distinct Ottoman style only in the second half of the sixteenth century – and that this in itself was a dissemination of the earlier Ming influence.

[61] Burak (2013a).   [62] Black (2011, p. 204).   [63] Tezcan (2010, p. 84).

tradition, so in this case the two traditions amplified each other. Mehmed II also adopted new titles, such as 'the ruler of the two seas and the two continents',[64] which 'not only firmly established the unquestionable and absolute authority of the House of Osman over the entirety of the Ottoman realm but also heralded dynastic claims of universal sovereignty'.[65] In other words, Mehmed II – like Bayezid I before him – tilted the empire away from the frontier practices towards an even more imperial conception of universal sovereignty, by drawing from as many wells of legitimation as were available.

Another significant accomplishment of Mehmed II was the development of 'the akçe zone between the Danube and the Euphrates, an area in which many different currencies had been in place'.[66] This allowed for Mehmed II to recreate the Islamic practice of the *mamluk*[67] in a rather innovative manner: he 'developed a new army and bureaucracy, based on recruitment of non-Muslim youths as loyal servants of the Sultan without social connections ... These provided the Sultan's personal troops ... Janissaries; and they staffed the central bureaucracy.'[68] The development of such a slave bureaucracy could not have happened in the absence of a strong monetary economy that financed it.[69] Mehmed's (vertical and spatial) centralisation and bureaucratisation strategies inevitably weakened the power of the frontier (*akinci*) families who had been instrumental to the empire's expansion in the fourteenth century:[70] 'One such strategy was the incorporation of the *akinci* troops into the centralized imperial army, which transformed the relatively independent soldiers of fortune of the past into agents of the highly centralized imperial structure of the future.'[71] Private estates were transformed into imperial fiefs (*timar*).[72] All of this was debated and resisted. Within the political justice literature of the period, the main 'bone of contention [at the time] was the Sultan Mehmed the Conqueror's (1451–1481) centralization of land-revenue grants in a quest for funds to expand his army (which was well equipped with gunpowder weapons)'.[73]

Mehmed's successor, Bayezid II (r. 1481–1512), continued the bureaucratisation of the empire, but he had to tread more lightly, given ongoing resistance. He cut a more scholarly figure, sponsoring a new

---

[64] Çıpa (2017, p. 102).   [65] Ibid.   [66] Tezcan (2010, p. 89).
[67] See Crone (1980).   [68] Tezcan (2010, p. 89).   [69] Ibid., p. 91.
[70] Cipa (2017, p. 102).   [71] Ibid., p. 103.   [72] Ibid.
[73] Darling (2008, p. 513).

imperial historiography.[74] Bayezid II wanted to project the image of a fair and triumphant warrior-sultan. Under his reign, the popularity of universalist ideologies that Mehmed II had been advancing decreased.[75] The opposite was true about his son and successor Selim I (r. 1512–20), who left a much bigger mark despite a much briefer reign. But before we get to Selim the Grim, let us first turn to the Safavids, who would be the primary rivals of the Ottomans in the sixteenth century, and the Mughals, whose time to make their greatest mark would come a bit later but who nevertheless constituted the core of the sixteenth-century world order along with them.

The Rise of the Mughals and the Safavids (Early Sixteenth Century)

Compared to the Ottomans, the Safavids and the Mughals were relatively recent arrivals on the historical scene. These houses rose in the sixteenth century, but they caught up fast with their western rival. The IR literature[76] has neglected them even more than the Ottomans. This is a direct consequence of Eurocentrism: on material grounds, no good case could be made for ignoring the Mughalsin favour of the Ottomans or any of the European powers in the sixteenth or the seventeenth century, as the Mughal dynasty ruled over more subjects and commanded more wealth than any other Great House of the period with the exception of the Ming.[77] And the Safavids influenced the sixteenth-century zeitgeist more than any others.

Babur: Last of the Timurids, First of the Mughals

In the sixteenth century, the fortunes of Safavid Iran and Mughal India were deeply intertwined: 'The cultural institutions that the Mughals

---

[74] Cipa (2017, p. 115).

[75] Şahin (2013, p. 27). There is some debate about the traditional understanding of Bayezid's reign. See Kafadar (2019).

[76] For recent and excellent exceptions on the Mughals, see, for example, Pardesi (2017, 2019); Phillips and Sharman (2015); Sharman and Phillips (2020); Sharman (2019). The Safavids are ignored in global history as well. Matthee (2010, p. 234).

[77] Ibid., p. 237. See also Subrahmanyam (2000). By the seventeenth century, the Mughals ruled over a population three to four times as populous as the Ottomans did.

used in South Asia to deal with a diversity of religious practice were not
invented wholesale in the "syncretistic" religious environment of India
but largely brought over from the heterogeneous conditions of Timurid
and Safavid Iran.'[78] The Mughals traced their lineage back to Babur
(1483–1530; r. 1526–30), the last independent Timurid prince, so we
could call them the House of Babur (they called themselves
Gurkhaniyya after Timur, or Gurkhani). Note that Babur wrote his
memoir, *Baburnama*, in Chagatai Turkish.[79] Of course, he was also a
Muslim: 'In his personality, sustained drinking bouts with Mughul and
Turkic companions, public encounters with ... women and explicit
evocations of legitimizing Chingizid customs coexisted with a visceral
distaste for Mongol and Uzbek crudity ... and a genuine if ordinary
piety marked by [a] characteristic steppe reverence for sufi shaykhs.'[80]
And by his own account, he was very much driven to reestablish the
Timurid Empire, animated by the legacy of his ancestors. He was
moved to write his memoir to demonstrate to readers that he lived up
to this ideal and that he had divine favour.[81]

By the time of Babur, the Timurids had been reduced to a limited
urban presence, barely surviving after the crisis of the mid-fifteenth
century. As a young man, Babur tried to reassert and even expand
Timurid control over their traditional realms. In fact, it could be argued
that the main preoccupation of his life was reacquiring Samarqand,[82] a
historically significant city for the Timurids, but he never managed to
hold onto it for very long. He could not withstand the attacks of the
Uzbeks. An unlikely alliance with Shah Ismail I of the Safavids (more on
him in a moment) gave him a brief respite, but eventually he lost his last
grasp on Transoxiana and moved south (to the northern region of the
Indian subcontinent), defeating first the rulers of the Delhi Sultanate
(the House of Lodi) and later the Rajput confederacy, and established
the 'Mughal Dynasty'.

From the very beginning, Babur was very much animated by
Chinggisid-Timurid notions of universal sovereignty along with other

[78] Moin (2012, p. 19).
[79] Dale (1998, p. 45). See Thackston (2007); Babur and Dalrymple (2020).
[80] Dale (1998, p. 45). Dale's language is problematic here, but the passage gets
across the point that Babur was exhibiting the Timurid synthesis described in the
previous chapter.
[81] Ibid. See also Moin (2012). Reminiscent of a US presidential memoir.
[82] Moin (2012, p. 70).

local and religious elements. Babur's lineage made it easier to launch such justifications. As we have seen with the early Ottoman rulers, Babur also mentions a number of dreams in his memoir: 'Babur fought countless battles in his life, but he narrated his dreams only during his early and desperate struggle for Samarqand. These dreams, then, must be viewed as marking the rite of passage of a budding Timurid sovereign.'[83] As in the other cases, Babur's dreams proved 'prophetic' and the Mughals evolved from their humbler beginnings into a large empire in South Asia, though the empire would not reach the height its expansion until the seventeenth century, during the reign of Alamgir/Aurangzeb (r. 1658–1707).[84]

During its expansion into the subcontinent, the House of Babur settled into local practices just as other Chinggisid and post-Chinggisid Great Houses had done before them, as we saw in the example of the Yuan Dynasty in China: 'If the first Mughal ruler, Babur (d. 1530), had come to India speaking and writing in Turkish and hunting wild ass on horseback, his great-grandson, Jahangir (d. 1627), was most comfortable speaking in "Hindi" and shooting tigers while perched on an elephant.'[85] What still united these two men were their immersion in the post-Timurid Persianate ecumene.[86] Between Babur and Jahangir, however, there were a number of other Mughal rulers significant both in their own right and for what they contributed to the advancement of the post-Timurid fusion of Mughal sovereignty: among them, Humayun (r. 1530–40; 1555–6) and especially Akbar I (the Great; r. 1556–1605). As we will see, Humayun and Akbar went to great lengths to expand the post-Timurid charisma of their house. But before we turn to them, let us first catch up on the Safavids as well.

Ismail: The Shah as a Messianic Cult Leader

The Safavids did not have a direct connection to Timur. But what they lacked in terms of pedigree, they made up for in their messianic

---

[83] Moin (2012, p. 74).

[84] The Mughal expansion into South Asia post-dates the arrival of the Portuguese in Calicut by about a quarter-century. Subrahmanyam (2005a). And the Ottomans started exploring the Indian Ocean around the same time as the Portuguese. See Casale (2007).

[85] Moin (2012, p. 17).

[86] Chagatai Turkish ceased to be widely used in India by the end of the sixteenth century. Persian remained the court language. Dale (1998, p. 51).

founder, Shah Ismail (1487–1524; r. 1501–14). An almost identical contemporary of Babur, he revolutionised the understanding of kingship in west Asia. Like Babur, who had been given command of Fergana when he was twelve, Shah Ismail came into rule early in his life, also at twelve. And even though he was not descended from Timur (or Genghis), he could claim a lineage which connected him with Ali[87] and also one of the previous dynasties ruling Iran – the Aq Qoyunlu, a strong Turkic house whose fortunes had fallen in the second half of the fifteenth century.[88] The new Safavid state borrowed liberally from its Aq Qoyunlu predecessor,[89] but it was also something new: an amalgamation of cult and polity.

Ismail had also inherited from his father the spiritual leadership of Safaviyya – the Safavid Sufi Order: 'The Safavid Sufi order had become militarized under Shah Isma'il's grandfather, Junayd, who had gathered a number of devotees among nomadic Turkmen tribes.'[90] Furthermore, 'the Safavids had developed an extensive network of preachers and proselytizers targeting the Turkmen tribes of Anatolia, the southern Caucasus, and Azerbaijan'.[91] The Safaviyya had started out as a Sunni Muslim movement (the Ottomans and the Mughals were also Sunni) but had transformed into 'militant Shi'i conquering force during the second half of the 15th century'[92] as a result of absorbing popular messianic belief swirling in Iran and Transoxiana during that period. In the preceding century, popular Sufism had become increasingly characterised by an apocalyptic tenor, which came with the expectation of the imminent manifestation of the messiah (*Mahdi*).[93] The Safavid now believed Ismail to be that messiah, the reincarnation and embodiment of 'divine truth (*haqq*), Ali, Jesus, the twelve Shi'i Imams, and ... great warriors and emperors of the pre-Islamic Iranian past',[94] Ismail also had a seemingly unlimited supply of conqueror's charisma, at least until his defeat in the Battle of Chaldiran (1514) by the Ottoman Sultan Selim I. Ismail's warriors may have been more devoted, but Selim's Ottoman armies had more experience and more

---

[87] See also Babayan (2002).
[88] Moin (2012, p. 76). His grandmother, the Aqqoyunlu queen Despina Khatun, was a Christian princess from the small Greek kingdom of Trebizond on the Black Sea coast.
[89] Melvin-Koushki (2018a, p. 363).   [90] Moin (2012, p. 76).   [91] Ibid.
[92] Melvin-Koushki (2018a, p. 364).
[93] Arjomand (2016). See also Babayan (2002).   [94] Moin (2012, p. 77).

artillery. Ismail escaped with his life, but the defeat punctured his messianic charisma, though not enough to completely sever the loyalty of his followers.[95] He fell into a depression for the rest of his reign. A heavy drinker, Ismail died at the young age of thirty-six. Before the Battle of Chaldiran, Ismail had managed to reunite most of the territory corresponding to modern-day Iran under his rule, ending the political fragmentation in this area which had lasted for much of the fifteenth century.

Ismail and Babur's paths also crossed in a significant way. Like Babur, Ismail had ambitions of expanding his reach into Transoxiana. After he defeated the Uzbek ruler Shaybani Khan, he turned to Babur for an alliance in a campaign to conquer Samarqand, promising Babur that he could keep any territory he conquered. This put Babur into a subservient position vis-à-vis the Safavids, but at the time he was a struggling prince from a dying Great House, not the founder of the next one. He essentially had to become a 'disciple' of Ismail in order to wage the wars he wanted. Babur's memoirs are silent when it comes to this period, so we do not know what Babur really made of Ismail's messianic ambitions. However, Moin notes that rituals practised by the Ismail's followers were not that different from Timurid custom,[96] which may explain why Babur was willing to wear the *Qizilbash taj* (hat or crown – more on this to come) and did not take it off when he conquered Samarqand.[97] His unwillingness to remove it may also partially explain his difficulties in holding onto the city, the population of which was not on board with the Safavid movement.

Qizilbash was what Ismail's warrior devotees (or disciples) were called. They were initially drawn from Turkmen tribes previously under the control of the Aq Qoyunlu.[98] These warrior devotees subscribed to a number of religious practices that were far from orthodox and more in line with the Safavid missionary preachers: they shaved their 'facial and body hair ... wore nose rings, pierced their bodies, carved out signs on their flesh, tattooed themselves ... took intoxicants, and danced in circles, holding hands and singing'.[99] Their name – literally 'redhead' in Turkish – was derived from a hat that they wore: 'According to Safavid tradition, Ali had come in a dream to Shah Isma'il's father, Shaykh Haydar, in 1487 and given him

---

[95] Matthee (2010, p. 247).   [96] Moin (2012, p. 86).   [97] Ibid., p. 87.
[98] Melvin-Koushki (2018a, p. 363). See also Matthee (2010, p. 246).
[99] Moin (2012, p. 78).

instructions to make a distinctive *taj* [crown]. This consisted of a
hat topped by a tall red baton with twelve facets (*tark*), around
which a turban could be tied.'[100] Wearing this hat was a sign of
devotion to Ali and also to Shah Ismail, who was considered to be
Ali's heir incarnate (both were depicted with red hair). Ismail's
crown was called *Taj-i Haydari*. They also wore collars around
their necks to show that they were slaves of Ali. They went into
battle without armour.[101] There were reports of other rituals as
well: 'Another more grisly way of demonstrating loyalty to the
shah consisted of the frenzied devouring of the body of his
enemy. Reportedly, one victim of this ritual act was the Uzbek
ruler Shaybani Khan, whose muddied and bloodied corpse was
eaten by a stampeding crowd of Qizilbash soldiers.'[102] Moin
observes that these rituals were also processes of incorporating
outsiders into the Safavid order.

Ismail named his sons after pre-Islamic Persian kings, another
signal that his claims to universal sovereignty were drawing from
multiple wells. He also commissioned a personalised epic
(*Shahnama-i Ismail*) commemorating his own deeds, echoing not
only earlier *shahnamas* ('books of kings') but also Timurnama
('Book of Timur'). He was thus reinventing Timurid sovereignty for
the sixteenth century. In sum, unlike the other rulers we have discussed thus far, Shah Ismail commanded a cult first and then went on
to conquer. He was a sacred king, but, while Ottoman and Mughal
kings in this period moved into the sacral sphere by usurping religious
titles around them, Ismail was first a religious cult leader who then
moved into the realm of the political.[103] But all roads lead to
Baghdad/Rome, so to speak: all three houses ended up claiming
millennial sovereignty one way or another in the sixteenth century.
I will return to what that means exactly in a moment.

Ismail's Ottoman Mirror: Selim the Grim

In many ways, Selim I (the Grim) was a real throwback to the Turco-
Mongol vein within the House of Osman, operating in ways well

---

[100] Ibid., p. 81. Note the dream connection.
[101] Melvin-Koushki (2018a, p. 363).   [102] Moin (2012, p. 82).
[103] See the centralisation discussion in Chapter 1.

within the Chinggisid sovereignty mould as discussed in the previous chapters. As such, he cut quite a different figure from his more placid father Bayezid II and mirrored the messianic fervour of Shah Ismail. In many ways, he (along with Ismail and Babur) set the stage for sixteenth-century world-ordering efforts.

As we have seen in previous chapters, the Chinggisid mode of succession was not primogeniture but the encouragement of members of the ruling house to fight each other for the throne: the norm of '"tanistry," which prescribed, usually via murder or war, the transition of supreme rule of the empire to the most competent member of the ruling family'.[104] Mehmed II had even codified this practice.[105] As was Ottoman tradition,[106] princes were given governorships to rule while the Sultan was alive. 'Each contender sought to outmaneuver his rivals by scoring a gubernatorial appointment to the province nearest Istanbul',[107] because proximity to the capital was an advantage in the case of the Sultan's death for reaching the city, claiming sovereignty and the resources associated with it. For instance, Selim I's father, Bayezid II, had bested his brother's claim by arriving in Constantinople before him after Mehmed II's death. Selim I went a step further and moved against Bayezid II while the latter was still alive.

Selim I was the youngest son of Bayezid II, and he had been relegated to the farthest princely governorate,[108] Trabzon, indicating the Sultan's disfavour. This remote posting proved to be a blessing in disguise, because it allowed Selim to raise his profile and support among common people and the *janissaries* (soldiers) by openly taking on the Safavids, who were an increasing threat. Shah Ismail's politico-religious movement appealed to many segments of the population in Anatolia, even members of some leading families. Ottoman conquest of Anatolia was relatively recent, and local power holders resisted the aforementioned moves towards centralisation and taxation of the fifteenth century.[109] Bayezid II 'did not trust Isma'il, whose letter … referred to the aging sultan as his "illustrious and noble father", and kept Anatolian soldiers on alert against a possible Safavid invasion',[110]

[104] Fletcher (1979); Çıpa (2017, p. 31).
[105] Çıpa (2017, p. 33); Şahin (2013, p. 23). Kafadar (1995) calls this 'unigeniture'.
[106] As we also saw with the appanages in the Chinggisid and Timurid empires, and as was also the case with the other post-Timurid houses we will discuss later.
[107] Çıpa (2017, p. 33).   [108] Çıpa (2017, p. 35).   [109] Şahin (2013, p. 25).
[110] Çıpa (2017, p. 35).

but he did not want an open confrontation. By contrast, Selim's belligerence towards the Safavids made him unpopular in the court but gave him an advantage when he reached for the throne[111] while his father was still alive (in contravention of norms of succession). Selim openly challenged his father by moving into the Balkan territories and demanding a governor's seat there. This brought him near military confrontation with his father. Eventually Bayezid II abdicated. This was because the *janissaries* openly supported Selim and pressured Bayezid II to abdicate:[112] '[Selim's] nearly self-destructive campaign against his father further solidified his image as a warrior prince.'[113] In other words, the emerging rivalry with the Safavids, which reinforced 'post-Timurid' or 'Chinggisid' sovereignty norms, worked in Selim's favour. Compared to his father, Selim I signalled a return to the warrior khan side of the universal empire claims rather than the more bureaucratic settled kingship side.

On his way to the throne, Selim had gathered supporters from the frontier families in Rumelia (the European part of the Empire) and had secured an alliance from the Crimean khan north of the Black Sea.[114] Once on the throne, Selim I sent Bayezid away from the capital, but Bayezid died soon after, rather suspiciously. By 1514 Selim I had eliminated his remaining brothers and nephews. He ruled very much as a 'Chinggisid sovereign' (as I am labelling it), as a strong ruler who recognised no other authority: when, for instance, the Şeyhülislam (the head of *ulama*) 'protested against the decision by Selim to have 150 treasury officials executed, the Sultan replied that this was "a violation of the Sultan's authority ... No-one [has] the right or competence to question what the Sultan commands or forbids." The men were executed.'[115] His military victories served to enhance his charisma both as conquests and because they increased his claim to sacred kingship.

In 1514, Selim I met the rising threat of Safavids at the Battle of Chaldiran and defeated Shah Ismail, as discussed previously. Then, in

---

[111] The episode is murky because overthrowing the sultan was illegitimate, so later historiography made it seem like Bayezid II abdicated voluntarily. Çıpa (2017, p. 49). We can compare this with a similar move in Yongle historiography – see Chapter 2 and also Brook (2019).
[112] Çıpa (2017, p. 56).   [113] Şahin (2013, p. 25).
[114] The Crimean Khanate is going to be discussed in the next chapter, along with Muscovy. The Crimean khan at the time was the father-in-law of Selim's son (and successor) Süleyman.
[115] Black (2011, p. 204), citing İnalcık (1973, p. 94).

the battles of Marj Dabik (1516) and Ridaniyya (1517), he defeated the Mamluks definitively, conquering Mecca and Medina, doubling the extent of the Ottoman realm. These conquests would eventually put the Ottomans into a rivalry with European actors who were starting to permeate Asian spaces: 'His capture of parts of the Arabian Peninsula and the Red Sea coast pitted the Ottomans against the Portuguese in the Indian Ocean',[116] but, given the focus of his military campaigns, it is clear that Selim believed the Safavids and the Mamluks to be his real competition, and not any Europeans. The defeat of the Mamluks and subsequent Ottoman conquest of the holy cities of Islam – as well the military defeat of Ismail – meant additional support for the Ottoman claim vis-à-vis the other post-Timurid houses. Now the Ottoman sultans could even more legitimately claim religious authority in addition to political authority.[117]

Many historians believe that Ottoman imperial ideology as thus developed during Selim's reign 'began to revolve increasingly around the notions of messianism, universal monarchy, the caliphate, and the ultimate politico-religious leadership of the ruler'.[118] Çıpa, while not disputing the evolution of Ottoman sovereignty in this direction, argues that the attribution of labels such as '"Master of the Auspicious Conjunction" (*sahib-kıran*) ... "Messiah of the Last Age" (*mehdi-yi ahir-i zaman*)' and so on to Selim was done by later-era historians, as they are found exclusively in works from the reign of his son Süleyman I: 'There is no definitive contemporaneous textual evidence that "Selim and his court ... participated in the process of fitting Ottoman sovereignty to a messianic model using the imagery of the *tarikat* religious-military brotherhood".'[119] In any case, there is no dispute that his son and successor Süleyman I definitively moved in this direction.

Mid-Sixteenth Century: Süleyman the Magnificent (the Ottomans)

Selim's son Süleyman I (the Magnificent, the Lawgiver; r. 1520–66) took Ottoman universal sovereignty claims to their limit, at least in the

---

[116] Şahin (2013, p. 27), citing Hess (1973).
[117] Indicating even more political centralisation of the (fused) vertical type. See Chapter 1.
[118] Şahin (2013, p. 27), citing Fleischer (1992).   [119] Çıpa (2017, p. 228).

first two-thirds of his reign. The reign of Süleyman is remembered as the period during which Ottoman claims of sovereignty reached their greatest territorial span; this is the closest the Ottomans came to manifesting world empire and universal sovereignty.

Süleyman competed with Charles V (Habsburgs) in the West[120] and with Shah Tahmasp I (Safavids) in the East.[121] In a string of victories, he pushed well into Europe, all the way to Vienna. He firmed up Ottoman control over Anatolia and the Levant. The naval forces (and corsairs) under Ottoman control also led many campaigns along the Horn of the Indian Ocean, attempting to displace the Portuguese from the trade routes with the Mughals. Other campaigns were advanced in the Mediterranean, bringing Rhodes as well as much of North Africa under Ottoman control as well, at least nominally. From 1524 until 1536, Süleyman I was guided in his many endeavours by his very influential grand vizier, İbrahim Pasha, who was also his longtime companion and confidante.[122]

As with the Safavid and Mughal rulers (as well as the Timurid and the Ming), Süleyman I invested in many public rituals as demonstration of his claim to universal sovereignty: 'between 1521 and 1528 ... Italian visitors to Istanbul noticed an increase in the pomp and cere-monialism around the Sultan'.[123] In 1524, İbrahim Pasha's wedding celebration to 'Muhsine Hatun, a member of the family that had initially purchased him as a slave boy'[124] was used as such an occasion to display the sultan's might. Celebrations were public and lasted for days, featuring exhibits of war booty taken from the Safavids and the Mamluks, mock fights, artistic exhibitions, wrestling matches, archery contests and incredible feasts.[125] There was also a public debate by scholars about his claim to the caliphate, marking the first time 'when Süleyman openly and publicly assumed this mantle'.[126] The title was used to bolster the divine backing of the sultan's political authority, another form of sacred kingship: 'The political center presented the sultan as, alternatively, the caliph of Sunni Islam, a messianic con-queror with a claim to universal sovereignty, and the renewer of

---

[120] See Chapter 5.
[121] To a lesser extent, John III of Portugal in the Indian Ocean. Casale (2007, 2010).
[122] Şahin (2013, p. 45).   [123] Ibid., p. 51.   [124] Ibid.   [125] Ibid., p. 52.
[126] Ibid., p. 53.

Islam (*mujaddid*).'[127] Safavid and Mughal rulers were making similar claims and invoking some of these same titles, as we will see.

Süleyman's domestic reforms flowed from this perspective. Especially in the early period of his reign, his main preoccupation was creating an official version of religious doctrine which would supersede alternative interpretations. He actively adapted a particular school of jurisprudence (Hanafi) and facilitated the development of an 'imperial learned hierarchy with fairly standardized career and training tracks'.[128] In 1556, Süleyman even took the unprecedented step of specifying which text the students of the imperial education system were to study: 'By specifying an imperial jurisprudential canon, the Ottoman sultans, and more generally the dynasty, sought to point to specific texts and opinions within the Hanafi school that members of imperial hierarchy were to consult and teach.'[129] Moreover, he also extended the Sultan's non-religious lawmaking authority further; hence his Turkish title as *Kanuni* (literally, lawgiver). The dynastic law (*kanun*) allowed for the creation of charitable cash endowments, for example, which sharia forbade due to the involvement of interest. This was in contravention of the Islamic tradition of kings not asserting their authority over *ulama*, as discussed in a previous section.[130]

The History of Islamic Political Thought[131] observes that Ottoman 'Sultans used the language of world sovereignty' and Süleyman I in particular 'boasted: "In Baghdad I am Shah, in Rum Caesar, in Egypt Sultan, who sends his fleets to the seas of Europe, the Maghrib and India"'.[132] Yet the book also claims the Ottomans got these notions from the 'ancient imperial tradition' they inherited, by which we could presume he means Rome and maybe Persia. This was of course the received wisdom about the Ottomans until recently, entirely missing the alternative Chinggisid tradition of universal sovereignty and its influence on Asia, including on the Ottomans. Reducing the Ottoman visions of universal empire in the sixteenth century only to its 'European' or 'Western' antecedents also badly misses the fact that the *strongest* universal empire claims in this period were emanating

---

[127] Ibid., p. 72.   [128] Burak (2013b, p. 584).   [129] Ibid., p. 586.
[130] Ibid., p. 584.
[131] Black (2011) – a book that, despite its specialist labelling, mischaracterizes the empires we are discussing in this chapter almost as badly as Kennedy's *Rise and Fall*.
[132] Ibid., p. 207.

not from Europe but rather from our post-Timurid trio: 'in the context of the Ottoman and Safavid empires, as well as Mughal India, millenarianism drew force from the fact that the last century of the Muslim millennium started in 1495 CE ... and was to end in 1591/92 CE. The expectations of an imminent apocalypse enhanced the imperial competition in the sixteenth century, bestowing it with soteriological significance.'[133] It was this millenarian competition that 'gave rise to the phenomena of confessional polarization and Sunnitization in the Ottoman empire'.[134]

This is not to say that the Ottomans were not drawing from European traditions: this was an empire 'European and Asian in equal measure'.[135] Just as the Mughals drew from Hindu traditions in addition to their post-Timurid norms, and just as the Safavids were animated by the post-Ilkhanid Sufi fervour of Iran, the Ottomans were heir to local ideas from the territories they controlled: for example, 'the Christian and Jewish traditions of apocalypticism pervading the Mediterranean zone'.[136] The fact that these three empires all mixed Timurid notions of sovereignty with other occult traditions goes some way towards explaining the variation in their imperial visions. For instance, 'where Mughal and Safavid imperial millenarianism was cyclical and reincarnationist in orientation, ... its Ottoman cognate was linear and teleological: the Ottoman Empire as world empire, the last in human history, expectant host of the mahdi and Jesus, sacral midwife of the eschaton'.[137] Despite these differences, the Ottomans also turned to the same occult sciences to back up their claims: lettrism and geomancy, for instance.[138] Practitioners of these sciences claimed Süleyman to be 'both the *sahib-qiran* and the *sahib-zaman*, a messianic Lord of the Age combining irresistible military and spiritual potency, as well as the *qutb al-aqtab* or axis mundi, whose universal dominion must needs prompt the *parousia* of the *mahdi* and the second coming of Jesus'.[139] The idea that Süleyman stood at the end of time as *sahib-zaman* or 'Last World Emperor'[140] became especially central to his image.

As we will see in the next chapter, there is no doubt that Süleyman was at least partially driven by his rivalry with Charles V in mounting such

---

[133] Krstić (2009, p. 39).   [134] Krstić (2011, p. 12).
[135] Melvin-Koushki (2018, p. 368).   [136] Ibid., p. 369.   [137] Ibid.
[138] Ibid., p. 370, citing Fleischer (2009, p. 240).
[139] Melvin-Koushki (2018a, p. 370).   [140] Ibid., p. 371.

claims (and vice versa). Yet, it is also undeniable that the Ottomans, like the Mughals, were primarily responding to something unleashed by the revolutionary model of sacred kingship as inherited from Timur and further innovated by Shah Ismail in the beginning of the sixteenth century. And it was the rivalry with the Safavids that kept the fire burning in the Ottomans. In 1534, the Ottoman forces quickly captured Tabriz, the Safavid capital, forcing Shah Tahmasb to retreat.[141] This was seen as proof by Ottoman chroniclers[142] that it was Süleyman I who had the powers of sainthood and prophecy and not the Safavid Shah. Baghdad, the seat of the caliphate before the Mongol invasions of the thirteenth century, fell to the Ottomans soon after, which was again interpreted as divine favour. Mosques and shrines were publicly Sunnified.

Soon after this campaign, Grand Vizier İbrahim Pasha – who had played a significant role in advancing the vision of universal sovereignty – fell out of favour with Süleyman, reportedly because of his hubris in claiming for himself the title 'sultan' and attempting to position himself similar to how Ferdinand had in the Habsburg Empire.[143] He was executed in 1536. For the next decade, the Ottomans were mostly engaged in European rivalries.[144] After 1547, Süleyman turned east once again, enticed into another campaign against Tabriz by Shah Tahmasp's brother Alqas Mirza who had sought refuge in his court. Though the campaign was successful, plans to install Alqas in Tahmasp's throne proved unsuccessful when he showed himself to be an incapable ruler.[145] The campaign finished in 1549 without much to show for it. In 1555, Süleyman and Tahmasp signed the Peace of Amasya, acknowledging the legitimacy of each other's dynastic and religious claims:[146] 'With this treaty the new religious divisions within Islamdom became increasingly territorialized, while Ottoman and Safavid rulers devoted themselves to the multipronged projects of state and confession building backed up by various measures of social disciplining.'[147] Note that the Peace of Amasya happened in the same year as the Treaty of Augsburg, in which Charles V recognised the territorial

---

[141] This was not as devastating a blow as it seems because the Safavid court was peripatetic until 1590. Matthee (2010, p. 237). This is another way the Safavid continued Chinggisid traditions. On peripatetic courts in the steppe tradition, see also Neumann and Wigen (2018).

[142] For example, Mustafa Ali. See Şahin (2013, p. 97).

[143] Şahin (2013, p. 101).   [144] For more on this, see Chapter 5.

[145] Şahin (2013, p. 119).   [146] Ibid., p. 135.   [147] Krstić (2011, p. 97).

rights of Protestant princes. The next chapter will deal with the similarities between Süleyman I and Charles V in more detail.

It goes without saying that there is a fundamental tension between mutual recognition arrangements such as treaties and universal sovereignty claims, no matter how court chroniclers try to spin the former. Even the Ottoman historian Mustafa Ali (1541–1600) was aware that Süleyman fell short of his universalist ambitions. Fleischer finds in his writings an understanding that 'far from being the last world empire, the Ottoman Empire was but the political equal of the Safavid Empire of Iran, the Uzbek Empire of Central Asia, and the Mughal Empire of India – all of whose competing universalist platforms, millennial or otherwise, had similarly failed to achieve the promise of true world empire held out by their shared Chingizid-Timurid model'.[148] It is important to underline once again that, for sixteenth-century Ottoman thinkers, their peers and chief rivals were these other post-Timurid sovereigns, not the Europeans.

Having failed to achieve universal sovereignty of Chinggisid or Timurid scale, Süleyman's last decade on the throne saw him embrace the pious Sunni side of his identity over millennial sovereignty. At the end of his reign Süleyman 'rerouted the full force of his millenarian kingship into his status as Lawgiver'.[149] The millenarian rivalry was channelled into something else: the Süleymaniye Mosque Complex he had built in this period aimed to demonstrate 'the civilizational superiority [of the Ottomans] over the Safavids and the European Christians'.[150] After 1550, austere references to bureaucracy, order and law displaced ostentatious displays of wealth and sacred kingship: 'the excitement, polyphony, eclecticism, innovation, and universalist dreams of the first three decades were replaced ... with a new gravity of tone and a formalizing impulse to establish consistency of imperial style'.[151] We could thus conclude that, when it became clear towards the end of his reign that he could not defeat his Habsburg and Safavid rivals for world sovereignty, Süleyman 'began to replace his messianic persona with a ruling persona whose majesty was derived from faithful implementation of justice and law'.[152]

---

[148] Melvin-Koushki (2018a, p. 371), paraphrasing Fleischer (2008, pp. 273–92).
[149] Melvin-Koushki (2018a, p. 370). Echoes of Genghis Khan as lawgiver.
[150] Şahin (2013, p. 142).
[151] Fleischer (1992, p. 171); Necipoğlu (1989); Şahin (2013, p. 143). It probably did not help that Süleyman, like Charles V, was in ill health for much of this period and had become withdrawn as a result.
[152] Krstić (2011, p. 106).

The second half of the sixteenth century also 'witnessed a boom in heresy trials and concerted efforts to define the boundaries of belief'[153] by, for instance, 'the promulgation of a new criminal law code that policed the boundaries of orthodoxy and public morality, the promotion of mosque worship through the imposition of new fines for irregular attendance, and the construction of an unprecedented number of mosques in order to stabilize mosque congregations and monitor them easily'.[154] Towards the end of Süleyman's realm, imperial law (*kanun*) began to be harmonised with holy law (sharia), a feat that could not (and would not) be achieved by lesser sultans. This insustainability of the world-conqueror mode of legitimation is one that we have encountered before with both the Chinggisids and the post-Chinggisid legacy houses, and it is one we can also trace in the Mughal and Safavid timelines. I will return to this theme at the end of the chapter.

Süleyman's Contemporaries: Humayun (Mughals) and Tahmasp I (Safavids)

Turning back to the Mughals, the reader will recall that Babur, failing to hold onto Samarkand, which he had conquered with the help of Shah Ismail, had moved into northern India instead in 1526, conquering Delhi and Agra. In 1530, Babur was succeeded by his son Humayun (r. 1530–40, 1555–6), who had to fight his brothers both before and after he took the throne (another manifestation of the tanistry norm). Humayun then designed a special crown for himself and his followers reminiscent of the Safavid crown: 'Taj-i 'Izzat (Crown of Power and Glory)',[155] clearly inspired by his father's experience with Ismail and the Safavids as described already.

This is good point to note that there was considerable movement between the Mughal and Safavid courts (as well as the Ottomans) by the intelligentsia as well as artists and artisans. For example, the historian Khand-Amir left the Safavids for the Mughals and brought with him his treatise about sacred kingship, renaming it *Qanun-i*

---

[153] Ibid., p. 107.

[154] Ibid. This is a period of increased Sunnitisation, parallel to other similar developments of confessionalisation in Europe as well as the Safavids (and later the Mughals). For more Ottoman sunnitisation, see Krstić and Terzioğlu (2020).

[155] Moin (2012, p. 124).

Humayun.[156] Edris Bedlisi, an important scribe in the Aq Qoyunlu court, defected to the Ottomans after the Safavids took over Iran and produced works for both Selim I and Süleyman I, including *Qanun-e shahanshahi.*[157] In other words, debates and theoretical treatises about sovereignty circulated across Ottoman, Safavid and Mughal lands. Perhaps due to such influences, in order to demonstrate that he was a sacred king deserving this type of adulation from his followers, Humayun increasingly dabbled in the occult and astrology and sponsored occult scientists.[158] He also performed sovereignty by 'touring the realm with his grand entourage, hunting, conquering, and feasting, taking in the sights, sounds, and tastes of its various locales while imposing upon it a new order of color and rhythm'.[159] We have seen that the Ottoman and Safavid rulers also engaged in similar displays of claims to universal sovereignty.

Circumstances, however, forced Humayun, like his father, to swallow the bitter pill and submit to the Safavids in order to gain their support. In 1540, Humayun was ousted from Delhi by Sher Shah of Sur and had to go into exile for more than a decade, eventually moving into the Safavid realms and seeking Shah Tahmasp's protection. By the time Humayun had sought refuge in the Safavid court in 1544, Shah Ismail had died and had been replaced by his ten-year-old son, Tahmasp I. Not that this was of much help to Humayun in 1544: when Humayun took refuge in Tahmasp's court, he had 'to give up his own crown and instead wear the emblem of Safavid discipleship, much as his father had done before him', and this was an expression of personal submission rather than a religious conversion.[160] Tainted by this submission, Humayun never wore his own crown again, even after he reconquered Delhi in 1555 with the help of the Safavids and reinstituted Mughal presence in northern India.[161] The House of Babur was haunted by the subservience of Babur and Humayun to the Safavids for generations, but later Mughal historiography downplayed this memory.[162]

Tahmasp's reign (r. 1524–76) over Safavids had also started rocky, with Qizilbash elites fighting each other to be his regents, but he would

[156] Arjomand (2016, p. 13). [157] Ibid., p. 14. [158] Moin (2012, p. 124).
[159] Ibid., p. 110. [160] Ibid., p. 127. [161] Ibid.
[162] Ibid. This is similar to how the Ilkhanid and Timurid experience had been downplayed in Ottoman historiography (or Golden Horde in Russian – more on that in the next chapter).

go on to have the longest reign of all Safavid shahs, even longer than his Ottoman contemporary Süleyman the Magnificent (r. 1520–66). While the Safavid territorial claims did not greatly expand this period, Tahmasp I nevertheless managed to keep the Ottoman threat in the West and the Uzbek threat in the East at bay, despite having to retreat several times from Tabriz in the face of Ottoman campaigns, as already discussed. He also entered into an alliance with Charles V of the Habsburgs against the Ottomans.

Especially in the first half of his reign, Tahmasp institutionalised many of the ritualistic aspects of Ismail's cult.[163] He had to continue invoking sacred kingship, the main source of legitimacy for Safavid rulers after Ismail: 'Shah Tahmasb remained for his Qizilbash followers the perfect guide (*murshid-i kamil*), to whom they submitted corporeally in the ritual of the Stick of the Path (*Chub-i Tariqat*).'[164] To back up these claims, Tahmasp referred in his memoirs to dreams in which the Prophet and Ali appeared to him. However, compared to Ismail, it was harder for Tahmasp to claim a conqueror's charisma or a messianic aura (especially given that even Ismail's image had been dented in the Battle of Chaldiran). To solve this problem, Tahmasp turned to the occult sciences: he was 'particularly obsessed with the divinatory science of geomancy (*ilm al-raml*) ... [He] had not left his palace for a decade, so devoted was he to practicing the science as substantiation of his claim to prophet-like sanctity and vision.'[165] His teacher in these matters was Haydar Rammal,[166] who later became an important fixture at the court of Süleyman the Magnificent, another example of the high levels of circulation between the Safavid, the Ottoman and the Mughal courts.[167] Perhaps because his claim to messianism was weaker, Tahmasp was more subdued about this in public compared to Shah Ismail.[168]

In his later years, especially after the Peace of Amasya (1555) with the Ottomans, Tahmasp became more pious, issuing decrees of public morality. Ottoman Sunnitisation in this period was paralleled in the Safavid realms by a similar Shi'itisation. However, despite this turn, notions of millennial sovereignty did not go out of circulation: 'The close identification of occultism with both Sufism and Shi'ism remained

---

[163] Melvin-Koushki (2016, p. 142).   [164] Moin (2012, p. 125).
[165] Melvin-Koushki (2018a, p. 364); see also Melvin-Koushki (2016, 143).
[166] Melvin-Koushki (2018a, p. 364); Melvin-Koushki (2018b); Fleischer (2009).
[167] Melvin-Koushki (2018b).   [168] Moin (2012, p. 126).

in effect through at least the height of Shah Abbas's reign.'[169] In sum, though neither Tahmasp I nor Humayun were the larger-than-life figures as their contemporary Ottoman ruler Süleyman was, they still operated in the post-Timurid millennial ecumene and thus reproduced it by trying to live up to its norms and expectations.

Closing the Sixteenth Century: Akbar the Great

Both Babur and Humayun had relatively brief reigns in northern India. It was Akbar I the Great who would break that pattern, with nearly half a century (r. 1556–1605). As did many other rulers we discussed, Akbar I ascended to the throne at a young age, in his case with the support of the military general Bairam Khan.[170] As we have seen in other cases discussed in this chapter, in the early years of his rule Akbar also had to contend with challenges from his brothers and other relatives. His sovereignty was thus precarious initially, and so was Mughal presence in India. The Mughals still saw Kabul as their real base, but Akbar decided that they were in the subcontinent to stay, first consolidating his hold over Delhi and then launching a south-facing military campaign in 1560.

During Akbar's reign the territory over which the Mughals claimed sovereignty nearly tripled in size, as rival houses in both north and central India were defeated and incorporated into the Mughal order. Significantly, the Mughal realm was extended over Rajputana, Gujarat and Bengal, bringing most eastern trade under Mughal control. He even went as far as the Deccan sultanates (south-west India).[171] Extending Mughal reach into the Indian subcontinent, Akbar ensured that the House of Babur would go on to control a world-leading manufacturing economy, one without rival until the Industrial Revolution[172] (not even the Ming could compete with India). In the meantime, Akbar also held the Uzbeks at bay in the north by negotiating a pact with them to stay neutral in their campaign against the Safavids in 1586. Relations with the latter were not what they used to be in the days of Babur and Humayun; Akbar gave refuge to Rustem

---

[169] Melvin-Koushki (2018a, p. 365).   [170] Akbar dismissed him in 1560.
[171] For more on the Deccan frontier, see Alam and Subrahmanyam (2004).
[172] Matthee (2010, p. 236).

Mirza, a Safavid prince, and took Kandahar, considered an ancestral homeland, back from the Safavids in 1595.

It was thus Akbar and his military conquests who delivered for the Mughals[173] the most plausible claim of millennial, universal sovereignty towards the end of the sixteenth century, rivalling as *sahibkıran* Shah Ismail of the early sixteenth century and Süleyman the Magnificent of the mid-sixteenth century. As was the case with Süleyman, Akbar's governance style was as significant as the military conquests. True to Chinggisid influences, Akbar encouraged debate among scholars of different faiths, founding in 1575 the House of Worship, where he 'allowed free-ranging discussion on all points of doctrine and metaphysics, not excepting even the most central tenets of Islam',[174] sitting himself as lone spectator, referee and judge.[175] When this approach caused controversy and religious edicts were issued against him, he put at least two Muslim jurists to death,[176] clearly asserting his authority over them. He also introduced wide-sweeping classificatory schemes: he famously organised the nobility into numbered ranks (*mansab*) based on merit and service, but he also organised his animals into categories by weight and food consumed.[177]

Akbar deliberately fashioned himself as *the sahibkıran*, building his sovereignty claims from 'conjunction astrology, messianic and millennial myths, and claims of royal and saintly authority combined in the person of the monarch'.[178] As we will also discuss in the next section, the idea that the Islamic Millennium was approaching at the end of the sixteenth century (1591/2) loomed large in the sovereignty narratives of all three houses, but Akbar also inaugurated his own 'Divine Religion (*din-i ilahi*): a reincarnationist, vegetarianist doctrine centered on the worship of Akbar as divine' in 1583, a year marked by the great Saturn–Jupiter Conjunction, heralding the end of the first Islamic millennium.[179] He commissioned a thousand-year history,[180] starting with the year of the Prophet's death and ending with the reign of

---

[173] On this matter, see also Balabanlilar (2007).   [174] Moin (2012, p. 133).
[175] Ibid., p. 151.   [176] Ibid., p. 133.
[177] Ibid., p. 151. This is form of centralisation as well, falling under heading C (centralisation by homogenisation). Categorisation is an act of rendering continuous and relational (usually hierarchical) what used be disparate and unrelated.
[178] Ibid., p. 166.   [179] Melvin-Koushki (2018a, p. 367).
[180] For a comparative take on world histories and historians in the sixteenth century, see Subrahmanyam (2005).

Akbar, and issued coins stamped with the word 'thousand'.[181] In the millennial history he had commissioned, 'Akbar was declared to be the Renewer of the Second Millennium (Mujaddid-i Alf-i Thani)'.[182] *Akbarnama* (Book of Akbar, completed in 1598) also claimed that Akbar had been born to inaugurate the new millennium:[183] 'In essence, Akbar celebrated his imperial achievements as a millennial being who had ushered in a new world order, as a Lord of Conjunction like his ancestor Timur, as a savior like the expected heir of Ali, as an avatar like Rama, as a messiah like Jesus, and as a Renewer of the Second Millennium (Mujaddid-i Alf-i Thani) of Islam.'[184] Like Humayun, he not only 'patronized astrologers, geomancers and other occultists' but 'also sought to royally mirror the celestial realm by means of elaborate astral-magical enactments'.[185] In 1579 an imperial decree declared Akbar 'the imam and mujtahid of the age', which 'were unusual titles for a monarch, ... [implying] an authority to decide matters of religious doctrine', especially given the fact that Akbar was illiterate.[186] Akbar played up his illiteracy because it was reminiscent of Prophet Muhammad, who also was famously illiterate.

Here we see an act parallel to one we have already discussed in the Ottoman context, to that of the Sultan Süleyman's assertion of his own *kanun* over the decisions of the *ulama*, the Islamic jurists. In elevating himself over all religious authority, including the *ulama*, Akbar was equally in contravention as Süleyman was of traditional Islamic practice, if not more so.[187] This decree caused considerable controversy, as expected, but Akbar did not retreat from his position 'as supreme spiritual guide of the realm'.[188] In this we can find another parallel, this time with Shah Ismail as the sacred cult leader of the Safavids. *Akbarnama* 'openly acknowledged his patronage of radical and anti-nomian Sufi groups who venerated him as divine; his support for the arguments of the Jesuit priests against their Muslim adversaries; his impatience with traditional Islamic law; his need to recruit and patron-ize men from all creeds and castes across India, Iran, and Transoxiana;

---

[181]   Moin (2012, p. 133).
[182]   Ibid., p. 134. Remember that Süleyman was also called a renewer.
[183]   Ibid., p. 137.   [184]   Ibid.
[185]   Ibid., p. 121; Melvin-Koushki (2018a, p. 367); see also Truschke (2016).
[186]   Moin (2012, p. 139).
[187]   Melvin-Koushki (2018a, p. 367) argues that Akbar went further than Süleyman.
[188]   Ibid., p. 144.

and, finally, his thinly veiled performance as the saintly guide and spiritual master of all humanity'.[189] This new vision was not consistently presented as a religion, however, and Akbar did not advance a new theology. All of it was very much centred on the idea of Akbar as a sacred, divine world emperor, a millennial sovereign.

Moving into the Seventeenth Century

Turning back to the Ottomans, readers will recall that Süleyman's long reign ended in 1566. One of his sons, Bayezid, had openly rebelled against him in 1561 and then had sought refuge in the court of Tahmasp, who had used him as a leverage to maintain the peace until Bayezid's death at the hands of an Ottoman assassin in 1562. Süleyman was thus succeeded by his son Selim II (1566–74), who then was followed by his son Murad III (r. 1574–95). Selim II is considered to have been an alcoholic by most historians. His otherwise unremarkable reign witnessed the increase of power of the Ottoman administrators, a trend which had begun during Süleyman's reign. Administrators were now increasingly 'able to pass their political influence to their families, creating alternative loci of power'.[190] Among them was Grand Vizier Sokollu Mehmet Pasha, who practically ruled the empire from Süleyman's death in 1566 until his own in 1579.

Murad III, who came on the throne in 1576, was not happy with this status quo and attempted to undermine it by frequently dismissing viziers after Sokollu's death.[191] He also created anew court offices as counterbalances to existing networks of vizier patronage, offices such as the chief white eunuch (*kapu agasu*), the superintendent of the harem (also a eunuch), the chief gardener and so on. Furthermore, 'this rise of the court as a center of administrative power was also reflected in the role that royal women were playing in politics'[192] – women who, like other personalities of the courts, frequently interfered with judicial and other bureaucratic appointments.[193] Murad III also meddled in financial management, farming out various lucrative sources of taxation to people close to the court. From one perspective, it could be argued that what Murad III was doing was no different from what Selim I and Süleyman I had done before him: he was asserting his sovereignty and

---

[189] Ibid., p. 145. [190] Tezcan (2010, p. 96). [191] Ibid., p. 100.
[192] Ibid., p. 104. [193] Ibid., p. 106.

promoting the power of his court over the bureaucracy and *ulama* alike. Like Süleyman and also Akbar, Murad III was also 'highly sensitive to his own status as king of the millennium, heavily investing to this end in both Sufism and the occult sciences, particularly astrology and oneiromancy, and identifying his royal persona with 'Ali in the time-honored Timurid-Safavid manner'.[194] However, something had shifted: in Ottoman historiography, 'Murad III later came to be remembered as the sultan during whose reign respect for the kanun disappeared and the decline of the empire started.'[195] I will discuss the reasons why in a moment.

Turning to the Safavids, Tahmasp's reign was followed by those of Ismail II (r. 1576–7) and (after a three-month interregnum) Muhammad Khodabanda (r. 1578–87). There is a parallel here to the Ottoman case discussed earlier in that the tumultuous period which followed Tahmasp's death laid the bare the influence of royal women (e.g. Pari Khan Khatum, who had de facto rule for a period) as well as the Qizilbash leaders in succession matters and the court. The continued infighting between the Qizilbash factions in this period exposed the Safavids to external threats as well, from both the Ottomans under Murad III and their allies, the Crimean Khanate under the Giray dynasty. Between 1578 and 1590, the Safavids were once again at war with the Ottomans, and the war did not end in the Safavids' favour.

The Safavid state fared better under the next shah, Abbas I (the Great, r. 1588–1629), who provides an interesting contrast with his Mughal counterpart and contemporary Akbar, discussed in the previous section, as well as Murad III of the Ottomans. The reign of Abbas is considered to be 'the apogee of Safavid power and imperial glory'.[196] Though enthroned at a young age as a result of a Qizilbash coup, Abbas' reign is marked for the transition away from the messianic *sahibkıran* model and Qizilbash influence towards 'a more routinized Imami Shi'ism',[197] the culmination of an internal tension that dates to the end of Tahmasp's reign. Though he promoted political centralisation and absolute power, Abbas shied from sacralising 'his royal

---

[194] Melvin-Koushki (2018a, p. 367).
[195] Tezcan (2010, p. 56). See also Fleischer (1992); Felek (2017). See also Melvin-Koushki (2018a, p. 367).
[196] Melvin-Koushki (2018a, p. 365). See also Babayan (2002).
[197] Moin (2012, p. 161).

persona to a degree that would be competitive with those of his Mughal and Ottoman counterparts'.[198] He was more expansionist than his predecessors (at least since Ismail): he conquered the southern Caucasus and inserted a more visible Safavid presence into the maritime competition in the Persian Gulf and the Indian Ocean. In previous decades, the main dynamic here had involved the Portuguese, the Mughals and the Ottomans.[199] Abbas cooperated with the English and the Dutch to oust the Portuguese.[200]

Abbas instituted a number of bureaucratic reforms in order to undercut the power of the Qizilbash. For example, he 'built a loyal military of Caucasian slave soldiers captured from neighboring Georgia, converted to Shi'ism, and trained by European military advisors' which decreased his reliance on the Qizilbash. He increased Safavids' military strength[201] but also invested in trade and commerce by building *caravanserai* and enhancing road safety.[202] Abbas selected a new, permanent capital in Isfahan,[203] and there he built a new imperial complex, which included not only a commercial and administrative arrangements[204] but also a special chamber for Qizilbash to repent and ask for forgiveness from the Shah.[205] Abbas also did not tolerate others in his realm who claimed messianic titles, which prompted Akbar to write him with advice to 'practice the policy of sulh-i kull (universal peace)' and to tolerate those from different faiths. All of this points to an increased Shi'itisation trend during Abbas' reign. Historians caution us, however, to see transition to 'a newly constructed Twelver Shi'i orthodoxy'[206] as less abrupt than it has been traditionally portrayed.[207] Though both Sufism and, to a lesser extent, occultism were marginalised in this period, many of the agents of the transformation were previously of those worlds: 'As elite and popular forms of piety in Iran were thus rerouted from persophilic and imamophilic Sunni Sufism into doctrinaire Twelver Shi'ism, the scholars responsible for this rerouting emerged as religiopolitical counterweights to their Safavid patrons, whose absolutist claims were thereby

---

[198] Melvin-Koushki (2018a, p. 366).   [199] Casale (2010).
[200] Matthee (2010, p. 249).   [201] Ibid., p. 248.
[202] Ibid., p. 249. *Caravanserai* are essentially roadside hotels for trade caravans.
[203] Tabriz was once again under Ottoman command at this time.
[204] Ibid., p. 248.   [205] Moin (2012, p. 162).
[206] Melvin-Koushki (2018a, p. 365).
[207] This is similar to revisionist readings of Aurangzeb of the Mughals. Truschke (2017).

impaired.'[208] A similar development also occurred in the Ottoman Empire in the seventeenth century, with the jurists (*ulama*) reasserting their influence, even intervening on decisions about who should be enthroned.[209]

In both contexts, then, jurists and scholars increasingly acted as a check on what I have called the Chinggisid sovereignty model (or its sixteenth-century manifestation). That development would come also for the Mughals, but later in the seventeenth century. In the first half of the seventeenth century, the Mughals still kept up with notions of millennial sovereignty,[210] with Jahangir (r. 1605–27) assuming his father's style of sacred kingship, for example by presiding over inter-faith debates.[211] Shah Jahan (r. 1627–58) called himself the 'Second Lord of Conjunction', even if he is remembered for 'establishing an "Islamic political culture"'.[212] However, it is undeniable that even if the titles were being used, the polity was moving in the same direction as the Ottomans and the Safavids in terms of Islamisation: in this case, Sunnitisation like the Ottomans. Shah Jahan's successor, Aurangzeb (r. 1658–1707), is notorious 'for his lifelong pursuit of a forbidding and austere form of Islam that had little place for wine, women, and merri-ment – nor, more significantly, for music, mysticism, and astrology'.[213] Though Aurangzeb is not usually associated with Mughal decline – as the empire reached its territorial and economic peak during his reign – the period right after him is.

Millennial Sovereignty as a Sixteenth-Century 'World Order'

To summarise, what these three Great Houses shared in the sixteenth century was something more than belief in Islam and Turco-Mongol ethno-linguistic pedigree. They were defined by their immersion in a post-Timurid ecumene; until the seventeenth century, they were operating – as inflected via cultural repertories more specific to each – with a version of the Chinggisid sovereignty model of universal empire

---

[208] Melvin-Koushki (2018a, p. 365).   [209] Tezcan (2010).
[210] They also never gave up on tanistry as a mode of succession.
[211] Moin (2012, p. 178).
[212] Ibid., p. 212. In addition to Moin, both Truschke (2017) and Subrahmanyam (2006) dispute this characterisation of Aurangzeb which they consider too one-dimensional. But for our purposes the point stands.
[213] Moin (2012, p. 214).

that the previous chapters have elaborated. Ottoman, Safavid and Mughal rulers in this period understood themselves to be millennial sovereigns and world conquerors: 'For the first time in history, world domination was within reach, this by combining the irresistible military potency of Alexander, Chingiz (r. 1206–27), and Timur (r. 1370–1405), the great Lords of Conjunction, with the irresistible spiritual potency of the Shi'i imams and the saints, true emperors of the world.'[214] They took turns at having a go at this vision throughout the sixteenth century: Shah Ismail with the Safavids (r. 1501–24), Süleyman the Magnificent with the Ottomans (r. 1520–66), and Akbar the Great with the Mughal (r. 1556–1605) came closest to projecting millenial sovereignty.

All of the post-Timurid Great Houses were marked by beliefs that associated sovereignty with the Timurid title *sahibkıran* and were competing for that title. Their competition, informed by shared norms about how a Great House behaves, reinforced a world order organised around this particular sovereignty model for anyone who lived in their realms – a third of the world's population – and beyond (as we will see in the next chapter). The three empires were connected to each other via military competition (in changing configurations) and also trade networks. More importantly, rulers of each house were acutely aware of the other's universal sovereignty claims, and, as we have seen, likely cared about those rival claims much more than similar power projections by European actors (more on this in the next chapter). They wrote to each other, exchanging letters, sometimes for advice, sometimes to show off. Princes took refuge in rival courts. Artists, artisans, historians, chroniclers, scholars – the intelligentsia of the day – constantly circulated between the three empires.[215] This is what explains the question I posed in the introduction to this chapter: why was the art of the Ottomans, the Mughals and the Safavids in this period so similar (while still distinct)? Because they were not the empire islands ('power-centres') they were presumed to be by the IR literature. People of these realms lived in a world order underwritten by a shared ecumene that extended from political theology to artistic taste, as we do today globally.

---

[214] Melvin-Koushki (2018a, p. 355); see also Subrahamyam (1997, p. 755).
[215] On intellectual networks between the empires, see also Binbaş (2016). For more accounts of travels in this shared space, see Alam and Subrahmanyam (2007).

It is in the title *sahibkıran* (Lord of Conjunction) that we can most closely discern the connections of the sixteenth-century world order as I have described in this chapter and the Chinggisid and post-Chinggisid 'world orders' as described in the previous chapters. There were accompanying labels also: 'last world conqueror', 'lord of time', 'letterlord', 'supreme pole' (*qutb al aqtab*) and so on. (It seems IR realists were not the ones to introduce the notion of poles to world politics.) These labels were not just affixed to particular rulers randomly but backed up by meticulous scholarship in occult sciences: astrology, lettrism, geomancy.[216] To bolster their claims, Ottoman, Safavid and Mughal rulers competed over a shared pool of occultist scholars: for example, 'Iranian scholar-occultists were even more in demand at the neighbouring Mughal and Ottoman courts, both far wealthier and more cosmopolitan than the Safavid, and many accordingly decamped to seek their fortunes abroad'.[217] Conjunction astrologers (as well as lettrists and geomancers) were thus consulted to help make sense of world events, as sort of the IR scholars or political scientists of their time.[218] At a time when astrology and astronomy, science and religion, history and myth had much more porous boundaries, those who studied astrology, lettrism and geomancy were among the intelligentsia of their day, and their predictions about politics relied on the rigorous study of star charts, historical events, mathematics and letter patterns. They were thus quite 'scientific' in their approach, perhaps in a way that should not be entirely alien to those of us who aim to study IR and politics scientifically today. They seemed to have a good empirical basis for their conjunction theories in the various correlations they had identified: Alexander the Great was a 'Lord of Conjunction', so was Chinggis Khan and Timur, and a conjunction had also signified the birth of Islam. One could even say this is not that different from the Great Power thinking of our day.

Decline of the Millennial Sovereigns?

So, what happened to these 'Lords of Conjunction'? The Islamic Millennium came and went. The astrologers were perhaps onto

---

[216] Melvin-Koushki (2016, p. 144).   [217] Ibid., p. 146.
[218] But better respected and in more demand. Note also the parallels to the Timurid-Ming interest in astronomy discussed in Chapter 3.

something, however: it does seem that the fortunes of these empires turned afterwards, though their trajectory of subsequent 'decline' is rarely analysed comparatively.[219] Let us take each in turn to start with.

In twentieth-century Indian historiography, there were at least[220] two explanations of Mughal's sudden 'decline' in the eighteenth century. The seventeenth century for the Mughals was an internally turbulent one in terms of especially succession struggles, but externally it was essentially a period of growth. The relative weakness of the polity in the eighteenth century in the face of the intrusion of others, by contrast, seemed to require explanation. One group of historians argued that 'later Mughal princes were molly-coddled in the harem, given to debauchery, excessively fond of music and the arts, and thus incapable of being the vigorous warrior-leaders that such an empire required. In presenting such an analysis, historians delved into the writings of chroniclers from the early eighteenth century, who often were crushingly contemptuous in their judgements of rulers such as Muhammad Shah (1719–1748).'[221] Similar condemnations exist of Ottoman and Safavid rulers as well. Yet other historians of India pointed at a 'great "agrarian crisis" of the late seventeenth century . . . derived in turn from the over-exploitation of the peasantry by the fiscal apparatus that the Mughals had developed in the late sixteenth century'.[222] But both accounts have been challenged in recent years, and what seems a better explanation is the fact that centralising efforts of the Mughal state were successfully resisted in the lead-up to the eighteenth century by the rural gentry in alliance with some sections of the Mughal elite, leading to a process of decentralisation by 1720.

Safavid 'decline' is not as well interrogated, but certain themes with similarities to the Ottomans and the Mughals emerge. Despite a relatively stable seventeenth century (in comparison to the Ottomans and the Mughals), they were replaced as the ruling house in 1722. It is sometimes argued that their gradual weakening followed an inward turn: 'The last Safavid shahs spent virtually all their time immured in their palaces, invisible to the public and inaccessible to all but their most immediate entourage. Since the empire was not just the shah but the shah who actively engaged in battle, this led to a great loss of

---

[219] Matthee (2015) is an exception.
[220] See also Pearson (1976) for an overview.
[221] Subrahmanyam (2000, p. 349).   [222] Ibid.

prestige and legitimacy among his fellow warriors, the Qezelbash.'[223]
The military was neglected, and the Qizilbash were increasingly relegated to the sidelines. Religion became more prominent as state ideology. However, while the Great House of the Safavid may have declined,
the polity they controlled bounced back, in a manner, under the rulership of another *sahibkıran*, Nader Shah (r. 1736–47), who managed to
conquer much of west Asia, including Delhi, in a short period.
Subrahmanyam sees in Nader Shah a precursor of Napoleon
Bonaparte and argues that, had Nader Shah not withdrawn after
conquering Delhi, the East India Company would not have been able
to control India.[224] More on this later.

Interestingly enough, even though the Ottomans well outlasted the
Safavids and even the Mughals, it is the Ottoman Empire that is most
closely associated with a decline paradigm. In modern official Turkish
historiography,[225] the decline of the Ottoman Empire starts in the
sixteenth century with the death of Grand Vizier Sokollu Mehmet
Pasha in 1579 (and goes on until the official end of the empire in
1922). Number of different causes have been given by historians,
with varying degrees of plausibility, and echoing explanations already
discussed here: the increased power of the viziers and the bureaucrats
and the subsequent withdrawal of the sultans from government
affairs;[226] the switch to a new succession system in the middle of the
seventeenth century (the oldest male member of the family would now
inherit the throne); the feminisation of heirs (now raised among the
women in the harem); the replacement of the fief-based land-grant
system with tax farming; the evolution of the *janissary* cadres into
major social strata (initially a 'slave' army of *devshirme*,[227] the ranks
of the *janissary* corps eventually opened to Muslims; soldiers increasingly started families and even set up shops); corruption of officials

[223] Matthee (2015, p. 291).   [224] Subrahmanyam (2000, p. 368).
[225] I mean the textbook version. The Ottoman decline paradigm has been
successfully questioned by Ottoman scholars (within and outside Turkey) for
several decades now. See, for example, Kafadar (1997–8); Tezcan (2009).
[226] Note that these complaints about increased power of bureaucracy (as well as
corruption within the ranks) parallel also those about the decline of the Ming
around the same time. See Atwell (1988). For a comparative take on Ming and
Ottoman crises, see Goldstone (1988).
[227] Christian children converted and raised by the Ottoman state, usually as
soldiers but sometimes in other administrative roles.

and extensive involvement of the Empire in European trade, and so on.[228]

Decline *was* a subject of concern among sixteenth- and seventeenth-century Ottoman elites: 'Starting with Lütfi Pasa's *Asafname* completed in 1542, during the "peak" of the Empire's power and grandeur, consecutive authors took to writing about "dissolution of order" they observed in the affairs of state and society.'[229] Writers such as 'Mustafa Ali in 1581 ... Koci Beg in 1631 and again in 1640, Katip Celebi in 1653'[230] and others generated a 'decline treatise' genre. This decline genre had some common themes: 'an absolutist model of politics, recognizing the sultan as the only legitimate political actor; any challenge to the hierarchical working of politics and to the balance of social elements are perceived as a deviation and sign of dissolution'.[231] These observations were then picked up by European travellers to the Ottoman Empire and repeated almost verbatim in their reports in the next centuries, establishing 'the grand narrative of Ottoman decline and fall'.[232] These treatises were also reprinted in the nineteenth-century Tanzimat period of the Ottoman Empire, indicating a rekindled interest in the theme.[233]

As in the Mughal case, for the last several decades, Ottoman historians have been successfully challenging the decline paradigm, arguing that, despite some tumultuous years from the end of the sixteenth to the middle of the seventeenth centuries, the empire by no means entered a linear trajectory of decline. Most of the troubles of the period, including the *Jalali* rebellions that shook the countryside for decades, are explained by reference to structural factors instead, especially the effects of the Little Ice Age[234] on the empire, causing demographic downturns and other troubles.[235] But there is a general agreement that by the end of the seventeenth century the Ottomans had managed to recover from the crisis. Tezcan even argues that this was a period of positive transformation and that what emerged in the eighteenth century – once the *ulama* and the *janissary* corps managed to check the

---

[228] See Topal (2017) and Tezcan (2010) for an overview.
[229] Topal (2017, p. 23).   [230] Ibid.   [231] Ibid., p. 28.   [232] Ibid., p. 23.
[233] Ibid., p. 24.
[234] On the links between the Little Ice Age and the 'Seventeenth-Century General Crisis', see Parker and Smith (1997); Parker (2013); Blom (2019).
[235] For an argument linking the effects of the Little Ice Age with the Jalali rebellions, see White (2011). See also Özel (2016). See also Goldstone (1991).

power of the absolutist court – was a more bureaucratic, but less
autocratic and much more decentralised, version of the empire ('The
Second Ottoman Empire') that was more favourable for political,
economic and social conditions within.[236] Though most perhaps
would not go as far as Tezcan, most Ottoman historians now agree
that the eighteenth century for the empire was not the century of never-
ending decline it has been depicted to be but was one full of economic
and cultural potential.[237]

In each case, then, two contradictory things seem to be true at the
same time. One, if recent historians are correct, there are not sustained centuries of linear 'decline' that predate the fall of these houses
in the eighteenth, nineteenth and twentieth centuries respectively.
Two, some Ottoman and Mughal observers (and perhaps the
Safavid) seem to have nevertheless thought that they were facing a
decline in the seventeenth century (even though our modern-day
historians do not agree, and for good reason) and to have given
similar explanations for why: a general decrease in the role, stature
and strength of sovereign, coupled with increased bureaucratisation.
And their explanations have been picked by European observers from
the eighteenth century onwards, and later even incorporated into
national(ist) historiographies of the successor states of these empires,
animating our understanding of these Asian polities for much of the
twentieth century. Note also that what is considered to be the root
cause of decline by Eastern observers of their own polities – deper-
sonalisation of sovereignty, increased bureaucratisation of the state
and so on – is precisely one of the explanations given for *progress* in
European historiography. In Europe, for from being associated with
decline, such developments have been hailed for ushering in an age of
enlightenment and rational state behaviour. How do we square these
circles?

Pointing to the material damage of the 'Seventeenth-Century
General Crisis',[238] which I will discuss in the next chapter, gets us

---

[236] Tezcan (2010).
[237] See, for example, Yaycıoğlu (2016); Abou-El-Haj (2005); Barkey (2008);
        Aksan and Goffman (2007).
[238] The 'Seventeenth-Century General Crisis' spans the end of the sixteenth
        century and two-thirds of the seventeenth century. It was a period of upheaval
        and unrest throughout Eurasia. Some historians now attribute this crisis to the
        cooling caused by the peak of the Little Ice Age. See Parker and Smith (1997);
        Parker (2013); Blom (2019).

only partially to a solution. The damaging impact of this crisis – whatever its real underlying cause – is evident from recent Ottoman historiography. Yet the Ottomans recovered. The impact of the crisis on the Mughals' subsequent troubles is murky at best and, from what we know, seems to have been negligible in the case of the Safavid. Thus we cannot easily conclude that a structural crisis caused the internal 'decline' of these polities, even if temporarily. As Chapter 5 will also discuss, what seems to me to be a much plausible story is that the seventeenth-century crisis period fragmented the sixteenth-century world order as it had come to exist, fraying well-established connections between these three empires (and others), turning the attention of some key nodal actors such as the Ottomans 'inward' (and to their regions) rather than to the world. To put it another way, what the seventeenth-century crisis caused was loss of the sixteenth-century world order and not necessarily the irreversible material decline of any particular polity.

There is, however, another shared story here; it is not one of 'decline', necessarily, but it is one that is perceived as such. The Chinggisid sovereignty model – as I have been tracing through the ages – rested on the twin pillars of extreme political centralisation around the supreme authority of the ruler (the Great Khan or *sahibkıran*), on the one hand, and world conquest and universal empire, on the other. The two things were always inherently linked in the minds of those who had been socialised to this model. If one promise was compromised, so was the other, at least in the minds of some. Thus in all of our cases, at least some observers perceived the decrease in political centralisation due to the inevitable bureaucratisation and institutionalisation of their polity (as well as its spatial-relational decentralisation due to the successful resistance of the peripheries) as 'decline', and especially so if this development happened to coincide with a period of external non-expansion or, worse, retrenchment. Alternative models of sovereign legitimation, in applying a more orthodox, austere form of Islam as state ideology, also ran against the Chinggisid sovereignty model in that such choices forced assimilationist centralisation measures in empires that had been very pluralist until that point. Such moves were vigorously resisted, causing further decentralisation.

This may be why the perception of decline is strongest in the Ottoman Empire in the sixteenth century: almost all[239] 'early modern' polities throughout Eurasia are experiencing increased bureaucratisation in this period (due to demographic expansion, coupled with downturn and resource scarcity at the end of century), but it is particularly in the case of the Ottomans that these trends got especially associated with decline. Why was that? It could be because their inevitable period of transition from Chinggisid sovereignty, which demanded extreme centralisation of political power in individual rulers as well as universal empire projects, to a different model, a more bureaucratic, decentralised model, coincided with 'the Seventeenth-Century General Crisis', a period of retrenchment for all empires. Thus, seventeenth-century developments in bureaucratisation, decentralisation, the increased role of *ulama* in lawmaking (initially a check on absolutism) and so on were understood as decline by some Ottoman observers of the period. These observers of 'decline' were not judging their conditions by the standards of the post-nineteenth-century international order as Bernard Lewis wrongly presumed in his (unfortunately) well-known article on the subject;[240] they were judging them according to their own normative standards of 'greatness', standards they had inherited from their own particular history of world orders, as explained in this book.

As we know from later European history, world domination does not necessarily require extreme political centralisation at home, and empire-building can very well be legitimated by other ideologies besides Chinggisid universal sovereignty, for example civilisational hierarchies, the 'white man's burden' and so on. Furthermore, the discussion of this chapter should not be taken to imply that Asian states were doomed in a cycle of reproducing sovereignty models from the thirteenth century; normative models are not static, and I think Subrahmanyam is right in speculating that Nader Shah (of Iran) or somebody else (Qianlong Emperor of China perhaps) could have found a compromise between the Timurid model and the demands of the eighteenth century, had certain contingencies had been played out differently. Yet that was not be. The next chapter will give us more ways to speculate as to why.

---

[239] Bureaucratisation in any given polity is driven both by endogenous dynamics and globally experienced structural conditions.

[240] Lewis (1962).

5 | How the East Made the World: Eurasia and Beyond

Chinggisid Influences on a Globalising World (Sixteenth Century)

The signs are that the age of the ṣāḥib-zamān will see unprecedented ordering and building of the world. There will be an unbelievable accumulation of wealth, not only from conquest, but also from mines and hidden treasures that will appear all over the world; and their appearance is one of the signs of the Last Age. The time will be one of prosperity, peace, pleasure in all things, including hunting and love. The ṣāḥib-zamān will be assiduous in the founding and construction of all things that seem good: mosques, bridges, travellers' khans and the like will spring up everywhere . . .

From Haydar the geomancer's address to Süleyman
I the Magnificent (1535)[1]

Introduction

The previous chapter described how Chinggisid sovereignty norms had given rise in the sixteenth century to a rivalry between three Great Houses with universal empire ambitions: the Ottomans, the Safavids and the Mughals. Each of these houses had rulers who claimed the Timurid title of *sahibkıran* – that is, an association with the Saturn–Jupiter conjunction believed to bestow great sovereign charisma, a title made even more significant in the sixteenth century by its additional association with the Islamic millennium (1591) and thus the 'Last Days' of the age. This title was invoked in service of universal empire projects much in the mould of the ones discussed in Chapters 2 and 3. The three empires together had under their sovereign umbrella most of the land area between western Europe (plus North Africa) and East Asia, and they controlled 'over a full third of the human race (some 160 million of 500 million souls)',[2] most of whom were not even Muslims. Together (though the Safavids are more negligible in this regard), they

---

[1] As quoted and explained by Fleischer (2018, pp. 71–2). Part of the same quote opens Chapter 4.
[2] Melvin-Koushki (2016, p. 148).

also controlled much of the world's economy and resources, and oversaw the most significant trade routes.[3] This was a 'world order' also because it was reaching into the rest of the world, however. Not only had the Ottomans, the Safavids and the Mughals created their own world order in the middle of Eurasia, but their world also linked other regional orders of Europe and Asia.[4] In the sixteenth century, it was not yet obvious that it would be the Europeans who would come to dominate the globe in the future. The world was still Asiacentric, and Chinngisid sovereignty norms were still very much in circulation. As we will see in this chapter, even Europe was not free from their influence. Had it not been for the developments of the seventeenth century, 'globalisation' could have continued along this Eurasian axis, rather than in the Eurocentric form it took after the eighteenth century.

This chapter will thus expand our gaze beyond the three houses of 'millennial sovereignty' discussed in Chapter 4, to the connections between the post-Timurid world order of the Ottomans, the Safavids and the Mughals, on the one hand, and other key political actors of the sixteenth century in the west, north and east of the post-Timurid core, on the other. First, we will turn to Europe. Because Europe was peripheral to Asian politics between the thirteenth and fifteenth centuries, European actors have not featured very much in the historical narrative of this book. This section brings them into the timeline by showing the ways Europeans, and especially the Habsburgs, were influenced by the post-Timurid ecumene of the Ottomans, the Safavid and the Mughals. Next, we will move north to Muscovy, and then we will briefly check in with the khanates in Inner Asia and the Ming in East Asia. The chapter concludes with a discussion of the 'Seventeenth-Century General Crisis' and its impact on the sixteenth-century Asian world order.

Looking to the West of the Millennial Sovereigns

Writing IR history with an exclusive focus on Europe in the sixteenth century leaves out some of the most significant and central dynamics of a globalising world. But it is not enough to label IR treatments of history as Eurocentric; if they are to be improved, we need alternative accounts. Here I advocate replacing the familiar IR timeline of the

---

[3] Ibid.
[4] Likely Africa as well, given the extensive presence of the Ottomans there.

closed box of European order expanding outwards with an account rooted in global historical sociology that underlines the points of connection between Europe and the post-Timurid world order in the sixteenth century. Even a cursory review demonstrates that, in the early modern period, European actors still depended on the East not only for material goods but also for *ideas*,[5] especially in the realm of universal sovereignty and world empire. As Melvin-Koushki notes: 'it is only because all the potentialities contained within the universalising Mongol model were so fully actualised by Turko-Mongol Perso-Islamic societies as a single cultural continuum, from the Timurids onwards, that Europeans were finally able to join the era of globalisation inaugurated by the Mongols in the thirteenth century'.[6] In other words, here we have an example of a non-European world order expanding *into* Europe, rather than the other way around.

An even better way of thinking about sixteenth-century dynamics is that the Ottomans acted as a two-way conduit between the smaller European regional order and the much larger post-Timurid world order in (south-)west Asia (and beyond). The previous chapter showed that the traditional historiographical view that Ottomans borrowed their ideas of universal empire from Europe is misplaced. The Ottomans in the sixteenth century were reacting above all else to the Safavid innovation of sacred kingship as manifested by Shah Ismail, a modified version of the Timurid sovereignty model. Their real power competition thus originated from the East but was adopted increasingly to the European theatre involving the Habsburgs. Much of the European 'Silk Road' trade passed through the Ottoman realms, but there was also considerable ideational transmission: they (and their subjects) also helped disseminate Eastern (Chinggisid) notions of universal sovereignty westwards (even as they themselves fused Western/ Roman imperial heritage with those models). Many European developments in the sixteenth century could be traced back to the Ottoman/ post-Timurid influence on the European regional order.

The Habsburgs and Charles V

Traditional narratives of the sixteenth century often observe that within it was the Habsburgs and more than anyone Charles V

[5] On this, see also Malcolm (2019). [6] Melvin-Koushki (2016, p. 148).

(r. 1516–56 [Holy Roman Emperor; also Archduke of Austria, King of Spain and Lord of the Netherlands]) who properly reintroduced notions of universal empire to the continental political landscape, with other European monarchs articulating their own visions in reaction to him. In this section, I am going to argue that, without the Ottomans (and their Chinggisid heritage), Charles V may not have been remembered for these 'innovations'. Charles' competition with Süleyman I (r. 1521–66) had a profound influence on him, thus also on the Habsburgs and the broader European trajectory of political development.

In contrast to most rulers discussed previously, Charles V was not exactly a military 'conqueror': he had inherited his many titles. His father was Philip from the House of Habsburg and his mother was Spanish royalty, the daughter of Isabella I of Castille and Ferdinand II of Aragon. Thanks to this inheritance, for much of the sixteenth century Charles V, and thus the House of Habsburgs, controlled much of continental Europe. Via Spain, he also controlled the Atlantic corridor to the West Indies. Spanish fleets reached via overland crossing of Panama the Pacific Ocean, the Philippines and, from there, the Ming economy. In the sixteenth century, the Atlantic trade had not yet started to rival the Mediterranean one in goods from the Levant. The primary commodity that came from Habsburg overseas territories was silver.[7] The overseas activities of the Spanish (as well the Portuguese) in the West were relatively marginal to European affairs: 'In the sixteenth century four times as many books were published about the Turks and Asia than about America.'[8] But even so, the Habsburgs and Charles V absolutely dominated *European* political affairs in the first part of the sixteenth century.

This is another way of saying that it was not *in Europe* that Charles V had his primary competition – later exaggerations of the sixteenth-century importance of various subsequently significant European houses notwithstanding. Most potential European rivals were in alliances with the Habsburgs at this point. For example, the Portuguese House of Aviz was tied to the Habsburgs via marriage. They were technically an overseas empire as Manuel I (r. 1495–1501) had claimed

---

[7] Tobacco, potatoes and tomatoes did not appear until the end of the sixteenth century; tea and coffee until the seventeenth. Koenigsberger, Mosse and Bowler (2014, p. 262). The silver of course would lead to problems for Spain later on.

[8] Ibid., p. 262.

the title 'Lord of the Conquest, Navigation and Commerce of Ethiopia, India, Arabia and Persia' in 1501. In reality they 'rarely held more than coastal fortresses and trading stations'[9] overseas and continued to be impressed by the opulence of the post-Timurid rulers they observed.[10] The only potential rival to Charles V on the Italian peninsula was the pope, Clement VII (born Giulio de' Medici). The pope resisted Charles' attempts to speak in the name of the Catholic Church and also to reform it, an authority grab which 'derived directly from Charles's view of his imperial dignity as transcendental'.[11] Clement VII thus conspired at times to undermine the power of Charles but remained generally tethered to him in an alliance against the Ottoman infidels. North-western European houses were also comparatively minor at this point in the sixteenth century, even though the Tudors in England, for instance, and Henry VIII (r. 1509–47) in particular loom large in our historical imagination. This is not to minimise Henry VIII's break from the Catholic Church and creation of the Church of England, but this development itself needs to be understood as part of larger, continental trends, including Charles V's aforementioned claim to speak for the Catholic Church, which, as I will demonstrate, cannot be understood as separate from his rivalry with Süleyman the Magnificent.

In omitting the East entirely from their view, traditional IR accounts of the emergence of Westphalian sovereignty in Europe have thus missed big parts of the story (if not the real story altogether).[12] In explaining the development of exclusive and supreme political authority – a prerequisite of Westphalian sovereignty – in England and elsewhere, the IR literature relies either on the history of political thought literature, which treats this as an ideational revolution associated especially with Bodin and Hobbes,[13] or on historical sociology, which documents novel and aggressive processes of centralisation.[14] Some IR accounts have drawn from both to argue for the importance of shifts in religious belief in making possible supreme political authority.[15] Within the European context, the development of the ideal[16] of

[9] Ibid., p. 256.
[10] Ibid., p. 258. See also Phillips and Sharman (2015); Sharman (2019) on the limitations of European activities in Asia at this point in history.
[11] Koenigsberger, Mosse and Bowler (2014, p. 232).
[12] See also Zarakol (2018a).   [13] See, for example, Skinner (2008).
[14] Too many examples to name altogether, but see, for example, Elias (2000 [1939]); Mann (1986); Tilly (1993).
[15] Philpott (2001).   [16] See, for example, Skinner (2008).

an absolutist state[17] in the sixteenth century is considered one of the
first steps in this direction because the preceding centuries were marked
by competing authority claims by the pope, the Holy Roman emperor
and various monarchs.[18] Because the IR literature says little about
what was happening outside of the European context but abounds
with claims of novelty and revolution in that context,[19] readers inevitably assume that philosophical justifications of supreme political
authority and/or political centralisation in western Europe must have
been without parallel in human history.

The previous chapters should have demonstrated just the opposite,
however. We saw that Islamic tradition had its own version of divided
sovereignty claims between kings, jurists and the caliph, and it was the
Chinggisid/Timurid influences from the thirteenth century onwards that
pushed a new form of political centralisation by Muslim rulers. This
process gained speed in the fifteenth century and culminated in the sixteenth century, with millennial sovereigns who, starting with Shah Ismail,
truly combined political and religious authority in their person, innovating
a highly centralised sacred kingship with Islamic (as well as astrological)
flavours. And it was the competition between millennial sovereigns that
pushed the process of social disciplining along confessional lines that the
realms under the control of the Ottomans and the Safavids went through
the second half of the sixteenth century, especially after the Peace of
Amasya (1555). The fact that 'the process of formation of distinct confessional territorial blocks and forging of religious "orthodoxies" unfolded
simultaneously in both Muslim and Christian empires in the sixteenth
century'[20] not only poses serious questions for IR theories which see the
root causes of the emergence of the Westphalian state and the state system
in such 'revolutionary' ideational trends thought to be exclusive to Europe
but also shows that the trend of elevating the authority of kings above all
challengers *was not* originating in western Europe. If anything the 'revolution' in sovereignty (in combining political and religious authority) spread
from *East to West*[21] via the Ottoman–Habsburg rivalry.[22] Habsburgs

[17] Scholarship has cast doubt on whether this ideal was ever fully realised. For an
IR version of this argument, see Nexon (2009).
[18] See, for example, Croxton (1999, p. 571); Ruggie (1983).
[19] Philpott's book, for instance, is called *Revolutions in Sovereignty*.
[20] Krstic (2011, p. 14).   [21] See also Zarakol (2018a).
[22] Confessionalisation may be the bit that went the other way. Post-Timurid
empires did not emphasise conversion in the same way as the Europeans. More
on this in a moment.

mirrored Ottoman universal empire claims, and lesser European houses got increasingly drawn into the rivalry on either side.

The only (western) European house[23] that properly challenged the continental dominance of Charles V was the House of Valois in France under Francis I, whose aspirations to become the Holy Roman emperor himself had been defeated by Charles V's election to this position in 1519.[24] In fact, in traditional accounts, the sixteenth century is described as being dominated by either the Habsburg–Valois rivalry, as manifested especially in the struggle over the control of the Italian peninsula. The years from the 1520s to the 1540s were marked with confrontations between Habsburg forces and Francis I, with the English, the pope and various Italian cities changing sides more than once.[25] While the forces of Francis I resisted the imperial attacks, the dominance was most certainly on the Habsburg side. This may be why, in 1536, Francis I entered into an alliance with Süleyman the Magnificent, whose help he needed against Charles V.[26] But Francis was clearly the smaller partner in this alliance.

Charles V was already facing Süleyman I on multiple fronts. From the mid-1530s to 1547, Ottoman expansionary aims had turned mostly westward, taking a break from the Safavid campaigns discussed in the previous chapter. Hayreddin Barbarossa, 'a merchant turned corsair and self-made ruler on the Maghribi coast',[27] had sought Ottoman protection and was appointed the official governor-general of the Aegean and Eastern Mediterranean islands, many of which the Ottomans now controlled thanks to him. He captured Tunis from another Muslim house, who sought refuge with Charles V, who then took it back from Hayreddin. In return, the Ottomans pressured Venice to turn against Charles V in favour of Francis I. This backfired when Venice joined the papacy, the Hospitaller knights and Charles V to create the Holy League against the Ottomans.[28] Süleyman countered

---

[23] The Jagiellonian Dynasty ruling over Poland-Lithuania should also get a mention. Sigismund I (1506–48) and Sigismund II (1548–72) were capable rulers and Poland-Lithuania played an important role in the geopolitics of the sixteenth century (more on this in the next section). They were an ally to Francis and, despite an agreement with Maximillian, a potential rival to the Habsburgs. Their present-day omission from most historical IR accounts of the European order is another version of reading into the past what we consider important in the present.

[24] Koenigsberger, Mosse, and Bowler (2014, p. 230).　　[25] Ibid., pp. 230–5.
[26] Şahin (2013, p. 104).　　[27] Ibid., p. 103.　　[28] Ibid., p. 106.

with a two-pronged attack in modern-day Romania and the Mediterranean (Battle of Preveza), both parts of of which resulted in victories for the Ottoman side. Good news also came from the Indian Ocean. These auspicious victories on the Ottoman side were marked in 1539 by grandiose celebrations in Constantinople marking the circumcisions of two princes, celebrations marked with more millennial sovereign symbolism.[29]

The sudden death of Ottoman ally John Szapolyai in Hungary in 1540, just two weeks after the birth of his son, brought Süleyman into yet newer tensions with Charles V, whose brother, Ferdinand of Austria, had a treaty-based claim to the throne of Hungary if Szapolyai had died without an heir. (Ferdinand also had an alliance with Shah Tahmasb of the Safavids). Süleyman captured Buda and annexed Hungary in 1541. But more tension and skirmishes followed in the next decade, as both sides continued to contest sovereignty of Hungary. Charles reached out to the Safavids for an alliance. In 1544, Francis I agreed in the Peace of Crepy to support Charles V against the Ottomans in return for the promise of his second son marrying a Habsburg princess and getting various territorial claims recognised. Commentators find this arrangement remarkable: 'after four successful wars against France Charles was willing to concede nearly all French territorial claims and to contemplate the cession of his own original Burgundian inheritance, all for the sake of achieving effective leadership of a Catholic and united Christendom'.[30] Why would Charles V agree to such an arrangement if he believed Francis I to be his main rival?

Charles V's aspirations only make sense in the context of his rivalry with Süleyman the Magnificent. Charles V's notions of universal sovereignty could not help being shaped by his competition with Süleyman, just as in the much better-documented[31] fact that Süleyman's were by his rivalry with Charles V. For example, in 1532, Süleyman purchased for an enormous sum of 144,400 ducats a 'spectacular golden helmet' from Venetian goldsmiths.[32] The helmet was not in the Ottoman tradition. Other ceremonial objects were also

---

[29] Ibid., p. 109.
[30] Koenigsberger, Mosse, and Bowler (2014, p. 239). The promise did not come to pass because the son died.
[31] It is a common stance in Ottoman historiography to look for European influences, whereas the opposite is true in European historiography.
[32] Necipoğlu (1989, p. 401).

acquired: horse furnishings, a sceptre and a golden throne.[33] Süleyman used these objects – symbols of sovereignty alien to the Islamic tradition – in his march to Vienna, donning them when he entered cities such as Belgrade and Nish: 'So powerful was the effect of this carefully staged reception ceremony that the Hapsburg ambassadors, stupefied by the abundance of jewels and gold, turned into "speechless corpses," according to a Venetian report.'[34] Necipoğlu observes that all of this was carefully staged to outshine Charles V's 1529 coronation in Bologna as Holy Roman emperor, which had featured four plumed "helmets of Caesar" and a joint procession with Pope Clement VII.[35]

After receiving reports of the coronation, the vizier İbrahim Pasha is reported to have 'remarked indignantly: "How can there be an emperor other than my grand signor?"'[36] Ottoman historians vigorously disputed Charles V's claim to the title of Caesar, and, 'refusing to recognize this ambitious title in his official correspondence, Süleyman addressed his rival simply as "King of Spain"'.[37] The golden helmet was designed against this background, to bolster Süleyman's claim that there could be only one (world) emperor, one 'Caesar'. Within the Ottoman context, it was also referred to as a 'trophy of Alexander the Great'.[38] Süleyman wore it to announce to Europeans that he was the second Alexander and that he was superior to Charles V. I think it has been a mistake to read such moves by the Ottomans as merely borrowing European symbols. A more apt diagnosis is that they were translating their millennial sovereignty claims for the benefit of European actors and audiences.[39]

Charles V as Would-Be Sahibkıran?

Given what we know of social dynamics, Charles V must also have[40] changed through his interactions with and observations of Süleyman.

---

[33] Ibid., p. 407.   [34] Ibid., p. 409.   [35] Ibid., p. 410.   [36] Ibid., p. 411.
[37] Ibid.
[38] Necipoğlu notes: 'Such a ceremonial plumed helmet-crown, reminiscent of the ones worn by ancient monarchs, is depicted in an early seventeenth-century Mughal painting where the emperor Jahangir holds it as an emblem of sovereignty allegedly belonging to his ancestor Timur' (Necipoğlu 1989, p. 411).
[39] Converts like Vizier İbrahim Pasha facilitated this translation.
[40] I have to be a bit more speculative here because the literature has not really entertained the possibility. But I think the evidence that follows is highly suggestive.

His grand-chancellor, Gattinara, a humanist from Piedmont and arguably İbrahim Pasha's counterpart on the Habsburg side, said to Charles
V in 1519: 'God has set you on the path towards world monarchy.'[41]
Many accounts of the Habsburg and Charles V note the unusualness of
such a claim within the European context: 'there was the quite novel
and, to many contemporaries, a rather sinister idea of a world empire.
Charles V himself denied such pretensions, but many of his supporters
made the claims for him.'[42] The post-Timurid notions of millennial
sovereignty and universal empire must have been seeping into the
Habsburg realms and interacting with local normative repertoires
there to make new ideational hybrids.

Recall from the previous chapter how the title of *sahibkıran*, specifically associated with the Timur and the post-Timurid milieu and
representing universalist notions of politico-religious leadership, had
come to dominate Ottoman, Safavid and Mughal political thought and
justifications of sovereignty in the period leading up to the Islamic
Millennium (1591), which was believed to be marked also by a grand
Saturn and Jupiter conjunction (1582). There was an apocalyptic tenor
to these sovereignty claims as well because, as we have seen, the Saturn–
Jupiter grand conjunction was believed to mark the end of ages and
coming of the Last Days: 'a renovation (tajdīd) that would compass
religious and political institutions, and establishment by conquest of a
universal empire that would be literally as well as figuratively millennial in this tenth century of the Muslim era (1494–1592 CE)'.[43] That
the end of the Islamic age may be near gave an urgency to the military
campaigns of Islamic millennial sovereigns, especially so when they
were fighting the infidels.

Thus the Hungarian campaign(s) had particularly apocalyptic over-
tones for the Ottomans and the Habsburgs. It was in this campaign that
Süleyman I was specifically called "'the messiah of the End Time
(mehdi-yi ahiru'z-zaman)" and "the master of the auspicious conjunction (sahib-kiran)"'.[44] What is more interesting for our purposes here is
that Ottoman millennial sovereignty visions about Hungary 'corres-
ponded with various prophecies about Turks that circulated in

---

[41] Koenigsberger, Mosse, and Bowler (2014, p. 231).
[42] Ibid., p. 236. There is a lot that is written on the Habsburgs, but there is a general
silence about where this novel notion comes from. See, for example, Curtis
(2013).
[43] Fleischer (2018, p. 19).   [44] Şahin (2013, p. 61).

Europe'.[45] After the fall of Constantinople in 1453, there had emerged in Europe a corpus of apocalyptic prophetic texts, and the Ottomans played a prominent place in this literature as evidence that an apocalyptic confrontation was near.[46] On the European side, there was hope that Charles 'would reunite and purify the western Roman Empire, then retake Constantinople and bring Eastern Rome under his rule, and finally gain the crown of Jerusalem; Christian political and spiritual salvation would be capped, in this millennial empire, by universal conversion of Muslims and Jews to purified Christianity'.[47]

The Ottoman chronicler Mustafa Ali believed that Charles V, along with Ferdinand, was fixated on taking Hungary because not having it kept Charles from using the title of *sahibkıran* (lord of conjunction), which shows that this was the primary ontological framework through which the Ottomans were reading the Habsburgs and Charles V. Mustafa Ali's speculation was not that far-fetched. It seems that Ferdinand, brother of Charles V, did use the title after his capture of Buda.[48] This may have been partly to irritate Süleyman, but – given the significance of this title in the sixteenth century milieu for a third of the world's population – even in Europe there would be those who would responded to it. A truce was finally signed in 1547, in which both 'the Ottomans and the Habsburgs recognized each other's possessions in Hungary'.[49] The Ottoman chronicler Mustafa Ali related this development as proof that Süleyman was a genuine *sahibkıran* and that he 'had superseded the glory of all the legendary Persian kings. Thanks to divine support, he equaled the military successes of Muhammad and attained the stature of [his namesake] Solomon. Even the Caesar of the Christians had become one of his slaves.'[50] This is not to say that Süleyman and Charles V were competing *only* over the title of *sahibkıran*; they also competed to be the 'last Roman Emperor'.[51] The titles themselves are not the issue here – except for showing that for Ottomans the main referent was not Europe – as both rulers were code-switching depending on the audience; rather, what matters is the rivalry between the two sides and how that competition elevated the stakes, especially for the Habsburgs.

---

[45] Ibid.   [46] Fleischer (2018).   [47] Ibid., p. 29.   [48] Şahin (2013, p. 76).
[49] Ibid., p. 114.   [50] Ibid., p. 116.   [51] Ibid., pp. 81–7.

Epistemological Networks of the Apocalypse

How did the two sides learn so much about each other? In the previous chapter, we saw that the intelligentsia were circulating across the Ottoman, Safavid and Mughal courts. There was a similar ideational circulation among the Habsburg and the Ottoman worlds as well, but for slightly different reasons and via another set of actors.

Italian merchants, especially those from Venice,[52] networked much of the Mediterranean especially in the first half of the sixteenth century, as they had done in periods before.[53] The trade of the Italian city states connected both the east and the west of the Mediterranean region but also connected the Mediterranean with continental Europe.[54] However, the balance of trade was not evenly distributed: the East – that is, the post-Timurid world order – was the primary source of goods for the West. What Braudel underlines in terms of the relationship between southern and northern Europe in the first half of the sixteenth century was even truer in terms of the relationship between Europe at the time and the west Asian zone of universal empires (replace 'North' with 'West' and 'South' with 'East'): 'A balance of trade unfavourable to the North was wholly to be expected. The towns, merchants, and artisans of the North were as if under apprenticeship, looking for guidance to the towns of the South. Southern businessmen were for a long time able to exploit local ignorance and backwardness.'[55] Italian merchants dominated northern German towns (as well the English and Flemish markets), but they were able to do so thanks to their connections to the Levant and their ability to control trade through the Mediterranean.

The Venetians did not only transmit goods: they were the connective stitches in the ontological fabric of the sixteenth-century world order.[56] For example, in the golden helmet affair described already, they played an important role not only in manufacturing the helmet but also in

---

[52] See Rothman (2014). Venetians regarded the Ottoman sultan as a ruler worthy of respect for being just and wise in addition to being powerful, and they described him as a Renaissance prince. Valensi (1993).
[53] Malcolm (2015) paints an even denser picture of a network of knights, corsairs, Jesuits and spies.
[54] Braudel (1972, p. 210).   [55] Ibid., p. 214.
[56] Italian spies – sometimes even of Jewish ancestry – also went back and forth between the two empires. See Cassen (2017). On spy networks in the Mediterranean, see also Malcolm (2015).

describing various ceremonies on both sides to the other. The Venetian diplomatic mission reported on the activities of Süleyman: 'Ramberti praised the wealth, power, and extraordinary obedience commanded by Süleymān, adding the pious sentiment that surely God would not permit the sultan to realize his dream of universal empire because the unprecedented signs of his authority were such that, were he indeed divinely designated to such state, all people would be bound to render him obeisance.'[57] Furthermore, the Venetians, like other European travellers[58] to Istanbul in this period, were very intrigued by and reported on a book of prophecies, the *Miftāḥ al-jafr al-jāmiʿ* (The Key to the Comprehensive Prognostication), 'a text that foretold the events of the Last Days and predicted that the last universal ruler would come in the tenth century from the Ottoman house'.[59] As Fleischer notes, this suggests that Europeans considered Ottoman apocalyptic prognostication valid (likely because it validated similar notions on the Christian side). The Venetian mission also reported that Istanbul was teeming with prophets and prophecies, and astrological speculations (for reasons discussed in the previous chapter).

Prophets and astrologers were not confined to Istanbul (or the post-Timurid zone); in the sixteenth century, Italy too 'was awash with prophets, often itinerant, who preached the fullness of time and the imminent arrival of the antichrist ... [and that] the apocalypse was at hand, and with it the revolutionary transformations and upheavals ... that must precede Last Judgment'.[60] Note how reminiscent this millennial ontology is of the Ottoman (and the post-Timurid) one discussed in the previous chapter. Is it plausible that Italians, with all their connections to the East, came by these notions entirely independently? To give just one example, Francesco da Meleto, a popular prophet whose father was a Florentine merchant and his mother a Russian slave, had lived in Istanbul at the end of the fifteenth century. He returned to Florence to preach that, just as 'renovation is universal, so was the circulation and validity of prophecy'.[61] Everyone expected a new age, and any prophecy pointing to that end, regardless of origin, seemed to confirm those expectations.

[57] Fleischer (2018, p. 22). [58] For example, the French mission. Ibid., p. 24.
[59] Ibid. [60] Ibid., p. 26. [61] Ibid., pp. 26–7.

Limits of European Learning

Obviously such a short sketch cannot do justice to the complicated world of sixteenth-century interactions between Europe and the post-Timurid world of the Ottomans, the Safavid and the Mughals. The main takeaway should be that Europe was receiving not only commodities but also ideas from the post-Timurid world spanning North Africa to Delhi, a sixteenth-century 'world order' covering a third of humanity, home to 'revolutions of sovereignty' as well as economic commodities. The millennial fervour transcended any boundaries, giving meaning to the universal empire claims of the Ottomans, the Safavids and the Mughals and now also the Habsburgs.

Three caveats are in order, however. The first is simply a reminder that the transmission of ideas (or goods) from the East to the West had not started in the sixteenth century; as is well known, the conquest of Constantinople in 1453 had pushed a number of scholars to move to Italy, but, as discussed in Chapter 2, there is no good reason to think of the Byzantine world as being entirely separate from the Chinggisid and post-Chinggisid orders of west Asia (or the Persianate world in general). *Reconquista* was yet another point of contact, even if the degree of transmission was obscured by later events. And of course merchants of all backgrounds connected Europe and Asia throughout all of the periods this book has been investigating.

My second caveat is that, in arguing that various European actors borrowed ideas from the post-Timurid world as they interacted with it, I do not mean to imply that the European regional order had become an exact replica of the post-Timurid order, because many differences remained. My contention is rather that these orders were ontologically porous in a way that is almost entirely overlooked in the IR literature, with implications for the understanding and development of state sovereignty.[62] I also contend that, at least up until the sixteenth century, Europe was the junior partner in matters of borrowing, and we need to stop projecting modern social hierarchies between the West and the East back onto earlier periods. To the extent that the first wave of political centralisation (in all senses of the word as I have defined in Chapter 1) in Europe was instigated by Charles V (and the various

[62] On the impact of the Ottomans on Western political thought, see also Malcolm (2019).

responses to him throughout the continent), we could argue that it might not have even happened without Ottoman presence.

However, the universal empire claims as developed on the continent remained different in practice from the Asian and Eurasian ones. For example, the post-Timurid order discussed in the previous chapter was much more culturally pluralist and heterodox compared to Europe, despite its preoccupation with the Islamic millennium. Perhaps they had to be: both the Ottomans and the Mughals ruled over populations in which the majority were not Muslims. However, it bears noting that, as discussed in previous chapters, a latitudinarian attitude in religious affairs has been a sustained feature of Chinggisid and post-Chinggisid sovereignty models and world orders. The Chinggisid, post-Chinggisid, Timurid and post-Timurid notions of universal empire never involved mass-scale conversion or religious purification. By contrast, such notions came up rather frequently in the apocalyptic narratives on the European side and as part of the divine plan for Charles V.

This comparatively higher ideational tolerance in Asia (especially until the last quarter of the sixteenth century) extended not only to religions other than Islam but also to occult sciences. In this period, Europe, too, was dominated by prophecies, astrological and other occult sciences (many of which, as we have seen, were resonating with similar teachings from the East), made accessible to popular audiences more than ever before thanks to advances in printing. Yet, unlike in post-Timurid realms, in Europe 'as magic boomed, so did its prosecution. A peculiar feature of Latin Christendom ... was its reigning obsession with discovering, and brutally prosecuting, "witchcraft" as essentially, demonically anti-Christian.'[63] Reformation specifically was anti-occult (and thus anti-pluralist), equating Catholicism with sorcery.[64] Occultists were prosecuted in Europe, but not in the 'post-Mongol Islamdom ... : the witch trials and book-burnings that so deranged the former were simply inconceivable in the latter'.[65] Even the Renaissance was marked by a type of close-mindedness which did not have its corollary in the post-Timurid realm (at least in the sixteenth century), which is rather ironic because much of twentieth-century historiography blamed the 'decline' of post-Timurid empires on their supposed rigidity and attributed the rise of Europe to the intellectual curiosity of its scientists.

[63] Melvin-Koushki (2019b, p. 141).   [64] Ibid.   [65] Ibid., p. 142.

In reality, the European Renaissance was defined by a struggle between two camps: the humanist one, which wanted to entirely discount Arabic sources in their study of Greek sources, and the science-and-philosophy-leaning one, which favoured independent inquiry and thus had to use Latin editions of Arabic texts.[66] Neither approach really gave credit where it was due to Eastern sources. The boom in Arabic-sourced scholarship in Europe the fifteenth and sixteenth centuries, 'as evidenced by the printing of editions, university curricula, biographical writing and a new Arabic-Latin and Hebrew-Latin translation movement'[67] was met with a humanist backlash in various fields ranging from astrology to medicine. Arabic sources were charged with being error-ridden, adding things to the text that Greeks did not intend or being mere plagiarists.[68] Astrology especially bore the brunt of these criticisms, with humanists advocating a return to Ptolemy. Yet, Ptolemaic astrology did not meet the demands of the day; as we have seen in the previous chapter, in the sixteenth century post-Timurid astrology had become almost the political science of its day, a way of legitimising imperial projects by making sense of history and predicting the future. Ptolemy, by contrast, dealt 'primarily with meteorology and agriculture'.[69] So the humanists could not exactly escape Eastern sources. What they did instead was 'the purging, suppressing or camouflaging of Arabic "accretions" – if usually only at the level of theory, not of praxis'.[70] To put it another way, the insights from these sources they could not really be dismissed as inferior, so they were reclaimed, 'culturally appropriated', so to speak: 'the forcible hellen- or hispanization of those Arabic authorities who proved theoretically and practically indispensable, served most notably to sever all association of Arabic learning with the Ottoman Empire' (and by extension, the post-Timurid ecumene). The anti-Arabic polemics of this period may indeed be at the genesis of the decline narrative of the East in Europe.[71]

The third caveat has to do with the direction of transmission. By replacing the narrative of only 'the East' borrowing from 'the West' with the above argument, I am not advocating a reverse-Eurocentric view of the sixteenth century but rather one of a connected world. In other words, I am not claiming that only Europe was borrowing from

[66] Melvin-Koushki (2018c, p. 195). [67] Ibid. [68] Ibid., p. 206.
[69] Ibid., p. 210. [70] Ibid., p. 211.
[71] Ibid., p. 195. Also see Hasse (2016). See also Rothman (2021).

Asia: both sides influenced each other to varying extents. A candidate for post-Timurid borrowing from Europe is the trend towards confessionalisation. We saw in the previous chapter that imperial competition between the Ottomans and the Safavids drove both sides to homogenise their Muslim populations in the second half of the sixteenth century: 'the continued expectations of spiritual renewal [due to millenarianism] as well as continued inter-imperial competition gave rise to the phenomena of confessional polarization and Sunnitization in the Ottoman empire'[72] as well as the parallel development of Shiʿitisation in Safavid Iran. Historians have long argued that the sixteenth century was a turning point for Europe for similar reasons: as alluded to in the earlier example of Henry VIII, churches cooperated with political centralisation efforts to delineate confessional boundaries, and these confessional communities later constituted the backbone of national communities in Europe upon which the territorial claim of the nation state was placed.[73] Is it a coincidence that the post-Timurid empires moved to confessionalise at the same time as their European counterparts? Given all the connectivity we have discussed, it seems unlikely that these parallel developments were unlinked. That suggests either that one side was learning from the other or that there were structural drivers pushing confesionalisation throughout Europe and (west) Asia.

If one side was learning from the other, this more exclusionary ethos underwriting confessionalisation is a good candidate for having European origins, rather than west Asian ones. As discussed, Europe was generally much less tolerant of religious difference to begin with. Late-sixteenth-century Ottoman and Safavid homogenisation drives took the shape of measures such as the promulgation of new criminal law codes that policed the boundaries of orthodoxy and public morality, the promotion of mosque worship through the imposition of new fines for irregular attendance, and the construction of an unprecedented number of mosques in order to stabilise mosque congregations and monitor them.[74] The Ottoman sultans did toy with the idea of punishing non-Muslim groups in the empire (especially foreign

---

[72] Krstic (2011, p. 12).

[73] On confessionalisation, see, for example, Lotz-Heumann (2001); Schilling (2001); Krstić (2009).

[74] Ibid., p. 107. See also Zarakol (2020b) for a comparison with the nineteenth century.

residents) in response to Habsburg measures against Muslims, but they decided against harsh measures.[75] A poll tax was instituted in 1613 but later rescinded. We can think of these developments as being parallel to European homogenisation measures of the same period – such as the expulsion of Jews and Muslims from Spain, the Inquisition, or the St. Bartholomew's Day massacre – but the fact remains that the Ottoman Empire (or the Safavids or the Mughals) did not go to the European extremes in persecuting interfaith heretics, let alone peoples of other faiths (at least in the sixteenth century).

Looking to the North and the East of the Millennial Sovereigns

Now we turn our gaze to the north of the post-Timurid zone, first to Muscovy and Caspian steppes, then to Transoxiana, then finally moving east to Inner Asia and to Ming China. Again, it is not possible to do justice to all of the complicated political dynamics across Asia in the sixteenth century or even to mention all the key political players by name. My goal in this section therefore is to highlight the ways Chinggisid and/or Timurid legacies were still alive throughout the continent and the nodes of interaction between the world order of the millennial sovereigns in west Asia and the rest of Asia. On this side, we have a number of houses that could be even more easily grouped together with the millennial sovereigns discussed in Chapter 4.

'Post-Chinggisid' Rise of Muscovy

Readers will recall from Chapter 2 that the territory that is now called Russia was under the control of the Jochid branch of the Chinggisid (the Golden Horde).[76] However, the Jochids, unlike the Ilkhanate in Persia or the Yuan in China, did not eventually assimilate into the local culture, preferring to rule Russian[77] towns from a distance, as

---

[75] Krstić (2013); also Tezcan (2010).
[76] Sometimes also called the Kipchak Khanate. For relations of the Rus to the Golden Horde until independence, see Ostrowski (2002).
[77] Neumann and Wigen (2019, chapter 4) argue that the influence of the steppe on the Rus polity well predates the arrival of the Chinggisid. Ostrowski (2012) observes that Sneath's (2007) characterisation of Mongol succession applies equally well to the early Rus.

vassals.[78] This governance choice strengthened Muscovy over other principalities as they collected tribute and taxes in the name of the khan.[79] The Golden Horde was also the most durable of the Chinggisid khanates, but their power over Muscovy had started fading after the Timurid invasions in the early fifteenth century. For Muscovy, the fifteenth century was a period of political consolidation (under Rurik dynasty) and territorial expansion, though of a more modest scale compared to what would come later. In 1480, Muscovy defeated the forces of the Golden Horde definitively at the 'Great Stand on the Ugra River' and shook off its vassal status. After that point, the Rurikids too would chase dreams of universal sovereignty.

There are many similarities between the Russian and Ottoman time-lines.[80] Ivan III (the Great; r. 1462–1505), who oversaw Muscovy's independence, was, like his near-contemporary Mehmed II (the Conqueror; r. 1444–6, 1451–81), a centraliser, taking considerable amount of power from established families, boyars[81] and princes (and even repossessing his own brothers' lands). He defeated the Republic of Novgorod to the north, an area that had not been fully under control of the Golden Horde, and annexed other significant cities such as Tver and Rostow.[82] Especially after 1480, he experimented with calling himself Tsar (Caesar) and Muscovy the Third Rome, just as Mehmed II had experimented with similar titles after the conquest of Constantinople. He was married to Sophia Palaiologa, the niece of the last Byzantine emperor, a match made by the pope, who, along with the Holy Roman emperor, hoped for Muscovy's help against the Ottomans to the south.[83] But Muscovy did not yet have the military power to challenge the Ottomans.

---

[78] The relationship also extended to the Russian church: 'a number of *iarlyks* or charters given by various Tatar khans ... based ... on the tradition established by the law code of Chingiz-khan himself ... [placed] the Russian church ... under the immediate jurisdiction of the khan-tsar, retaining a universal rather than a national-territorial character under a ruler of many states and peoples. In return for all these privileges the church had but one duty-to pray for the khan' (Cherniavsky 1959, p. 467).

[79] Halperin (2019, p. 15).   [80] See also Neumann and Wigen (2018).

[81] 'The boyars, from approximately twenty to forty families, constituted the upper elite' (Halperin 2019, p. 19). 'The ruler called his boyars his "slaves"' (Halperin 2019, p. 27).

[82] This is not unlike the Ottoman conquest of Anatolia, though the territory is larger, if less densely populated.

[83] Halperin (2019, p. 17).

It was Ivan III's grandson Ivan IV (the Terrible [or Fearsome]; r. 1533–84) – and not his son and immediate successor Vasily III (r. 1505–33) – who pushed these universal sovereignty claims to their limit. But Vasily played his part as well. It was during his reign that the title Tsar[84] was officially adopted by the House of Rurik, and Philotheos of Pskov explicitly articulated the 'Third Rome' argument.[85] The first two Romes – Rome and Constantinople – had fallen due to betraying the true Christian faith: 'This left the Russian Orthodox Church as the only true and direct heir, with its centre in the blessed city of Moscow, the city where the holy Virgin Mary had died.'[86] It was also claimed that the House of Rurik had descended from Emperor Augustus of Rome and had been also blessed by the Byzantine emperor in the twelfth century.[87] Vasily expanded Muscovy's control over the remaining cities of Rus and took Smolensk from the Lithuanians; he also actively meddled in the affairs of the khanates to the south, especially that of Kazan.[88]

Inner Asia, Still an Order of Chinggisid Khanates

Let's pause here and note that much of the territory to the south and east of Muscovy in the Pontic-Caspian steppes, territory that used to be controlled by the Golden Horde had come to be claimed in the fifteenth century by smaller 'khanates'. In fact, what could be called the khanate belt of Asia (i.e. the remnants of earlier Chinggisid khanates) extended all the way from Crimea to the boundaries of the Ming realm, flanking also (and thus connecting) the Ottomans, the Safavids and the Mughals to the south and an expanding Muscovy to the north. In this middle part of Asia, the Chinggisid and Timurid sovereignty models still ruled the day, even if in an only aspirational sense, and perhaps in an even 'purer' form than the empires we discussed in the previous chapter, who had hybridised it via cross-fertilisation of other cultural repertoires.[89] Some of the ruling houses of these lesser khanates were not necessarily Chinggisid in lineage, but Genghis Khan's world conqueror

[84] As well the double-headed eagle.   [85] Halperin (2019, p. 45).
[86] Koenigsberger, Mosse, and Bowler (2014, p. 249).   [87] Ibid.
[88] Halperin (2019, p. 17).
[89] For example, Rome in the case of the Ottomans; Hindu traditions in the case of the Mughals etc.

charisma still lingered in a powerful way, and houses would claim relations to him when they could.

The Uzbek Khanate[90] has already made some appearances in the previous chapter as a threat to the Timurid/Mughals as well the Safavids. The Shaybanids who ruled it were one of the greater houses of Inner Asia in the sixteenth century, and they were related to the Jochid branch of the Chinggisids (the Golden Horde). There is an argument to be made that the Shaybanids should have been discussed in the previous chapter on post-Timurid sovereignty, as they were very much part of the ecumene, but for our purposes here it is also fine to think of them as yet another Chinggisid link in the sixteenth-century chain of millennial sovereigns with world-ordering ambitions. Transoxiana, where the Uzbeks were located, was deeply connected to both Persia and India via various land and sea routes; as we saw in Chapter 3, Samarkand and Bukhara were trade centres for goods going from east to west, but they were also centres for Indian merchants from the south looking to trade with the north.[91] Indian merchants brought textiles from as far as Bengal and Gujarat, and these goods made their way from Transoxiana to the Safavids and the Ottomans as well.[92] Additional trade items included spices, sugar, precious stones, animals and slaves, such as Indian stonemasons.[93] In return, horses, fruits and fur were imported from Transoxiana back into India.[94] The horse trade was so valuable that horse traders in the subcontinent often had political power: for example, the Lodi and the Sur challengers of the Mughals.[95] The trade between India and Transoxiana as facilitated by the Mughals[96] and others, including by road building, allowed the considerable development of the northern Indian economy in the sixteenth century: 'The entire area then came to be linked, on the one hand, to India's eastern and western seashores, while opening up, on the other, to Central Asia and Persia through Kabul and Qandahar.'[97] Urban centres began to grow as well as emerge: the expansion of Lahore is a good example. Yet it was not just the

---

[90] See Subrahmanyam (2000), who considers them the fourth corner of a square made up also of the Ottomans, the Mughals and the Safavid.

[91] Representatives of the Muscovy company (discussed later) also made their way here. Jenkinson (1886).

[92] Alam (1994, p. 206).

[93] By the eighteenth century, most Indian slaves were replaced by African slaves in Central Asian markets.

[94] Ibid., p. 208.   [95] Ibid., p. 210.   [96] See also Rossabi (2014a, p. 208).

[97] Alam (1994, p. 221).

north: 'the production centres of almost the entire subcontinent were involved in this trade and ... the merchants from Central Asia – Khrusan, *Mawara al-Nahr* [Transoxiana] and Turkistan – reached as far south as "Malibar"'.[98] By the sixteenth century, economic production was in line with the demand from Transoxiana as well as Persia. As for Persia, trade between the Uzbeks and the Safavids continued even in times of animosity: 'they regularly informed each other of the details of their caravans to ensure appropriate protection in each other's territory'.[99] Uzbek, Safavid and Mughal rulers were all keen to encourage trade and to participate in it.[100]

To the east of the Uzbeks and to the west of the Ming, we can point to yet others as part of the same chain of khanates linking northern, western and eastern Asia as an ecumene, such as Dayan Khan (r. 1479–1517), a descendant of Kubilai Khan who fashioned himself the Great Khan of the Yuan Dynasty, or his grandson Altan Khan (r. 1542–82),[101] who united the western Mongol houses.[102] As discussed in Chapter 3, the claims of these neighbouring khans to be 'Great Khan' presented a legitimacy challenge as well as a military threat to the Ming. Yet the Mongols were also rather keen on trading with the Ming – as always, they wanted Chinese silk and the Ming needed horses. Altan Khan's raids in 1542 were in part a response to his tributary overtures being rejected.[103] In 1550, the Ming 'finally made a concession by permitting a border trade in Mongol horses and Chinese silk'[104] but revoked it soon after when the Mongols requested grain, which the Ming feared was intended for Chinese defectors on the Mongol side.[105] Altan Khan's raids continued until 1571, when a settlement was reached, and trade markets were permitted.[106]

Ming (2.0) in the Sixteenth Century

Having mentioned the Ming, let's also take a moment to bring them into the sixteenth-century timeline. As noted in Chapter 3, the Yuan

---

[98] Ibid., p. 225.   [99] Ibid., p. 215.
[100] Ibid., p. 218. This is also in keeping with the Chinggisid norms.
[101] See Rossabi (1987).
[102] Or even Nurhaci (r. 1616–26), the founder of the Qing Dynasty.
[103] Rossabi (2014b, p. 162).   [104] Ibid., p. 163.
[105] The fact of Chinese defectors on the Mongol side once again points to the connectivity of these realms.
[106] Ibid., p. 164.

Dynasty's Chinggisid influences on the Ming Dynasty rulers had slowly faded in the second half of the fifteenth century, and the Ming Dynasty 2.0 was much more isolationist, at least in ideology, if not always in practice. Neo-Confucian bureaucrats had increasingly gained power vis-à-vis the emperors, considerably limiting their room for manoeuvre and thus their sovereign prerogative[107] (at least as compared to the Yuan and the early Ming period).

It bears pointing out, however, that not all sixteenth-century Ming emperors fit this isolationist mould. A notable exception was Zhengde (r. 1505–21), who challenged the very stylised rituals he found himself entangled in when ascended to the throne. He started openly contesting them. In 1508, he moved out of his palace quarters. He sought the company of 'eunuchs, courtesans, Lamaist monks, and magicians from other lands'.[108] In a manner reminiscent of the early Ming (and Yuan) emperors, he loved hunting and field exercises with his battalion of mounted archers. A 1517 incursion into the northern frontier by Batu Mengke Khan gave Zhengde the opportunity to go into the field, despite great opposition from the establishment: 'an imperial censor overseeing the defense on the Great Wall refused to let emperor go beyond the barrier, as he had no business there', so Zhengde removed him from his position.[109] When Zhengde returned from the field, he held triumphant celebrations, though the members of Hanlin Academy and state officials refused to congratulate him.[110] This did not stop Zhengde from going on a second campaign in 1519 for nine months; in fact, in order to overcome the bureaucratic opposition, he proclaimed himself 'Grand Preceptor, and thus the senior civil official of his own court, outranking all ministers and grand-secretaries'.[111] When officials petitioned against the campaign, he 'retaliated by giving the order that the 146 demonstrators be beaten with whipping clubs for thirty strokes each'.[112] Zhengde died unexpectedly in 1521, at the age of thirty. Having no children, he was succeeded by his cousin, the Jiajing Emperor (r. 1521–67), who, despite a strong centralising move in the beginning of his reign,[113] checked out of ruling altogether after he

---

[107] Yet another version of the competing sovereignty models tension. The diagnosis about Ming decline was also very similar to those discussed in the previous chapter.

[108] Huang (1982, p. 96). See also Geiss (1988).   [109] Huang (1982, p. 97).

[110] Ibid.   [111] Ibid., p. 98.   [112] Ibid., p. 99.

[113] The 'Great Rites controversy'. See, for example, Dardess (2016).

survived an assassination attempt by his concubines in 1542. He had built a new residence, and he pursued Daoist alchemy to prolong his life.

It is interesting to question what direction the Ming would have gone in had Zhengde not passed away prematurely. By his time, the Ming Dynasty notion of sovereignty had evolved such that the 'character and personality [of the emperor] must be hidden behind the image of the Son of Heaven', yet Zhengde managed to separate 'himself as an individual from the monarchy as an institution ... disrupted the standing practice of the bureaucracy'.[114] The steps he took to make the monarchy more independent (or more centralised) alienated his officials. As a latter-day Ming emperor, Zhengde's choices are often attributed to his youth and the appeal of military pursuits over staid bureaucracy, but, as we have discussed in Chapter 3, this Chinggisid-inflected understanding of sovereignty had been celebrated in the early Ming Dynasty. Perhaps the memory of it was not completely forgotten. When Emperor Wanli (r. 1572–1620) came to the throne, officials worried about him going a similar way to Zhengde, but he 'lacked the physical courage, exuberance, and aggressiveness of his granduncle',[115] and his reign became marked by his passivity instead.

There is an inherent tension between the Chinggisid mode of sovereign practice of centralised, personalised control of the realm versus the increased bureaucratisation of the state that happens over time, especially if the latter supports power-holders whose authority is justified with respect to other sets of legitimising principles (neo-Confucianism in the case of the Ming). Suffice it to say that Ming China, despite its official isolationism, remained loosely linked to our ecumene for a couple of reasons: first, its main foreign policy concerns were the Mongol khans active on its north-eastern frontiers (one of which was about to take over and establish the Qing Dynasty); and second, because its Yuan legacy, though much faded, had not entirely disappeared in the sixteenth century. Furthermore, the realm did not shut down to trade and tribute: the activities of Europeans taking advantage of the loophole in Macau in the sixteenth century are better studied,[116] but the Ming never fully stopped trading with (or accepting 'tribute' from) Inner Asia either,[117]

---

[114] Ibid., p. 100.   [115] Ibid., p. 102.   [116] Brook (2019).
[117] There is less research on this, but Chinese-Indian trade had a long history and no doubt it continued in this period. See, for example, Sen (2014).

even if they did not always document it. Even wars did not disrupt the trade for very long periods.[118]

Ivan IV, the Tsar of Rus

Turning back to Muscovy, in the sixteenth century the immediate threat was from the neighbouring khanates: Crimea, Kazan, Astrakhan and Sibir, as well the nomadic Nogai who frequently raided Muscovite territory and took slaves.[119] In the previous chapter, we saw that the Crimean Khanate under House of Giray were allied to the Ottomans. During Vasily's reign, Muscovy managed to install a puppet ruler in the Kazan khanate, but the Girays intervened, took control of Kazan and sacked Muscovy in retaliation in 1521, forcing Vasily to retreat. Though not as powerful as the Shaybanids, the Girays also fit the mould of ambitious houses operating in the sixteenth-century Chinggisid ecumene. Mehmed Giray I (r. 1515–23) entertained dreams of reuniting Crimea, Kazan, Astrakhan and the Nogai. When he died, his brother Sahib Giray (r. 1532–51), who had been briefly installed the Khan of Kazan, became the Crimean Khan.[120] The alliance with the Ottomans remained tight.[121] In the meantime, the Safavids were exploring the possibility of alliance with Muscovy against the Ottomans. Kazan and Astrakhan were to be conquered later by Ivan IV (the Terrible [or Fearsome]; r. 1533–84), in 1552 and 1556 respectively.

Ivan IV became the ruler of the Grand Duchy of Muscovy when he was three years old. The story of his regency period carries echoes of others we have discussed. Ivan III's father, Vasily II (the Blind; r. 1425–72), who also acceded to the throne as a minor, had faced a serious sovereignty challenge from his uncles, creating essentially a civil war that lasted almost thirty years (1425–53). Different sides even appealed to the Golden Horde for intervention and support. Vasily lost power for intervals and was even blinded by his rival cousin, but he managed to reclaim the throne, making his son Ivan III a co-ruler to

---

[118] Rossabi (2014b, p. 165).   [119] Halperin (2019, p. 16).
[120] Inalcik (1979).
[121] See Chapter 4. See also Karateke (2019), who demonstrates that Crimean khans were treated much better than those from other tributary states in Ottoman protocol well into the eighteenth century due to their Chinggisid lineage.

compensate for his own disability. It should be obvious to the reader by now that this war between uncles, nephews and cousins carried echoes of the Chinggisid institution of tanistry,[122] versions of which we have seen in many other contexts (even the early Ming). Once the dust settled, collateral succession was abandoned, and 'brothers and nephews of the grand prince of Moscow became holders of appanages, hereditary semiautonomous domains with their own institutions',[123] another Chinggisid practice, though in modified form here. These appanage princes became a major threat during Ivan's regency.[124]

Yet Ivan survived; he was declared the Tsar of Rus when he was sixteen, in 1547. As noted, this title was derived from the Byzantine model: 'The Rus' translated the Byzantine title *Basileus* as "tsar" … The Muscovites understood the universal aspirations of the title "basileus".'[125] Yet Ivan did not use the 'Third Rome' concept.[126] Ivan's coronation featured Monomakh's Cap – yet another notable headgear in our narrative – 'supposedly given to Ivan's ancestor Vladimir Monomakh by the Byzantine emperor Constantine Monomachos in the twelfth century'.[127] In reality, this cap likely had Central Asian origins.[128] Yet another lineage that was claimed was from the Kievan rulers St. Vladimir and Vladimir Monomakh. In all these hybrid ways of justifying a highly centralised form of sovereignty, he fits the post-Chinggisid pattern of rulers in this book. As tsar, Ivan felt himself 'superior to almost all contemporary rulers, especially those who ascended the throne via election'[129] and he did not at all think that Europe was better than Muscovy.[130] Ivan's long reign indeed overlapped with the other would-be universal sovereigns with long reigns that we have discussed, such as Süleyman the Magnificent (r. 1521–66), Charles V (r. 1519–56) and Akbar the Great (r. 1562 – 1605), and it's likely that he harboured similar ambitions.

Ivan IV led an ambitious military campaign in the West, fighting a long and ultimately unproductive war against a coalition Denmark, Sweden, Poland-Lithuania and the Hanseatic League over the control of Livonia (present-day Baltic states). In Western accounts, it is the Livonian War that gets most of the attention in terms of Ivan IV's foreign policy. It is true that Poland-Lithuania, under the control of

---

[122] See also Neumann and Wigen (2018, p. 177). [123] Halperin (2019, p. 18).
[124] Ibid., p. 32. [125] Ibid., p. 46 [126] Ibid. [127] Ibid., p. 47 [128] Ibid.
[129] Ibid., p. 44. [130] Ibid., p. 151.

the Catholic Jagiellonian Dynasty, was the main sixteenth-century rival of the rising Muscovy *to the West*. However, from the perspective of sixteenth-century Muscovy, the annexation of Kazan and Astrakhan (as well as further expansion into Siberia) would likely have balanced some of the disappointment from the Livonian War. We have to remember that, until the fifteenth century, the main threat to Muscovy had come from this direction. More importantly, conquering Kazan and Astrakhan allowed Ivan to become 'khan' himself,[131] even if he did not use that title openly.

Second, the Astrakhan Khanate, which sat at the mouth of the Volga, was an important trading city for commodities such as astrakhan fur,[132] honey, fish, salt and wax, as well as Indian spices and Iranian silk.[133] But even more significantly, the Astrakhan Khanate – like the Crimean Khanate – was home to one of the largest slave markets in the region, if not the world. Slaves were captured in war or in raids from surrounding areas all the way to Finland. Female slaves were many times more expensive than male slaves, and in general slaves were more valuable commodity than most others.[134] All of the neighbouring states (e.g. initially Byzantium, later the Ottomans, the Safavids and Muscovy)[135] participated in the slave trade. And this regional slave trade lasted for centuries, though its effects are very understudied. For our purposes here, let us conclude by noting that expansion into Kazan and especially Astrakhan would have been both symbolically and economically important for Muscovy.

Ivan IV is not known necessarily for the success of his foreign campaigns, however, but rather for his 'domestic' ones. Most notorious of these was the period the *oprichnina* (1565–72), which took place well into Ivan's reign, during the aforementioned Livonian War. In 1564, Ivan engineered a situation where he first left Moscow and then agreed to return only on the condition that he be allowed to establish 'a separate realm in which only his authority obtained' (i.e. *oprichnina*) and where he 'would create a personal corps of servitors and bodyguards'.[136] Areas outside this zone were expected to fund its

[131] Ibid., p. 45.
[132] This is a type of fur made from baby lambs, sometimes cut from their mother's womb. In the West it was especially popular in Victorian times, and it is still used in the region.
[133] Ibid., p. 148.   [134] See Kołodziejczyk (2006).   [135] Stanziani (2014).
[136] Ibid., p. 168.

operations. Once it was established, Ivan started eliminating the boyars as well as religious figures who challenged him, often by trumped-up charges.[137] In 1569, he moved against the north-western cities such as Tver and Novgorod, incorporated into the realm under Ivan III and Vasily. Novgorod received a particularly brutal treatment, subjected to massacres, tortures and looting for weeks, with surrounding fields burned. The city never fully recovered.

At the same time, Ivan was facing a threat from his southern flank, as the Crimean Khanate, with the support of the Ottomans, attempted to retake Astrakhan in 1569. In 1571, the Crimean forces (including Ottoman reinforcements) under the control of Devlet Giray (r. 1551–77) reached Moscow, raiding and burning the city, causing great damage as well as loss of life. Ivan's forces managed to defeat the Crimean forces next year at the Battle of Molodi when they attempted a similar raid.[138]

In 1572, Ivan IV abandoned *oprichnina* and turned his efforts into uncovering the 'pro-Crimean conspiracy', targetting Muscovy nobility suspected of having sympathies for the khanate.[139] This is of course evidence of Ivan's growing paranoia, but the fact that it was plausible gives us hints of the degree to which Muscovite nobility had intermarried with Chinggisid lineages.[140] Another interesting figure in this period was Elijah Bomel, or Eliseus Bomelus, who was either from Holland or Westphalia and was educated at Cambridge University. He was a physician but also a humanist and astrologer (or a magician, according to some). He was arrested in England due to opposition from the London College of Physicians, but, hearing his reputation, the Russian ambassador sought and gained permission to take him to Muscovy. Once there, Bomel quickly made a fortune as an advisor during the *oprichnina*.[141] He may have been the first person to introduce Ivan to astrology. Later Russian historiography saw Ivan's dabbling in astrology and the occult[142] as more evidence of his psychological deficiencies that led to the terror of *oprichnina*, but we can posit other explanations: as we saw in the previous chapter, in the sixteenth century astrology and occult sciences played a role similar to

---

[137] Ibid., p. 169. He had the metropolitan strangled.   [138] Ibid.
[139] Skrynnikov (2015, p. 452).
[140] Many nobles were of mixed heritage. See Cherniavsky (1959); Ostrowski (2012).
[141] Skrynnikov (2015, p. 451).   [142] Ryan (2012).

what political science does today in both studying but also legitimating sovereign power.

All the rulers dreaming of world empire that we discussed in Chapter 4 had astrologers (or astronomers) and other occultists in their courts. It would be more surprising, therefore, if an aspirant to universal sovereignty such as Ivan seems to have been had also not latched onto an astrologer, especially one such as Elijah Bomel. Bomel was peddling cyclical theories about eclipses and conjunctions which sound suspiciously similar to the conjunction astrology underwriting the millennial sovereignty projects discussed in Chapter 4. Bomel's writings have been lost, and very little of the research into Ivan's turn to the occult takes it seriously as a political act, but given Bomel's continental background, he might even have had access to the Eastern occult books circulating in Europe at the time. Given the growing rivalry between Muscovy and the Ottomans, not to mention the connections to the Safavids, it would also be unusual if Ivan IV had not been exposed at all to notions of *sahibkıran* and millennial sovereignty by this point, but on that score I can only speculate. Let's observe that most contemporaries noted Ivan's erudition and book knowledge.[143] Ivan's relation to occultists seems more similar to his European than his Asian counterparts, however, in the sense that he both consulted and also persecuted them.[144] Bomel fell out of favour and was accused of conspiracy. After being severely tortured, he implicated many boyars and died in the dungeons.[145] The Russian public did not know Bomel had died and believed him to be behind the executions of the boyars.[146]

Ivan's solution to deal with the 'Crimean conspiracy' was to abdicate in favour of the Tatar nobleman Simeon Bekbulatovich, who was given the title 'Grand Prince of All Rus' but not tsar.[147] (Simeon Bekbulatovich was also Tatar nobility, a descendant of Genghis Khan in fact.) Ivan, now as the Prince Ivan Vasil'evich of Moscow, petitioned Simeon, in effect asking for permission (or declaring) to resurrect the *oprichnina*.[148] This allowed him to confiscate more territory, especially that of the church. A large number of executions also took place, directed at the nobility.[149] This second *oprichnina* targeted nobles

---

[143] Skrynnikov (2015, p. 465). There is, however, some debate among historians as to how Muscovite culture in the sixteenth century should be characterised. See Halperin (1974).

[144] Ryan (2012, p. 25). [145] Ibid., p. 454. [146] Ibid., p. 452.

[147] Ibid., p. 455. [148] Ibid., p. 457. [149] Ibid., p. 460.

who had been elevated into the vacancies created by the first one. In 1576, Ivan told the English ambassador that he could resume office if he wished to do so because Simeon had not been crowned.[150] At the same time, Ivan IV was negotiating with the English ambassador the possibility of taking refuge there.[151] The second *oprichnina* came to an end at the end of 1576; Simeon was demoted to be the grand prince of Tver. Ivan would stay in power for nearly another decade. In 1581, he accidentally killed his son Ivan, leaving the mentally deficient Fyodor as his only heir.

Ivan the Terrible as a Chinggisid Sovereign?

Ivan IV is many ways comparable to the rulers we have discussed previously. Yet his reign also had many distinct features specific to the Russian context. Like others we have discussed, he was an almost unstoppable centraliser; after the two periods of *oprichnina*, there was hardly anyone left to resist him: '"I think that even the Turk is not obeyed as the Muscovite is, because he is a great tyrant," wrote a Venetian envoy.'[152] Yet in emphasising Ivan's power, we should not overlook the fact that he had to concoct excuses and pretences to get what he wanted. For instance, in the first *oprichnina*, he had to pretend to abdicate and get the regular people on his side to pressure the boyars and the metropolitan to accept his demands. This suggests that absolute power was not assumed to be natural in the Russian context; to the contrary, princes, boyars and even the Church – not to mention other cities such as Novgorod – had considerable independent authority in Russia at the time Ivan came to power. The idea that absolutism or autocracy comes naturally to Russians is as false as the idea that it comes naturally to Muslim societies.

The fact that the Russian timeline for centralisation followed the Ottomans closely is also unlikely to be an accident. In fact, Neumann and Wigen argue that Muscovy was borrowing from the Ottoman model in the sixteenth century. There were a number of texts petitioning Ivan IV to copy the Ottomans' 'superior political organisation'.[153] So while Ivan IV is often compared to Henry VIII of England (r. 1509–47) or Gustav Vasa of Sweden (r. 1523–60) by European historians, he

---

[150] Ibid., p. 456.   [151] Ibid., pp. 463–4.   [152] Ibid., p. 466.
[153] Neumann and Wigen (2018, p. 196); for a review of changes proposed, see pp. 196–8. Ostrowski (1992) argues that elements of the land-grant system were borrowed from the south.

really should also be understood in the larger context of the post-
Chinggisid millennial sovereigns of the last chapter: Süleyman I of the
Ottomans, Ismail I of the Safavids or Akbar of the Mughals. This is not
to say, of course, that comparison to European rulers is totally wrong.
As the Bomel episode demonstrates, Muscovy was connected to Europe
in the sixteenth century. However, the preceding discussion should also
have made clear that sixteenth-century Muscovy was part of a much
larger world – it was not *just* on the periphery of Europe. It had rivalries
with Poland-Lithuania (as well the Nordic kingdoms) but also with the
Ottoman Empire. It had alliances with the pope but also with the
Safavids. The post–Golden Horde khanates were an important factor
in Muscovy's calculations well, and Moscow society included nobles of
Tatar (Mongol) descent (who had converted to Christianity).[154]

It is not straightforward to ascertain to what extent the developments in
Muscovy in the sixteenth century were linked to the legacy of the
Chinggisid, post-Chinggisid and post-Timurid ecumene. That is partly
because unlike, say, the Mughals, after independence from Golden
Horde, Russian historiography denied[155] that Muscovy owed anything
to the Mongols, characterising the Golden Horde period as 'the Tatar
Yoke',[156] seeing this as a period of disruption in the natural course of
Russian history. Russia was more explicitly understood as an heir to the
Byzantine Empire. However, for those who could read between the lines,
the Chinggisid influence was definitely there. Muscovite rulers did not
start calling themselves 'tsar' immediately after the fall of Constantinople
and the death of the last 'basileus' in 1453. The title was not even officially
adopted until 1547.[157] Cherniavsky argues that this was because during
the 'Tatar Yoke' the khan came to replace the basileus in the Russian
imagination. The two concepts of universal sovereignty (i.e. Roman-
Christian and the Chinggisid) merged within the Russian context.
Russian princes stopped minting coins during the Golden Horde period;
this activity was resumed in the fifteenth century, but the early coins had
on the one side 'the name of the reigning khan, sometimes accompanied by

---

[154] Cherniavsky (1959, p. 474). He notes this continued until the nineteenth
century.
[155] On this point, see Halperin (1987); Neumann and Wigen (2018, pp. 191–2).
This is a bit reminiscent of the Ming (who did not deny the Yuan but
assimilated them into the historiography, which is also similar to how eastern
sources were Latinised during the Renaissance).
[156] Cherniavsky (1959).   [157] Ibid., p. 463.

the slogan: "May he live long".[158] After independence, new coins appeared, with the khan replaced by an inscription that declared Ivan III 'Sovereign of all Russia'.[159] To put another way, having lived under Jochid control for more than 200 years, Russians' understanding of sovereignty and its symbols was inevitably transformed by the Chinggisid tradition. The references to basileus allowed independent rulers of Muscovy from Ivan III onward to claim the universal sovereignty mantle via an alternative path while there were still others khans who also could claim it via their Chinggisid pedigree. After Ivan IV conquered Kazan and Astrakhan, he had yet another justification for his claim to be a Great Khan.[160] Muscovy also used Chinggisid practices in its diplomacy, especially in its communications with the Ottomans.[161]

Muscovy: A Post-Chinggisid (or Post-Timurid) State?

In sum, it is not hard to make the case of Chinggisid influence on Muscovy and Russia, even though such influences were downplayed after the fall of the Golden Horde. Muscovy's trajectory was a bit different from the post-Timurid empires we discussed in Chapter 4, however. They had inherited the Chinggisid legacy by way of the Jochid khanate (Golden Horde), the Chinggisid branch that became autonomous before the other three, and also the branch that waged war on the Ilkhanate, the precursor of the Timurids. For that reason, Muscovy's path was also a separate one from the empires of (south-)west Asia.

The Timurid and post-Timurid space there was a product of the fusion of the Islamic Persianate world with the Ilkhanate and the Chagataid legacies. Timur's campaigns did move north as well: Timur's forces defeated Toqtamish Khan numerous times and essentially caused the fragmentation of the Golden Horde. It is possible therefore that Timurid influences could have spread northward with these campaigns just as they did to Ottomans in the south. The Timurid influence on the latter was less due to battlefield interaction, however, and more by way of artisans, scholars, Sufi dervishes and other occultists who moved to the Ottoman realm as the power of the Timurid Empire waned. Could some of these types have made their way north? When Timur sacked Sarai (capital of the Golden Horde), he took craftsmen back with him to Samarkand. Some of

---

[158] Ibid., p. 469.   [159] Ibid.   [160] Ibid, p. 473.
[161] Halperin (1987, p. 92), as also quoted by Neumann and Wigen (2018, p. 193).

the descendants of these craftsmen (and others) could have returned, if not to Muscovy, then to the neighbouring khanates which later were absorbed by Muscovy. Finally, there is the occult sciences connection discussed previously: many sources note the popularity of the occult arts in Muscovy and Ivan's court in the sixteenth century, but Russian historiography on this subject is rather old-fashioned. The prevailing assumption seems to be that Russian interest in the occult was an even more primitive version of what was going on in Europe, rather than the more plausible explanation of Muscovy's participation in much larger sixteenth-century ecumene about millennial sovereignty as a rising house. We will have to wait for more research on the subject.

As far as the trajectory of political centralisation goes, it is true that in intervening years, especially in the twentieth century, the autocratic tradition in Russia has been blamed on Mongol influence on Russian society. It is indeed hard to argue that there was not a type of Chinggisid sovereignty model at play in sixteenth-century Muscovy.[162] However, that does not that the Mongols are 'to blame' for Russian autocracy.[163] As noted in Chapter 1, there are would-be centralisers and resisters in every society, aided or hindered both by structural conditions (of which deep normative repertoires are a part) and existing institutions. Throughout this book, we have seen that centralisation around a supreme political authority was favoured by the various iterations of the Chinggisid ecumene, so we do find this pattern over and over in areas that were under the control of the Chinggisid or one of their successor states, at least initially. Sixteenth-century Russia does fit this pattern as well.

However, not all of what Ivan IV did could be laid at the feet of the influence of the Chinggisid ecumene. There is no parallel episode to *oprichnina* in any of the other successor states. In conjuring up a *state of exception*, Ivan IV seems to have been a political innovator on the same level as Ismail I (or even Genghis Khan). Furthermore, compared to their Chinggisid and post-Timurid counterparts, Muscovite rulers were much less tolerant of religious differences. In annexing various khanates and expanding eastward, Muscovy, like the Ottomans and the

---

[162] See also Ostrowski (1990, 2012).
[163] The idea that Russians (as a white, therefore Western people) were doomed forever by their medieval association with the Mongols (an Asiatic, Eastern people) to autocracy is a stigmatising construct I criticised in my first book; see Zarakol (2011, chapter 5). As noted already, even among the Mongols, the Chinggisid model alternates with periods of decentralisation.

Mughals, came to rule over large swaths of population who were not Christian: 'The Tatars in Kazan and the volatile nomadic Nogai Tatar hordes adhered to Islam, and many of the Finnic and Ugric ethnic groups living along the middle Volga River practiced animism.'[164] Yet in Russian discourse this was framed as a Christian victory over Islam, and houses of worship were taken down. Jews had it even worse: 'When a Muscovite army conquered Polotsk, [Ivan] ordered the drowning of all Jews who refused to convert.'[165] These attitudes were much more in keeping with the European Christian ethos at the time (with the possible exception of Poland) than they were with the post-Timurid empires.

Fragmentation of the Sixteenth-Century Order

To sum up, the sovereignty model diffused by the empire of Genghis Khan in the thirteenth century was still giving shape to projects of world ordering in the sixteenth century. At the core of the sixteenth-century world order were the millennial sovereigns of west Asia: the Ottomans, the Safavids, the Mughals. Europe was filled with ambitious houses, but in the sixteenth century only the Habsburgs could rival the post-Timurid Great Houses of west Asia. Meanwhile, much of the rest of Asia also still carried various Chinggisid legacies. In Transoxiana, the Uzbeks were another post-Timurid house with ambitions just as great. In the north, having finally gained its independence from the Golden Horde in the previous century, Muscovy was chasing similar dreams. And in the east, the Ming Dynasty still carried some traces of the Chinggisid ecumene and remained linked into it via its Inner Asian neighbours.[166] When I look at the sixteenth century, I do not see a world order of Europeans originating from the West[167] but rather an 'Eastern' world order of 'Asians' and 'Eurasians', beaming (for better or worse) with the activity and promise of universal empire projects (see Figure 5.1). So what happened to that order?

---

[164] Halperin (2019, p. 53).   [165] Ibid.
[166] This is not to deny that the Ming were part of other dynamics as well, for example including the Joseon Dynasty in Korea or the *daimyo* in Japan. For more on regional dynamics in Asia, see Kang (2010). The account I have given in the book inevitably leaves out a lot of Asian history.
[167] It is true that, in the same century, Portuguese and Spanish excursions had started to reach around the world via maritime connections (to Africa, Asia and the Americas). It does bear remembering, however, that European presence in any of these geographies, and especially Asia, remained limited until at least the next century and even later.

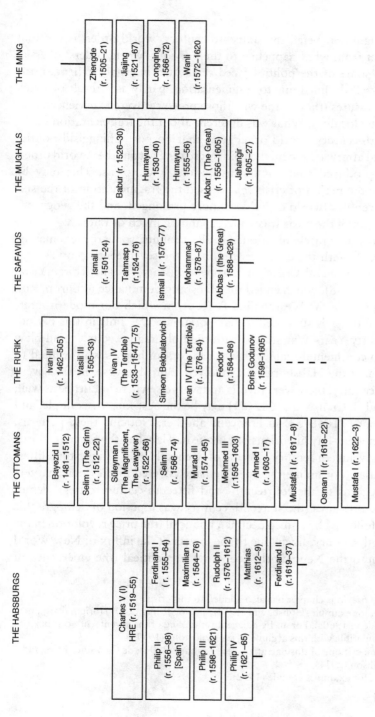

Figure 5.1 A Eurasian world

THE HABSBURGS

Charles V (I)
HRE (r. 1519–55)

Ferdinand I
(r. 1555–64)

Maximilian II
(r. 1564–76)

Rudolph II
(r. 1576–1612)

Matthias
(r. 1612–9)

Ferdinand II
(r. 1619–37)

Philip II
(r. 1556–98)
[Spain]

Philip III
(r. 1598–1621)

Philip IV
(r. 1621–65)

THE OTTOMANS

Bayezid II
(r. 1481–1512)

Selim I (The Grim)
(r. 1512–22)

Süleyman I
(The Magnificent,
The Lawgiver)
(r. 1522–66)

Selim II
(r. 1566–74)

Murad III
(r. 1574–95)

Mehmed III
(r.1595–1603)

Ahmed I
(r. 1603–17)

Mustafa I (r. 1617–8)

Osman II (r. 1618–22)

Mustafa I (r. 1622–3)

THE RURIK

Ivan III
(r. 1462–505)

Vasili III
(r. 1505–33)

Ivan IV
(The Terrible)
(r. 1533–[1547]–75)

Simeon Bekbulatovich

Ivan IV (The Terrible)
(r. 1576–84)

Feodor I
(r.1584–98)

Boris Godunov
(r. 1598–1605)

THE SAFAVIDS

Ismail I
(r. 1501–24)

Tahmasp I
(r.1524–76)

Ismail II (r. 1576–77)

Mohammad
(r. 1578–87)

Abbas I (the Great)
(r. 1588–629)

THE MUGHALS

Babur (r. 1526–30)

Humayun
(r. 1530–40)

Humayun
(r. 1555–56)

Akbar I (The Great)
(r. 1556–1605)

Jahangir
(r. 1605–27)

THE MING

Zhengde
(r. 1505–21)

Jiajing
(r. 1521–67)

Longqing
(r. 1566–72)

Wanli
(r.1572–1620)

The fate that befell the sixteenth-century 'world order' is not that different from what happened to the previous 'world orders' of Asia. Just as some of the polities faced their own internal challenges, the order itself declined due to fragmentation, partly as a result of structural pressures (though the way those pressures were experienced also varied by locality). What was different about the fragmentation of the sixteenth-century 'world order' was that no post-Chinggisid polities emerged afterwards to fill the void by creating yet another 'world order' that reproduced some of its institutions and norms. This may be because the period of crisis that caused the fragmentation of the sixteenth-century 'world order' was more prolonged, and the geographical spread of the crisis was wider, spanning much of Eurasia.

Though it is rarely mentioned in IR accounts, some readers may be familiar[168] with the characterisation of the seventeenth century as a period of 'General Crisis' in European history.[169] The Thirty Years War (1618–48), which ended the Habsburg dominance in Europe and made possible the Westphalian Peace from which our modern international order is supposed to have originated,[170] falls in this period. The Thirty Years War started with the Bohemian revolts[171] and blew up into continental-scale war when European houses who wanted to undermine the Habsburgs got involved. But of course, in the seventeenth century, there were revolts and wars elsewhere in Europe as well: the English Civil War (1642–51) may be the best-known example, and the Fronde (1648–53) in France is another. Noticing these patterns, some modern-day historians of Europe had labelled the first two-thirds of the seventeeth century a period of 'General Crisis', suggesting different causes (not unlike the ones we have covered in previous chapters with regards to the fourteenth- and fifteenth-century crises): demographic pressures (the sixteenth century was a period of demographic boom followed by a steep decline), financial (the price revolution in the sixteenth century, likely due to the effects of the influx of New World silver into the New World economy) or political (the emergence of

---

[168] The previous chapter has also alluded to this crisis.
[169] See, for example, Hobsbawm (1954); Trevor-Roper (2001) (original argument made in 1960s). For an IR-adjacent rethinking of the seventeenth century compatible with this argument, see Goldstone (1991).
[170] For a critique of this narrative, see Osiander (2001); de Carvalho, Leira and Hobson (2011).
[171] See, for example, Ogilvie (1992).

strong centralised states in Europe and the resistance they generated).[172] But the thesis met resistance from other historians of Europe
who disagreed with the periodisation or the notion that these events
were driven by a common cause or even were connected.

With the recent global history turn, the 'General Crisis' thesis has
gained new life,[173] however, as some historians of Eurasia noticed that
other settings had their own similar troubles in the same time period. In
East Asia, economic and agricultural disasters led to rebellions which
brought the end of the Ming Dynasty, who were replaced by the Qing
in 1644. Japan and Korea also experienced difficulties in this period.[174]
In north Eurasia, Muscovy, which had expanded for much of the
sixteenth century, fell into chaos as the last Rurik tsar, Fyodor I, died
without an heir at a time of economic hardship and famine, ushering in
a period known as 'The Time of Troubles' (1598–1613), which ended
with the establishment of the Romanov Dynasty. The Ottomans also
experienced a particularly severe version of their own crisis as well:
from the late sixteenth century to the middle of the seventeenth century,
the countryside was rocked by the *Jalali* rebellions, demographic
decline, economic downturns and agricultural shortages (as well as
disease).[175] The Ottoman Dynasty did manage to hold on to power,
even if it emerged from the period of crisis transformed.

Noting these periods of pronounced chaos and political tumult
throughout Eurasia (including examples not otherwise mentioned
here, e.g. Japan), some global historians now argue that we should
think of the seventeenth century as a period of global crisis.[176] The
connective tissue in all these problems is believed by many to be climate
change, underlying other demographic, financial and political problems already identified. The seventeenth century is the coldest period in
the middle of a much longer cold period in the northern hemisphere
known as 'the Little Ice Age', which is held by many climatologists to
have extended from the thirteenth to the nineteenth centuries.[177] Some

[172] See, for example, Parker and Smith (1997) for an overview of different
explanations.
[173] See, for example, de Vries (2009).
[174] See, for example, Atwell (1990) for an overview for the discussion of East Asia
during the 'General Crisis'.
[175] See White (2011); Ozel (2016). See also Goldstone (1987) for a comparison of
the Ming, Ottoman and English crises in this period. See also Goldstone (1991).
[176] See, for example, Parker (2013); Parker and Smith (1997).
[177] See, for example, Matthews and Briffa (2005); Parker (2013).

historians even argue that the divergence between Europe and Asia, East and West could be traced back to this period. Geoffrey Parker and Phillip Blom both conclude that intellectual developments in north-western Europe turned the period of crisis into an opportunity for Europe, compared to the rest of Eurasia.[178]

Impact of the 'Seventeenth-Century General Crisis'

Whether one agrees with those conclusions or not, it is clear that something did happen in the seventeenth century in Asia; in fact, in recent years, historians of the Ottoman Empire and China especially have been taking the Little Ice Age thesis as an explanation for seventeenth-century political developments very seriously, such as the Jalali rebellions or the collapse of the Ming Dynasty in 1644, following crop failures, floods and the Great Plague.[179] But the crisis had broader effects as well. Let's start with the decline[180] of the Eurasian overland trade (the 'Silk Road'), usually dated to the late sixteenth and early seventeenth centuries. Rossabi notes that this decline is usually[181] 'attributed to competition from the European oceangoing vessels that began to reach China in the sixteenth century' but proposes instead that 'political disruptions and the religious and social changes of the time' also played a role in diminishing this trade.[182] In other words, this trade may have been another casualty of the 'Seventeenth-Century General Crisis'.

Traditional overland trade throughout Eurasia was slow (in the fifteenth century, it could take up to a year for a traveller from Herat under the control of the Timurids to reach Peking, the seat of the Ming court) and thus was very expensive, as both the animals and the people in the caravans had to be fed throughout that time. Nevertheless, there

---

[178] See, for example, Wakeman (1985); Parker and Smith (1978); Steensgaard (1978, 1990); Reid (1978); Atwell (1978, 1986); Blom (2019); Parker (2013); de Vries (2013). The argument is also reminiscent of Goldstone's early work (1987, 1988, 1991, 1998).

[179] See, for example, White (2011); Brook (2010).

[180] Millward (2013) observes that trade continued even beyond this point of attributed decline. Rossabi (2014b [1990], p. 202) also notes that short-distance trade continued.

[181] See, for example, Steensgaard (1975). See Millward (2013); Sharman and Phillips (2020).

[182] Rossabi (2014b [1990], p. 201).

was a steady flow (with a few disruptions) in the three centuries we have examined, benefitting from the relative stability of the Eastern 'world orders' the previous chapters have covered. Even during periods of conflict, most Chinggisid and post-Chinggisid Great Houses tended to use their resources to protect merchants and trade routes even when they were involved in military campaigns with their rivals.[183] Lodgings and other safety measures were put in place to help merchants travel with ease and to protect them from bandits.[184] Naval trade, which existed in various forms long before the Europeans came on the scene, had arguably more unpredictable risks, from corsairs to shipwrecks. The overland route, by contrast, had remained relatively predictable (even if expensive and slow) over the centuries. The early sixteenth century was a growth period for this overland trade. The post-Timurid empires we discussed in Chapter 4 were great consumers of Ming products (and also passed on some of this trade to Europe). As Rossabi observes: 'It is no accident that two of the finest collections of Ming porcelains in the world are located at the Topkapi Museum in Turkey and at the Ardebil Shrine in Iran.'[185] The Mughals had also inherited an enthusiasm for Ming porcelains from the Timurids.[186]

Rossabi attributes the decline of the overland trade to increasing turmoil in Eurasia starting in the latter part of the sixteenth century and continuing in the seventeenth. The political instability along the major routes 'led to greater unpredictability in costs for merchants',[187] rendering the trade less profitable. It is true that naval trade starts increasing in the second half of the sixteenth century, and it is not only the European merchants: for example, as we saw previously, the Safavids under Abbas I became more invested in seaborne commerce in this period. Though the debate about the climatological explanation for the 'Sevententh-Century General Crisis' is far from settled, we could at least speculate that extreme weather conditions in this period may

---

[183] Chapter 2 mentioned the postal station route instituted by the Mongol Empire. To give an example from the sixteenth century, the Safavids exported silk to the Ottomans throughout the conflict years. Rossabi (2014b [1990], 211).

[184] Ibid., p. 206.

[185] Ibid., pp. 207–8. He also notes: 'Though precise statistics on Eurasian trade are unavailable, this commerce must have been extensive, judging from the Ming court's knowledge of conditions in the Middle East and central Asia' (p. 209).

[186] For more on Mughal–Ming (as well as Timurid–Ming) trade, see Guy (2018). I am grateful to Manjeet Pardesi for the suggestion.

[187] Ibid., p. 210.

have also played a role in creating delays and driving up expenditures in overland trade. In linking the 'General Crisis' to the peak period of the Little Ice Age, Geoffrey Parker notes extreme cold weather and snow-storms throughout Eurasia during this period.[188]

Extreme cold as well as snow along the overland routes in the seven-teenth century would have made overland travel more difficult, and accompanying problems of food shortages would have made it even more expensive to feed the caravans. Maritime routes, by contrast, were further to the south, in warmer seas, and the risks of inclement weather had been baked into seaborne commerce since its inception, and thus various insurance schemes and shipping technologies were intro-duced to deal with it. As political turmoil unsettled the overland route and increased the likelihood of banditry, the threat of pirates and cor-sairs would have seemed more tolerable as a result. All of this could have given seaborne commerce the edge it needed to subsequently take over in an irreversible manner. Some of this is speculation, and we will have to wait for historians to revisit the question with fresher eyes. But whatever the cause, it is a fact that overland trade networks from eastern to western Asia (and to some extent northern and southern) that held together the Eastern 'world orders' (and beyond) covered in this book frayed during the period labelled the 'Seventeenth-Century General Crisis'. That itself is not a particularly new observation: I even remember reading in my secondary school history text book that the decline of the 'Silk Roads' was one of the causes of the decline of the Ottoman Empire. Is that what I am arguing here?

Not exactly. The difficulty arises from the fact that, regardless of what happened to overland trade, the seventeenth-century picture is not one of straightforward decline in Asia. First, revisionist historio-graphies of all Asian polities we have discussed have shown that – if they did indeed experience a crisis in the seventeenth century – they *recovered* from it subsequently, if we define recovery in generally material terms. The eighteenth century was a period of expansion for Russia under the Romanovs and China under the Qing Dynasty. Both houses were rising in the seventeenth century. The Safavid realms do not seem to have experienced a major material crisis in the seventeenth century, though the Safavids did decline as a house. Nader Shah Afshari, who gained control of Safavid realms in the eighteenth

---

[188] Parker (2013, p. xxiv).

century, was able to wage a successful military campaign conquering much of west Asia. The Mughal empire controlled its largest territory at the end of the seventeenth century, during the reign of Aurangzeb (r. 1658–1707). Even the Ottomans, who among the houses discussed here probably faced the worst of what the seventeenth century had to offer, generally recovered from the crises of the period, at least well enough to survive as a house until the twentieth century.

Furthermore, locating the decline of Asia/the East and the rise of Europe/the West in this century also retrospectively overestimates the importance and material strength of European actors of the time as relative to the rest of the world. Recent scholarship is overwhelming in its finding that European actors were not more powerful or economically advanced than their (Eur)Asian counterparts until at least the second half of the eighteenth century.[189] European empires (at least in Asia) were not a product of military or economic or intellectual domination until the nineteenth century. It is also clear that the Westphalian peace in Europe did not play the definitive turn it is imagined to have played in IR; its importance was retroactively conjured by nineteenth-century jurists.[190] To reiterate, despite what IR textbooks claim, the modern international order was not created in the seventeenth century by European states from scratch in a world that had not known that kind of ambition before.

The loss of the overland trade still matters, but for another reason entirely. I contend that the main consequence of the 'Seventeenth-Century General Crisis' was to temporarily but seriously fragment some of the networks of the increasingly global world order of the sixteenth century that connected much of Eurasia and beyond as described in this chapter. Whatever its main cause – likely a combination of the factors we have discussed here, all of which amplified each other – the decades of political tumult forced major Great Houses of the sixteenth century to struggle to hold on to their realms of influence, facing rebellions, food shortages, demographic decline, taxation problems and so on. They ceased competing with each other over universal sovereignty claims and thus also engaged each other less. This was especially true for the Habsburgs and the Ottomans. The Safavids

---

[189] In addition to what has been cited already, see also Sharman (2019); Sharman and Phillips (2020); Buzan and Lawson (2015); Phillips (2021); Sivasundaram (2020).
[190] Osiander (2001).

turned reticent, became small. The Mughals moved further into the warmer Indian subcontinent, and Muscovy turned its attention its own neighbourhood. In other words, Eastern universal visions of 'world order' were increasingly replaced by 'regional' concerns (amplified in places by the increasing cultural homogenisation in subject societies due to confessionalisation). The loss of overland Asian and Eurasian trade as described already and its replacement with bilateral trade via European shipping installed this fragmentation of the broader social space as a permanent feature of the continent.

In other words, it was the sixteenth-century Eastern world order that was lost in the seventeenth-century crisis, not any particular empire. The ecumene that gave shape to the ambitions of the post-Timurid empires fragmented, and with it the promise of the underlying structure that connected 'Asia' politically, socially and culturally from the thirteenth century until the seventeenth. Chinggisid notions of universal sovereignty did not fully die out[191] – they continued to animate various Eastern actors, but they did not have the same weight after the seventeenth century. No other universalising project since then has come close to truly reconstituting 'Asia' as a whole (though the USSR tried to an extent). The East became a fragmented political space of regional orders, left vulnerable to the stigmatising dynamics of the nineteenth century.

[191] 'The title sahib-qiran ("Lord of Conjunction") ... was still routinely brandished by the likes of Nader Shah Afshar (r. 1736–1747), Fath 'Ali Shah Qajar (r. 1797–1834), and Nasr Allah Khan Mangït (r. 1827–1860) to mark their Chingizid-Timurid legitimacy (Moin 2012: 23–55; Subrahmanyam 2000: 367)'. Melvin-Koushki (2018a, 357).

PART II

Lessons of History

6 | Rise and Fall of Eastern World Orders

Lessons for International Relations

Introduction

In Part I, *Before the West* reconstructed a *longue durée* history of world politics (or international relations) from an Asian or Eastern perspective. In this chapter, I will use this history to intervene in some of the current debates in IR, especially those that pertain to the rise and decline of Great Powers and the crises of international orders. But let's first recap some of the contours of the history as developed in Part I, which focused on the Great Houses of Asia and Eurasia and the world orders they created between the thirteenth and the seventeenth centuries.

Chapter 2 argued that the empire of Genghis Khan created a Chinggisid world order centred in Asia in the thirteenth and fourteenth centuries. The Chinggisid world order facilitated an exchange of people, goods, arts, technology and ideas from one end of Asia to the other, from modern-day China to Iran to Russia and anywhere in between. Even regions that were not directly under the control of the Great House of Genghis Khan were transformed by their interactions with those that were. Most importantly, this world order diffused throughout the continent a particular sovereignty model. Chinggisid sovereignty was highly centralised around the person of the Great Khan, who was understood to be *the* lawgiver (and thus also above even religious authority). As the lawgiver, the Great Khan was also expected to be a world conqueror, which proved to his would-be aristocratic challengers (and, less importantly, subjects) that he had heaven's mandate to claim such awesome power. This meant that the Chinggisid sovereignty model relied greatly on 'external' dynamics for legitimation, and Chinggisid rulers were thus particularly invested in claiming universal sovereignty. They were not particularly interested in homogenising the ruled population, however, most of whom were hardly understood to be any different than cattle. The Chinggisid sovereignty model also came with a number of secondary institutions: tanistry as a succession norm, sponsorship of astronomy/astrology, facilitation of trade etc. The next three chapters then traced the influences of the Chinggisid sovereignty norm as well as the accompanying institutions within the various successor polities of the empire and the world orders they created.

Chapter 3 argued that, from the late fourteenth century to the mid-fifteenth century, Asia was dominated by the 'post-Chinggisid' world-ordering projects of the Timurids and the early Ming, two Great Houses which were operating generally according to the expectations of the Chinggisid sovereignty model. The chapter placed early Ming excursions into Asia, including the so-called treasure voyages, and the Ming tributary system in this larger historical and continental context. It showed that we need to understand the influence of the (Chinggisid) Yuan Dynasty on the Ming, as well as the significance of early Ming competition with Inner Asia, in order to make sense of the ruling styles of Hongwu and Yongle emperors. In west Asia, Timur more deliberately fashioned himself after Genghis Khan. The empire he founded was not long-lived, fragmenting around the same time as the Ming turned more isolationist, around the middle of the fifteenth century. Nevertheless, up until that point we can point to a world order constituted by post-Chinggisid norms as reproduced by the Timurids and the Ming at either end of Asia, with relatively robust trade networks and smaller khanates connecting the two in the middle.

The Timurid-Ming world order may have been looser than the Chinggisid one before it, but it too had a significant legacy, particularly in west Asia. Islamic and Chinggisid practices were an uncomfortable fit when first merged in the thirteenth century. As explained in Chapter 4, while Islam had its own universal traditions, the idea of the ruler as the ultimate lawgiver went against much of Islamic theology and practice (at least as in the Sunni tradition until that point in time). Timur introduced a new twist to the Chinggisid sovereignty model: he found a way to reconcile Islam and the Chinggisid-style supreme authority by using (Islamic) astrology and other occult sciences. The title of *sahibkıran* (Lord of Conjunction) marked world conquerors; they were supposed to have been born under a Saturn–Jupiter conjunction, which also marked the end of ages. The title gave special status, authority and power to rulers so marked. This mode of legitimation made sense both within Chinggisid ecumene and Islamic ontology. The title *sahibkıran* came to be very closely associated first with Timur and gained even greater importance in west Asia after his death, as Muslims were anticipating major events to coincide with the Islamic millennium at the end of the sixteenth century, also supposedly marked by a Saturn–Jupiter conjunction.

Within this millennial ecumene shaping the late fifteenth and early sixteenth centuries, the Chinggisid model found yet another life as rising Great Houses in west Asia started laying claim to the *sahibkıran* title and building world orders in the Chinggisid mould. Chapter 4 traced precisely this rivalry among the millennial sovereigns of three post-Timurid Great Houses: the Ottomans, the Safavid and the Mughals. The strongest claim to the *sahibkıran* title was passed from Shah Ismail of the Safavids to Süleyman the Magnificent (or the Lawgiver) of the Ottomans to Akbar the Great of the Mughals. Chapter 4 also argued that, together, these three empires constituted the core of the sixteenth-century globalising order. Between them, they ruled over a third of the world's population (most of them not even Muslim) and controlled much of the world's economic resources. They also shaped the sixteenth-century global political ecumene around post-Chinggisid and post-Timurid notions of universal, millennial sovereignty. In other words, this chapter pushed back against the traditional narrative in IR which casts the Ottomans, the Safavids and the Mughals as peripheral actors to Europe within this period, arguing that it was rather Europe that was peripheral to the western Asian core of the sixteenth-century world order.

Chapter 5 illustrated the influence of this core (as well as Chinggisid universal sovereignty norms) on the globalisation dynamics of the sixteenth century by first tracing the influence of these post-Timurid Great Houses on Europe, and especially the Habsburgs. It showed that Charles V's universal sovereignty aspirations – as well the subsequent developments in Europe in response to the Habsburg bid for hegemony – cannot be understood without reference to the Ottomans and the post-Timurid order of millennial competition. This is where the timeline offered in this book lines up with the traditional IR account of the emergence of the modern international order, dated back to the developments of the Thirty Years War and the Westphalian Peace. Part I made clear, however, that the traditional IR notion that European actors suddenly innovated a centralised sovereignty model and in the seventeenth century created a globalising international order for the first time in history is simply wrong. Sovereignty and order-making developments which until now have only been studied in the European context are in fact an offshoot of longer trends that originate from Asia (and likely elsewhere) and thus need to be understood within a global historical sociology of world orders. Chapter 5 also caught up with the rest of Eurasia/Asia in the sixteenth century and demonstrated that Chinggisid and/or Timurid norms were still at play in places on the continent, especially Muscovy to the north, but also in Inner Asia and to a lesser extent East Asia.

Finally, Chapter 5 also argued that this sixteenth-century 'world order' fragmented during the period of the 'Seventeenth-Century General Crisis', a tumultous period lasting from the latter quarter of the sixteenth century to the latter part of the seventeenth. Even though Asian empires materially recovered from this period of upheaval (and they were affected by it to varying degrees to begin with), Eurasian trade networks that made possible and reproduced the Eastern orders of the previous three centuries irreversibly declined. More significantly, the social fabric of the sixteenth-century 'world order' decayed as its Great Houses turned inwards and/or to regional conflicts and ceased competing with each other for universal sovereignty. Even though Chinggisid sovereignty norms continued to circulate in the East beyond the 'Seventeenth-Century General Crisis' and motivated individual rulers such as Nader Shah in the eighteenth century, no sustainable 'world order' projects organised by these notions came into being after early modernity.

Lessons for International Relations

This reconstructed history of the East opens up a lot of historical real estate to general IR inquiry. Yet before we go gallivanting in this new space looking for lessons that are applicable to the present, we need to think about how exactly such lessons may be derived from a period which – even this book admits – is different from ours in significant ways. The question then is: what logics were operating in this era that are still operating in ours?

How to Approach Macro-Historical Comparisons

In IR, we often approach history in one of two problematic ways.[1] In one camp are those who assume that our modern-day concepts such as

---

[1]   On the problematic uses of history in IR, see also Hobson and Lawson (2008); Lawson (2012).

'Great Power' or 'state' can be projected seamlessly onto any historical period or geography. Discussions around 'Thucydides' Trap', for example, operate with the notion that our concepts easily cover Ancient Greek city-state system dynamics (and vice versa).[2] Such an assumption at a minimum can lead us to focus on historical time periods and dynamics that are either inherently similar to our own and/or verifying our present-day beliefs, creating a selection bias effect. At a maximum, it causes presentist distortions in the treatments of history, in service of contemporary debates. In another camp are those who believe political institutions to be both temporally contingent and culturally specific. This camp doesn't believe in looking beyond what is understood to be a naturally bounded sphere: for example, churches of one kind can be compared with churches of another but not with mosques etc. There are several problems with this assumption also, but perhaps the most severe one is that it essentialises (with a presentist bias) various cultural and geographical categories, assuming them to be unchanging and given.

As I have tried to demonstrate in this book, there is no reason for these to be our only choices when we approach history in IR theory. Some concepts – such as centralisation or hierarchy – *can* travel relatively seamlessly across time and space (though we still have to be sensitive to the myriad forms they can take in different settings). Most concepts, however, do not. That does not mean we are doomed to stay away from transhistorical and transcultural comparisons. With some additional work, some foundational concepts for IR can be rethought to allow for such comparisons. The general concept of sovereignty, as laid out in Chapter 1, is one such example. Once abstracted as such, we are no longer limited to thinking about sovereignty in terms of the modern-state or European practices, and we can introduce other variations to our accounts, such as the Chinggisid sovereignty model discussed in this book. The fact that both modern-state sovereignty and Chinggisid sovereignty are versions of a centralised type of sovereignty creates a certain degree of commensurability between the two. Some may say of course that this commensurability makes the focus on Chinggisid sovereignty (and universal empire/world order projects) a bit suspect: it can reproduce some of the existing Eurocentric biases in the IR scholarship. That worry is correct

---

[2] See Zarakol (2020a) for a critique.

to the extent our current understanding of sovereignty is more closely associated with the European trajectory, but we need to rethink that.[3] Hopefully seeing a similar version elsewhere will spell the end of the exceptionalism narrative. Moreover, future projects could and should follow other paths and look at sovereignty models that deviate even further from what we take for granted.[4]

For other concepts, a different strategy is required. What I have in mind here are concepts that do have a certain temporality and/or cultural specifity built into them: 'international order' is such a term, because it inevitably presumes the existence of nations and/or nation states. Therefore, given that nations are of relatively recent vintage in history, the term 'international order' does not travel well. But in the sense that international orders are orders with global ambitions, the idea itself does: this is why I tried to capture the historical corollaries of modern international orders with the term 'world order'. 'World orders' can consist of empires, houses, cities and so on and can thus be found – at least in principle – in many different historical settings. My criterion in this book for labelling an order as a 'world order' was the universality of the vision of the orderers, coupled with a material reach that at least briefly made the vision seem attainable.

'Great Power' is yet another temporally bound term, both because it has a particular history[5] and because analytically it assumes a certain type of state/sovereignty model. Much of traditional IR scholarship assumes 'Great Power' to be a transhistorical term, though it does not bother to use it as such, because it believes Great Powers to have only existed from the seventeenth century onwards. As we have seen, the historical reality is much more complicated. Once we acknowledge the existence of a world outside of Europe, we also have to confront the fact that most European states which were called Great Powers were not in fact Great Powers in a global sense before the nineteenth century but were regional powers at best, no matter how they labelled themselves. If we insist on calling early modern European states Great Powers in order to salvage the claims of the IR literature, we would also have to confront the fact that there were other powerful polities in Asia before the eighteenth century that fit description equally as well or

[3] Though hopefully this book has convinced the reader that the European trajectory did not exist in a vacuum.
[4] Sneath (2007) shows how we could study decentralised sovereignty.
[5] Keene (2013); Leigh (2019).

better. In other words, reading the ending of the story (i.e. eventual Western domination) has created in the IR Great Power literature either an under- or over-counting problem, depending on how the concept of Great Power is understood. We are over-counting if we rely on the self-designation of European actors and are under-counting if we try to deploy the category as a transhistorical one with some basis in material measurements. That is one of the problems I am trying to address in this book. To solve these issues, I have proposed (following Keene and Sneath) that 'House' and 'Great House' may be more flexible terms to travel with before modernity in discussing political units across time and space.[6] In *Before the West*, we have thus zoomed in on a successive set of 'world orders' within a particular time period that were created by Great Houses which had universalising visions that were not identical but bore some familial resemblance to each other. Other, lesser houses also materially and ideationally participated in and reproduced those 'world orders' (until they did not).

Other concepts that were critical to the theoretical framework I used in this book were 'structure' and 'ecumene'. As explained in Chapter 1, I do not use 'order' and 'structure' interchangeably. I defined 'order' as the (man-made) rules, understandings and institutions that govern (and pattern) relations between the primary actors of world politics.[7] Orders are more deliberately created by its various actors (but not always in a top-down manner) and/or reflexively maintained (or undermined), though in practice they rarely function the way were designed. In other words, there is a strong link between orders and human agency. By contrast, I have used the term 'structure' to denote dynamics, processes and pressures that are not at all (or are hardly) susceptible to modification by (individual) human agency. Structural dynamics include collective human processes that emerge without deliberate design, as subject to material forces beyond deliberate human agency, such as climatological or environmental pressures, macro-economic processes (e.g. of capitalism), long-term demographic trends, and technological and scientific raptures. Though some aspects of such processes may be manipulated or challenged by human agency (or at least attempted), most of these processes are by definition beyond (at that moment

---

[6] Though in this book I have also at times used the terms 'empire', 'polity' and 'realm' to capture different dimensions of power projection by ruling houses.

[7] See also Adler (2019) for a discussion of the concept of order.

of time) human control or even full comprehension, and they cannot be eradicated or replaced by agency alone.

Its relative autonomy from human agency makes it easier to conceptualise 'structure' transhistorically in comparison to some of the other concepts discussed. However, there is a temporality to the relationship between 'order' and 'structure' that is often overlooked. What is subject to human manipulation is not a transhistorical category; as human agency has increased over time, so has our ability to design institutions and orders that solve (some) structural problems. Certain phenomena that would have been 'structural' at another period in time (e.g. capital flows or demographic outcomes) have increasingly become subject to ordering and institutional design. Whether an international-level arrangement is better classified as ordered or structural is therefore not given and needs to be evaluated within its particular historical frame. The modern international order is inevitably more complex and differentiated with its various institutions compared to the Chinggisid and post-Chinggisid world orders covered in this book for this reason, but that does not mean these world orders are not comparable. The question to be asked about all world orders is whether they were designed to shape what was (or was believed to be) within the control of the actors of the time and, if so, to what extent they did. We cannot judge orderers in history for not being able to manipulate dynamics that we consider orderable but were not understood as such in previous time periods.

Finally, a word about the term 'ecumene', which you have encountered in Part I, as in 'a Chinggisid ecumene'. I have resurrected the term, with some modification, from Arnold J. Toynbee[8] to capture something deeper than world orders, something that belongs to *longue durée*. I use 'ecumene' to denote a deep-settled way of seeing and inhabiting the world, operating at a more structural level (as defined previously), something close to 'culture' or 'civilisation' but (hopefully) without the troubling connotations of those terms. The way I understand it, an ecumene can span several world orders which, if so, exhibit some degree of continuity in their deep norms – that is, unwritten and intersubjective rules that gradually emerge over time, which come to be perceived as *natural* by the actors in the system and therefore as not being subject to agency. In other words, norms take

---

[8]   More on Toynbee in the next chapter.

a structural flavour when they have been around for a long time and are no longer remembered to be changing but instead are described as the underlying (and unchangeable) logic of world politics. For example, the 'Westphalian System' has been the backdrop of a number of successive modern 'international orders', characterised by deep political norms such as anarchy, territorial sovereignty, nationalism and various notions about 'Great Power' politics (not to mention various economic and sociological norms,[9] all of which together amount to 'modernity'). Such deep norms were thus understood by many observers in the twentieth century as structural, which they pretty much were/are (according to the definitions set out here). 'Chinggisid' sovereignty norms discussed in this book had a similar power within the Chinggisid ecumene spanning the Eurasian continent for several centuries, until they did not. This example should demonstrate that there is a problem in conflating the structural nature of such an ecumene for *the time being* with an assumption of its universality or transhistoricity.

General Lessons about the Rise and Fall of World Orders

Having thus established the tools for comparison, let's turn to some general lessons about what IR theory can learn from the reconstructed history of the East offered in this book and its comparison to what we already know about international relations in modernity. Though technically this history can be used to refine theories in many different directions, in this book I am focused on the rise and fall of political actors and orders, so this section will limit itself to some interventions in those debates.

When IR (and IR-adjacent) scholars discuss 'rise and decline', they are almost invariably referring to particular states (i.e. Great Powers).[10] For the most part, IR scholarship defines Great Power in strictly material terms: military strength, economic resources and so on. Power transition is said to occur when one Great Power loses its

---

[9]   For example, race.

[10]   Obviously the literature on Great Powers is too vast to be covered here, but for a start, see, for example, MacDonald and Parent (2018a, 2018b); Lake (2006, 2013); Brooks and Wohlforth (2016); Kennedy (1988); Gresh (2021); Itzkowitz Shifrinson (2018); Kennedy (1991); Orlovsky (1989); Levy (1983); Mearsheimer (2014); Scott (2006); Goddard (2018); Kegley and Raymond (2020).

material capabilities and others rise up to take its place.[11] The historical examples are familiar to anyone who has ever picked up a book on the rise and fall of Great Powers: a declining France was replaced by a rising Great Britain; or as European Great Powers waned at the end of the long nineteenth century, the United States and the USSR took over as the new 'great' – or even 'super' – powers in the second half of the twentieth century and so on. Decline is not always matched by a simultaneous rise: when the USSR collapsed at the end of the Cold War, no other power took its place in the international system, at least immediately. As far as most IR scholarship on Great Powers is concerned, however, whether replacement happens is a more important question than who is a Great Power at any given moment, because the number of Great Powers in the system is assumed to determine the basic character of international politics.[12] Multipolar systems are supposed to be different from bipolar and unipolar systems (and vice versa). It hardly needs repeating that these expectations about Great Power behaviour, balance-of-power, polarity and so on are derived from studying European history.

At first glance, the account offered here does not radically challenge the basic building blocks of this literature. Allowing for 'Great Houses' to stand in for 'Great Powers', we do see some groupings that could be analysed in traditional IR language: the thirteenth century has unipolarity (or hegemonic stability) in the Chinggisid world empire; the early fourteenth century has mulipolarity with the four khanates balancing against each other; the late-fourteenth- to mid-fifteenth-century period has bipolar competition between the Timurids and the Ming; the sixteenth century has another form of multipolarity, with the Ottomans, the Safavids and the Mughals competing with each other,

---

[11] See, for example, Organski and Kugler (1981); Tammen (2008); DiCicco and Levy (2014); Kim and Gates (2015); Kim (1991); Lebow and Valentino (2009); Chan (2007); Lemke (1997, 2001); Lemke and Reed (1996); Lemke and Tammen (2003).

[12] Or perhaps this used to be the claim back in the day when US hegemony seemed very secure. The literature on Great Powers has become increasing concerned with the USA versus China rivalry and is driven by policy considerations (as they apply to the United States) to a greater extent. See, for example, Brooks and Wohlforth (2002, 2016); Lake (2006); Mearsheimer (2006, 2010); Nye (2010); Walt (2011); Schweller and Xiaoyu (2011); Buzan (2010); Kroenig (2020); Cooley and Nexon (2020). There is also more writing on US decline; see, for example, Merand (2020).

as well as the Habsburgs. And in the transition between one arrangement to the next, there are stories of the rise and decline of particular
houses: as the Yuan decline, the Ming take over; the Timurids decline,
and the Mughals rise; and so on. In other words, there is a certain
legibility to this history already for IR.

However, theories derived from the European experience do not
necessarily fare well when the potential universe of cases is thus
expanded. Power transition theory, for instance, has already been
challenged in the East Asian historical context,[13] and it seems to me
unlikely that it would do well if tested on the history covered in Part I.
As far as Great Houses are concerned, the more common power-
transition pattern in the East seems to be fragmentation/decay and
then replacement (usually by another dynasty). Even the applicability
of balance-of-power logic as previously described is highly questionable: constructivists argue that balance-of-power thinking,[14] even if
presented as transhistorical, is a product of nineteenth-century grand
strategy culture. We do not have to settle any of these debates here.
Rather, my point is that all of these IR-type questions could be investi-
gated in this historical space also: expanding the potential universe of
eligible cases would thus inevitably refine our existing theories about
the 'rise and fall' of Great Powers.

But the realisation that there were Eastern 'world orders' allows us to
do something more than just engage in existing IR debates with more
data. It forces us to look beyond the rise and fall of Great Powers to
'world orders'. Broadening our temporal and geographical horizon
helps us to think about how 'world orders' come about and how they
are replaced. As a discipline, we have focused too much on the decline
of Great Powers and, until recently, barely thought about the decline of
international or 'world orders'. Simplifying a bit, this is partly because
realist IR has assumed that whatever order exists automatically flows
from Great Powers (and thus concluded there was no reason to study
orders separately). IR liberalism, on the other hand, while much more
interested in the emergence and mainenance of international orders,
had not really imagined their demise. Because of the teleological
assumptions implicit in liberalism, scholars working within this vein

---

[13] See Kang and Ma (2018); Kang (2020); Huang and Kang (2020).
[14] Realists could counter that the *sahibkıran* millennial sovereigns in the sixteenth
century were also described as 'poles' (*kutb*), so perhaps there is something
transhistorical to polarity logics.

228 Lessons of History

had not really imagined that international orders may unravel and even less so that they may be replaced by Liberal International Orders. The developments of the last decade have finally forced us to entertain the possibility. What that outcome would look like is still an under-theorised question, however. The history of Eastern world orders can help us think about such scenarios by offering examples of different patterns of world order decline.

Reviewing the trajectory of Eastern world orders, for example, it is hard to overlook the fact that major crises punctuate the end of each order (even if the exact chain of causality is hard to ascertain). The fragmentation of each Eastern world order seems to at least *correlate* with a 'general crisis' that affected large areas of the northern hemisphere. The original Chinggisid world order fragmented at a time when the plague was spreading across Asia (and then Europe), and it came to an end during a period that some historians label the 'Fourteenth-Century Crisis'; the post-Chinggisid world order fragmented during a period some historians call the 'Fifteenth-Century Crisis', the effects of which seem to have been felt especially in west Asia and Europe. Finally, the sixteenth-century post-Timurid world order as described in Chapters 4 and 5 fragmented in the 'Seventeenth-Century General Crisis'.

We can make several observations about this pattern. First, under-lying all of these 'general crises' were structural pressures[15], at least in the way I have defined the term 'structure' in this book. The benefit of *longue durée* hindsight, coupled with a global vision, allows us to see that political turmoil during these crises (and during the ensuing frag-mentation of the existing order) was not really caused by specific Great House rivalries or 'power transition' (i.e. the things IR worries most about as being corrosive to order) but rather structural dynamics such as climate change, epidemics, demographic decline, monetary prob-lems and so on (i.e. the things IR has not worried at all about until recently). Contrary to the assumptions of the IR literature about Great Powers, rivalries by Great Houses that shared the same understanding of 'greatness' in fact *strengthened* and *reinforced* the existing world order (even when those rivalries turned violent). A similar observation can be made about Great Power competition during the nineteenth century or the Cold War. Rivalry is *constitutive* of order (especially if

---

[15] On structural pressures, see also Goldstone (1991).

rivals are shaped by the same ecumene); order decline almost always originates from elsewhere and is exogenous to the rivalry. A third observation is that Eastern world orders were not immediately replaced after fragmentation; there were periods without 'world order'-ers around (or even if they were around, their presence was not yet felt by other actors as such). The 'Seventeenth-Century General Crisis' period lasted the longest without the next order emerging, and perhaps this is why the Chinggisid ecumene declined along with the last world order it had produced.

This brings us to ecumenical decline: a type of decline even less theorised in IR than the decline of international orders. Paradigmatic debates in the discipline have forced IR scholars to make artificial choices between studying material and studying ideational dynamics that give shape to world politics. In reality, both matter, just not consistently so across time and space. How those respective roles are allocated in any given historical setting should be a question approached empirically, rather than decided a priori. The ecumene is the deep normative well from which notions of 'power', 'sovereignty', 'legitimacy' and so on are derived at any given time.[16] As long as a particular ecumene exists, it seems like (or is) structure: it appears natural, unchanging, with alternatives unthinkable. The 'Westphalian' ecumene has been the backdrop of a number of successive 'international orders' in modernity. The 'Chinggisid' ecumene was the backdrop of the Eastern 'world orders' that were scrutinised in this book. The actors socialised to the 'Chinggisid' ecumene had their own understanding of what 'greatness' entailed, which was comparable to but different from our notions. Such beliefs shaped the actions of the participants in that ecumene in ways that were recognisably similar across time. Just as Westphalian norms shape the globe now, Chinggisid norms used to be so powerful that they organised political behaviour throughout the East for centuries. Yet today they are obscured from our view. What happened in the seventeenth century in the East therefore is bigger than even order fragmentation: it is the decline of an 'ecumene' that had existed from centuries, a macro shift of social and normative gravity from Asia to Europe. That is the kind of

---

[16] I don't mean to imply that power and greatness are universally valued; some cultures encourage modesty and restraint. But they are less likely to create world orders.

decline that IR has even failed to imagine could happen (again), because the discipline is shaped by its assumption that nothing of significance existed before Westphalia and outside of Europe. Now you know that assumption is wrong.

The fact that an ecumene of this continental scale declined before, to be almost completely forgotten, suggests that it could happen again. I will conclude the chapter by entertaining the possibility for the trajectory of world politics today, but before we get to that we need to review what exactly happened in the East after the point we left off in Chapter 5 – that is, after the 'Seventeenth-Century General Crisis'. As Chapter 5 noted, Eastern empires materially recovered from this crisis and were not really dominated by European actors until the latter part of the eighteenth century (or later). Why, then, do we think that they have been declining for centuries? It turns out that sorting out the story of the 'decline of the East' has interesting implications for thinking about the future 'decline of the West'.

Rethinking 'the Decline of the East'

As also noted in Chapter 5, in recent decades revisionist histories have strongly challenged the traditional decline narratives of Asian and Eurasian polities. The substantiveness of the challenge varies depending on the particular historiography, but challengers share some common insights. First, most regional historians question the post-nineteenth-century idea that Eastern decline (as seen from their particular regional vantage point) extends back centuries, as well the belief that (Eur)Asian polities stagnated or did not politically develop for centuries. Second, there is considerable evidence that many – if not most – major Asian polities remained materially powerful well into the eighteenth century, a number of them even considerably extending their territorial holdings at a time that is considered to be marked by European expansion. Third, we now know that many of the socio-economic and political processes (e.g. centralisation or confessionalisation – that were thought to be unique to the European political development trajectory were unfolding at the same time (or even earlier) in Asia. All that is well and good. Yet, as also noted in Chapter 1, such realisations, when put together, pose a new puzzle – or should do so, if the assumed inevitability of European domination did not create such blind spots in our thinking about the past.

The new puzzle is this: if Asia was not really that far 'behind' Europe in terms of material, social and political indicators, why then did Asian elites so easily fold ontologically in (especially the second half of) the nineteenth century when faced with narratives of European civilisational superiority? Why did the narrative of Asia having declined for centuries become so widely accepted? To put it another way, why did (Eur)Asians become so easily *stigmatised*[17] by Western actors? Why did they internalise the civilisational schema which found them inferior, even as they challenged their own countries' particular placement within that schema? Why did this process unfold so rapidly and so evenly (all things considered) throughout (Eur)Asia, given the varying material strengths of the actors in Asia as well as the differing degrees of trauma in their interactions with European colonialism? If Asia was indeed a residual category genuinely created by European colonialism, if Asia was unified as a continent for the very first time via its encounters with European actors in the nineteenth century, as it is always assumed in IR, why were actors throughout (Eur)Asia so similarly susceptible to European stigmatisation?

Let us consider some possible explanations for this puzzle before I return to my own theory, based on the alternative reading of history offered in this book. I think most people assume – to the extent that they think about this question at all – that the feelings of social, cultural and civilisational inadequacy that the elites in (Eur)Asian states developed vis-à-vis Europe are a natural consequence of the fact that these states were bested by the superior technology of the European powers in the nineteenth century, especially in the military realm. Yet this seemingly commonsensical explanation becomes extremely puzzling if you pause to consider it. Societies (or individuals) do not abruptly develop feelings of inadequacy vis-à-vis other cultures just because they are falling short in some economic accomplishment or even due to military defeat. After the Vietnam War, Americans did not suddenly start viewing Vietnamese culture in a different light: they had their own narratives as to why they lost (or 'failed to win') the war that had

---

[17] For more on stigmatisation, see my earlier work, especially Zarakol (2011, 2014). Stigmatisation is not just discrimination: those who are stigmatised also internalise that judgment, even if they want to change or reject it.

nothing to do with the superiority of the Vietnamese culture. Even in the face of undeniable defeat, then, our common tendency as human beings is to come up with narratives that justify the situation as well as promises that better days are around the corner. Rare is the group of people who are militarily defeated (or otherwise beaten) by another group of people and then say, 'Well, we really deserved that beating because our culture is clearly inferior, so let us emulate the victors'. Remember the initial US response to the COVID-19 pandemic: in its early days in 2020, most Americans, even those critical of the government response, had difficulty imagining other countries could be handling things better, especially countries they understood to be 'less developed' than the United States. All of this is to say: our assessments of our own culture and how well we are doing are not based on objective comparisons of merit.

This suggests to me that, despite the attention we have paid lately in IR to the nineteenth century as a formative moment for modern international relations, the relative uniqueness of that century in the world historical sense is still underestimated. The extremely unlikely scenario I have described of rapidly coming to want to emulate the life and governance style of a group that has materially bested you is what seems to have happened all over Eurasia (to elites) in the nineteenth century. But, you may counter, was the East not lagging behind the West for a long time, at least intellectually? Perhaps it was a realisation that sunk in gradually. As we have discussed in Part I, and as recent historical scholarship has clearly demonstrated, this long-held notion (shared by the West and the East) that Asia had materially (or intellectually) lagged behind western Europe for centuries is just not correct.[18] The Industrial Revolution was one of the most important breakthroughs in world history, but it happened relatively late. The material gap industrialisation created between the West and the non-West (and especially between Europe and Asia) in the nineteenth century has been retroactively exaggerated, while the gap between the forerunners of industrialisation in western Europe and Western latecomers has been minimised.

It was only in the second half of the nineteenth century and the early twentieth century that major Asian polities suffered from substantive economic (and political) backsliding, as well de-industrialisation, due

---

[18] See also Goldstone (2002, 2015).

often to predatory behaviour by western European powers. In the twentieth century, nationalist historical narratives of successor states in the East projected such economic backwardness back in time, often centuries back, thus justifying to respective domestic audiences why the ancien régimes had to be replaced by nationalist or communist regimes with modernising visions. Aided also by European visions of civilisational hierarchies, the political and economic losses of the nineteenth century, spanning a handful decades at most, were turned into narratives of Eastern civilisational backwardness, a backwardness that was supposed to have been predestined for centuries. For many non-Western societies, this imagined gap of centuries became a source of great shame,[19] as well as the motivation for subsequent political pursuits in the twentieth century (seducing funds and resources that could be used elsewhere), but there was nothing inevitable about such an outcome. Had they not been thus turned to ontological and existential dilemmas implicating 'national' and 'civilisational' standing, such material differences in the nineteenth century may not have mattered that much in the long run (as it did not for many European laggards, such as Spain or Austria, who were spared many of the effects of this process of stigmatisation).[20]

We may be tempted to blame Europeans at this juncture: after all, it was European law that imposed 'the standard of civilisation' on the world. There is no denying that in the nineteenth century, especially towards the end of it, certain segments within the European 'civilisation' had reached the apex of feeling superior vis-à-vis other cultures and peoples. Late-nineteenth-century and early-twentieth-century European/Western cultures were – broadly speaking – more racist and exclusionary compared to those of the twentieth century, but they were also these things compared to those of the eighteenth century. But as easy as it would be to blame Europe entirely for the creation of this social/civilisational hierarchy and the imposing of it on the rest of the world in the nineteenth century (and Europe does deserve a sizeable portion of the blame), none of that explains why many on the *receiving* end of the civilisational judgement also internalised it as such. One group of people judging another group of people for not being like

[19] Zarakol (2011).
[20] Such as Spain/Habsburg dominions, despite having followed a similar trajectory.

them is nothing new, and – whatever we think of Western smugness in the nineteenth century and afterwards – history is replete with self-congratulation. The past is also peppered with examples of one group of people needing to borrow technology from another group of people without feeling at all stigmatised by that necessity. It was not always (or even often) that the borrower of a military technology ended up feeling existentially inadequate by the fact that their diet or clothing or hair-style was different from who came up with the technology.

The question we are left with, then, is as follows: why in the *nine-teenth* century did so many people around Asia come to see themselves as not just in need of military technology but also as *civilisationally inferior*?[21] As noted already, the question becomes doubly difficult to answer if one continues to buy into the standard narrative – radically challenged by this book – that it was the expansion of the European international society (or, from a critical perspective, European coloni-alism) that created a global international order encompassing Asia for the very first time. This would mean that Asian polities were not in any way connected to each other previously, which should make it even more surprising that they should have such similar (and similarly timed) responses to European encroachment. The alternative historical account I have reconstructed in this book, as well as the analytical framework I have offered for thinking about different types of sover-eignty models, helps us explain this 'puzzle'. The reasons why Asian elites were vulnerable to stigmatisation by Europeans in the nineteenth century were twofold, both having to do with the history of sovereignty models in Asia and ecumenical decline.

First, Eastern polities, especially the Ottomans and the Chinese, had long-standing internal narratives of 'decline' preserved in their own historiography. A lot of these decline debates were associated with the political tumult during the seventeenth century. But they were not just about that crisis. In Chinggisid and post-Chinggisid polities, such perceptions of decline were often generated by the inevitable transition from the Chinggisid mode to some alternative arrangement of legitim-ation. World conquest is not infinitely sustainable. Because the Chinggisid sovereignty norm relied on extreme political centralisation in the person of specific rulers, on the one hand, and the idea that such rulers had to be world conquerors on the other hand, the deviation

---

[21] For more on this and the consequences, see Zarakol (2011).

from either expectation, whether due to endogenous causes or facilitated by macro-sociological conditions, almost always created instability. Such transitions also drove the perception of decline, at least among some internal observers who understood 'greatness' along these Chinggisid norms. These perceptions of decline were in fact relatively untethered from the objective economic or political health of the polity. Such handwringing about decline is not of course unique to Chinggisid sovereigns: decline debates happen in every society that needs to switch from one package of institutional arrangements (or sovereignty model) that worked well in the past to another as demanded by the pressures of the moment.[22] And ruling elites everywhere, especially those that have achieved 'greatness' as they understand it, always fear future demise. We could speculate, however, that the reliance on 'external recognition' in the form of world conquest made Chinggisid polities particularly more vulnerable to perceptions of decline if expansion or external competition stopped, even in the absence of absolute decline in material prosperity in said conditions. There may be parallels there to our modern order.

Such decline debates in the East from previous periods in history (but especially from the sixteenth and seventeenth centuries) found new life in the long nineteenth century, when they were repurposed due to their encounter with emerging European narratives about the superiority of the West and the stagnation of the East. In the nineteenth century, the externally imposed European narrative of civilisational hierarchies and the internal decline debates in the political thought and historical literatures of Asia *seemed* to corroborate each other, even if they were pointing at entirely different understandings of 'greatness' and causes of 'decline'. The result was an amplification[23] of the notion of 'Eastern decline' from the nineteenth century onwards and its rereading back into history as fact, even to periods it did not apply, and to geographies to which it could not be generalised. A good example of this type of problematic finding of seeming corroboration is Bernard Lewis' famous 1962 essay 'Ottoman Observers of Ottoman Decline', also mentioned in Chapter 4, where he credits Ottoman thinkers at the peak of the empire's power in the sixteenth century for having foreseen

---

[22] The United States has a lot of decline debates of its own. See, for example, Cox (2001, 2007).

[23] More research is needed to explore this argument in each national setting – the degree would have varied by location.

Ottoman decline centuries later, completely overlooking the periods of growth and expansion in the four centuries that stood in between.

More significantly, the fact that the East no longer existed as a shared space organised by its own 'world orders' and the fact that (Eur)Asian politics had become increasingly regionalised from the seventeenth century onwards rendered Asian polities 'anomic' when dealing with a group narrative of civilisational superiority emanating from Europe. Groupness is *the* greatest advantage when it comes to wielding the power to stigmatise.[24] By the nineteenth century, European states, though still in competition with each other, were operating in a relatively consistent manner when dealing with other regions of the world and together were pushing a narrative of group superiority about European/white civilisation. It is very difficult if not impossible for sole actors on the weaker side of an emerging hierarchy to resist such group narratives of normative superiority if they cannot advance alternative group narratives of their own. In the nineteenth century, because the East no longer existed in a coherent space, Eastern elites could not successfully advance such a counter-narrative, though towards the end of the century there were attempts to do so, as I discuss in the next chapter. At the same time, the sociological ghosts of past Eastern 'world orders' were present enough for Asian states to seem similar enough to each other as far as Europeans were concerned and to be tainted by association with each other. The subjugation of any one polity (or any Asian 'race') contributed to the understanding it was the East *altogether* that was lagging behind the West. It was the worst of all worlds from a stigmatisation perspective: not enough groupness to mount a defence, but just enough to be damned by the association.

A final point that is often missed in present-day debates: in this period, many Asian polities were able to emulate European sovereignty models relatively easily once they got going (whether by coercion or choice) because many developments seemingly unique to the European trajectory were actually historically and sociologically driven by struc-tural conditions operating at much larger scale in the northern hemi-sphere (if not globally). If we accept that Asia was not lagging behind Europe by centuries but was simply suffering the adverse effects of various contingent policy choices as well as relatively small

---

[24] See Zarakol (2011), building on the theories of Elias and Scotson (1965) and
      Goffman (1963).

technological gaps that had emerged in the long nineteenth century, then it seems clear that many of the changes either imposed by Western colonialism or self-imposed by local elites to escape that fate could or would have happened in Asia anyway. Emulation of the West was a way of speeding up those developments by locals who desired them against the arguments of locals who did not. The problem is that the consequences of such choices accumulated over time and completely distorted our understanding of pre-nineteenth-century international relations.

Complicating the story of 'the decline of the East' thusly has implications beyond setting the historical record; it forces us to rethink the concept of 'decline' altogether. Decline is often retrospectively projected back onto the past, to periods that would have been experienced very differently by the people living through them. In other words, there is very much a *social* (constructed) element to 'decline'. In other words, ecumenical decline has the potential to distort our understanding of other types of decline in history. This brings us back to the final remaining question for this chapter. If ecumenical decline is a real possibility in world politics, what does that mean for our order? Could what happened to 'the East' happen to 'the West' as well?

The End of the Western Order?

It is almost banal to observe these days that uncertainty haunts world politics in the face of global challenges (and challengers) to the Liberal International Order. The irrational exuberance (in the West) of the post–Cold War decade has become a distant memory. We are still working through the repercussions of 9/11, America's 'War on Terror' and the ensuing conflicts in Afghanistan and Iraq, and the still-open wounds from the so-called Arab Spring from Syria to Yemen. Our order may have survived (for the time being) the Global Financial Crisis of 2007–8, but we had never fully recovered from the traumas it wrought, even before the COVID-19 pandemic hit and brought the world economy to a standstill. Even before then, the major financial players in the West were all bogged down in their own institutional quagmires; it was not at all clear that the financial system had been properly repaired or reformed. Emerging markets that were seen for a while by analysts as the salvation out of that malaise have now come to face their own economic slowdowns. In the meantime, global

income inequality has continued to grow and reached historic propor-
tions. Millions of economic migrants as well as refugees from political
and criminal violence around the world push against (and through) the
borders of the more economically privileged countries of our international system. The COVID-19 pandemic has only exacerbated
these problems, perhaps even for decades to come.

These global problems have had domestic political repercussions as
well: populism and nativism have been on the rise around the world.
Democracies are 'backsliding'. 'Strongmen' have come to power in
every continent, and no regime type – not monarchy (obviously), not
single-party rule (more expectedly), but also not presidential democracy and not even parliamentary democracy – has proven a reliable
bulwark against the takeover of such leaders. These 'strongmen' have
tended to be contemptuous of existing international agreements, treaties and institutions; as a result, international organisations and regimes
thought to be well-established are now threatened, and their continued
existence can no longer be taken for granted. Long-standing alliances
are falling apart and being reconfigured. Major structural challenges
even beyond the current pandemic loom ahead: there is a worldwide
scientific consensus that transformational climate change, specifically
global warming, is well underway and may soon be reaching – if it has
not already – irreversible levels. Technological innovation, specifically
in the realm of artificial intelligence and robotics, also seems poised to
challenge the traditional operating logic of capitalism by displacing
workers out of the consumer base at unprecedented levels. Finally, the
emergence of 'surveillance capitalism' may signal a fundamental shift
of power between nation states and global corporations, with the latter
controlling (and having the capacity to manipulate) more data than
most governments can dream of accessing. It is unlikely that the
COVID-19 pandemic has reversed any of these trends.

All of this adds to a general sensation that the problems we face at
our current juncture may be more than superficial, that they may
actually extend beyond specific politicians and institutions, that we
may be at a real historical juncture, a moment of profound global
change. I say 'sensation' because, while IR scholars have been rather
good at compiling a laundry list of current global problems and
challenges such as the one I just provided, we have not yet developed
a framework for understanding how they are related to each other or
for separating cause and effect. Uncertainty and dread underwrite

our scholarly meetings where we grope for (but ultimately fail to find) ways of thinking about these global challenges within the toolkit of the established IR canon, which suggests one of two explanations.

The first thing we are told by (some) IR scholars is that all of this uncertainty is rooted in an ongoing power transition between the United States and China. As noted in the previous section, Great Power decline and its consequences is well-trodden ground in IR scholarship. A consensus has emerged relatively recently that the United States is in decline as a 'superpower' and that China (and perhaps others) are rising powers. There are those who foresee conflict between the United States and China as inevitable, with danger lurking everywhere in periods of transition, and yet others who argue that American decline can be managed peacefully or even reversed. As interesting as this debate may be, however, it has a number of shortcomings in terms of explaining our current moment. First, the consensus about American decline seems to have emerged after the 2016 presidential election. Given former president Trump's foreign policy decisions and reversals and the damage they did to the image of the United States around the world, the perception of decline is understandable, but it should be noted that the facts underwriting such projections remain debatable within a traditional realist framework as long as US material and military capability outstrips China and others. Second, even if we agree – and I do – that the United States is declining and China is rising (and also that these trajectories will remain as they are for the foreseeable future), the power gap between these countries has not yet closed to the extent that it could be responsible for all of the aforementioned challenges in our international system. In fact, it could even be argued that America's decline is more the *result* of certain global challenges rather than the cause of them. Furthermore, despite increasing consensus in Washington DC that China is a threat, it still debatable whether China is actively trying to undermine the international system in the traditional mould of a 'revisionist power'. Russia, which is not a 'rising power', seems to fit that description better. In any case, both Russia and China – not to mention other 'rising powers' – exhibit high degrees of buy-in to the fundamental norms ('ecumene') of the existing order, such as sovereignty and nationalism, and therefore cannot reasonably be held solely responsible for the current levels of volatility within our system.

If we turn to the second explanation we are given by IR scholars, we find that current global challenges may have something to do with the ongoing crisis of the 'Liberal International Order'. While this is inevitably related to American decline, those who are concerned about the demise of the Liberal International Order are worried about more than the decline of the United States as a Great Power. It had been long maintained, especially within liberal institutionalist IR circles, that hegemonic institutions could outlast the hegemon and in fact alleviate the downsides of Great Power decline. In other words, there was a long-standing belief that the rules, the norms and the institutions of the Liberal International Order would long outlast the peak of the United States' material power and eventually would have been taken over by some of the 'rising powers'. In this vision of the future, the rise of China (or others) was not seen as a threat as long as the new Great Powers bought into the fundamental rules and institutions of the existing international order. What was not anticipated, however, was the current scenario we are living through, where the Liberal International Order is being simultaneously undermined from within and without, with anti-liberal forces in the West constituting even more of a threat than those outside.[25] In other words, while there is a broad consensus that the Liberal International Order is being undermined by current global trends, that consensus is more of a diagnosis as to what is happening rather than an explanation as to how and why.

To sum up, IR has been telling us a lot about the Great Power rivalry between the United States and China, but the debate is not settled as to whether China will act like a typical Great Power. IR has also been telling us that something has unexpectedly gone awry with the Liberal International Order and that it may be falling apart, but it is not able to say much more about what will come next. The literature is just not familiar with historical circumstances in which 'world orders' are not replaced with better, more expansive, versions of themselves, with similar actors in positions of privilege. One of the things I have tried to suggest in this book is that IR should not only fill in those blanks but also imagine other kinds of decline and fragmentation, because they have *happened before*.

For example, IR as a discipline cannot imagine the end of Western domination (to the extent that this is not the same thing as the rise

[25] See Adler-Nissen and Zarakol (2021).

of China), having long pretended that the social, epistemic, ontological centring of the West was not even a factor in international politics. Our discipline has mostly ceded the speculative ground on this issue to kooks and white supremacists of various stripes. I am hoping that the historical account I offer here can help us think about it by comparison to the decentring of the East in world politics, but without the self-congratulation of late-nineteenth- and early-twentieth-century accounts of civilisational decline.

Admittedly, Western-centrism is so embedded in the modern international order that it is hard, if not impossible, to truly imagine a world where this is not a given. Even this book has not been able to escape its terminology and thus has reproduced many of its assumptions and binaries. The social hierarchy between the West and the rest of the world has been around for barely three centuries (if that), yet our social sciences have no idea how the world would function in its absence or in the presence of another social hierarchy with some other centre (or multiple centres). IR continuously assumes the omniscient presence of Western social domination in the international order and then simultaneously forgets it. Western social domination is the 'secret sauce' that much IR (and other) theorising about how the world works relies on; many of our theories, though seemingly identifying other causal mechanisms, could cease to have power in a world where recognition by the West was not such a sought-after good (and also the cause of such resentment). Western-centrism is thus baked into our approaches; because of this, very few of us trained in twentieth-century IR traditions are able to genuinely imagine the end of the current order in an ecumenical sense. Fish cannot imagine the end of the oceans.

And it is not only mainstream IR that is constrained in its imagination of a post-Western future. Critical scholars – of especially decolonial sensibilities – may think they know what such a future looks like because they often advocate for it. However, they are also working with ahistorical assumptions. Such approaches often envision Western social hegemony as a blanket that has covered other parts of the world, and they assume that once that blanket is removed, so to speak (i.e. when the West declines), the non-West will find and reassert its 'authentic' self. This may have its political uses as a world view in the present for its proponents, but it has little resemblance to historical reality. The idea that there is an authentic Chinese or Turkish or Indigenous or non-white culture that can be recovered or defended overlooks how our notions of authenticity (as well as 'China' or 'Turkey' or 'Indigenous'-ness or non-whiteness) are just as much the products of the ecumene of modernity as anything labelled 'Western'. The charge that coercive world-ordering is a feature of only Western political projects is also severely contradicted by the historical account in *Before the West*. The idealisation of the 'non-West' is as problematic as its stigmatisation.

Nobody is free from this entirely: we all have assumed the centrality of the West in our world for the last two centuries. Since the nineteenth century, every other region has looked to the West first to make sense of its place in the world. People, states, regions felt they had 'arrived' when they were recognised by the West. The benchmarks they used to measure their own success all seemed to have Western origins. The international 'standard(s) of civilisation' have evolved over time from racial-religious markers of identity to seemingly more meritocratic ones upholding the Liberal International Order, but these standards always either emanated from the West or were at least disseminated by the West.[26] This has been one of *the* foundational blocks of modern world politics, one of the few main lines that truly demarcate our period from the previous ones.

Theories that do not acknowledge the significance of the 'West versus non-West' social hierarchy for the functioning of the modern international system since the nineteenth century end up assuming, erroneously, that the end of the Western order depends on who the Great Powers are. Many people – including both those who are conservative and those who are critical in their politics – think that if China surpassed the United States in terms of military or economic strength it would hail the arrival of a 'post-Western' future. But that is not how the world works; deep social hierarchies of the type that has existed between the West and the rest of the world for the last two centuries are not so easily dismantled. The election of Barack Obama did not mean that we had arrived at a post-racial United States, nor did Margaret Thatcher's prime ministership (or Theresa May's for that matter) signal the end of gender hierarchies in the United Kingdom. The social hierarchies that underwrite our ecumene could easily survive

---

[26] Zarakol (2011, chapter 2). I am not unsympathetic to the argument that the non-West has played a significant role in shaping those modern standards. I do think, however, that the West has been the primary arbiter of dissemination even in those cases.

(even in their current diluted forms) for many years beyond China's ascent.

Nay, a truly post-Western future (for better or worse) requires something else, something bigger than the rise of China as a Great Power. That sort of change is not about counting the number of American versus Chinese warheads (or banks). To conclude that we have arrived in that future, the assumption of Western centrality to global normative standards will first have to be entirely relaxed, and the belief that the West is 'ahead' of others in qualities deemed desirable by the international community abandoned. The decline of the West (for better or worse) will truly have come to pass when there is a convergence on standards and terminologies that are alternatives to those we have now by which we define, categorise and evaluate actors, places, geographies, communities. We will know it happened when those who live elsewhere forget to wonder what those of us who live in the West are doing or thinking, when they forget that we act at all, that the people who lived here once upon a time even produced world orders. For the East, that moment arrived in the seventeenth century, after a sustained, decades-long structural crisis, underwritten by multiple causes, including climate change. The decades of upheaval forced major polities – even those relatively unaffected by the political manifestations of the turmoil – to turn inwards and/or to burrow into their regions; existing material and ideational networks were severely disrupted. When the dust had settled, towards the end of the seventeenth century, material and political recovery was relatively easy. But the *social* fabric that connected the East (and more) around various shared understandings that gave meaning to the behaviour of actors had irretrievably frayed. Perhaps there is a lesson in that for the twenty-first century.

7 | Uses and Abuses of Macro History in International Relations

Am I a 'Eurasianist'?

An Epilogue

I am aware that my own identity may render some of the arguments in this book suspicious to the reader. I was born in Ankara and raised in Istanbul, Turkey, and now I have written a book that claims to excavate Asian and Eurasian Eastern 'world orders' which can be compared to the European and Western international orders of modernity. My account is mostly about a network of ethnolinguistically Turco-Mongol dynasties throughout Asia. I realise that it is thus possible that the reader has reached these final pages suspecting me of some kind of hidden agenda for a political project of Eurasianism or pan-Turkism or of justifying Asian unity under Turkish leadership in the twenty-first century. This is among the last things I would advocate, but I do not want to just casually dismiss the suspicion.

Another issue is whether the macro-history approach I adopted is defensible in an age where the social sciences have come to increasingly value micro approaches and methodologies, whether in the archives or experiments. What value can there be, after all, in synthetic work based on secondary sources? This is an objection that I often encounter implicitly: conventions of polite society usually prevent academic colleagues from raising the point when I am in the room, but I do want to take it head on here. I am not against micro-oriented approaches and methodologies in IR (to the contrary), but their superior virtue should not be assumed automatically in all contexts and for all questions.

In sum, there are some potential issues with the book that still remain unconfronted. First, there are the political and ethical questions. Are alternative or revisionist histories always political? If so, does this necessarily doom them? Does my own supposedly 'Eurasian' identity render my arguments automatically suspect? Second, there are the disciplinary and methodological questions. Can such a macro-synthetic account be

244

defended as 'good social science' in this day and age? Aren't macro accounts and sweeping generalisations about history intrinsically violent from an epistemological perspective, unjustly reductive of large patches of history, the dynamics of which are always more complex on closer inspection? Do they not inevitably get a lot wrong?

In this Epilogue, I want to get at these questions in a slightly unusual way. Instead of writing a methodology treatise defending my choices, I would like to first (re-)introduce the reader to a few other authors before me who have made macro-historical arguments which seem to me to be in the same family as those in this book. I thought that working through their biographies, as well as their successes and failures in terms of making these macro historical arguments (and also getting them heard), could be rather illustrative for the reader.

The first section will thus discuss three 'Eastern' authors from the late nineteenth and early twentieth centuries who advocated various historical notions about Eurasian and Asian interconnectedness that ran counter to received wisdom (back then and now): Kencho Suematsu, a Japanese scholar and politician who suggested a significant connection between Japanese medieval history and the Mongols; Ziya Gökalp, an Ottoman sociologist who advocated pan-Turanism and pan-Turkism for a while before settling into a state-based version of Turkish nationalism; and George Vernadsky, a respected historian of Russia who was a staunch Russian Eurasianist for a time before moving in a more pro-Western direction. I want to use them to think through both the larger intellectual currents in Asia in the period that they were writing in and also how my own identity and scholarly arguments intersect.[1] And of course, the label 'Eastern' is as misleading there as it is in my case (these biographies spanned many geographies, as do mine), but I nevertheless use it to denote that they had a different relationship to the project of reimagining (Eur)asia than supposedly more objective Western scholars.

The second section will move on to discuss three 'Western' authors from a slightly later period (early to mid-twentieth century) who broadly worked with civilisational arguments: Arnold J. Toynbee, Karl Wittfogel, and Owen Lattimore. All three were very well-known at points in their careers, but their works fell out of popularity in

---

[1] This is not intended as an exhaustive or definitive study of the history of Asian political thought in this period. See, for example, Aydin (2007b, 2013) for a more comprehensive overview.

the second half of the twentieth century. I am interested in this second set of authors partly because there are resonances between the approach I adopt here and their arguments about world history, but each author was also flawed – Wittfogel more than the others – and through their examples I am interested in exploring how and why macro history goes wrong.

The final section brings the discussion to the present and defends macro historical approaches in International Relations and revisionist pan-Asian/Eurasian history from both a social science and a normative perspective.

Eurasia or Pan-Asia As Defensive Self-Narrative

In the end of the nineteenth century and the early decades of the twentieth, many writers throughout Eurasia were toying with various accounts of the world that reached beyond the nascent nation-state mould while also manifesting growing degrees of nationalist attachment. Thus the three writers I have selected – Suematsu Kencho ('Japan'), Ziya Gökalp ('Turkey') and George Vernadsky ('Russia') – do not at all exhaust the possibilities of thinkers who could be discussed under this heading. The geographical distribution is not entirely accidental, however; though China, for instance, had some thinkers who were sympathetic towards pan-Asianism, such as Li Ta-chao,[2] pan-Asian or Eurasianist theories were more likely to emanate from the aforementioned three corners of Asia rather than its core. I think this has something to do with the dynamics I discussed in *After Defeat*: precisely because the Ottoman, Russian and Japanese empires occupied a liminal space in this period (i.e. both as victim and victimiser), so did their narratives of self that were being constructed. As we will see, Eurasian and pan-Asian narratives played a double function: they aimed at propping up the dignity of these countries vis-à-vis Europe/the West, while simultaneously justifying their colonial and expansionist projects in Asia.

Suematsu Kencho and Japanese Mongols

Mongol (Yuan) forces could not conquer Japan, despite attempting to do so twice in 1274 and 1281. Both times they were defeated by

---

[2] See, for example, Meisner (1965).

weather events, and they decided that the island was not worth the trouble. In other words, the Japanese archipelago constitutes one of the few areas in Asia never to have been under the direct rule of the Chinggisids. Given the marginality of Japan to the Chinggisid order, it may seem a bit odd that I am starting our tour of thinkers with inter-Asian connection theories with a Japanese scholar. However, I am interested in Suematsu Kencho as someone who relatively successfully 'fabricated' an inter-Asian connection where there was none, at least in the way he imagined it. By doing so, he inadvertently pointed to a particular historical narrative of Asia that could potentially be taken seriously by Europeans. He thus illustrates both the need for and the difficulty of imagining 'Asia' from an 'Eastern' vantage point at the end of the nineteenth century.

Suematsu (1855–1920) was a journalist who was sent to study at the University of Cambridge by the Japanese government. After returning to Japan in 1886 with a law degree, he married the daughter of Prime Minister Ito and entered politics. He later served the government in a diplomatic mission to Europe, tasked with counteracting anti-Japanese propaganda. He features here because he *invented* the Japanese historical tradition that Minamoto no Yoshitsune (1159–89), the half-brother of the founder of the Kamakura Shogunate,[3] later became Genghis Khan. In telling his story, I am borrowing from a delightful article by Junko Miyawaki-Okada entitled 'The Japanese Origin of the Chinggis Khan Legends',[4] which notes that the notion that Yoshitsune and Genghis Khan were the same person remains popular with the public, even though the theory has long been discredited by scholars.

The invented connection had somewhat of a plausible basis in Japanese history. Yoshitsune (also called Gen Gikei) was considered a military genius by his contemporaries. He had a falling-out with his brother Yoritomo, who then had him killed in 1189, at the age of thirty-one. But Yoshitsune's legend lived on, and by the fifteenth century there was a widespread belief that he had not in fact been killed. Eventually, people came to believe that he crossed from the north into continental Asia proper. In the seventeenth century, a pseudo-history

---

[3] From 1185 to 1333, sovereignty rested with the shoguns (originally a military title). This is yet another sovereignty model.
[4] Miyawaki-Okada (2006).

claimed that a grandson of Yoshitsune had later become the commander of the Qing, replacing the Ming in 1644 to rule China until
the Republican period. This account gained some popularity in Japan
despite being discredited soon after publication. Though Miyawaka-
Okada does not comment on this point, we can surmise that the claim
of Japanese descent for the Qing was an attempt to rethink Japan's
traditional relationship with (the ruling dynasty of) China and put the
two on more equal footing. The supposed Japanese origins of the Qing
were then 'reconfirmed' by the nineteenth-century traveller Mamiya
Rinzo, who reported back continental rumours with the same premise
(i.e. the Manchu were Japanese).[5]

In other words, by the time Suematsu arrived on the scene at the end
of the nineteenth century, there had been a well-established myth in
Japan that the Qing (Manchu) Dynasty in China and the Japanese
people were somehow connected. It was Suematsu, however, who
brought all these threads together in a treatise published during his
time at Cambridge called 'Genghis Khan was Minamoto no Yoshitsune
or Gen Gikei'.[6] Drawing upon the work of Yasuo Nagayama,[7]
Miyawaka-Okada suggests that Suematsu was driven to claim this
heritage in order to impress his British hosts. According to Suematsu,
Yoshitsune's death was a deception, and he had indeed escaped to Asia
as the legend claimed. There, he had become Genghis Khan. In evidence
of this transformation, Suematsu put forward the following evidence:
'that there were no written records of the first half of [Genghis Khan's]
life; that his name read in Chinese characters, Gen was comparable to
Genghis; that the Japanese name of a god, tenjin, was turned into
Temüjin ... that the Mongolian custom of valuing number nine was
the fact that Yoshitsune was Kurô or the ninth son, and on'.[8]
Suematsu's book was translated into Japanese and became
a bestseller in 1885.

In the 1920s, during the Japanese excursion into Siberia, another
writer called Mataichiro Oyabe picked up the same theme. Oyabe
travelled areas of Asia occupied by the Japanese army: 'those places
where there were said to be sites of the Chinggis Khan legends ...
explaining to the Japanese reader that in each case the customs of the

[5] Ibid., p. 128.   [6] Ibid., p. 129.
[7] Nagayama (1998), as cited by Miyawaki-Okada (2006, p. 129).
[8] Miyawaki-Okada (2006, pp. 130–1).

Mongols he met resembled Japanese ones, with the final aim of establishing his theory Chinggis Khan was Minamoto no Yoshitsune'.[9] Miyawaka-Okada suggests that this line of reasoning was especially popular in that period because it gave comfort to the Japanese soldiers who were moving through the same region. This was a period where Japanese pan-Asianism also drew considerable influences from Russian Eurasianism: a number of works were translated from Russian to Japanese, including Trubetskoi's[10] *Europe and Mankind*.[11]

Miyawaka-Okada also speculates that claiming kinship with the Mongols was a way of impressing on the Europeans the greatness of Japan, because to the Europeans the Mongols had represented *Asia* since the thirteenth century: 'To the Japanese, raised in an insular nation, it was encouraging [to believe] that their race had once spread as far as Europe . . . [and] the fantasy inspired [the] Japanese to travel to the strange land of continental China. Moreover, this theory greatly increased the strong affinity felt towards the Mongol people by the Japanese.'[12] Indeed, the invented links between Japan and the Mongols are not limited to the attributed Japanese identity of Genghis Khan. After the Second World War, the Japanese historian Namio Egami advanced another similar theory, the 'Horsemen Theory', claiming that the Japanese Imperial family were descended from horsemen from the Mongol steppes.[13] Despite the absence of evidence, the theory remains popular in Japan to the present day, precisely because it again links the Japanese ruling class with the Mongols who ruled over the world – and especially over China.[14]

Suematsu was writing at a time when Japan was forging its nation-state identity and was both emulating and competing against European empires. The invented connection to render Genghis Khan Japanese raised the historical profile of Japan both vis-à-vis Europe *and* China, while seemingly legitimising Japanese colonialism in areas historically subjected to Mongol rule. I would wager that he did not outright lie and actually believed that he had discovered a connection between Genghis Khan and Yoshitsune. If looking at history a particular way gives you exactly the secret sauce you need for present-day political purposes, it is very difficult not to look at history that way. At the same time, it is

---

[9] Ibid., p. 131.   [10] We will return to Trubetskoi later.
[11] For more on the connections between Russian Eurasianism and Japanese pan-Asianism, see Saito (2017).
[12] Miyawaki-Okada (2006, p. 133).   [13] Ibid., p. 124.   [14] Ibid., p. 126.

equally problematic to shy away from particular historical narratives that get us closer to a more comprehensive understanding just because they could be abused for political purposes by present-day actors.

Ziya Gökalp and Pan-Turanism

Ziya Gökalp (1876–1924) was an Ottoman thinker whose work some have described as entirely derivative from Durkheim; yet others have named him the founder of Turkish sociology.[15] He is a figure very closely associated with Turkish nationalism, as he advocated the Turkification of the Ottoman Empire, contrary to the other trends of his time such as pan-Ottomanism and pan-Islamism, which were initially more popular. Many of his arguments were picked up and reproduced by Kemalism after the collapse of the Ottoman Empire and the founding of the Turkish Republic.

Gökalp was well-versed in Western social sciences, and he was particularly influenced by Durkheim but also Tönnies. Topal criticises the temptation to read Gökalp only with reference Western sociology and locates Gökalp in a long-standing tradition of Ottoman thinkers who conceptualised decline and revival, often with a Khaldunian reflection.[16] My interest in Gökalp, however, stems from the fact that, before Gökalp had settled into a state-oriented understanding of the Turkish nation, he flirted with pan-Turkism and Turanism, ideologies that could be considered Eurasianist. He was by no means the only Turkish/Ottoman thinker to do so, but he is among the more serious, and thus he offers a decent entry point for thinking about a number of racialised nineteenth-century conceptions about Asia/Eurasia.

To give some background, pan-Turkism originated in the second half of the nineteenth century among Turkic intellectuals living in the Russian Empire, as a response to pan-Slavism, another popular ideology of the time.[17] Pan-Turkism had its golden age at the beginning of the twentieth century, with pan-Turkic intellectuals in the Russian Empire making connections with their Ottoman counterparts.[18] Pan-Turkism advocated the collaboration and eventual unity of the Turkic people. Leaders of the Committee of Union and Progress (CUP), which was the governing party of the Ottoman Empire during the Second

---

[15] Topal (2017).   [16] Ibid., p. 288.   [17] Landau (2004, pp. 30–1).
[18] Tokluoğlu (2012, p. 106).

Constitutional Era (1908–1912), were very sympathetic to this ideology.[19] The 'Three Pashas' triumvirate that usurped de facto power with the 1913 coup and ruled over the empire during the First World War (and who were responsible for the Armenian Genocide of 1915) were especially attached to pan-Turkism. Indeed, after the triumvirate was ousted from power at the end of the First World War, Enver Pasha went into exile and travelled to Bukhara in 1921. He eventually took up the leadership of the Basmachi (or the Turkestan Liberation Organisation) movement's uprising against Moscow. He would be killed near Dushanbe in 1922.

Pan-Turanism, on the other hand, is a broader ideology than pan-Turkism and superficially shares more elements with the argument I have made in this book (more on this disturbing thought later).[20] Turan is originally a geographical term, used from the eighteenth century onwards to refer to Inner Asia. According to pan-Turanism (or Turanism), which had its origins in the early-nineteenth-century linguistic works of the Finnish ethnologist/nationalist Matthias Alexander Castren (1813–52),[21] a number of peoples – including the Finns – originate from Turan (Central Asia) and thus should eventually be reunited or brought under the same political rule in order to attain future greatness. As was the case with pan-Turkism, pan-Turanism also originated in regions under Russian rule (or threat) as a response to pan-Slavism.

In a 1917 *APSR* article on 'Pan-Turanism', the American white supremacist[22] T. Lothrop Stoddard took this designation at face value and described 'Turanians' as 'the Ottoman Turks of Constantinople and Anatolia, the Turcomans of Central Asia and Persia, the Tartars of southern Russia and Transcaucasia, the Magyars of Hungary, the Finns of Finland and the Baltic provinces, the aboriginal tribes of Siberia, and even the distant Mongols and Manchus'[23] and remarked that, though these people seem diverse in appearance and culture, they shared common traits (e.g. language but

---

[19] The CUP also looked up to Meiji Japan. Gökalp was also initially a member of the CUP, and he also admired Japan as a model for the Ottoman Empire. See Aydın (2007b).

[20] Though the terms are at times used interchangeably by some authors.

[21] During Castren's lifetime, 'Finland' was part of the Russian Empire, which allowed him to conduct field research in Siberia.

[22] He was a member of the Ku Klux Klan.   [23] Stoddard (1917, p. 16).

also temperament). According to Stoddard, the Turanians were phys-
ically tough and tenacious in character but lacked imagination and
artistic sense. This is what made possible the military capacity of the
Turanians who 'certainly have been the greatest conquerors and
empire-builders that the world has ever seen. Attila and his Huns,
Arpad and his Magyars, Isperich and his Bulgars, Alp Arslan and his
Seljuks, Ertogrul and his Ottomans, Genghis Khan and Tamerlane with
their "inflexible" Mongol hordes, Baber in India, even Kubilai Khan
and Nurhacu in far-off Cathay: the type is ever the same.'[24]
Interestingly, Stoppard also paused to consider whether such
a diverse group could actually form a 'genuine race' but then concluded
that the threat remained the same as long as they thought they did.
Stoppard especially blamed Hungarian scholars such as Armin[ius]
Vambery (1832–1913)[25] for awakening these groups to their common
Asiatic origins. It was true that pan-Turanism was rather popular in
Hungary at the time, seen as an alternative to pan-Slavism, and
a magazine called *Turan* was published in Hungary from 1913 to
1970 with support from the Hungarian government.[26]

Gökalp was certainly influenced by both pan-Turkism and pan-
Turanism in his early career. Pan-Turkism was being propagated by
émigrés to the Ottoman Empire from the Russian Empire, thinkers
such as Yusuf Akçura, a Tatar writer who studied with Ernest Renan
in Paris and advocated a common blood-based Turkish union. Gökalp
built on Akçura's arguments but shed some of the more racialised
aspects, arguing that nations have never been racially pure.[27] Another
influential figure at this time was Ahmet Ağaoğlu, who emigrated to the
Ottoman Empire from the Russian Empire in 1908. Ağaoğlu was also
a student of Ernest Renan and an avid pan-Turanist.[28] In the same
period, there were also a number of political associations within and
outside the Ottoman Empire advocating these views and circulating
publications with these messages. In terms of Gökalp's personal intellectual journey, he seems to have been initially very attracted to pan-
Turanism, going even so far as to publish a poem in 1911 with the title

---

[24] Ibid.
[25] Vambery was a Hungarian Turkologist who travelled through the Ottoman
Empire in the mid-nineteenth century and made his way all the way to
Samarqand. He advocated the theory that Turks and Hungarians shared
common linguistic origins in Asia.
[26] Tokluoğlu (2012, p. 110).   [27] Ibid., p. 116.   [28] Ibid., p. 120.

'Turan'.[29] At the time, he defined Turan as the ideal homeland[30] that contained all the lands where Turks/Turan lived and Turkish/Turanian was spoken.[31] However, as pan-Turanism started gaining a more political flavour globally, Gökalp distanced himself from the label. In 1923, he explicitly stated that Turanism was only an ideal for Turks, while leaving open the future possibility that other peoples may one day be united under this banner.[32] Gökalp eventually settled on the position that the most defensible ideology was a more pragmatic Turkey-ism, making a marked distinction between 'Turks-in-here' and 'Turks-out-there'.[33] This distinction would also become the official position of Turkish nationalism within the Republic of Turkey.

Pan-Turkism and pan-Turanism fell out of official favour in the Republic years, partly because they were strongly associated with Enver Pasha and the Committee on Union and Progress, as well as their disastrous military and political campaigns, which are blamed for the demise of the Ottoman Empire. They also fell out of favour partly because these ideologies put Turkey right in the crosshairs of the USSR by advocating the unity of Turkish Turks in Turkey with the Turkic Turks in the Central Asian Soviet Republics. Pan-Turanism became less popular also in Finland and Hungary. These ideologies never fully went away, however, and they would sometimes resurface among certain groups – especially military officers – throughout the twentieth century. Eurasianism has been enjoying a much greater resurgence in Turkey in the last few decades especially[34] and may even be partially responsible for the recent pivot in Turkish foreign policy towards Russia. Interestingly, at the same time, pan-Turanian notions have made a comeback in Hungary as well and have been at times advocated by the Orban government.[35]

---

[29] Ibid., p. 126.
[30] One of the Turkish words for homeland is *yurt* (the same Mongolian origin as the word that means 'tent' in English).
[31] Ibid., p. 128.
[32] Gökalp (1973 [1923], p. 27), as cited in Tokluoğlu (2012, p. 129).
[33] 'İç Türkler' and 'Dış Türkler'. For more, see Tokluoğlu (2012).
[34] For more on the links between Turkish and Russian Eurasianism, see Yanık (2019).
[35] For more, see Korkut (2017).

George Vernadsky and Eurasianism

Russian Eurasianism – 'the idea that Russia was neither Europe nor Asia but a world unto itself'[36] – also has nineteenth-century roots, but – unlike the examples discussed – the origins of Russian Eurasianism are not in the study of genealogy or linguistics but rather in the discipline of geography. Nineteenth-century geographers started conceiving of Eurasia as one continent, and in the twentieth century this geographical categorisation became an answer to the problem of belonging that had plagued Russia for centuries.[37] Thinkers such as Nikolai Trubetskoi (1890–1938) and Peter Savitskii (1895–1968) advocated Eurasianism as Russia's real cultural identity, with the former arguing in favour of the positive influence of the Mongols on the Russian ethos and against Peter the Great's modernisation efforts.[38] For my purposes here, however, George Vernadsky (1887–1973) is the most interesting Eurasianist. What sets Vernadsky apart from the others is the fact that, though he was trained at Moscow University and then worked at the Academy of Sciences in St Petersburg, he emigrated in 1920 first to Europe and then in 1927 to the United States, to Yale University, where he became a respected historian of Russia. He thus also creates a bridge between the 'local' or 'native' scholars of Eurasia I have discussed in this section and the scholars I will discuss in the next section.

In the early part of his career, Vernadsky produced a number of articles in which he argued 'that the Russian national character per-force changed as the Russians moved eastward, "against the sun." Experience with varying geographic and climatic zones and intermarriage with native Siberian peoples altered the Russian personality of necessity.'[39] More importantly, he presented 'the Mongol conquest of Russia as the pivotal development in the course of Russian history'.[40] According to Vernadsky, by transforming Russian relationship with the steppe, 'the Mongols solved what had been the problem of Russia's eastward expansion during the Kievan period . . . . The Mongols organized the disorganized steppe, which in the long run facilitated Russian expansion eastward.'[41] The Mongols also weakened Russian principalities and the aristocracy and thus allowed the rise of a strong

---

[36] Halperin (1982a, p. 477).   [37] Laruelle (2016). See also Yanık (2019, p. 35).
[38] Laruelle (2016).   [39] Halperin (1982a, p. 478).   [40] Ibid., p. 479.
[41] Ibid.

centralised government in Muscovy. In other words, according to Vernadsky, Russians wanted and needed to expand into the steppe before Mongol rule but lacked the state capacity to do so. Having been transformed by the Golden Horde period, they started moving towards Asia in the sixteenth century and did not stop moving until they crossed into North America in the nineteenth century.[42]

After the Bolshevik Revolution, Vernadsky made his way to Prague, where he stayed for five years, during which time he became associated with the aforementioned Eurasianists Trubetskoi and Savitskii, who were arguing that 'Eurasia was a self-contained geographical entity whose boundaries coincided roughly with those of the Russian Empire in 1914 .... [Russia's] geopolitical destiny was to unite all of Eurasia under its authority, to recreate the empire of Genghis Khan. The Russians had more in common with their fellow Eurasian, Inner Asian peoples.'[43] According to the Eurasianists, 'Eurasian peoples instinctively obeyed a centralized autocratic authority' but Marxism as a European import was doomed to fail and when it did Russian greatness would be restored by those who understood her true nature.[44] Halperin comments on the anomaly of Vernadsky's affiliation with the Eurasianists given his Westernised background and education (it was no more anomalous than French educated Turkic émigrés from Russia taking up Pan-Turanism as discussed earlier). Most of the émigré community rejected these views.

During his time in Europe, Vernadsky authored a number of articles focused on the Catholic–Orthodox hatred, one of which is especially relevant to our discussion here. In an article on Alexander Nevsky (1221–63), prince of Novgorod and a key figure in medieval Russian history, Vernadsky argued that 'Nevskii's two feats were fighting off the Latin enemies and submitting in all humility to the Mongols, thus saving Russian national consciousness and Orthodoxy.'[45] Unlike the Teutonic and Livonian knights from the West who forced Russians to convert, the Mongols did not threaten the Russian soul because they practised religious toleration. In 1934, Vernadsky published a book called *Opyt istorii Evrazii* which 'attempted to integrate histories of all the peoples of Eurasia'[46] by drawing parallels between Russian and Inner Asian history and arguing once again that 'Russia is the

---

[42] Ibid., p. 480.   [43] Ibid., p. 481.   [44] Ibid., p. 481–2.   [45] Ibid., p. 485.
[46] Ibid., p. 486.

geopolitical heir of the Chinggisid Empire'.[47] However, later, in the five-volume history of Russia (published starting in 1948 over nearly three decades) he is best known for, Vernadsky modified his argument to one that was more favourably disposed towards Western influences on Russia as well as one that underlined the democratic values within Russian history.[48] He also toned down his arguments about the positive influence of the Mongols on Muscovite state structure. In the United States, Vernadsky distanced himself from the authoritarian politics of the Eurasianists.

In sum, just as Gökalp had moderated his views from a more grandiose pan-Asian/Turkic ideology towards a state-based Turkish nationalism due to a degree of political realism on his part, Vernadsky moderated his views from a more grandiose and proud Eurasian/pro-Mongol conception of Russia towards one that embraced greater degrees of Westernism. Political realism played a role in Vernadsky's case as well. Vernadsky had been exiled from Russia due to the Bolshevik takeover, and the West had given him a new home. While it was surely not only political expediency that made him change his views, allowing for the positive historical influence of Westernisation of Russia made the same leverage more rhetorically applicable in the twentieth century. Unadulterated Eurasianism, by contrast, did not make for fertile ground when it came to criticising the Soviet model. The Soviet model did in fact render Eurasianism somewhat superfluous in the twentieth century, because communism itself seemed to provide the needed all-encompassing ideological tent to unite all the disparate peoples across the geographies of not only Eurasia but the entire world against 'the West'. Thus, as was the case in Turkey as discussed, Eurasianism fell out of favour in Russia/USSR for most of the twentieth century, only to make a strong comeback in the last few decades, after the end of the Cold War.[49]

Some General Observations

These were all men of their time. Their thinking inevitably reflected their and their countries' geopolitical positions and problems, and each suffered from certain blind spots specific to their time when it came to their understanding of world history and their own identities

---

[47] Ibid., p. 487.   [48] Ibid., p. 488.   [49] See, for example, Laruelle (2016).

(as do we all). We could not justifiably claim, however, that these men had political motivations only. Their theories had elements of historical 'truth' (some more than others), and their desire to find a basis for identity that superceeded the state and could match those emanating from western Europe in the nineteenth century was an understandable one. After all, from the second half of the nineteenth century to the Second World War, certain overlapping groups were explicitly privileged within the international order – imperial powers, whites, (Western) Europeans, Anglo-Saxons, Christians, Westerners and so on – and each of these in-groupings generated alternative visions along the same axes of categorisation.[50]

Many of the pan-ideologies that were developed at the turn of the century in response to the various Western justifications for the privilege of the core were discredited along with the originals, and perhaps rightly so. The trouble is that alternative visions of community often got buried with these flawed attempts. I think we can count the possibilities of a certain sort of pan-Asianism or Eurasianism among these lost promises; it is possible to imagine visions of Asia that were not ethnicised or racialised or religious (Lattimore in the next section approximates such a vision), possibilities which could have provided a simultaneously more ecumenical and more unifying vision of regional community than those based on religion (e.g. the Muslim World) or postcolonial understanding of regions (e.g the Third World).

We should not forget that having to embrace the nation state but each having to do so *alone* in the face of the relative cohesiveness of Europe/the West is one of the factors that contributed to the weakened social status of Eastern states in the twentieth-century international order. The great bait-and-switch of modernity is to promise individualism (or anarchy in the case of nation states) but to hide, in the midst of all that discourse about individual rights and sovereign inequality, various status clubs, members of which benefit greatly from their exclusivity and cohesion. To put it another way, 'groupness' already exists in the international order in the form of 'the West', so not having comparable 'groupness' has been a great social, economic and political disadvantage; hence the continued experiments throughout the last century with Third Worldism or the Global South or the Muslim World. The problem with many such efforts, however, is that they

---

[50] See Aydın (2007a).

overlook genuine alternative historical connections and conceptualisations that could be emphasised in favour of manufactured rhetorical schemas that replicate and mirror the hierarchies of the modern international order.

World History, Civilisations and (Eur)Asia

This section briefly covers three Western thinkers who took the notion of civilisation seriously as well as the idea that (Eur)Asia had its own distinct history: the British historian Arnold J. Toynbee; the German-American historian Karl Wittfogel; and the American scholar Owen Lattimore. Though macro-oriented comparative world history has never entirely disappeared (and now has made a comeback of sorts), having some very notable practitioners throughout the twentieth century to the present – such as Fernand Braudel (1902–85) and the Annales School, William H. McNeill (1917–2016), Marshall Hodgson (1922–68, but most of his seminal scholarship was published posthumously in the 1970s), Joseph Fletcher (1934–84, but much of his scholarship was also published posthumously), Janet Abu-Lughod (1928–2013), Patricia Crone (1945–2015), Victor Lieberman (1945–), Jack Goldstone (1953–), Sanjay Subrahmanyam (1961–) and so on – I wanted to return to these earlier writers because they were arguably in what we could call the golden age of macro world history, driven by the increasing encounter between the West and the rest of the world and the need to make comprehensive sense of it all. If the trajectory of world history is one from immense popularity until the middle of the twentieth century to increased marginalisation in the second half to a possible resurgence now under the banner of global history, it makes sense to first understand what made it appealing initially.

Arnold J. Toynbee and Civilisations

Toynbee (1889–1975) was an Oxford-educated British historian and one of the most popular writers of his time:[51] 'in 1947, *Time* magazine considered his historical significance to be on par with Marx'.[52] He fell

---

[51] See, for example, McNeill (1988, 1989).
[52] Lang (2011, p. 747). On how Toynbee lost Luce's support by not agreeing with him, see McNeill (1988, pp. 23–4).

out of favour in the second half of the twentieth century. Michael Lang opens his 2011 essay on Toynbee and 'global history' by noting that most world historians regard Toynbee 'like an embarrassing uncle at a house party [who] gets a requisite introduction by virtue of his place on the family tree, but ... is quickly passed over for other friends and relatives'.[53] Unlike, for instance, Wittfogel, who we will discuss next, however, Toynbee does every now and then get revisited by those who find things to recommend about his approach to history.[54]

Toynbee was writing against a background wherein evolutionary idealism dominated scholarly debates. Evolutionary idealists saw increasing global integration from late nineteenth century onwards as evidence of human 'progress'[55] and the advance of European civilisation.[56] Toynbee was exposed to these notions in Oxford and at first was rather taken with them. He saw the First World War as a confirmation of these views, arguing that European peoples would soon arrive 'into a "post-nationalist" phase of cooperation and peace' and that 'those in the "outer darkness" would now "find their own souls," while Europeans broadened theirs'.[57] However, midway through the war, he was shifted into a government position that required him to study the Ottoman Empire. Toynbee's views underwent considerable change as a result: 'The intractable demands and then violent failure of many postwar arrangements pushed him to question whether the Europeanization of the world necessarily entailed its unification.'[58] In *The Western Question in Greece and Turkey*,[59] Toynbee raised questions about whether 'the "Western formula" of national governance' had helped Greece and Turkey or had brought them into further conflict. Also in this book he started questioning the notion of convergence on Western civilisation, though he still noted that Western civilisation was transforming the planet: 'omnipresent and indefatigable in creation and destruction, like some gigantic force of nature'.[60] According to Toynbee, this was a material transformation but not a spiritual one: 'Consequently, the world's different

---

[53] Lang (2011, p. 747).

[54] Among these, Lang notes Arnaldo Momigliano, who 'pointed to Toynbee's "single-handed achievement in deprovincializing history"', as well as Benedikt Stuchtey, Eckhardt Fuchs and Jürgen Osterhammel. Lang (2011, p. 781).

[55] Lang (2011, p. 754).   [56] Ibid., p. 755.   [57] Ibid., p. 761.   [58] Ibid., p. 765.

[59] Toynbee (2019 [1922]).

[60] Lang (2011, p. 766). See also McNeill (1988, p. 18).

civilizations were each ruptured within, "Westernized in every limb and organ – except the heart".'[61] Toynbee argued that 'civilizations were all "offspring of the same family," and this biological condition constituted a "universality" across them', but they could not be entirely translated into each other because each civilisation had its own essence, its own 'spiritual' character.[62]

In the multi-volume *A Study of History*, which he started sketching on the way back from his trip to Turkey, Toynbee found the same dynamics in social orders of the past, arguing against the 'unity of history' thesis. Toynbee traced extinct civilisations as well as living ones (twenty-one in total) to argue that civilisations were movements which evolved from the interaction between an environmental stimulus and a creative solution:

> The 'human psyche', under pressure from natural conditions, created the first civilizations, which themselves then generated new kinds of natural and social pressures, requiring ever-fresh responses from the 'inner creative factor'. Additional civilizations then arose when such reactions failed and the conditions of ruin acted as a foundational stimulus for initiating a new endeavor.[63]

Civilisations would thus be born, grow and die,[64] and 'in the process throw up their successors'.[65] They also had spiritual endeavours: 'Each civilization envisioned salvation in a discrete and original way, and this constituted its "qualitative uniqueness", its "own different destiny". On the other hand, the commonality of the goal unified these differences into knowable comparability.'[66] For Toynbee, Europe's civilisation was not unique or historically superior.[67]

Yet, though he devoted his entire career to it, Toynbee could not find a satisfactory solution to the problem of reconciling the universalist demands of Western civilisation with the particularities of other civilisations. His work became increasingly unpopular both due to the 'mystical' qualities of his argument but also because the discipline of

[61] Lang (2011, p. 767).   [62] Ibid., p. 769.   [63] Ibid., p. 771.
[64] See also McNeill (1988, p. 15). Spengler had similar notions of life cycles but was much more deterministic and did not give any explanations as to how this process originated or unfolded. Also Toynbee rejected the individual analogy.
[65] Kumar (2014, p. 830).   [66] Lang (2011, p. 773); McNeill (1988, p. 15).
[67] Kumar (2014, p. 837). He also came to see Japanese Buddhism as superior to Christianity, Islam and Judaism because of its pluralism. See McNeill (1988, p. 25).

history changed: 'Postwar historians ... increasingly turned away from ideas, synthesis, and narrative for the "modernism" of impartial evidence, minute focus, and delimited claims of significance.'[68] At the same time, IR moved in a more 'scientific' direction as well. Toynbee's humanistic macro approach increasingly did not fit in either camp. Lang argues that Toynbee anticipated the challenges of doing the history of the global: 'The integrative narrations of world history thus easily surpass the older methodological atomism, but even as they highlight diversification, they cannot represent the antinomy of these global circumstances.'[69] McNeill credits Toynbee for moving in the right direction over the course of his career, towards an acknowledgment that civilisations are not really separate.[70] McNeill, himself a great world historian, even wrote a biography of Toynbee in order to redeem Toynbee's scholarly reputation. Krishan Kumar suggests that the renewal of interest[71] in the concept of 'civilisation' should also re-spark an interest in Toynbee: 'The return of civilization as a form of analysis is at least partly bound up with the return of the old questions: "What is the West?" and "What is the relation of the West to 'the rest'?".'[72] He writes that 'when asked by a journalist in 1965 how he would like to be remembered, Toynbee replied: "As someone who has tried to see it whole, and ... not just in Western terms"'[73] and suggests that Toynbee, perhaps more than anyone else, was the pioneer of global, comparative, history.

Karl Wittfogel and Oriental Despotism

Though hardly anyone[74] ever reads him anymore, in the first half of the twentieth century Wittfogel (1896–1988) was one of the best-known names in the study of Asia.[75] Born in Hanover in 1896, Wittfogel had been very active in the communist movement as a young man. After Hitler came to power, he escaped, making his way eventually to the United States. He took the Molotov–Ribbentrop pact as a personal

---

[68] Lang (2011, p. 780).   [69] Ibid., 782.   [70] McNeill (1988).
[71] See, for example, works by Huntington, Ferguson, Pagden, Morris, Fernandez-Armesto etc.
[72] Kumar (2014, p. 818).   [73] Ibid., p. 838.
[74] Once again, I am the exception. Zarakol (2011) has both Toynbee and Wittfogel.
[75] See Smith (1987).

betrayal. Wittfogel became a public denouncer of communism, even
testifying before the Senate Committee during the McCarthy years and
implicating fellow academics, such as Owen Lattimore (whose career
we will discuss next).[76] He also spent his career developing a theory of
'Oriental Despotism' within a Marxian framework, possibly in order
to reconcile his earlier attachment to Marx with his later disillusion-
ment with the USSR.

Simplifying a bit, according to Wittfogel what distinguished Asia
from Europe was the fact that agriculture in Asia necessitated irrigation
due to ecological factors, and irrigation of this scale necessitated hierarchical and despotic social organisation.[77] Asian states were thus
'hydraulic' bureaucracies under 'Oriental Despotism', and this is why
the USSR or China had turned out the way they did (i.e. coercive,
authoritarian). In fact, in my first book, *After Defeat*, I used
Wittfogel as a prime example of Russia's stigmatisation during the
Cold War years, quoting from his 1950 article 'Russia and Asia', in
which Wittfogel argues that Russia was made into an Asiatic society by
the Mongols.[78] In *After Defeat* I argued that 'it is difficult not to come
away from this passage with a feeling that it was the (Asian, Eastern,
Oriental) Mongols who "ruined" it for the Russians who may otherwise have turned out as all white races are supposed to',[79] and it was
problematic, to put it mildly, to attribute everything that was wrong
with the USSR to the Mongols. I must admit now, as we have seen in
this book, that there was a kernel of truth in what Wittfogel argued (but
he was wrong assuming that that influence was inherently ruinous),
and how to discuss these matters without slipping into racist reductionism or essentialism à la Wittfogel or Stoddard is exactly the crux of
matter.

Wittfogel had broken with 'with the emerging Stalinist orthodoxy
over the latter's insistence on universal adherence to a unilinear path of
history based on the European model',[80] and after half a century
disproving every facet of modernisation theory I think we can all
agree that unilinear path models derived from the experience of
Europe are bad scholarship. The question then becomes: how should

---

[76] 'Wittfogel argued that Lattimore's use of "feudal" and "feudal survival" to
describe Chinese society betrayed an orthodox marxist conception of history
and society' (Smith 1987, p. 129).
[77] Ibid., p. 127.   [78] Wittfogel (1950, p. 450).   [79] Zarakol (2011, p. 216).
[80] Rowe (2007).

we acknowledge that there may be certain historically common experiences that make (parts of) Asia different from (parts of) Europe and similar to each other without also reading into that difference some kind of racial or civilisational hierarchy or teleology?

Wittfogel's reductionism about Asia was challenged in his lifetime as well. For example, in a 1963 essay, Maurice Meisner, a well-respected historian of China and communism, questioned whether Wittfogel's theories applied to China at all and challenged Wittfogel's claim of indebtedness to Marx for his theories. Meisner observed that neither Marx nor Engels applied the theories derived from India to China: 'Between 1857 and 1862 Marx and Engels wrote at least twenty articles dealing with China ... Nowhere does Marx directly refer to China as "Orientally despotic".'[81] Thus, Wittfogel was mistaken in arguing that these societies could be reduced to each other: 'The theory that if a society is not feudal according to the Western European pattern then it must ... be described as of the "Orientally despotic" variety is an assumption that has been made by Karl Wittfogel and not by Karl Marx.'[82] Meisner also noted that 'Marx insisted upon the necessity of studying the particular characteristics of diverse paths of historical development .... Analogous events taking place in different historical surroundings lead to totally different results.'[83] Meisner also used Marx to challenge Wittfogel's contention that 'traditional Chinese social structure was (and is) essentially immutable'[84] by noting that 'not only were the founding fathers of Marxism convinced that China was experiencing a capitalist economic revolution, Marx went so far as to express fears that the socialist revolution in Europe might be inhibited by the ascendancy of capitalism in the vast non-European areas of the world'.[85]

Given the prescience of the quote for our times, it should suffice to conclude that Marx – though he too is often accused[86] of Eurocentrism as he was operating with hardly more than secondary knowledge of most regions he wrote about – got much more of the picture right than Wittfogel, a supposed expert in Asian politics. The next sections may shed some light as to why.

---

[81] Meisner (1963, p. 102). [82] Ibid., p. 103. [83] Ibid., p. 105.
[84] Ibid., p. 107. [85] Ibid., p. 109.
[86] See, for example, Lindner (2010, pp. 27–41) for an overview.

Owen Lattimore and the Asian Freedom Bloc

Owen Lattimore (1900–89) was born in Washington DC but spent his childhood in China. He made significant contributions to our under-standing of Inner/Central Asia and in fact defined that field of study.[87] Though he also at times held influential policy advisory positions, Lattimore is perhaps best remembered for the period he was targeted by Joseph McCarthy. By President Roosevelt's recommendation, Chiang Kai-Shek made Lattimore his political adviser in 1940. The relationship lasted only a year and made Lattimore more sceptical of the Kuomintang. It was Lattimore's criticisms of the Kuomintang that put him in the crosshairs of McCarthy and McCarran, who, with the support of the China lobby in the United States, named him 'as "the top Russian espionage agent in the US" and as "a principal architect" of American Far Eastern policy, one of those responsible for having "lost China" to communism'.[88] As a result, Lattimore lost his directorship of Johns Hopkins University's Page School of International Relations and left the United States, not to return until 1985, a few years before his death. His scholarly work fell out of favour after his denouncement, but later his influence was acknowledged by new generations of com-parative historians.[89]

Like others we have discussed, Lattimore 'was a key participant in the vogue of an especially ambitious kind of generalized historical comparison, a "search for the morphology of history"'.[90] William T. Rowe, an eminent historian of China, observes that 'this kind of audacious historical vision has largely disappeared from Sinological scholarship in the West and perhaps to a large extent, from historical writing more generally'.[91] Rowe likens Lattimore's approach to the French *Annalistes* and notes that 'Lattimore's attempt at a transcendent perspective impels him to actively resist all ethnocentr-isms, not only that of the West but also that of his sources – emphatic-ally, those of the Chinese textual tradition.'[92] In his early years, Lattimore was influenced by writers such as Huxley, Spengler and even Wittfogel; though he denied it later, likely also Marx. His greatest

---

[87] Kahin (1989).   [88] Ibid., p. 945.
[89] 'He was acknowledged as a pioneer by exponents of comparative or "world history" such as Moore, McNeill, and Curtin; less commonly so by new ecological historians such as Braudel, Crosby, or Cronin' (Rowe 2007, p. 782).
[90] Rowe (2007, p. 759), citing Grew (1980, p. 764); Sewell (1967).
[91] Rowe (2007).   [92] Ibid., p. 760.

influence according to Rowe, however, was Toynbee. Lattimore was Toynbee's protege: 'it was from Toynbee that he adopted his distaste for national histories, his basic notion of historical change'.[93]

Though Lattimore was initially rather attracted to a view of ecological determinism, over the years he grew increasingly uncomfortable 'with such a monocausal view of Asian – and human – historical development'.[94] Lattimore grew more aware of how humans can shape their environment (possibly due to his observations about the American Dust Bowl): 'it is important to stick to the fact that nature is passive and that the active factor is man'.[95] Similarly, even though he seemed to embrace racial explanations of historical processes that were very much in vogue at the time in his early career, Lattimore later decisively rejected them.[96] Increasingly he used 'cultures' as a unit of analysis: cultures were formed as 'a response to the specifics of the ecology inhabited by the group and the economy and technology developed in adaptation to that ecology'[97] and also via a process of 'differentiation' from other cultures; and once formed, cultural features became causally determinative.

Lattimore was against teleological accounts of human civilisation, however, challenging 'the presumed historical sequence from hunting-gathering to pastoral nomadism to shifting agriculture to sedentary agriculture', and he criticised not only American anthropology on these assumptions but also Chinese governmental policy directed towards assimilating the steppe nomads.[98] He rejected the view that agriculture was an evolution from pastoral nomadism. He also rejected the Marxist idea of 'feudalism as a universally observable stage toward the development of capitalism and socialism', arguing instead that feudalism was an administrative system created when 'a society develops the military technology to stake claims to a larger unit of territory than its economic or logistical technology can effectively integrate';[99] societies could devolve into feudalism just as well as they could evolve into it. Despite his rejection of teleology, like other near contemporaries (e.g. Spengler) Lattimore did view societies as 'organisms' who could 'mature', and these views led him, as they did other students of

[93] Ibid., p. 761; Lattimore (1948, pp. 104–5); McNeill (1989).
[94] Rowe (2007, p. 763).   [95] Ibid., p. 765, citing Lattimore (1962, p. 532).
[96] Rowe (2007, pp. 769–70). See also Rosenboim (2014, p. 760).
[97] Ibid., p. 773.   [98] Ibid., p. 771.   [99] Ibid., p. 778.

civilisation in that period, to the conclusion that the West was past its prime.

Lattimore held the view that Asia was due for a comeback after the Second World War, as land powers (rather than naval empires) reasserted themselves due to railway and airplane technology. Western imperialism 'came across the sea to Asia and looked at the vast territory from boats and ports in the littoral zone', whereas 'local Asian powers established their political centre in the land masses, looking outwards from the continental core towards the coasts'.[100] The former was exploitative; the latter was constructive. He advocated for a new world order where different 'civilisations' could co-exist 'democratically' (i.e. free from imperial domination), an order in which Asia and especially China would play an important part: 'The world would be divided into three dynamic democratic regions, the United States, Russia, and an Asian 'Freedom Bloc' of small states led by China. Each region would be governed, possibly as a federation, according to its own political and economic philosophy.'[101]

Some General Observations

Toynbee, Wittfogel and Lattimore were influential in different ways in the early to middle part of the twentieth century and who fell out of favour in the second half. If we compare them with the 'local' theorists of Eurasia, I think it is fair to say that their distance to the geographies they were discussing did not necessarily render them more objective as historians or theorists. Whereas the former group of scholars were especially interested in finding alternative sources of macro-community in the international order, the latter group were especially interested in the 'decline' or survival of civilisations, understandable given the shocks of the world wars for the West.[102] Their situated-ness also determined their views in other ways: Wittfogel's career was driven by his traumatic experience around the Second World War; Toynbee's views were shaped by his government assignments in Turkey and Greece; and Lattimore's open-mindedness stemmed to some degree from his early and frequent exposure to China and Inner Asia.

[100] Rosenboim (2014, p. 750).   [101] Ibid., p. 757.
[102] On this point, see also Costello (1992).

Of all the scholars whose views I have discussed, Wittfogel fares the worst in my estimation, even worse than Suematsu, even though the latter's scholarship was both based on a false conjecture *and* was later used to justify Japanese imperialism in Asia. The problem with Wittfogel was that he used his scholarship to argue that vast parts of the world were not only inferior to the West but immutably so, just as he did not have any problem publicly denouncing colleagues for being alleged communists. And while our 'local' scholars wore their 'nationalism' on their sleeve, Wittfogel hid behind the seemingly objective analysis of sociological models. For these reasons, I would say Wittfogel's scholarship was left behind for good reason. By contrast, there is much more to recommend in both Toynbee's and especially Lattimore's non-Eurocentric, un-'methodologically nationalist', fair-minded approach to comparative world history. Both men fell afoul of political currents in the United States and academic currents in history and social sciences, but not for very good reasons. It is no wonder then that both of their works are attracting fresh eyes these days, which brings us to the question of whether a comparative world history is possible and justifiable today, especially within International Relations but also in social sciences in general.

Macro-History as Global IR

More than three decades ago, in an article called 'The Mega-Historians', Randall Collins argued that historical sociology was experiencing a golden age but that much of historical sociology of the time was anti-theoretical: 'When we step into the rank and file of today's historical sociology, the belief is all too frequent that sheer, massive, specialized historical detail is the ideal, and that theoretical generalizations are out.'[103] According to Collins, historical sociologists were increasingly leaning that way in order to curry favour with the historians, and historians were forced down this path because of their sheer numbers: 'This is the Durkheimian process of size fostering specialization.'[104] Collins bemoaned, however, the fact that historians had come to see specialisation as a good in and of itself as a result: 'There is a scorn of secondary sources – as if historians themselves were not the authors of these same secondary sources. There is the

---

[103] Collins (1985).   [104] Ibid., p. 115.

ritual glorification of the dirt of the archives: in short, an ideology of intellectual "manual labor".'[105] I think Collins is right about this, but his reasoning gives us only partial explanation because the same development has happened in International Relations (IR) as well, but the fetishisation of methods is not limited to archives or history adjacent IR scholars.

It can be found in IR scholarship of all stripes. What varies is the method that is vaunted at any given time by any IR sub-community – the latest statistical innovation, a cool experimental design, new archives, and so on – but the idea that real cutting-edge scholarship happens through methodological manual labour is one of the rare commonly shared values of our discipline. I think the main culprit is fragmentation of the discipline and our growing inability to judge each other's arguments. When you cannot evaluate the quality of the substance of the work because it is outside of your epistemological expertise, methods become the primary way to evaluate whether the scholarship is 'good' and is 'publishable'. Of course, this then becomes a self-fulfilling prophecy, in that having to constantly catch up with new methods and the labour required by each – not to mention the need to continuously publish research – comes at the expense of acquiring the knowledge base that could help us evaluate colleagues' work on more substantial grounds.

Collins advocated another approach, one that is also applicable to IR. He suggested not only that grand history – the archetype of which is Gibbon, Herodotus and Livy – is where history comes closest to addressing the theoretical concerns of historical sociology but also 'that accomplishments of specialized historiography have made possible grand history on a level that is technically much more impressive than what has existed before'.[106] One of the main improvements was in the accumulation of knowledge about parts of the world beyond Europe. Collins argued that mega-historians (of 1985) were less Eurocentric than their predecessors: here, his examples are Fernand Braudel and William McNeill (compared favourably in this regard to Oswald Spengler and Arnold Toynbee, though Collins still favours Weber overall). Braudel showed, for instance, 'the remarkable extent to which markets, shops, fairs, promissory notes, maritime insurance, and networks of credit existed outside Europe',[107] and McNeill looked

---

[105] Ibid. See also Sachsenmaier (2006).   [106] Collins (1985, p. 117).
[107] Ibid., p. 119.

to all of world history and ended up contextualising Europe in the process: 'the most ambitious historian of all ... the author of the best book ever written on the history of the entire world'.[108] Attempting to turn Spengler and Toynbee on their heads, as Marx had done with Hegel, McNeill weaved a picture of world history wherein civilisations were not separate entities and wherein knowledge diffused and accumulated over time.[109] They also changed in response to external stimulus – for instance, from the environment – but also due to political and military competition.

Collins did not mention them, but we could also count many of the names in this Epilogue as examples of approaches similar to that of McNeill (e.g. Hodgson), each showing us the possibilities of macro, comparative, grand world history. Increasingly, there are more names to be added to that list. Collins does discuss Wallerstein, but he would have done even better to point at the works of other, less Eurocentric world systems theorists such as Gunder Frank, Denemark and Abu-Lughod. In anthropology, one could point to the likes of Jack Goody or David Sneath. In history we have people like Nicolo DiCosmo, Tim Brooks, Pamela Crossley, Sanjah Subrahmanyam, Charles Halperin, Donald Ostrowski, Cemal Kafadar, Cornell Fleischer, Linda Darling, Tijana Krstic, Matthew Melvin-Koushki or Cemil Aydın.[110]

For those who know where to look, there is a sizeable corpus of literature scattered across different disciplines – not all of it in agreement with each other, but all sharing a certain *je ne sais quoi* ambition in terms of their comprehensive vision – that model what kind of a knowledge revolution non-Eurocentric, comprehensive understandings of the world can help us achieve. Yet while the social sciences in general – and IR in particular – have become more acutely aware of the pervasiveness of Eurocentric assumptions as both a methodological and an epistemological problem in its theorising, macro-historical approaches are hardly ever posed as the antidote. Macro history is even more rarely encountered in social sciences (and certainly in IR) than it was in 1985, despite the growth of interest in recent decades in what is called 'global history' – that is, the attempt to globalise historiography by focusing on '"ecumenical" perspectives on history ... to

---

[108] Ibid., p. 120.
[109] On McNeill, see also Costello (1992, p. 104). See also Collins (1985, p. 120).
[110] And many others cited in this book and beyond, including in IR.

"connected histories" ... , "entangled histories" ... , and *histoire croisee*" [crossed history]'.[111] The label 'global history' can be at times misleading because while some interpret it as taking a global vision of human history, others understand it as the history of globalisation.[112] Perhaps it is partly for this reason that much of the recent turn in 'global history' has focused on the period from the nineteenth century onwards. Another reason may be that more archival material is available the closer one is to modernity, but that is not a good enough reason not to study pre-nineteenth-century history.

What we need to acknowledge is that even though it is macro-history and grand theorising that is often (and often justifiably) accused of Eurocentrism, the reverse can also be true: the fetishisation of archival methods and micro-histories can also reproduce Eurocentrism. There is the very basic logistical problem that primary sources are not equally distributed or equally accessible or equally preserved (and the patterns that they are or are not often reproduce the inequalities and hierarchies of the last century), coupled with the fact that 'national' archives often reproduce methodological nationalism in ways that are very difficult to transcend unless one is already coming at them with an alternative vision. Second, there is the issue that Collins also recognised: historians writing about other parts of the world besides Europe inevitably are pushed towards grand history because there is still a lot of ground to cover; his example here was of Joseph Needham's *Science and Civilization in China* (1954–[2004]). Collins noted that Needham had to write a grand history because his work was pioneering the subject.[113]

Is it fair that hundreds or thousands of gallons of ink have been spilled parsing the meaning beyond – say – Hobbes' every word, whereas – a few token exceptions notwithstanding – most non-Western political thinkers of the same period (or before or after) languish in complete obscurity, perhaps only nowadays getting to be the subject of a PhD thesis here and there? No, it is not. I welcome every new page that is written on a non-Western historical figure, event or polity, however trivial, that has been unfairly neglected until now due to the social hierarchies of the modern order. Yet mountains of such

---

[111] Sachsenmaier (2006, p. 453), citing Erdmann (1987); Lepenies (2003); Subrahmanyam (1997); Werner and Zimmermann (2004).
[112] Sachsenmaier (2006, p. 454).   [113] Collins (1985, p. 117).

work are not enough to correct the epistemological damage we are dealing with, if the grand narratives of history remain undisturbed. Readings of archives or primary texts, including those of political theorists, cannot happen in a vacuum, without a bigger-picture background in which the text is to be located. One does not have to subscribe to the Cambridge School to believe this; even the most stridently textualist of Straussians are operating with an implicit grand narrative of history (otherwise, how could they distinguish between the ancients and the moderns?). That suggests to me strongly that the desire to move away from all macro history and synthetic work actually runs at times counter to the desire to move social sciences towards more global and less Eurocentric accounts. If we dismantle Eurocentric grand histories that have animated our modern international order without replacing them with anything but micro-oriented work, those macro-historical accounts that we think we have dismantled through our brilliantly devastating critiques of Eurocentrism will simply live on as zombie common-sense versions of themselves, filling in the blanks wherever there are some, and every account has blanks.

My purpose in writing this book was thus twofold. First, I wanted to create a non-Eurocentric version of international history and world politics as understood from an Eastern vantage point. Eurocentrism critiques have been well-made and are increasingly well-received in IR. But they are not enough by themselves. We need alternative narratives, but in generating these alternative narratives we have to tread carefully. This brings me to my second goal. Given the political and economic resurgence of Asia and the numerous dangerous alleys Asian historiography can travel down in the near future, I wanted to provide an account of Asian history that is not owned by any one 'nation', 'civilisation', 'race' or 'religion'. To the extent that the shared 'Chinggisid' legacy of Asian states have been acknowledged, it has been to make an argument for autocracy. Thankfully there is no present-day state strong enough to push such a narrative in a jingoistic manner similar to neo-Ottomanism or the Chinese tributary model. Rising powers of (Eur)Asia all deny their Chinggisid legacies, which is partly why I estimate the political risks of the historical narrative offered here to be relatively negligible. But I still do want to advocate for another way of viewing the shared Chinggisid legacy. Chinggisid-type 'world orders' were not organised by religion or ethnicity. This is why it is a shared heritage – like the Roman Empire – which could nominally be embraced by many. The narrative of that shared legacy, and one that emphasised the ideational and artistic connections facilitated by the experience, could be used to build interfaith and international bridges across Eurasia. There is enough common historical ground throughout Asia to build a more pluralist vision of the region; it is the political will to do it that is lacking.

I tried to remain as faithful to historical facts as I understand them, cross-checking claims across different historiographies wherever I could, but there is no doubt that I am as shaped by my own times and as captive to the historical knowledge production of this moment as are all the historians discussed in this chapter, if not more so. The possibility of being wrong about some details is not something I am too troubled by, however: first, I know that I must be, inevitably (but not deliberately); and second, I know of no other way that historical knowledge can accumulate except by advancing plausible accounts and then having them gradually corrected and filled in by others. At the end of the day, even though I am no historian, I agree with McNeill that the best historians (or, in my case, a historically oriented IR scholar) can hope to do is to provide 'sense of the past', a broad, meaningful interpretation of history as a basis for action now. Whether the historical account I have provided here will resonate with the larger scholarly community as well as the public thus ultimately depends on whether there is any current need for it and whether you are ready to hear it.

THOMASINA: ... the enemy who burned the great library of Alexandria without so much as a fine for all that is overdue. Oh, Septimus! – can you bear it? All the lost plays of the Athenians! Two hundred at least by Aeschylus, Sophocles, Euripides – thousands of poems – Aristotle's own library! .... How can we sleep for grief?

SEPTIMUS: Seven plays from Aeschylus, seven from Sophocles, nineteen from Euripides, my lady! You should no more grieve for the rest than for a buckle lost from a shoe! We shed as we pick up, like travellers who must carry everything in their arms, and what we let fall will be picked up by those behind. The procession is very long and life is very short. We die on the march. But there is nothing outside the march so nothing can be lost to it. The missing plays of Sophocles will turn up piece by piece, or be written again in another language.

From *Arcadia* (1993), Act 1, Scene 3, by Tom Stoppard

Bibliography

Abou-El-Haj, Rifa'at Ali. 2005. *Formation of the Modern State: The Ottoman Empire, Sixteenth to Eighteenth Centuries*. Syracuse University Press.

Abu-Lughod, Janet. 1989. *Before European Hegemony*. Oxford University Press.

Acharya, Amitav, and Barry Buzan. 2019. *The Making of Global International Relations*. Cambridge University Press.

Adler, Emanuel. 2019. *World Ordering: A Social Theory of Cognitive Evolution*. Cambridge University Press.

Adler-Nissen, Rebecca, and Ayşe Zarakol. 2021. 'Struggles for Recognition: The Liberal International Order and the Merger of Its Discontents'. *International Organization* 75(2): 611–34.

Adshead, S. A. M. 1988. *China in World History*. St. Martin's Press.

Aigle, Denise. 2005. 'The Letters of Eljigidei, Hülegü, and Abaqa: Mongol Overtures or Christian Ventriloquism?' *Inner Asia* 7(2): 143–62.

2006. 'Iran under Mongol Domination: The Effectiveness and Failings of a Dual Administrative System'. *Bulletin D'études Orientales* 57: 65–78.

Aksan, Virginia H., and Daniel Goffman. 2007. *The Early Modern Ottomans: Remapping the Empire*. Cambridge University Press.

Alam, Muzaffar. 1994. 'Trade, State Policy and Regional Change: Aspects of Mughal–Uzbek Commercial Relations, C. 1550–1750'. *Journal of Economic and Social History of the Orient* 37(3): 202–27.

Alam, Muzaffar, and Sanjay Subrahmanyam. 2004. 'The Deccan Frontier and Mughal Expansion, Ca. 1600: Contemporary Perspectives'. *Journal of Economic and Social History of the Orient* 47(3): 357–89.

2007. *Indo-Persian Travels in the Age of Discoveries, 1400–1800*. Cambridge University Press.

Al-Azmeh, A. 2001. 'Islamic Fundamentalism'. In *International Encyclopedia of the Social & Behavioral Sciences*, edited by James D. Wright, pp. 7931–4. Elsevier.

Allsen, Thomas. 1981. 'Mongol Census Taking in Rus', 1245–1275'. *Harvard Ukrainian Studies* 5(1): 32–53.

2001. *Culture and Conquest in Mongol Eurasia*. Cambridge University Press.

2004. 'Population Movements in Mongol Eurasia'. In *Nomads as Agents of Cultural Change: The Mongols and Their Eurasian Predecessors*, edited by Reuven Amitai and Michal Biran, pp. 119–51. Oxford University Press.

2019. *The Steppe and the Sea: Pearls in the Mongol Empire*. University of Pennsylvania Press.

Amitai, Reuven. 1994. 'An Exchange of Letters in Arabic between Abaγa Īlkhān and Sultan Baybars (A.H. 667/A.D. 1268–69)'. *Central Asiatic Journal* 38(1): 11–33.

2004a. 'Did Chinggis Khan Have a Jewish Teacher? An Examination of an Early Fourteenth-Century Arabic Text'. *Journal of the American Oriental Society* 124(4): 691–705.

2004b. 'The Impact of the Mongols on the History of Syria, Politics, Society and Culture'. In *Nomads as Agents of Cultural Change: The Mongols and Their Eurasian Predecessors*, edited by Reuven Amitai and Michal Biran, pp. 228–51. Oxford University Press.

Amitai-Preiss, Reuven. 1996. 'Ghazan, Islam and Mongol Tradition: A View from the Mamlūk Sultanate'. *Bulletin of the School of Oriental and African Studies* 59(1): 1–10.

Anderson, James A. 2014. 'Man and Mongols: the Dali and Đại Việt Kingdoms in the Face of the Northern Invasions'. In James A. Anderson and John K. Whitmore (eds.), *China's Encounters on the South and Southwest: Reforging the Fiery Frontier over Two Millennia*, pp. 106–34. Brill.

Anievas, Alex, and Kerem Nişancıoğlu. 2015. *How the West Came to Rule*. University of Chicago Press.

Anooshahr, Ali. 2014. *The Ghazi Sultans and the Frontiers of Islam*. Routledge.

Arjomand, Saïd Amir. 2016. 'Unity of the Persianate World under Turko-Mongolian Domination and Divergent Development of Imperial Autocracies in the Sixteenth Century'. *Journal of Persianate Studies* 9(1): 1–18.

Assmann, Jan. 2003. *The Mind of Egypt: History and Meaning in the Time of the Pharaohs*. Harvard University Press.

2014. *From Akhenaten to Moses: Ancient Egypt and Religious Change*. Oxford University Press.

Atwell, William S. 1978. 'A Seventeenth-Century "General Crisis" in East Asia?' In *The General Crisis of the Seventeenth Century*, edited by Geoffrey Parkey and Lesley M. Smith, pp. 236–56. Routledge & Kegan Paul.

1986. 'Some Observations on the "Seventeenth-Century Crisis" in China and Japan'. *Journal of Asian Studies* 45(2): 223–44.

1988. 'Ming Observers of Ming Decline: Some Chinese Views on the "Seventeenth-Century Crisis" in Comparative Perspective'. *Journal of the Royal Asiatic Society of Great Britain & Ireland* 2: 316–48.

1990. 'A Seventeenth-Century "General Crisis" in East Asia?', *Modern Asian Studies* 24(4): 661–82.

2002. 'Time, Money, and the Weather: Ming China and the "Great Depression" of the Mid-Fifteenth Century'. *Journal of Asian Studies* 61(1): 83–113.

Atwood, Christopher P. 2004a. *Encyclopedia of Mongolia and the Mongol Empire*. Facts on File.

2004b. 'Validation by Holiness or Sovereignty: Religious Toleration as Political Theology in the Mongol World Empire of the Thirteenth Century'. *International History Review* 26(2): 237–56.

2015. 'The Administrative Origins of Mongolia's "Tribal" Vocabulary'. https://repository.upenn.edu/cgi/viewcontent.cgi?article=1012&context=ealc.

Aydın, Cemil. 2007a. 'A Global Anti-Western Moment? The Russo-Japanese War, Decolonization, and Asian Modernity'. In *Competing Visions of World Order: Global Moments and Movements, 1880s–1930s*, edited by Sebastian Conrad and Dominic Sachsenmaier, pp. 213–36. Palgrave Macmillan.

2007b. *The Politics of Anti-Westernism in Asia: Visions of World Order in Pan-Islamic and Pan-Asian Thought*. Columbia University Press.

2013. 'Globalizing the Intellectual History of the Idea of the "Muslim World"'. In *Global Intellectual History*, edited by Samuel Moyn and Andrew Sartori, pp. 158–86. Columbia University Press.

Babayan, Kathryn. 2002. *Mystics, Monarchs, and Messiahs: Cultural Landscapes of Early Modern Iran*. Harvard Center for Middle Eastern Studies.

Babur, and William Dalrymple. 2020. *The Babur Nama*. Translated by Annette Susannah Beveridge. Everyman's Library.

Balabanlilar, Lisa. 2007. 'Lords of the Auspicious Conjunction: Turco-Mongol Imperial Identity on the Subcontinent'. *Journal of World History* 18(1): 1–39.

Barkey, Karen. 2008. *Empire of Difference – The Ottomans in Comparative Perspective*. Cambridge University Press.

Bartelson, Jens. 1995. *A Genealogy of Sovereignty*. Cambridge University Press.

2009. *Visions of World Community*. Cambridge University Press.

2018. 'Dating Sovereignty'. *International Studies Review* 20: 509–13.

Baumann, Brian. 2013. 'By the Power of Eternal Heaven: The Meaning of Tenggeri to the Government of the Pre-Buddhist Mongols'. *Extrême-Orient Extrême-Occident* 35: 233–84.

Beaulac, Stephane. 2000. 'The Westphalian Legal Orthodoxy – Myth or Reality?' *Journal of the History of International Law* 2: 148–77.

Benabdallah, Lina. 2020. *Shaping the Future of Power: Knowledge Production and Network-Building in China–Africa Relation.* University of Michigan Press.

Ben-Dor Benite, Zvi. 2008. 'The Marrano Emperor: The Mysterious Bond between Zhu Yuanzhang and the Chinese Muslims'. In *Long Live the Emperor! Uses of the Ming Founder across Six Centuries of East Asian History*, pp. 275–308. Society for Ming Studies.

Bennison, Amira. 2014. *The Great Caliphs: The Golden Age of the 'Abbasid Empire*. Yale University Press.

Benton, Lauren. 2009. *A Search for Sovereignty: Law and Geography in European Empires, 1400–1900.* Cambridge University Press.

Binbaş, İlker Evrim. 2016. *Intellectual Networks in Timurid Iran: Sharaf Al-Dīn 'Alī Yazdī and the Islamicate Republic of Letters.* Cambridge University Press.

Biran, Michal. 2007. *Chinggis Khan.* Oneworld Publications.
  2013. 'The Mongol Empire in World History: The State of the Field'. *History Compass* 11(11): 1021–33.

Black, Antony. 2011. *History of Islamic Political Thought: From the Prophet to the Present.* Edinburgh University Press.

Blom, Philipp. 2019. *Nature's Mutiny: How the Little Ice Age of the Long Seventeenth Century Transformed the West and Shaped the Present.* Liveright Publishing Corp.

Bonine, Michael E., Abbas Amanat and Michael Gasper, eds. 2011. *Is There a Middle East? The Evolution of a Geopolitical Concept.* Stanford University Press.

Branch, Jordan. 2011. 'Mapping the Sovereign State: Technology, Authority, and Systemic Change'. *International Organization* 65(1): 1–36.
  2013. *The Cartographic State: Maps, Territory, and the Origins of Sovereignty.* Cambridge University Press.

Braudel, Fernand. 1972. *The Mediterranean and the Mediterranean World in the Age of Philip II, Vol 1.* Collins.

Broadbridge, Anne F. 2013. 'Mongolian Conquests Review'. *Journal of World History* 24(3): 696–99.

Brook, Timothy. 2010. *The Troubled Empire.* Harvard University Press.
  2019. *Great State: China and the World.* Profile Books.

Brook, Timothy, Michael van Walt van Praag and Miek Boltjes. 2018. *Sacred Mandates: Asian International Relations since Chinggis Khan.* University of Chicago Press.

Brooks, Stephen G., and William C. Wohlforth. 2002. 'American Primacy in Perspective'. *Foreign Affairs* 81(4): 20–33.

2016. 'The Rise and Fall of the Great Powers in the Twenty-First Century: China's Rise and the Fate of America's Global Position'. *International Security* 40(3): 7–53.

Buell, Paul. 2009. "Mongols in Vietnam: End of One Era, Beginning of Another". First Congress of the Asian Association of World Historians. Osaka University Nakanoshima-Center.

2012. 'Qubilai and the Rats'. *Sudhoffs Archiv* 96(2): 127–44.

2015. 'Early Mongolian Geographical Conceptions'. *Journal of South Asian Natural History* 49(1–2): 19–29.

Bull, Hedley. 1977. *The Anarchical Society: A Study of Order in World Politics.* Palgrave.

Bull, Hedley, and Adam Watson. 1984. *The Expansion of International Society.* Clarendon Press.

Büntgen, Ulf, and Nicola Di Cosmo. 2016. 'Climatic and Environmental Aspects of the Mongol Withdrawal from Hungary in 1242 CE'. *Scientific Reports* 6(25606): 1–9.

Burak, Guy. 2013a. 'Faith, Law and Empire in the Ottoman "Age of Confessionalization" (Fifteenth–Seventeenth Centuries): The Case of "Renewal of Faith"'. *Mediterranean Historical Review* 28(1): 1–23.

2013b. 'The Second Formation of Islamic Law: The Post-Mongol Context of the Ottoman Adoption of a School of Law'. *Comparative Studies in Society and History* 55(3): 579–602.

Buzan, Barry. 2010. 'China in International Society: Is "Peaceful Rise" Possible?'. *Chinese Journal of International Politics* 3(1): 5–36.

Buzan, Barry, and George Lawson. 2015. *The Global Transformation.* Cambridge University Press.

Buzan, Barry, and Richard Little. 2000. *International Systems in World History: Remaking the Study of International Relations.* Oxford University Press.

Buzan, Barry, and Yongjin Zhang. 2014. *Contesting International Society in East Asia.* Cambridge University Press.

Cabbuag, Samuel. 2016. 'Charisma and Charismatic Leaders: Weber and Beyond'. *Philippine Sociological Review* 64(1): 209–30.

Cannadine, David. 2002. *Ornamentalism: How the British Saw Their Empire.* Oxford University Press.

Çapan, Gülşah Zeynep, and Ayşe Zarakol. 2019. 'Turkey's Ambivalent Self: Ontological Insecurity in "Kemalism" versus "Erdoğanism"'. *Cambridge Review of International Affairs* 32(3): 263–82.

Casale, Giancarlo. 2007. 'Global Politics in the 1580s: One Canal, Twenty Thousand Cannibals, and an Ottoman Plot to Rule the World'. *Journal of World History* 18(3): 267–96.

2010. *The Ottoman Age of Exploration*. Oxford University Press.

Cassen, Flora. 2017. 'Philip Ii of Spain and His Italian Jewish Spy'. *Journal of Early Modern History* 21(4): 318–42.

Chan, Steve. 2007. *China, the US and the Power-Transition Theory: A Critique*. Routledge.

Ch'en, T. T. 1963. 'Sino-Liu-chiuan Relations in the Nineteenth Century'. Ph.D. diss., Indiana University. Cheng, Anne. 2020. 'Is Zhongguo the Middle Kingdom or Madhyadeśa?" In *India–China: Intersecting Universalities*, edited by Anne Cheng and Sanchit Kumar, pp. 38–55. Collège de France.

Cherniavsky, Michael. 1959. 'Khan or Basileus: An Aspect of Russian Mediaeval Political Theory'. *Journal of the History of Ideas* 20(4): 459–76.

Çıpa, Erdem H. 2017. *The Making of Selim: Succession, Legitimacy, and Memory in the Early Modern Ottoman World*. Indiana University Press.

Çırakman, Aslı. 2001. 'From Tyranny to Despotism: The Enlightenment's Unenlightened Image of the Turks'. *International Journal of Middle East Studies* 33: 49–68.

Clavijo, Ruy Gonzalez De. 1928. *Clavijo: Embassy to Tamerlane, 1403–1406*. Translated by Guy Le Strange. Routledge.

Collins, Randall. 1985. 'The Mega-Historians'. *Sociological Theory* 3(1): 114–22.

1997. 'An Asian Route to Capitalism: Religious Economy and the Origins of Self-Transforming Growth in Japan'. *American Sociological Review* 62(6): 843–65.

Cooley, Alexander, and Daniel Nexon. 2020. *Exit from Hegemony: The Unraveling of the American Global Order*. Oxford University Press.

Costello, Paul. 1992. 'William McNeill's Ecological Mythhistory: Toward an Ambiguous Future'. *Historical Reflections* 18(1): 99–119.

Cox, Michael. 2001. 'Whatever Happened to American Decline? International Relations and the New United States Hegemony'. *New Political Economy* 6(3): 311–40.

2007. 'Still the American Empire'. *Political Studies Review* 5(1): 1–10.

Crone, Patricia. 1980. *Slaves on Horses: The Evolution of the Islamic Polity*. Cambridge University Press.

2004. *God's Rule: Government and Islam*. Columbia University Press.

Crone, Patricia, and Martin Hinds. 2003. *God's Caliph: Religious Authority in the First Centuries of Islam*. Cambridge University Press.

Crossley, Pamela. 2000. *A Translucent Mirror: History and Identity in Qing Imperial Ideology*. University of California Press.

Crossley, Pamela Kyle, Helen F. Siu and Donal S. Sutton. 2000. *Empire at the Margins: Culture, Ethnicity, and Frontier in Early Modern China*. University of California Press.

Croxton, Derek. 1999. 'The Peace of Westphalia of 1648 and the Origins of Sovereignty'. *International History Review* 21(3): 569–91.

Curtis, Benjamin. 2013. *The Habsburgs: The History of a Dynasty*. Bloomsbury Academic.

Dale, Stephen Frederic. 1998. 'The Legacy of the Timurids'. *Journal of the Royal Asiatic Society of Great Britain & Ireland* 8(1): 43–58.

2006. 'Ibn Khaldun: The Last Greek and the First Annaliste Historian'. *International Journal of Middle East Studies* 38(3): 431–51.

Dardess, John. 2016. *Four Seasons: A Ming Emperor and His Grand Secretaries in Sixteenth-Century China*. Rowman & Littlefield.

Darling, Linda T. 2008. 'Political Change and Political Discourse in the Early Modern Mediterranean World'. *Journal of Interdisciplinary History* xxxviii(4): 505–31.

2011. 'Reformulating the Gazi Narrative: When Was the Ottoman State a Gazi State?' *Turcica* 43: 13–53.

Davis, Kathleen. 2008. *Periodization and Sovereignty: How Ideas of Feudalism and Secularization Govern the Politics of Time*. University of Pennsylvania Press.

de Carvalho, Benjamin, Halvard Leira and John M. Hobson. 2011. 'The Big Bangs of IR: The Myths That Your Teachers Still Tell You about 1648 and 1919'. *Millennium* 39(3): 735–58.

Dekkiche, Malika. 2014–5. 'New Source, New Debate: Re-evaluation of the Mamluk-Timurid Struggle for Religious Supremacy in the Hijaz (Paris, BnF MS ar. 4440)'. *Mamluk Studies Review* XVIII: 247–71.

2016. 'The Letter and Its Response: The Exchanges between the Qara Qoyunlu and the Mamluk Sultan: Ms Arabe 4440 (BnF, Paris)'. *Arabica* 63(6): 579–626.

Denemark, Robert. 1999. 'World System History: From Traditional International Politics to the Study of Global Relations'. *International Studies Review* 1(2): 43–75.

Deng, Kent. 2020. 'One-Off Capitalism in Song China, 960–1279 CE'. In *Capitalisms: Toward a Global History*, edited by Menon Yazdani, pp. 227–50. Oxford University Press.

Derman, Joshua. 2011. 'Max Weber and Charisma: A Transatlantic Affair'. *New German Critique* 113: 51–88.

de Vries, Jan. 2009. 'The Economic Crisis of the Seventeenth Century after Fifty Years'. *Journal of Interdisciplinary History* 40(2): 151–94.

2013. 'The Crisis of the Seventeenth Century: The Little Ice Age and the Mystery of the "Great Divergence"'. *Journal of Interdisciplinary History* 44(3): 369–77.

DiCicco, Jonathan M., and Jack S. Levy. 2014. 'The Power Transition Research Program'. In *The Realism Reader*, edited by Colin Elman and Michael Jenson, pp. 211–17. Routledge.

Di Cosmo, Nicola. 1999. 'State Formation and Periodization in Inner Asian History'. *Journal of World History* 10(1): 1–40.

2010. 'Black Sea Emporia and the Mongol Empire: A Reassessment of the Pax Mongolica'. *Journal of Economic and Social History of the Orient* 53(1/2): 83–108.

Drompp, Michael. 2005. 'Imperial State Formation in Inner Asia'. *Acta Orientalia Academia Scientarium Hungary* 58(1): 101–11.

Dunlop, Anne. 2015. 'European Art and the Mongol Middle Ages: Two Exercises in Cultural Translation'. 美育学刊 *Mei Yu Xue Kan* (Journal of Aesthetic Education) 6(31): 1–10.

2018. 'Artistic Contact between Italy and Mongol Eurasia: State of the Field'. *EWHA SAHAK YEONGU* 57: 1–36.

Eaton, Richard. 1993. 'Islamic History as Global History'. In *Islamic and European Expansion: The Forging of a Global Order*, edited by Michael Adas. Temple University Press.

Elden, Stuart. 2013. *The Birth of Territory*. University of Chicago Press.

Elias, Norbert. 2000 (1939). *The Civilizing Process*. Wiley-Blackwell.

Elias, Norbert, and John L. Scotson. 1994 [1965]. *The Established and the Outsiders*. Sage.

Endicott-West, Elizabeth. 1994. 'The Yüan Government and Society'. In *The Cambridge History of China*, Vol. 6, edited by Herbert Franke and Dennis C. Twitchett, pp. 587–615. Cambridge University Press.

Erdmann, Karl D. 1987. *Die Ökumene Der Historiker: Geschichte Der Internationalen Historikerkongresse Und Des Comité International Des Sciences Historiques*. Ruprecht Gmbh & Company.

Fancy, Nahyan, and Monica H. Green. 2021. 'Plague and the Fall of Baghdad (1258)'. *Medical History* 65(2): 157–77.

Favereau, Marie. 2021. *The Horde: How the Mongols Changed the World*. Belknap Press.

Felek, Özgen. 2017. 'Fears, Hopes, and Dreams: The Talismanic Shirts of Murad III'. *Arabica* 64: 647–72.

Fleischer, Cornell. 1986. *Bureaucrat and Intellectual in the Ottoman Empire: The Historian Mustafa Ali (1541–1600)*. Princeton University Press.

1992. 'The Lawgiver as Messiah: The Making of the Imperial Image in the Reign of Suleyman'. In *Soliman le magnifique et son temps, Actes du Colloque de Paris. Galeries Nationales du Grand Palais, 7–10 Mars 1990*, edited by Gilles Veinstein, pp. 159–77. La Documentation Francaise.

2008. *Bureaucrat and Intellectual in the Ottoman Empire: The Historian Mustafa Ali (1541–1600)*. Princeton University Press.

2009. 'Ancient Wisdom and New Sciences: Prophecies at the Ottoman Court in the Fifteenth and Early Sixteenth Centuries'. In *Falnama: The Book of Omens*, edited by Masumed Farhad and Serpil Bağcı, pp. 232–43, 329–30. Thames and Hudson Ltd.

2018. 'A Mediterranean Apocalypse: Prophecies of Empire in the Fifteenth and Sixteenth Centuries'. *Journal of Economic and Social History of the Orient* 61(1–2): 18–90.

Fletcher, Joseph. 1968. 'China and Central Asia, 1368–1884'. In *The Chinese World Order*, edited by John K. Fairbank, pp. 206–24. Harvard University Press.

1979. 'Turco-Mongolian Monarchic Tradition in the Ottoman Empire'. *Harvard Ukrainian Studies* 3/4: 236–51.

1986. 'The Mongols: Ecological and Social Perspectives'. *Harvard Journal of Asiatic Studies* 46(1): 11–50.

Frank, Andre Gunder. 1998. *ReORIENT: Global Economy in the Asian Age*. University of California Press.

Frank, Andre Gunder, and Barry K. Gills, eds. 1996. *The World System: Five Hundred Years of Five Thousand?* Routledge.

Franke, Herbert. 1951. 'Some Sinological Remarks on Rašîd Ad-Dîn's History of China'. *Oriens* 4(1): 21–6.

1966. 'Sino-Western Contacts under the Mongol Empire'. *Journal of the Hong Kong Branch of the Royal Asiatic Society* 6: 49–72.

1990. 'The Forest Peoples of Manchuria: Kitans and Jurchens'. In *The Cambridge History of Early Inner Asia*, edited by Denis Sinor, pp. 400–23. Cambridge University Press.

Frankopan, Peter. 2016. *The Silk Roads: A New History of the World*. Bloomsbury Paperbacks.

Fromherz, Allen James. 2011. *Ibn Khaldun: Life and Times*. Edinburgh University Press.

Geiss, James. 1988. 'The Cheng-Te Reign, 1506–1521'. *The Cambridge History of China* 7: 403–39.

Gellner, Ernest. 1980. *Nations and Nationalism*. Cornell University Press.

Go, Julian, and George Lawson, eds. 2017. *Global Historical Sociology*. Cambridge University Press.

Goddard, Stacie E. 2018. *When Right Makes Might: Rising Powers and World Order*. Cornell University Press.

Goettlich, Kerry. 2019. 'The Rise of Linear Borders in World Politics'. *European Journal of International Relations* 25(1): 203–28.

Goffman, Erving. 1963. *Stigma: Notes of the Management of Spoiled Identity*. Prentice Hall.

Goh, Evelyn. 2008. 'Power, Interest, and Identity: Reviving the Sinocentric Hierarchy in East Asia'. *Asia Policy* 6(1): 148–53.

Golden, Peter B. 2000. '"I Will Give the People unto Thee": The Činggisid Conquests and Their Aftermath in the Turkic World'. *Journal of the Royal Asiatic Society of Great Britain & Ireland* 10(1): 21–41.

Goldstone, Jack A. 1987. 'Cultural Orthodoxy, Risk, and Innovation: The Divergence of East and West in the Early Modern World'. *Sociological Theory* 5(2): 119–35.

   1988. 'East and West in the Seventeenth Century: Political Crises in Stuart England, Ottoman Turkey, and Ming China'. *Comparative Studies in Society and History* 30(1): 103–42.

   1991. *Revolution and Rebellion in the Early Modern World*. University of California Press.

   1998. 'The Problem of the "Early Modern" World'. *Journal of Economic and Social History of the Orient* 41(3): 249–84.

   2000. 'The Rise of the West-Or Not? A Revision to Socio-Economic History'. *Sociological Theory* 18(2): 175–94.

   2002. 'Efflorescences and Economic Growth in World History: Rethinking the "Rise of the West" and the Industrial Revolution'. *Journal of World History: Official Journal of the World History Association* 13(2): 323–89.

   2008. *Why Europe? The Rise of the West in World History 1500–1850: Global Change in a Global Context, 1500–1900 A.D.* 1st ed. McGraw-Hill Education.

   2015. 'Political Trajectories Compared'. In *The Cambridge World History*, edited by Jerry H. Bentley, Sanjay Subrahmanyam and Merry E. Wiesner-Hanks, Vol. VI, pp. 447–89. Cambridge University Press.

Gökalp, Ziya. 1973 [1923]. *Türkçülüğün Esasları* [*Fundamentals of Turkism*]. Varlık Yayınları.

Gresh, Geoffrey F. 2021. *To Rule Eurasia's Waves: The New Great Power Competition at Sea*. Yale University Press.

Grew, Raymond. 1980. 'The Case for Comparing Histories'. *American Historical Review* 85(4): 763–78.

Guy, John. 2018. 'China in India: Porcelain Trade and Attitudes to Collecting in Early Islamic India'. In *China and Southest Asia*, edited by Geoff Wade and James K. Chin, pp. 44–84. Routledge.

Hall, Martin. 2018. 'Steppe State Making'. In *De-Centering State Making*, edited by Jens Bartelson, Martin Hall and Jan Toerell, pp. 17–37. Edward Elgar.

Halperin, Charles J. 1974. 'A Heretical View of Sixteenth-Century Muscovy Edward L. Keenan: The Kurbskii-Groznyi Apocrypha'. *Jahrbucher Fur Geschichte Osteuropas* 22(2): 161–86.

1982a. 'George Vernadsky, Eurasianism, the Mongols, and Russia'. *Slavic Review* 41(3): 477–93.

1982b. '"Know Thy Enemy": Medieval Russian Familiarity with the Mongols of the Golden Horde'. *Jahrbucher Fur Geschichte Osteuropas* 30(2): 161–75.

1987. *Russia and the Golden Horde: The Mongol Impact on Medieval Russian History*. Indiana University Press.

2000a. 'The Kipchak Connection: The Ilkhans, the Mamluks and Ayn Jalut'. *Bulletin of the School of Oriental and African Studies* 63(2): 229–45.

2000b. 'The Missing Golden Horde Chronicles and Historiography in the Mongol Empire'. *Mongolian Studies* 23: 1–15.

2006. 'Rus', Russia and National Identity'. *Canadian Slavonic Papers* 48 (1/2): 157–66.

2019. *Ivan the Terrible: Free to Reward and Free to Punish*. University of Pittsburgh Press.

Hasse, Dag Nikolaus. 2016. *Success and Suppression*. Harvard University Press.

Hathaway, Jane. 2019. 'Eunuchs and the State in the Mamlūk Sultanate and the Ottoman Empire: A Comparison'. In *Ottoman War and Peace: Studies in Honor of Virginia H. Aksan*, edited by Frank Castiglione et al., pp. 315–26. Brill.

Hecker, Felicia. 1993. 'A Fifteenth-Century Chinese Diplomat in Herat'. *Journal of the Royal Asiatic Society of Great Britain & Ireland* 3(1): 85–98.

Heiskanen, Jaakko. 2020. 'The Ethnos of the Earth: Nationalism, Ethnicity, and International Order'. PhD thesis, University of Cambridge.

Hess, Andrew. 1973. 'The Ottoman Conquest of Egypt (1517) and the Beginning of the Sixteenth-Century World War'. *IJMES* 4(1): 55–76.

Hobsbawm, Eric. 1954. 'The General Crisis of the European Economy in the 17th Century'. *Past & Present* 5(1): 33–53.

Hobson, John M. 2004. *The Eastern Origins of Western Civilisation*. Cambridge University Press.

2009. 'Provincializing Westphalia: The Eastern Origins of Sovereignty'. *International Politics* 46(6): 671–90.

John M. 2012a. 'The Other Side of the Westphalian Frontier'. In Sanjay Seth, ed., *Postcolonial Theory and International Relations*, pp. 32–48. Taylor & Francis.

2012b. *The Eurocentric Conception of World Politics*. Cambridge University Press.

2020. *Multicultural Origins of the Global Economy': Beyond the Western-Centric Frontier*. Cambridge University Press.

Hobson, John M., and George Lawson. 2008. 'What Is History in International Relations?' *Millennium* 37(2): 415–35.

Hobson, John M., and J. C. Sharman. 2005. 'The Enduring Place of Hierarchy in World Politics: Tracing the Social Logics of Hierarchy and Political Change'. *European Journal of International Relations* 11 (1): 63–98.

Hodgson, Marshall. 1977. *The Venture of Islam 3: The Gunpowder Empires and Modern Times*. University of Chicago Press.

Hodous, Florence. 2013. 'The Quriltai as a Legal Institution in the Mongol Empire'. *Central Asiatic Journal* 56: 87–102.

Hope, Michael. 2016. *Power, Politics, and Tradition in the Mongol Empire and the Ilkhanate of Iran*. Oxford University Press.

Huang, Chin-Hao, and David C. Kang. 2021. 'State Formation in Korea and Japan, 400–800 CE: Emulation and Learning, Not Bellicist Competition'. *International Organization*. Published online first. https://doi.org/10.1017/S0020818321000254.

Huang, Ray. 1982. *1587, A Year of No Significance: The Ming Dynasty in Decline*. Yale University Press.

Hui, Victoria Tin-bor. 2005. *War and State Formation in Ancient China and Early Modern Europe*. Cambridge University Press.

2020. 'Cultural Diversity and Coercive Cultural Homogenization in Chinese History'. In *Culture and Order in World Politics*, pp. 93–112. Cambridge University Press.

Imber, Colin. 1987. 'The Ottoman Dynastic Myth'. *Turcica* 19(0): 7–27.

İnalcık, Halil. 1973. *Ottoman Empire: The Classical Age, 1300–1600*. Widenfeld & Nicolson.

1979. 'The Khan and the Tribal Aristocracy: The Crimean Khanate under Sahib Giray I'. *Harvard Ukrainian Studies* 3/4: 445–66.

Irwin, Robert. 1997. 'Toynbee and Ibn Khaldun'. *Middle Eastern Studies* 33 (3): 461–79.

2019. *Ibn Khaldun: An Intellectual Biography*. Princeton University Press.

Itzkowitz Shifrinson, Joshua R. 2018. *Rising Titans, Falling Giants: How Great Powers Exploit Power Shifts*. Cornell University Press.

Jackson, Peter. 1998. 'Marco Polo and His "Travels"'. *Bulletin of the School of Oriental and African Studies* 61(1): 82–101.

2018. *The Mongols and the West: 1221–1410*. Routledge.

Jahn, Karl. 1970. 'Rashid al-din and Chinese Culture'. *Central Asiatic Journal* 14(1/3): 134–47.

Jenkinson, Anthony. 1886. *Early Voyages and Travels to Russia and Persia by Anthony Jenkinson and Other Englishmen: With Some Account of the First Intercourse of the English with Russia and Central Asia by Way of the Caspian Sea*. Hakluyt Society.

Jordan, Carmel. 1987. 'Soviet Archeology and the Setting of the "Squire's Tale"'. *Chaucer Review* 22(2): 128–40.

Kafadar, Cemal. 1995. *Between Two Worlds: The Construction of the Ottoman State*. University of California Press.

1997–8. 'The Question of Ottoman Decline'. *Harvard Middle Eastern and Islamic Decline* 4 (1–2): 30–75.

2019. 'Between Amasya and Istanbul: Bayezid II, His Librarian, and the Textual Turn of the Late Fifteenth Century'. In *Treasures of Knowledge: An Inventory of the Ottoman Palace Library (1502/3–1503/4)*, edited by Gülru Necipoğlu, Cemal Kafadar and Cornell H. Fleischer, pp. 79–153. Brill.

Kahin, George McTurnan. 1989. 'Obituary: Owen Lattimore (1900–1989)'. *Journal of Asian Studies* 48(4): 945–6.

Kalpakian, Jack. 2008. 'Ibn Khaldun's Influence on Current International Relations Theory'. *Journal of North African Studies* 13(3): 363–76.

Kang, David C. 2003. 'Hierarchy, Balancing, and Empirical Puzzles in Asian International Relations'. *International Security* 28(3): 165–80.

2010a. *East Asia before the West: Five Centuries of Trade and Tribute*. Columbia University Press.

2010b. 'Hierarchy and Legitimacy in International Systems: The Tribute System in Early Modern East Asia'. *Security Studies* 19(4): 591–622.

2020. 'International Order in Historical East Asia: Tribute and Hierarchy beyond Sinocentrism and Eurocentrism'. *International Organization* 74: 65–93.

Kang, David C., and Xinru Ma. 2018. 'Power Transitions: Thucydides Didn't Live in East Asia'. *Washington Quarterly* 41(1): 137–54.

Karateke, Hakan T. 2019. 'The Peculiar Status of the Crimean Khans in Ottoman Protocol'. *Journal of the Ottoman and Turkish Studies Association* 6(1): 103–20.

Kauz, Ralph. 2015. 'Michel Didier's *Chen Cheng (1365–1457), ambassadeur des premiers empereurs Ming*: A Review Article, or Some Considerations of the Geographical Knowledge on the Silk Road during the Early Ming Dynasty'. *Journal of South Asian Natural History* 49 (1–2): 253–66.

Kayaoğlu, Turan. 2010. 'Westphalian Eurocentrism in International Relations Theory'. *International Studies Review* 12: 193–217.

Keene, Edward. 2002. *Beyond the Anarchical Society: Grotius, Colonialism and Order in World Politics*. Cambridge University Press.

2013. 'The Naming of Powers'. *Cooperation & Conflict* 48(2): 268–82.

Kegley, Charles W., and Gregory A. Raymond. 2020. *Great Powers and World Order: Patterns and Prospects*. 1st ed. Washington, DC: CQ Press.

Kennedy, Paul. 1988. *The Rise and Fall of the Great Powers*. Unwin Hyman.

1991. 'On the "Natural Size" of Great Powers'. *Proceedings of the American Philosophical Society* 135(4): 485–89.

Khazanov, Anatoly M. 1993. 'Muhammad and Jenghiz Khan Compared: The Religious Factor in World Empire Building'. *Comparative Studies in Society and History* 35(3): 461–79.

Kim, Woosang. 1991. 'Alliance Transitions and Great Power War'. *American Journal of Political Science* 35(4): 833–50.

Kim, Woosang, and Scott Gates. 2015. 'Power Transition Theory and the Rise of China'. *International Area Studies Review* 18(3): 219–26.

Kobata Atsushi. 1969. *Chūsei Nisshi tsūkō bōekishi no kenkyū [Studies on the History of Commercial Relations between Japan and China during the Medieval Period]*. Doko shoin.

Koenigsberger, H. G., George L. Moss and G. Q. Bowler. 2014. *Europe in the Sixteenth Century*. Routledge.

Kolff, Dirk. 1990. *Naukar, Rajput, and Sepoy: The Ethnohistory of the Military Labour Market in Hindustan, 1450–1850*. Cambridge University Press.

Kołodziejczyk, Dariusz. 2006. 'Slave Hunting And Slave Redemption as a Business Enterprise: The Northern Black Sea Region in the Sixteenth to Seventeenth Centuries'. *Oriente Moderno* 25(86): 149–59.

Korhonen, Pekka. 1997. 'Monopolizing Asia: The Politics of a Metaphor'. *Pacific Review* 10(3): 347–65.

2001. 'The Geography of Okakura Tenshin'. *Japan Review* 13: 107–27.

2008. 'Common Culture: Asia Rhetoric in the Beginning of the 20th Century'. *Inter-Asia Cultural Studies* 9(3): 395–417.

2014. 'Leaving Asia? The Meaning of Datsu-A and Japan's Modern History'. *Asia-Pacific Journal* 12(9): 1–18.

Korkut, Umut. 2017. 'Resentment and Reorganization: Anti-Western Discourse and the Making of Eurasianism in Hungary'. *Acta Slavica Iaponica* 38: 71–90.

Krasner, Stephen D. 1996. 'Compromising Westphalia'. *International Security* 20 (Winter): 115–51.

1999. *Sovereignty: Organized Hypocrisy*. Princeton University Press.

2001. Rethinking the Sovereign State Model. *Review of International Studies* 27: 17–42.

Kroenig, Matthew. 2020. *The Return of Great Power Rivalry: Democracy versus Autocracy from the Ancient World to the U.S. and China.* Oxford University Press.

Krstić, Tijana. 2009. 'Illuminated by the Light of Islam and the Glory of the Ottoman Sultanate: Self-Narratives of Conversion to Islam in the Age of Confessionalization'. *Comparative Studies in Society and History* 51(1): 35–63.

2011. *Contested Conversions to Islam Narratives of Religious Change in the Early Modern Ottoman Empire.* Stanford University Press.

2013. 'Contesting Subjecthood and Sovereignty in Ottoman Galata in the Age of Confessionalization: The Carazo Affair, 1613–1617'. *Oriente Moderno* 93(2): 422–53.

Krstić, Tijana, and Derin Terzioğlu. 2020. *Historicizing Sunni Islam in the Ottoman Empire, C. 1450–C. 1750.* Brill.

Kumar, Krishan. 2014. 'The Return of Civilization – and of Arnold Toynbee?' *Comparative Studies in Society and History* 56(4): 815–43.

Lake, David. 2006. 'American Hegemony and the Future of East–West Relations'. *International Studies Perspectives* 7: 23–30.

2013. 'Great Power Hierarchies and Strategies in Twenty-First Century World Politics'. In *Handbook of International Relations*, edited by Walter Carlsnaes, Thomas Risse and Beth Simmons, pp. 555–78. Sage.

Landau, Jacob M. 2004. *Exploring Ottoman and Turkish History.* C. Hurst & Co. Publishers.

Lane, George. 2012. 'Mongol News: The Akhbār-I Moghulān Dar Anbāneh Qutb by Quṭb Al-Dīn Maḥmūd Ibn Mas'ūd Shīrāzī'. *Journal of the Royal Asiatic Society of Great Britain & Ireland* 22(3/4): 541–59.

2014. 'Persian Notables and the Families Who Underpinned the Ilkhanate'. In *Nomads as Agents of Cultural Change: The Mongols and Their Eurasian Predecessors*, edited by Reuven Amitai and Michal Biran, pp. 182–213. Oxford University Press.

Lang, Michael. 2011. 'Globalization and Global History in Toynbee'. *Journal of World History* 22(4): 747–83.

Laruelle, Marlene. 2016. 'The Notion of Eurasia: A Spatial, Historical, and Political Construct'. In *Questioning Post-Soviet*, edited by Edward Holland and Matthew Derrick, pp. 127–42. Woodrow Wilson International Center for Scholars.

Laszlovszky, József, Stephen Pow, Beatrix F. Romhányi, László Ferenczi and Zsolt Pinke. 2018. 'Contextualizing the Mongol Invasion of Hungary in 1241–42: Short- and Long-Term Perspectives'. *Hungarian Historical Review* 7(3): 419–50.

Lattimore, Owen. 1948. 'Spengler and Toynbee'. *Atlantic Monthly* 181(4): 104–5.

1962. *Studies in Frontier History: Collected Papers, 1928–1958*. Mouton.

Lawson, George. 2012. 'The Eternal Divide? History and International Relations'. *European Journal of International Relations* 18(2): 203–26.

2019. *Anatomies of Revolution*. Cambridge University Press.

Lawson, George, and Robbie Shilliam. 2009. 'Beyond Hypocrisy? Debating the "Fact" and "Value" of Sovereignty in Contemporary World Politics'. *International Politics* 46(6): 657–70.

Lebow, Richard Ned, and Benjamin Valentino. 2009. 'Lost in Transition: A Critical Analysis of Power Transition Theory'. *International Relations* 23(3): 389–410.

Lee, Joo-Yup. 2016. 'The Historical Meaning of the Term Turk and the Nature of the Turkic Identity of the Chinggisid and Timurid Elites in Post-Mongol Central Asia'. *Central Asiatic Journal* 59(1–2): 101–32.

Leigh, Joseph. 2019. 'The Emergence of Global Power Politics: Imperialism, Modernity, and American Expansion 1870–1914'. PhD Thesis, London School of Economics.

Lemke, Douglas. 1997. 'The Continuation of History: Power Transition Theory and the End of the Cold War'. *Journal of Peace Research* 34 (1): 23–36.

2001. *Power Transitions: Strategies for the 21st Century*. CQ Press.

Lemke, Douglas, and William Reed. 1996. 'Regime Types and Status Quo Evaluations: Power Transition Theory and the Democratic Peace'. *International Interactions* 22(2): 143–64.

Lemke, Douglas, and Ronald L. Tammen. 2003. 'Power Transition Theory and the Rise of China'. *International Interactions* 29(4): 269–71.

Lentz, Thomas W., and Glenn D. Lowry, eds. 1989. *Timur and the Princely Vision*. Smithsonian Books.

Lepenies, Wolf. 2003. *Entangled Histories and Negotiated Universals: Centers and Peripheries in a Changing World*. Campus Verlag.

Levy, Jack S. 1983. *War in the Modern Great Power System: 1495–1975*. University Press of Kentucky.

Lewis, Bernard. 1962. 'Ottoman Observers Of Ottoman Decline'. *Islamic Studies* 1(1): 71–87.

1968. 'The Mongols, the Turks and the Muslim Polity'. *Transactions of the Royal Historical Society* 18: 49–68.

Lindner, Kolja. 2010. 'Marx's Eurocentrism: Postcolonial Studies and Marx Scholarship'. *Radical Philosophy* 161: 27–41.

Lopez, Robert, Harry Miskimin, and Abraham Udovitch. 1970. 'England to Egypt, 1350–1500: Long-Term Trends and Long-Distance Trade'. In *Studies in the Economic History of the Middle East from the Rise of*

Islam to the Present Day, edited by M. A. Cook, pp. 93–128. Oxford University Press.

Lotz-Heumann, Ute. 2001. 'The Concept of "Confessionalization": A Historiographical Paradigm in Dispute'. *Memoria Y Civilización* 4: 93–114.

MacDonald, Paul K., and Joseph M. Parent. 2018a. 'The Road to Recovery: How Once Great Powers Became Great Again'. *Washington Quarterly* 41(3): 21–39.

2018b. *Twilight of the Titans: Great Power Decline and Retrenchment.* Cornell University Press.

Mack, Rosamond. 2001. *Bazaar to Piazza: Islamic Trade and Italian Art, 1300–1600.* University of California Press.

MacKay, Joseph. 2016. 'The Nomadic Other: Ontological Security and the Inner Asian Steppe in Historical East Asian International Politics'. *Review of International Studies* 42(3): 471–91.

2018. 'Rethinking Hierarchies in East Asian Historical IR'. *Journal of Global Security Studies* 4(4): 598–611.

MacKay, Joseph, Jamie Levin, Gustavo de Carvalho, Kristin Cavoukian and Ross Cuthbert. 2014. 'Before and after Borders: The Nomadic Challenge to Sovereign Territoriality'. *International Political Science Review* 51(1): 101–23.

Malcolm, Noel. 2015. *Agents of Empire: Knights, Corsairs, Jesuits and Spies in the Sixteenth-Century Mediterranean World.* Oxford University Press.

2019. *Useful Enemies: Islam and the Ottoman Empire in Western Political Thought, 1450–1750.* Oxford University Press.

Mann, Michael. 1986. *The Sources of Social Power.* Cambridge University Press.

Manz, Beatrice F. 1988. 'Tamerlane and the Symbolism of Sovereignty'. *Iranian Studies* (1–2): 105–22.

1998. 'Temür and the Problem of a Conqueror's Legacy'. *Journal of the Royal Asiatic Society of Great Britain & Ireland* 8(1): 21–41.

1999. *The Rise and Rule of Tamerlane.* Cambridge University Press.

Masuya, Kadoi. 2017. 'Chinese and TurkoMongol Elements in Ilkhanid and Timurid Arts'. In *A Companion to Islamic Art and Architecture*, edited by Finbarr Barry Flood and Gülru Necipoğlu, pp. 636–67. John Wiley & Sons.

Matin, Kamran. 2007. 'Uneven and Combined Development in World History: The International Relations of State-Formation in Premodern Iran'. *European Journal of International Relations* 13(3): 419–47.

Matthee, Rudi. 2015. 'The Decline of Safavid Iran in Comparative Perspective'. *Journal of Persianate Studies* 8: 276–308.

2010. 'Was Safavid Iran an Empire?' *Journal of Economic and Social History of the Orient* 53 (1/2): 233–65.

Matthews, John A., and Keith R. Briffa. 2005. 'The 'little Ice Age': Re-evaluation of an Evolving Concept'. *Geografiska Annaler: Series A, Physical Geography* 87(1): 17–36.

May, Timothy. 2006. 'The Training of an Inner Asian Nomad Army in the Pre-Modern Period'. *Journal of Military History* 70(3): 617–35.

2012. *The Mongol Conquests in World History*. Reaktion Books.

2016. 'Color Symbolism in the Turko-Mongolian World'. In *The Use of Color in History, Politics, and Art*, edited by Sungshin Kim, pp. 51–77. University Press of North Georgia.

McNeill, William. 1988. 'Toynbee Revisited'. *Bulletin of the American Academy of Arts and Sciences* 41(7): 13–27.

1989. *Arnold J. Toynbee: A Life*. Oxford University Press.

Mearsheimer, John. 2006. 'China's Unpeaceful Rise'. *Current History* 105: 160–3.

2010. 'The Gathering Storm: China's Challenge to US Power in Asia'. *Chinese Journal of International Politics* 3(4): 381–96.

2014. *The Tragedy of Great Power Politics*. Updated edition. W. W. Norton & Company.

Meisner, Maurice. 1963. 'The Despotism of Concepts: Wittfogel and Marx on China'. *China Quarterly* 16: 99–111.

1965. 'Li Ta-Chao and the Chinese Communist Treatment of the Materialist Conception of History'. *China Quarterly* 24: 141–69.

Melvin-Koushki, Matthew. 2016. 'Astrology, Lettrism, Geomancy: The Occult-Scientific Methods of Post-Mongol Islamicate Imperialism'. *Medieval History Journal* 19(1): 142–50.

2018a. 'Early Modern Islamicate Empire: New Forms of Religiopolitical Legitimacy'. In *The Wiley Blackwell History of Islam*, edited by A. Salvatore, R. Tottoli, B. Rahimi, M. Fariduddin Attar and N. Patel., pp. 353–75. John Wiley & Sons Ltd.

2018b. 'Persianate Geomancy from Ṭūsī to the Millennium'. In *Occult Sciences in Premodern Islamic Culture*, edited by N. El-Bizri and E. Orthmann, pp. 151–99. Orient-Institut Beirut.

2018c. 'Taḥqīq vs. Taqlīd in the Renaissances of Western Early Modernity'. *Philological Encounters* 3(1–2): 193–249.

2019a. 'The Occult Sciences in Safavid Iran'. In *Empires of the Near East and India*, edited by H. Khafipour, pp. 348–65. Columbia University Press.

2019b. 'How to Rule the World: Occult-Scientific Manuals of the Early Modern Persian Cosmopolis'. *Journal of Persianate Studies* 11(2): 140–54.

Merand, Frederic, ed. 2020. *Coping with Geopolitical Decline*. McGill University Press.

Millward, James A. 2013. *The Silk Road*. Oxford University Press.

2020. 'Qing and Twentieth-Century Chinese Diversity Regimes'. In *Culture and Order in World Politics*, edited by Andrew Phillips and Christian Reus-Smit, pp. 71–92. Cambridge University Press.

Milwright, Marcus, and Evanthia Baboula. 2011. 'Bayezid's Cage: A Re-Examination of a Venerable Academic Controversy'. *Journal of the Royal Asiatic Society of Great Britain & Ireland* 21(3): 239–60.

Miyawaki-Okada, Junko. 2006. 'The Japanese Origin of the Chinggis Khan Legends'. *Inner Asia* 8(1): 123–34.

Moin, Azfar. 2012. *The Millennial Sovereign*. Columbia University Press.

Morgan, David O. 1982. 'Who Ran the Mongol Empire?' *Journal of the Royal Asiatic Society of Great Britain & Ireland* 1: 124–36.

1986 'The "Great 'Yāsā' of Chingiz Khān" and Mongol Law in the Īlkhānate'. *Bulletin of the School of Oriental and African Studies* 49(1): 163–76.

2001. 'Ibn Baṭṭūṭa and the Mongols'. *Journal of the Royal Asiatic Society of Great Britain & Ireland* 11(1): 1–11.

2009. 'The Decline and Fall of the Mongol Empire'. *Journal of the Royal Asiatic Society of Great Britain & Ireland* 19(4): 427–37.

2014. 'Mongol Historiography since 1985: The Rise of Cultural History'. In *Nomads as Agents of Cultural Change: The Mongols and Their Eurasian Predecessors*, edited by Reuven Amitai and Michal Biran., pp. 271–82. Oxford University Press.

Mote, Frederick W., and Denis Twitchett, eds. 1988. *The Cambridge History of China: Volume 7, The Ming Dynasty, 1368–1644, Part 1*. Cambridge University Press.

Munkh-Erdene, Lhamsuren. 2011. 'Where Did the Mongol Empire Come From? Medieval Mongol Ideas of People, State and Empire'. *Inner Asia* 13(2): 211–37.

Musgrave, Paul, and Daniel H. Nexon. 2018. 'Defending Hierarchy from the Moon to the Indian Ocean: Symbolic Capital and Political Dominance in Early Modern China and the Cold War'. *International Organization* 72(3): 591–626.

Necipoğlu, Gülru. 1989. 'Süleyman the Magnificent and the Representation of Power in the Context of Ottoman-Hapsburg-Papal Rivalry'. *Art Bulletin* 71(3): 401–27.

1990. 'From International Timurid to Ottoman: A Change of Taste in Sixteenth-Century Ceramic Tiles'. *Muqarnas* 7: 136–70.

Neumann, Iver. 2014. 'Europeans and the Steppe: Russian Lands under the Mongol Rule'. In *International Orders in the Early Modern World: Before the Rise of the West*, edited by Shogo Suzuki, Yongjin Zhang and Joel Quirk, pp. 12–33. Routledge.

Neumann, Iver B., and Einar Wigen. 2013. 'The Importance of the Eurasian Steppe to the Study of International Relations'. *Journal of International Relations and Development* 16(3): 311–30.

2015. 'Remnants of the Mongol Imperial Tradition'. In *Legacies of Empire: Imperial Roots of the Contemporary Global Order*, edited by Sandra Halperin, pp. 99–127. Cambridge University Press.

2018. *The Steppe Tradition in International Relations: Russians, Turks and European State-Building 4000 BCE–2018 CE*. Cambridge University Press.

Nexon, Daniel H. 2009. *The Struggle for Power in Early Modern Europe: Religious Conflict, Dynastic Empires, and International*. Princeton University Press.

Nye, Joseph. 2010. 'The Future of American Power: Dominance and Decline in Perspective'. *Foreign Affairs* 89(6): 2–12.

Ogilvie, Sheilagh. 1992. 'Germany and the Seventeenth-Century Crisis'. *Historical Journal* 35(2): 417–41.

O'Kane, Bernard. 2017. 'Architecture and Court Cultures of the Fourteenth Century'. In *A Companion to Islamic Art and Architecture*, edited by Finbarr Barry Flood and Gülru Necipoğlu, pp. 585–615. John Wiley & Sons.

Organski, A. F. K., and Jacek Kugler. 1981. *The War Ledger*. University of Chicago Press.

Orlovsky, Daniel. 1989. 'Selling American Anxiety: The Rise and Fall of the Great Powers'. *Southwest Review* 74(1): 110–21.

Osiander, Andreas. 2001. 'Sovereignty, International Relations and the Westphalian Myth'. *International Organization* 55(2): 251–87.

Ostrowski, Donald. 1990. 'The Mongol Origins of Muscovite Political Institutions'. *Slavic Review* 49(4): 525–42.

1992. 'The Military Land Grant Along the Muslim Christian Frontier'. *Russian History/Histoire Russe* 19(1–4): 327–59.

1998. 'The "Tamma" and the Dual-Administrative Structure of the Mongol Empire'. *Bulletin of the School of Oriental and African Studies* 61(2): 262–77.

2002. 'Troop Mobilization by the Muscovite Grand Princes (1313–1533)'. In *The Military and Society in Russia, 1450–1917*, edited by Eric Lohr and Marshall Poe, pp. 25–38. Brill.

2012. 'Systems of Succession in Rus' and Steppe Societies'. *Ruthenica* XI: 29–58.

Özel, Oktay. 2016. *The Collapse of Rural Order in Ottoman Anatolia: Amasya 1576–1643*. Brill.

Pamuk, Şevket. 2007. 'The Black Death and the Origins of the 'Great Divergence' across Europe, 1300–1600'. *European Review of Economic History* 11(3): 289–317.

Pancaroğlu, Oya. 2013. 'Devotion, Hospitality and Architecture in Medieval Anatolia'. *Studia Islamica* 108(1): 48–81.

Pardesi, Manjeet S. 2017. 'Region, System, and Order: The Mughal Empire in Islamicate Asia'. *Security Studies* 26(2): 249–78.

2019. 'Mughal Hegemony and the Emergence of South Asia as a 'Region' for Regional Order-Building'. *European Journal of International Relations* 25(1): 276–301.

Park, Seo-Hyun. 2017. *Sovereignty and Status in East Asian International Relations*. Cambridge University Press.

Parker, Geoffrey. 2013. *Global Crisis: War, Climate Change and Catastrophe in the Seventeenth Century*. Yale University Press.

Parker, Geoffrey, and Lesley M. Smith. 1978. *The General Crisis of the Seventeenth Century*. 1st ed. Routledge & Kegan Paul.

Parker, Geoffrey, and Lesley M. Smith, eds. 1997. *The General Crisis of the Seventeenth Century*. Routledge.

Peacock, Andrew. 2019. *Islam, Literature and Society in Mongol Anatolia*. Cambridge University Press.

Pearson, M. N. 1976. 'Shivaji and the Decline of the Mughal Empire'. *Journal of Asian Studies* 35(2): 221–35.

Pederson, Neil, Amy E. Hessi, Nachin Baatarbileg, Kevin J. Anchukaitis and Nicola Di Cosmo. 2014. 'Pluvials, Droughts, the Mongol Empire, and Modern Mongolia'. *Proceedings of the National Academy of Sciences of the United States of America* 111(12): 4375–9.

Peng Xinwei. 1965. *Zhongguo huobi shi* [*A History of Chinese Currency*]. 3rd ed. Renmin chuban she.

Phillips, Andrew. 2016. 'International Systems'. In *The Globalization of International Society*, edited by Christian Reus-Smit and Tim Dunne, pp. 43–62. Oxford University Press.

Phillips, Andrew. 2021. *How the East Was Won: Barbarian Conquerors, Universal Conquest and the Making of Modern Asia*. Cambridge University Press.

Phillips, Andrew, and Chris Reus-Smit, eds. 2020. *Culture and Order in World Politics*. Cambridge University Press.

Phillips, Andrew, and J. C. Sharman. 2015. *International Order in Diversity*. Cambridge University Press.

Philpott, Daniel. 2001. *Revolutions in Sovereignty: How Ideas Shaped Modern International Relations*. Princeton University Press.

Pijl, Kees van der. 2007. *Nomads, Empires, States: Modes of Foreign Relations and Political Economy*. Pluto Press.

Pinke, Zsolt, Laszlo Ferenczi, Beatrix F. Romhanyi, Jozsef Laszlovszky and Stephen Pow. 2017. 'Climate of Doubt: A Re-Evaluation of Büntgen and Di Cosmo's Environmental Hypothesis for the Mongol Withdrawal from Hungary, 1242 CE'. *Scientific Reports* 7(1): 1–6.

Pollock, Sheldon. 2005. 'Empire and Imitation'. In *Lessons of Empire: Imperial Histories and American Power*, edited by Craig Calhoun, Frederick Cooper, and Kevin W. Moore, pp. 175–88. The New Press.

Polo, Marco. 1948. *The Travels of Marco Polo the Venetian*, edited by Thomas Wright, translated by William Marsden. International Collectors Library.

Pomeranz, Kenneth. 2001. *The Great Divergence: China, Europe, and the Making of the Modern World Economy*. Princeton University Press.

Prazniak, Roxann. 2010. 'Siena on the Silk Roads: Ambrogio Lorenzetti and the Mongol Global Century, 1250–1350'. *Journal of World History* 21 (2): 177–217.

Putnam, Aaron E., David E. Putnam, Laia Andreu-Hayles, Edward R. Cook, Jonathan G. Palmer, Elizabeth H. Clark, Chunzeng Wang, Feng Chen, George H. Denton, Douglas P. Boyle, Scott D. Bassett, Sean D. Birkel, Javier Martin-Fernandez, Irka Hajdas, John Southon, Christopher B. Garner, Hai Cheng and Wallace S. Broecker. 2016. 'Little Ice Age Wetting of Interior Asian Deserts and the Rise of the Mongol Empire'. *Quaternary Science Reviews* 131: 33–50.

Quinn, Sholeh. 1996. 'The Dreams of Shaykh Safi Al-Din and Safavid Historical Writing'. *Iranian Studies* 29(1/2): 127–47.

Raphael, Kate. 2009. 'Mongol Siege Warfare on the Banks of the Euphrates and the Question of Gunpowder (1260–1312)'. *Journal of the Royal Asiatic Society of Great Britain & Ireland* 19(3): 355–70.

Reid, Anthony. 1978. 'The Crisis of the Seventeenth Century in Southeast Asia'. In *The General Crisis of the Seventeenth Century*, edited by Geoffrey Parkey and Lesley M. Smith, pp. 207–35. Routledge & Kegan Paul.

Reus-Smit, Christian. 1999. *The Moral Purpose of the State*. Princeton University Press.

Robinson, David M. 2012. 'Mongolian Migration and the Ming's Place in Eurasia'. *Journal of Central Eurasian Studies* 3: 109–29.

2019. *Ming China and Its Allies*. Cambridge University Press.

2020. *Culture, Courtiers, and Competition: The Ming Court (1368–1644)*. Brill.

Robinson, Francis. 1997. 'Ottomans-Safavids-Mughals: Shared Knowledge And Connective Systems'. *Journal of Islamic Studies* 8(2): 151–84.

Rogers, J. Daniel. 2012. 'Inner Asian States and Empires: Theories and Synthesis'. *Journal of Archaeological Research* 20(3): 205–56.

Rong Xinjiang. 2015. 'Reality or Tale? Marco Polo's Description of Khotan'. *Journal of South Asian Natural History* 49(1–2): 161–74.

Rosenboim, Or. 2014. 'Geopolitics and Global Democracy in Owen Lattimore's Political Thought'. *International History Review* 36(4): 745–66.

Rossabi, Morris. 1975. *China and Inner Asia: From 1368 to the Present Day.* Thames and Hudson.

1983. 'A Translation of Ch'en Ch'eng's Hsi-yii fan-kuo chih'. *Ming Studies* 17: 49–59.

1987. *Khubilai Khan: His Life and Times.* 1st ed. University of California Press.

1988. *Kubilai Khan: His Life and Times.* University of California Press.

1998. 'The Ming and Inner Asia'. In *The Cambridge History of China, Vol. 8: The Ming Dynasty, Part 2: 1368–1644*, edited by Dennis Twitchett and Frederick Mote, pp. 221–71. Cambridge University Press.

2009. *Khubilai Khan.* University of California Press.

2014a. 'Ming China and Turfan, 1406–1517'. In *From Yuan to Modern China and Mongolia: The Writings of Morris Rossabi*, pp. 39–58. Brill.

2014b. 'The 'Decline' of the Central Asian Caravan Trade'. In *From Yuan to Modern China and Mongolia: The Writings of Morris Rossabi*, pp. 201–20. Brill.

2014c. 'The Mongol Empire and Its Impact on the Arts of China'. In *Nomads as Agents of Cultural Change: The Mongols and Their Eurasian Predecessors*, edited by Reuven Amitai and Michal Biran, pp. 214–27. Oxford University Press.

2014d. 'The Tea and Horse Trade with Inner Asia during the Ming', In *From Yuan to Modern China and Mongolia: The Writings of Morris Rossabi*, pp. 59–88. Brill.

Rothman, Natalie. 2014. *Brokering Empire: Trans-Imperial Subjects between Venice and Istanbul.* Cornell University Press.

2021. *The Dragoman Renaissance: Diplomatic Interpreters and the Routes of Orientalism.* Cornell University Press.

Rowe, William T. 2007. 'Owen Lattimore, Asia, and Comparative History'. *Journal of Asian Studies* 66(3): 759–86.

Ruggie, John G. 1983. 'Continuity and Transformation in the World Polity: Toward a Neorealist Synthesis'. *World Politics* 35(2): 261–85.

Ryan, William F. 2012. 'Ivan the Terrible's Malady and Its Magical Cure'. *Incantatio* 2(1): 23–32.

Sachsenmaier, Dominic. 2006. 'Global History and Critiques of Western Perspectives'. *Comparative Education Review* 42(3): 451–70.

Şahin, Kaya. 2013. *Empire and Power in the Reign of Süleyman: Narrating the Sixteenth-Century Ottoman World.* Cambridge University Press.

Saito, Shohei. 2017. 'Crossing Perspectives in "Manchukuo" Russian Eurasianism and Japanese Pan-Asianism'. *Jahrbucher Fur Geschichte Osteuropas* 65(4): 597–623.

Saliba, George. 1995. *A History of Arabic Astronomy: Planetary Theories during the Golden Age of Islam.* New York University Press.

Sawma, Rabban. 2014. *The Monks of Kublai Khan Emperor of China,* edited and translated by E. A. Wallis Budge. I. B. Tauris.

Schamiloglu, Uli. 2004. 'The Rise of the Ottoman Empire: The Black Death in Medieval Anatolia and Its Impact on Turkish Civilization'. In *Views from the Edge: Essays in Honour of Richard W. Bulliet,* edited by Neguin Yavari, Lawrence G. Potter and Jean-Marc Oppenheim, pp. 255–79. Columbia University Press.

  2017a. 'The Impact of the Black Death on the Golden Horde: Politics, Economy, Society, Civilization'. *Golden Horde Review* 5(2): 325–43.

  2017b. 'Black Death and Its Consequences'. In *The History of the Tatars since Ancient Times in Seven Volumes: The Ulus of Jochi (Golden Horde): 13th Century–Mid-15th Century, Vol. 3,* pp. 714–19. Academy Sciences of Tatarstan.

Schilling, H. 2001. 'Reformation and Confessionalization'. In *International Encyclopedia of the Social and Behavioral Sciences,* edited by Neil J. Smelser and Paul B. Baltes, pp. 12891–5. Elsevier.

Schmid, Boris V., Ulf Büntgen, W. Ryan Easterday, Christian Ginzler, Lars Walløe, Barbara Bramanti and Nils Chr. Stenseth. 2015. 'Climate-Driven Introduction of the Black Death and Successive Plague Reintroductions into Europe'. *Proceedings of the National Academy of Sciences of the United States of America* 112(10): 3020–5.

Schmidt, Sebastian. 2011. 'To Order the Minds of Scholars: The Discourse of the Peace of Westphalia in International Relations Literature'. *International Studies Quarterly* 55: 601–23.

Schweller, Randall, and Xiaoyu Pu. 2011. 'After Unipolarity: China's Visions of International Order in an Era of U.S. Decline'. *International Security* 36(1): 41–72.

Scott, H. M. 2006. *Birth of a Great Power System.* Routledge.

Sen, Tansen. 2014. 'Maritime Southeast Asia between South Asia and China to the Sixteenth Century'. *TRaNS: Trans-Regional and -National Studies of Southeast Asia* 2(1): 31–59.

Sewell, William H. 1967. 'Marc Bloch and the Logic of Comparative History'. *History and Theory* 6(2): 208–18.

Sharman, J. C. 2019. *Empires of the Weak: The Real Story of European Expansion and the Creation of the New World Order*. Princeton University Press.

Sharman, J. C., and Andrew Phillips. 2020. *Outsourcing Empire: How Company-States Made the Modern World*. Princeton University Press.

Shim, Hosung. 2014. 'The Postal Roads of the Great Khans in Central Asia under the Mongol-Yuan Empire'. *Journal of Song-Yuan Studies* 44: 405–69.

Sivasundaram, Sujit. 2020. *Waves across the South: A New History of Revolution and Empire*. William Collins.

Skinner, Quentin. 2008. 'A Genealogy of the Modern State'. *Proceedings of the British Academy* 162: 325–70.

Skrynnikov, Ruslan G. 2015. *Reign of Terror: Ivan IV*. Leiden: Brill.

Slavin, Philip. 2012. 'The Great Bovine Pestilence and Its Economic and Environmental Consequences in England and Wales, 1318–501'. *Economic History Review* 65(4): 1239–66.

Smith, Neil. 1987. 'Essay Review: Rehabilitating A Renegade? The Geography And Politics Of Karl August Wittfogel'. *Dialectical Anthropology* 12(1): 127–36.

Sneath, David. 2007. *The Headless State*. Columbia University Press.

Sood, Gagan. 2011. 'An Islamicate Eurasia: Vernacular Perspectives on the Early Modern World'. In *Is There a Middle East? The Evolution of a Geopolitical Concept*, edited by Michael E. Bonine, Abbas Amanat and Michael Gasper, pp. 154–69. Stanford University Press.

Sophoulis, Panos. 2015. 'The Mongol Invasion of Croatia and Serb'. *Fragmenta Hellenoslavica* 2: 251–78.

Spruyt, Hendrik. 2020. *The World Imagined: Collective Beliefs and Political Order in the Sinocentric, Islamic and Southeast Asian International Societies*. Cambridge University Press.

Stanziani, Alessandro. 2014. 'Slavery and Bondage in Central Asia and Russia from the Fourteenth to the Nineteenth Century'. In *Bondage*, pp. 63–100. Berghahn Books.

Starr, Frederick S. 2013. *Lost Enlightenment: Central Asia's Golden Age from the Arab Conquest to Tamerlane*. Princeton University Press.

Steensgaard, Niels. 1975. *Asian Trade Revolution of the Seventeenth Century: East India Companies and the Decline of the Caravan Trade*. University of Chicago Press.

1978. 'The Seventeenth-Century Crisis'. In *The General Crisis of the Seventeenth Century*, edited by Geoffrey Parkey and Lesley M. Smith, pp. 32–56. Routledge & Kegan Paul.

1990. 'The Seventeenth-Century Crisis and the Unity of Eurasian History'. *Modern Asian Studies* 24(4): 683–97.

Stoddard, T. Lothrop. 1917. 'Pan-Turanism'. *American Political Science Review* 11(1): 12–23.

Subrahmanyam, Sanjay. 1997. 'Connected Histories: Notes towards a Reconfiguration of Early Modern Eurasia'. *Modern Asian Studies* 31 (3): 735–62.

2000. 'Un Grand Dérangement: Dreaming An Indo-Persian Empire In South Asia, 1740–1800'. *Journal of Early Modern History* 4(3–4): 337–78.

2005a. *Explorations in Connected History (Mughals and Franks)*. Oxford University Press.

2005b. 'On World Historians in the Sixteenth Century'. *Representations* 91(1): 26–57.

2006. 'A Tale of Three Empires: Mughals, Ottomans, and Habsburgs in a Comparative Context'. *Common Knowledge* 12(1): 66–92.

Tammen, Ronald. 2008. 'The Organski Legacy: A Fifty-Year Research Program'. *International Interactions* 34(4): 314–32.

Tanaka, Takeo. 1977. 'Japan's Relations with Overseas Countries'. In *Japan in the Muromachi Age*, edited by John W. Hall and Toyoda Takeshi, pp. 159–78. University of California Press.

Teschke, Benno. 2003. *The Myth of 1648: Class, Geopolitics, and the Making of Modern International Relations*. Verso.

Tezcan, Baki. 2009. 'Lost in Historiography: An Essay on the Reasons for the Absence of a History of Limited Government in the Early Modern Ottoman Empire'. *Middle Eastern Studies* 45(3): 477–505.

2010. *The Second Ottoman Empire*. Cambridge University Press.

Thackston, W. M., Jr. 2007. *The Baburnama: Memoirs of Babur, Prince and Emperor*. Modern Library.

Tilly, Charles. 1993. *Coercion, Capital, and European States, A.D. 990–1990*. 1st ed. Hoboken, NJ: Wiley-Blackwell.

Todorov, Tzvetan. 1999. *The Conquest of America: The Question of the Other*. University of Oklahoma Press.

Tokluoğlu, Ceylan. 2012. 'Ziya Gökalp: From Turanism To Turkism'. *Atatürk Araştırma Merkezi Dergisi* 28(84): 103–42.

Topal, Alp Eren. 2017. 'Against Influence: Ziya Gökalp in Context and Tradition'. *Journal of Islamic Studies* 28(3): 283–310.

Toynbee, Arnold. 1922. *The Western Question in Greece and Turkey: a Study in the Contact of Civilisations*. Constable And Company Ltd.

1957. *A Study of History: Abridgement of Volumes I–VI*, edited by David Churchill Somervell. Oxford University Press.

Trevor-Roper, Hugh. 2001. *The Crisis of the Seventeenth Century: Religion, the Reformation and Social Change*. Liberty Fund.

Truschke, Audrey. 2016. 'Translating the Solar Cosmology of Sacred Kingship'. *Medieval History Journal* 19(1): 136–41.

———. 2017. *Aurangzeb: The Life and Legacy of India's Most Controversial King*. Stanford University Press.

Tuchman, Barbara. 2011. *A Distant Mirror: The Calamitous 14th Century*. Reissue edition. Random House.

Twitchett, Denis C., and Frederick W. Mote. 1998. *The Cambridge History of China: Volume 8, The Ming Dynasty, Part 2, 1368–1644*. Cambridge University Press.

Valensi, Lucette. 1993. *The Birth of the Despot: Venice and the Sublime Porte*. Cornell University Press.

Varlık, Nükhet. 2017. *Plague and Contagion in the Islamic Mediterranean*. Arc Humanities Press.

Vásáry, István. 2014. 'The Tatar Factor in the Formation of Muscovy's Political Culture'. In *Nomads as Agents of Cultural Change: The Mongols and Their Eurasian Predecessors*, edited by Reuven Amitai and Michal Biran, pp. 252–70. Oxford University Press.

Vries, Peer. 2010. 'The California School and beyond: How to Study the Great Divergence?' *History Compass* 8(7): 730–51.

Wakeman, Frederic E. 1985. *The Great Enterprise: The Manchu Reconstruction of Imperial Order in Seventeenth-Century China*. Berkeley: University of California Press.

Walt, Stephen M. 2011. 'The End of the American Era'. *National Interest* 116: 6–16.

Waltz, Kenneth. 1979. *Theory of International Politics*. Addison-Wesley.

Wang, Gung-Wu. 1991. *China and the Overseas Chinese*. Time Academic Press.

———. 1992. *Community and Nation: China, Southeast Asia, and Australia*. Allen and Unwin.

Wang, Yuan-Kang. 2012. 'Managing Regional Hegemony in Historical Asia: The Case of Early Ming China'. *Chinese Journal of International Politics* 5(2): 129–53.

Watanabe, H. 1975. *An Index of Embassies and Tribute Missions from Islamic Countries to Ming China (1368–1466) as Recorded in the Ming Shih-lu Classified According to Geographic Area*. Toyo Bunko.

Weatherford, Jack. 2004. *Genghis Khan and the Making of the Modern World*. Crown and Three Rivers Press.

Weber, Max. 1965 (1919). *Politics as a Vocation*. Fortress Press.

Werner, Michael, and Bénédicte Zimmermann. 2004. *De la comparaison à l'histoire croisée*. Seuil.

White, Sam. 2011. *The Climate of Rebellion in the Early Modern Ottoman Empire*. Cambridge University Press.

Wight, Martin. 1977. *Systems of State*, edited by Hedley Bull. Continuum International Publishing.

Wills, John E., Jr. 1998. 'Relations with Maritime Europeans, 1514–1662'. In *The Cambridge History of China, Vol. 8: The Ming Dynasty, Part 2: 1368–1644*, edited by Dennis Twitchett and Frederick Mote, pp. 333–75. Cambridge University Press.

Wittfogel, Karl A. 1950. 'Russia and Asia: Problems of Contemporary Area Studies and International Relations'. *World Politics* 2(4): 445–62.

Wong, Bin. 2000. *China Transformed: Historical Change and the Limits of European Experience*. Cornell University Press.

Xiaonan, Deng, 部小南 and Christian Lamouroux. 2005. 'The "Ancestors' Family Instructions": Authority and Sovereignty in Song China'. *Journal of Song-Yuan Studies* 35: 79–97.

Yanık, Lerna K. 2019. 'Debating Eurasia'. *Uluslararası İlişkiler/ International Relations* 16(63): 33–50.

Yasuo Nagayama. 1998. *Hito wa naze Rekishi wo Gizôsuru no ka* [Why Men Try to Fabricate History]. Shinchô.

Yaycıoğlu, Ali. 2016. *Partners of the Empire: The Crisis of the Ottoman Order in the Age of Revolutions*. Stanford University Press.

Zachariadou, Elizabeth. 2013. 'The Mosque of Kahriye and the Eastern Inclinations of Its Late Byzantine Patron'. *Archivum Ottomanicum* 30: 281–301.

Zarakol, Ayşe. 2010. 'Ontological (In)Security and State Denial of Historical Crimes: Turkey and Japan'. *International Relations* 24(1): 3–23.

  2011. *After Defeat: How the East Learned to Live with the West*. Cambridge University Press.

  2014. 'What Made the Modern World Hang Together: Socialisation or Stigmatisation'. *International Theory* 6(2): 311–32.

  2017a. 'States and Ontological Security: A Historical Rethinking'. *Cooperation & Conflict* 52(1): 48–68.

  2017b. 'Why Hierarchy?' In *Hierarchies in World Politics*, edited by Ayşe Zarakol, pp. 266–74. Cambridge University Press.

  2018a. 'A Non-Eurocentric Approach to Sovereignty'. *International Studies Review* 3(20): 489–520.

  2018b. 'Sovereign Equality as Misrecognition'. *Review of International Studies* 44(5): 848–62.

  2019. 'Rise of the Rest: As Hype and Reality'. *International Relations* 33 (2): 213–228.

  2020a. 'Use of Historical Analogies in IR Theory'. ISSF Roundtable XII-2 on Steve Chan, *Thucydides's Trap? Historical Interpretation, Logic of Inquiry, and the Future of Sino-American Relations*. H-Diplo. November 9.

2020b. 'Ottomans and Diversity'. In *Culture and Order in World Politics*, edited by Andrew Phillips and Chris Reus-Smit, pp. 49–70. Cambridge University Press.

2021. 'Linking Up The Ottoman Empire with IR's Timeline'. In *Routledge Handbook of Historical International Relations*, edited by Julia Costa Lopez, Benjamin de Carvalho and Halvard Leira, pp. 464–76. Routledge.

Zhang, Yongjin, and Barry Buzan. 2012. 'The Tributary System as International Society in Theory and Practice'. *Chinese Journal of International Politics* 5(1): 3–36.

Index

Abbas I, Safavid Shah, 162–4, 211
Abu Sa'id Mirza, Timurid ruler, 116
Abu-Lughod, Janet, 258
Ağaoğlu, Ahmet, 252
Akbar I, Mughal Emperor, 143,
    158–61, 165
  as *sahibkıran*, 159
  Divine Religion of, 159
  millenarianism of, 159
  occult sciences and, 160
  religious tolerance of, 159
Akbarnama (Book of Akbar), 160
Akçura, Yusuf, 252
Alanquva, Mongol princess, 100
alchemy, 196
Alexander the Great, 55, 93, 134
  as Lord of Conjunction, 97, 165, 166
Ali, Fourth Caliph, 100
  Ismail and, 144
  qizilbah taj and, 145
Ali, Mustafa, 154, 169, 183
Alp Arslan, Seljuk Sultan, 252
Alqas Mirza, Safavid prince, 153
Altan Khan, Mongol ruler, 194
Amasya, Peace of (1555), 4n4, 153,
    157, 178
Anatolian beyliks, 70, 133n30, 133, 134
animism, 206
Annales School, 258, 264
apocalyptic fears, 182, 185
Aq Qoyunlu (white sheep) dynasty,
    108, 122, 144, 145
Arab Spring, 237
Arghun Khan, Ilkhanate ruler, 49
Ariq Böke, Chinggisid Khan, 67, 69
Armenian Genocide (1915), 251
Arslan Khan, Qarluq leader, 62
Asia, 5n7, 7n13. *See also* Eurasia
Asian 'Freedom Bloc' (Lattimore), 266
Astrakhan Khanate, 199

astrology, 19, 25, 31, 80. *See also*
    occult sciences
  Akbar and, 160
  apocalyptic fears and, 185
  conjunction, 97–100, 166
  Humayun and, 156
  Ivan IV and, 201
  post-Timurid, 188, 218
  sacred kingship and, 178
  sahibkıran and, 97
  Süleyman and, 152
astronomy, 19, 25, 49, 80
  Persian, 103
  Zhu Yuanzhang and, 102
Atatürk, Mustafa Kemal, 250
Attila the Hun, 252n
Augsburg, Treaty of (1555), 153
Aurangzeb, Mughal Emperor, 143,
    163n207, 164, 213
Aviz, House of (Portugal), 176
Ayn Jalut, battle of (1260), 67
Ayyubid Dynasty, 67

Babur, Mughal Emperor, 116, 142–3
  Ismail and, 144, 145
  Sufism and, 142
  Timur and, 142
Baghdad
  Mongols' sack of, 66, 87, 98
  Süleyman's conquest of, 153
Bairam Khan, 158
Bar Sauma, Rabban, 49
Barsbay, Mamluk Sultan, 110
Batu Khan, Golden Horde ruler, 68,
    74n117
Batu Mengke Khan (sixteenth-century
    Mongol ruler), 195
Bayezid I, Ottoman Sultan, 109, 134,
Bayezid II, Ottoman Sultan, 140, 147
Bekbulatovich, Simeon, 201

Bela IV, Hungarian king, 64
Belt and Road Initiative, 9. *See also* silk
  roads
Berke Khan, Golden Horde ruler, 69,
  70n103
Black Death, 29, 34, 87, 121
  Byzantine Empire and, 134n38
  feudalism and, 56
  Golden Horde and, 72
  Pax Mongolica and, 73
Blom, Phillip, 210
Blue Horde, 68
Bodin, Jean, 177
Bomel, Elijah, 201
Braudel, Fernand, 184, 258, 268
Brook, Timothy, 106, 108n87
Buddhism, 82
  Kumar on, 260n67
  Tibetan, 71n106
Bukhara, 193
Bulgars, 252
bullion 'famine', 31, 34, 122,
bureaucratisation, 172, 196
Byzantine Empire, 135, 139, 186
  Black Death in, 134n38
  Chinggisid ties of, 84

capitalism, 23, 53, 223
  feudalism and, 265
  in China, 263
  surveillance, 238
Castren, Matthias Alexander, 251
Çelebi, Katip, 48n1, 169
Chagatai Khanate, 53, 69
  end of, 72
  Timurids and, 73, 91
Chaldiran, battle of (1514), 144, 148, 157
Charles V, Holy Roman Emperor,
  175–81, 219
  as *sahibkıran*, 181–3
  Caesar helmets of, 181
  centralisation of, 186
  Clement VII and, 177
  family of, 176
  Francis I and, 179–80
  Süleyman I and, 150, 152, 154n151,
    176, 179–81
  Tahmasp I and, 157
  Treaty of Augsburg and, 153
  universal empire and, 176

Chaucer, Geoffrey, 47, 51
Chen Cheng, 107
Cherniavsky, Michael, 203
Chiang Kai-Shek, 264
China, 8, 56. *See also particular*
  dynasties
  as Great Power, 240, 242
  as rising power, 239
  capitalism in, 263
  international relations of, 8
  IR theories of, 8–10
  Marx on, 263
  tributary system of, 8–9, 90, 218, 271
  Wittfogel on, 263
Chinese Revolution (1794), 1
Chinggisid Empire, 53. *See also*
  Mongols
  as Great Power, 81
  end of, 71, 73
  fragmentation of, 68, 85–8, 110
  globalising influence of, 173–4
  Japan and, 246
  legacy of, 3, 271
  Muscovy and, 206
  political structure of, 73–8
  sovereignty model of, 18–22, 31, 54,
    59, 74, 80–2, 136, 137, 171, 217,
    225
  world order of, 71–3, 81, 82–5, 217,
    271
Chinggisid Exchange, 29, 73
Cihannüma, 48n1
'civilisation', 233, 261
Clement VII (pope), 177, 181
climate change. *See also* Little Ice Age
  as structural crisis, 120, 209, 238
Cold War, 30, 226, 262
Collins, Randall, 267–9, 270
colonialism, 10, 54, 231, 234, 257
  Hobson on, 11
  Japanese, 249
  nationalism and, 119n133
Columbus, Christopher, 51
Committee of Union and Progress
  (CUP), 250, 253
confessionalisation, 189–90
Confucianism. *See* neo-Confucianism
Constantinople, 134, 135
  conquest of, 135, 139, 186
COVID-19 pandemic, 53, 232, 237–8

Crepy, Peace of (1544), 180
Crimean Khanate, 148, 197. *See also*
    Girays
    Ivan IV and, 200
Crimean Khanate, 197n121
Crone, Patricia, 258

da Meleto, Francesco, 185
Daoism, 196
Dayan Khan, Mongol ruler, 194
Deccan frontier, 158
Delhi Sultanate, 83, 122, 158
    Babur's conquest of, 142
    Shah Rukh and, 110
    Timur's conquest of, 94
devshirme (Ottoman slave army), 168.
    See also Janissaries
dream interpretation
    Babur and, 143
    Ismail and, 145
    Osman and, 137
    Tahmasp and, 157
Durkheim, Émile, 250, 267

East India Company, 168
East, decline of the, 230–7
ecological determinism, 265
ecumene, 224–30, 239
    Chinggisid, 224
    Westphalian, 229
Edebali, Sufi sheikh, 137
Egami, Namio, 249
English Civil War (1642–51), 208
Enver Pasha, 251, 253
essentialism, 27n95, 221
Eurasia, 5n7, 7n13, 255
Eurasianism, 244
    authoritarian politics of, 256
    Chinggisid world order and, 85
    globalisation and, 174
    in Turkey, 253
    nationalism and, 246
    Russian, 254–6
    Vernadsky on, 254–6
Eurocentrism, 54
    big bang theory of, 11
    international relations and, 128n11,
        174
    macro-history and, 270
evolutionary idealism, 259

Fairbank, John King, 8
feudalism, 107
    Black Death and, 56
    in Japan, 130
    Lattimore on, 262n76
    Marx on, 265
    Wittfogel on, 263
Finland, 251, 253
Fleischer, Cornell H., 154, 185
Fletcher, Joseph, 24, 60n47, 258
Francis I, French king, 179–80
French Revolution, 1
Fronde (1648–53), 208
Fyodor I, Russian tsar, 209

Gattinara, Mercurino de, 182
Genghis Khan, 53, 137
    as lawgiver, 79, 98
    as *sahibkıran*, 97, 165, 166
    centralisation by, 78–80, 84
    death of, 63
    family of, 60, 64
    Japanese legend of, 247
    legacy of, 80–2, 192
    rise of, 59–62
    shamans and, 80
    Timur and, 94
geomancy, 97, 166
    Akbar and, 160
    in Ottoman Empire, 124, 152
    sahib-zaman and, 173
    Tahmasp and, 157
gerege (passport), 50
ghaza (holy war), 96, 133
Ghazan Khan, Ilkhanate ruler, 70
Gibbon, Edward, 268
Giray Dynasty, 162, 197, 200
Global Financial Crisis (2008), 237
global historical sociology, 27n93, 43,
        175, 220
global history
    definitions of, 269
    Toynbee on, 259, 261
globalisation, 7, 53
    Chinggisid influence on, 173–4
    Eurasianism and, 174
    history of, 270
    Mongols and, 82, 175
    proto, 11
Gökalp, Ziya, 245, 250

pan-Turanism and, 250–3
    pan-Turkism and, 256
Golden Clan (Altan Uruq), 80
Golden Horde, 53, 68, 190
    conversion to Islam of, 70n103
    decline of, 72
    Muscovy and, 204
    Timur's conquest of, 94
Goldstone, Jack, 258
Great Depression, 265
Great Houses, 32, 75, 165. *See also*
    specific dynasties
    aristocratic networks of, 83
    as Great Powers, 37, 226, 228
    Babur and, 143, 145
    charismatic rulers of, 27
    Chinggisid, 26, 63, 85
    definitions of, 223
    durability of, 76
    Ming, 29, 90, 114
    post-Chinggisid, 86, 90, 93, 211
    rise/fall of, 220, 227, 228
    Safavid, 168
    Sneath on, 60
    Timurid, 29, 90, 115
    universalist ambitions of, 39
    world orders of, 126
Great Mongol People (Yeke Mongol
    Ulus), 62n67, 77
Great Powers, 25, 129, 226
    China as, 240, 242
    Chinggisid Empire as, 81
    Cold War and, 30
    definitions of, 222, 225
    Great Houses as, 37, 226, 228
    hegemonic institutions of, 240
    international orders of, 39, 242
    millenarianism and, 166
    politics of, 225
    post-Chinggisid, 91
    rise/fall of, 36, 128, 217
    structural risks of, 120
Greece
    ancient city states of, 13
    Toynbee on, 259
'groupness', 41, 236, 257
guild networks, 6n11, 18
gunpowder empires, 127
Gürkani. *See* Timur
Gurkhaniyya, 142. *See* Mughal Empire

Gustav I, Swedish king, 202
Güyüg Khan, 66

Habsburg Dynasty, 32, 129, 175–81,
    219
    Süleyman I and, 150
    Tahmasp's alliance with, 180
    Thirty Years War, 208
    Valois rivalry with, 179
Halperin, Charles J., 255
Hanafi law school, 151
Haydar the geomancer, 124
Hayreddin Barbarossa, 179
Hegel, G. W. F., 17n62, 269
Henry VIII, English king, 14, 177, 189
    Ivan IV and, 202
heresy, 155, 187, 190. *See also* religious
    toleration
Herodotus, 268
hierarchy, 81, 90, 102, 221
Hobbes, Thomas, 177, 270
Hodgson, Marshall, 55n25, 127n6, 258
Holy League, 179
Holy Roman Empire, 131, 176, 181.
    See also Charles V
Hong Kong, 14
Hongwu Emperor. *See* Zhu Yuanzhang
Hongzhi Emperor, 114
'horde', 74
Hospitaller Knights, 179
'house society', 76
Hülegü Khan, 66, 67
    Berke and, 69
    Kubilai and, 70
humanism, Renaissance, 182, 188
Humayun, Mughal emperor, 143,
    155
    occult sciences and, 156
Hundred Years War, 88
Hungary, 68, 83
    Magyars of, 251
    Ottoman campaigns against, 180,
    182
    pan-Turanism in, 252, 253
Husayn Bayqara, Timurid ruler, 116

Ibn Battuta, 28, 47, 48, 50, 51–2, 84
Ibn Khaldun, 57, 98, 99
Ibrahim I, Ottoman Sultan, 131n22
İbrahim Pasha (Pargali), 150, 153

Ilkhanate, 53, 69
  Black Death in, 87
  Timurids and, 91
international orders, 217
  as world orders, 10, 22
  IR understanding of, 7, 10
  liberal, 237, 240, 242
  of Great Powers, 39, 242
  of modernity, 244
  post-Chinggisid orders versus, 91
international relations, 6
  Eurasianism in, 128n11
  Eurocentrism in, 174
  global, 128, 272
  institutionalist, 240
  millennial sovereigns and, 174–5
  sovereignty models and, 177
  theories of, 225–9
Iran, 56, 144. *See also* Persia
  messianism in, 144
  Shiitisation of, 189
Isa Kelemechi, 49
Iskandar Sultan, Timurid ruler, 103
Islam, 82, 125
  astrological conjunction of, 166
  demographics of, 132
  Shah Rukh and, 109
  sovereignty model of, 97, 135
  Sunni, 136
Islamic art, 118, 124
  Chinese influences on, 73, 118
  Chinggisid Exchange and, 73
Islamic Millennium (1591), 159, 173,
  182
Ismail, Safavid Shah, 142, 144–6, 175
  as *sahibkıran*, 159
  Babur and, 144, 145
  sacred kingship of, 178
  Selim and, 148
  Sufism and, 144
  Tahmasp and, 157
Italian Renaissance, 2, 117n125,
  188
Ivan III, Russian tsar, 122, 191, 197,
  204
Ivan IV, Russian tsar, 192, 197–202
  as Chinggisid sovereign, 202–4
  astrologer of, 201
  centralisation by, 202
  occult sciences and, 205

Jagiellonian Dynasty, 179n23, 199
Jahan, Safavid shah, 164
Jahangir, Mughal emperor, 143, 164
Jalali rebellions, 169, 209, 210
Jami'-i sultani (Sultanic Compendium),
  103
Jamuqa (Genghis Khan's rival), 61, 62
Janissaries, 140, 147, 168
Japan, 59n41, 70, 101
  colonialism of, 249
  feudalism in, 130
  Genghis Khan legend in, 247
  Kamakura Shogunate in, 88
  Mongol campaigns against, 246
  Onin War in, 122n147
  pan-Asianism of, 249
  Qing Dynasty and, 248
  seventeenth-century crises in, 209
  Tokugawa Shogunate of, 128, 129
Jaqmaq, Mamluk Sultan, 110
Jiajing Emperor (Zhu Houcoung),
  195
Jin/Jurchen Dynasty, 58, 61, 62, 70
  Ögödei's conquest of, 64
Jingtai Emperor (Zhu Qiyu), 114
Jochi Khan, 68
Jochid Khanate. *See* Golden Horde
John III, Portuguese king, 150n121
Jurchens. *See* Jin/Jurchen Dynasty
Juwayn-i, 79

Kabul, 158, 193
Kabul Khan, 62n67
Kandahar, 159, 193
kanun (imperial law), 155
kanunname (law code), 139
Karakorum, 19
Kennedy, Paul, 128–31
Kereyids, 59, 61
Khalil Sultan, Timurid ruler, 103
Khand-Amir, 155
Khitans, 61, 63
Khwarazm, 63, 68
Kipchaks, 63, 67, 68, 190n76. *See also*
  Golden Horde
kiswah, 110
Kitans, 76
Koçi Beg, 169
Korea, 70, 83, 101
  Goryeo dynasty in, 83, 88

Joseon dynasty of, 30, 108, 113, 114, 119, 206n166
  seventeenth-century crises in, 209
  Toyotomi's invasion of, 130
Kubilai Khan, Chinggisid Great Khan, 48, 66, 86, 91, 252
  Hongwu and, 101
  Hülegü and, 70
  successors of, 71
  Tibet and, 70
  Toluid Civil War and, 67, 69, 70
Kulikove Pole, battle of (1381), 72

Lattimore, Owen, 245, 264–6
  Toynbee and, 265
  Wittfogel and, 262
Lewis, Bernard, 172, 235
Li Ta-chao, 246
Lieberman, Victor, 258
Little Ice Age, 34, 88, 120, 169, 170n238, 209, 210, 212. *See also* climate change
Livonia, 198
Livonian Order, 255
Livy (Roman historian), 268
Lord of Conjunction. *See sahibkıran*
loyalty oaths, 61
Lumi, 112
Lütfi Pasa, Ottoman vizier, 169

Macau, 196
macro-history, 42, 220–5, 245–6
  as international relations, 267–72
  criticisms of, 245
  Eurocentrism and, 270
  golden age of, 258
  micro approaches and, 244, 270
  world history and, 258
Magyars, 251
Mahdi (Messiah), 144
Malacca (Malaysia), 105
Mamiya Rinzo, 248
mamluk (slave soldier), 67, 140
Mamluks, 83
  Chinggisid ties of, 84
  Hülegü's defeat by, 66
  Shah Rukh and, 109
Manuel I, Portuguese king, 176
Marj Dabik, battle of (1516), 149
Markos, Rabban, 49

Marx, Karl
  Hegel and, 269
  on China, 263
  on feudalism, 265
  Toynbee and, 258
May, Theresa, 242n
Mayans, 122n147
McCarthy, Joseph, 262, 264
McNeill, William H., 258, 268, 272
  on Toynbee, 261
Medieval Warm Period, 87
Mehmed II, Ottoman Sultan, 14, 135, 140
  centralisation by, 191
  conquest of Constantinople by, 139
  on tanistry, 147
Meisner, Maurice, 263
Melvin-Koushki, Matthew, 82, 175
Merkids, 59
messiah of the End Time (*mehdi-yi ahiru'z-zaman*), 182
messianism
  Süleyman I and, 182
  Tahmasp I and, 157
Miftāh al-jafr al-jāmi' (Key to the Comprehensive Prognostication), 185
millenarianism, 99, 152
  Great Power and, 166
  of Akbar, 159
  of Süleyman I, 154
  Timur and, 98
  world order and, 164–6
millennial sovereigns, 174–5. *See also sahibkıran*
millennialism, 219
  Charles V and, 183
Milward, James, 8
Minamoto no Yochitsune (Gen Gikei), 247
Minamoto no Yoritomo, 247
Ming Dynasty, 194–7, 227
  decline of, 209, 210, 230–7
  divisions of, 114
  founder of, 93, 115
  Great House of, 29, 90, 114
  heavenly mandate of, 104
  IR studies of, 90
  isolationism of, 93, 111–15, 116
  Kennedy on, 128

Ming Dynasty (cont.)
  religious toleration of, 102
  sovereignty notions of, 196
  Spanish trade with, 176
  tanistry and, 103
  treasure voyages of, 30, 101, 106,
    218
  Veritable Records of, 112
  Yuan legacy of, 30, 71, 91, 95
Miyawaka-Okada, Junko, 247–9
Moin, Azfar, 84, 97, 145, 146
Molodi, battle of (1572), 200
Molotov–Ribbentrop pact, 261
Möngke Khan, Chinggisid Great Khan,
  66–7, 69, 71
Möngke-Temür Khan, Golden Horde
  ruler, 70n103
Mongol studies, 57
Mongols, 251. *See also* Chinggisid
  Empire
  globalisation and, 82, 175
  Russia and, 63, 254–6, 262
  Secret History of, 59, 75n122
Monomakh's Cap, 198
Mughal Empire, 32, 133, 143, 213, 227
  decline of, 167, 171
  expansion of, 158
  Kennedy on, 128
  millenarianism of, 152, 219
Muhammad Khodabanda, Safavid
  Shah, 162
Muhammad, Prophet, 14, 97, 135, 160,
  183
  as *sahibkıran*, 99
Muhammad Shah, Mughal emperor,
  167
Muhammad, Sultan, 63
mujaddid (renewer), 108, 151
Murad III, Ottoman Sultan, 161–2
Muscovy, 33, 72, 92, 190–2. *See also*
  Russia
  Chinggisid influence on, 206
  Golden Horde and, 31, 204, 255
  Ivan III and, 122
  Ivan IV and, 197
  Kennedy on, 128
  religious toleration in, 205
  Rurik Dynasty in, 119
  Russian state formation and, 33
  seventeenth-century crises in, 209

  Timurid influences on, 220
  Vasily III and, 197

Nader Shah Afshari, Persian ruler, 34,
  168, 172, 212, 220
Naimans, 59, 61
Napoleon Bonaparte, 168
nationalism, 7n15, 267
  absolutism and, 135n43
  colonialism and, 119n133
  Eurasianism and, 246
  international system and, 11
  myths of, 7
Necipoğlu, Gülru, 139n60, 181n38
Needham, Joseph, 270
neo-Confucianism, 31, 119, 195, 196
Nestorianism, 49
Nevsky, Alexander, 255
nöker, 78
Novgorod, 191, 200, 202, 255

occult sciences, 25, 31, 103, 200. *See*
  also astrology
  Akbar and, 160
  Christian prosecution of, 187
  heavenly mandate and, 109
  Humayun and, 156
  in Ottoman Empire, 152
  Iranian, 166
  Ivan IV and, 205
  Sufism and, 157
  Tahmasp and, 157
Ögödei Khan, Chinggisid Great Khan,
  64–6, 69
Oirats, 113
Ong Khan, 61
Ongguds, 59
Opium War, 9
oprichnina, 199, 201, 205
'orda' (Mongol institution), 74
Orda Khan, Golden Horde ruler, 68
Oriental despotism theory, 130, 135,
  261–3
Osman, House of, 92, 133–5, 137
Ostrowski, Donald, 202n153
Ottoman Empire, 32
  as Ilkhanate vassal, 133
  as Timurid tributary, 109
  bureaucratisation of, 172
  centralisation of, 137–41

Chinggisid legacy of, 83
Crimean Khanate and, 197
decline of, 168–70, 212–14, 230–7
European trade and, 175
Hungarian campaigns of, 180, 182
Kennedy on, 128
longevity of, 133
millenarianism of, 152, 219
millet system in, 9n27
Second Constitutional Era of, 250
Sunnitisation of, 189
Three Pashas' coup in, 251
Timur's conquest of, 94
Turkification of, 250
Oyabe, Mataichiro, 248

pan-Asianism, 249
pan-Islamism, 250
panopticon, 48n1
pan-Slavism, 250
pan-Turanism, 252
    Gökalp and, 250–3
    in Hungary, 252
pan-Turkism, 244, 250–1
    Gökalp and, 252, 256
    origin of, 250
Parameswara, Malaysian king, 105
Pari Khan Khatum, Safavid princess, 162
Parker, Geoffrey, 210, 212
Pax Mongolica, 3, 51, 57
    beneficiaries of, 84
    Black Death and, 73
periodisation bias, 5n7
Persia, 71. *See also* Iran
    kingship models of, 20, 96
    Mongol conquest of, 66
Persian language, 109
Peter I, Russian tsar, 254
Philippines, 176
Philotheos of Pskov, 192
Pir Muhammad, Timurid ruler, 103
plague. *See* Black Death
Poe, Edgar Allen, 89
Poland-Lithuania, 64, 69, 179n23, 198, 203
Polo, Marco, 28, 48, 49, 50, 84
post-Chinggisid world orders, 90–3,
    192. *See also* Ming Dynasty;
    Timurid Empire

post-Timurid world orders, 124–7.
    See also specific ones, e.g. Mughal
    Empire
presentist distortions, 221
primogeniture, 24, 147, 168
Protestant Reformation, 177, 187, 190
Ptolemy, 188

Qanun-e shahanshahi, 156
Qanun-i Humayun, 156
Qara Khitai, 63
Qara Qoyunlu (black sheep) Dynasty,
    109
Qianlong Emperor, 172
Qing Dynasty, 71n108, 93, 212
    Japanese legends of, 248
Qizilbash, 162, 168
Qizilbash taj, 145
Qonggirads, 59
qurultai (assembly of nobles), 62, 80,
    81, 91
    Talas Covenant and, 69
    Toluid Civil War and, 67
    yasa of, 78
qutb (axis mundi), 100, 227
qutb al aqtab (supreme pole), 166

racism, 233, 241
    white supremacist, 241, 251
Rajput confederacy, 142
Red Turban Rebellion (1358), 93
religious toleration, 2, 80
    interfaith heresies and, 190
    Muscovite, 205
    occult sciences and, 187
    of Akbar, 159
    of Ming Dynasty, 102
Renaissance
    Italian, 2, 117n125, 188
    Timurid, 3–4, 116
Renan, Ernest, 252
Ridaniyya, battle of (1516), 149
Roman Empire, 2, 13, 93, 271
    Muscovy and, 192
    sovereignty model of, 175
Romanov dynasty, 209, 212
Rossabi, Morris, 210, 211
Rowe, William T., 264
Rum Seljuk sultanate, 66, 70, 92, 133
Rurik Dynasty, 191, 192, 209

Russia, 56. *See also* Muscovy
  as liminal country, 5
  as modern rising power, 239
  Mongols and, 63, 254–6, 262
  pan-Slavism and, 250
  rise of, 190–2
Russian Eurasianism, 254–6
Russian Orthodox Church, 191n78,
  192
Rustem Mirza, Timurid ruler, 159

sacred kingship, 80
  Ismail and, 178
Safavid Dynasty, 32, 133, 143–6, 155
  decline of, 167
  millenarianism of, 152, 219
  seventeenth-century crises and, 212
  Shiitisation of, 189
sahibkıran (Lord of Conjunction), 26,
  80, 97, 100, 137, 165–6
  Akbar as, 159
  as *qutb*, 227
  centralisation by, 171
  charisma of, 173
  Charles V as, 181–3
  decline of, 166–72
  Ismail as, 159
  Ivan IV as, 201
  post-Timurid empires and, 127
  Süleyman as, 124, 183
  Timur as, 219
sahib-zaman (Last World Emperor),
  124, 152, 173
Saint Bartholomew's Day Massacre
  (1572), 190
Samarkand, 102, 193, 204
  Ismail's campaign against, 145
  Ulugh Beg and, 115
Savitskii, Peter, 254, 255
Schamiloglu, Uli, 134n38
Secret History of the Mongols, 59,
  75n122
Sejong, Joseon king, 113
selection bias, 221
Selim I, Ottoman Sultan, 141, 144,
  146–9
Selim II, Ottoman Sultan, 161
Seljuk Dynasty, 56, 58, 252
Seventeenth-Century General Crisis,
  33, 170n238, 208–10, 220, 229

  impact of, 210–14
Shah Rukh, Timurid ruler, 100, 103,
  108–10, 115, 120
Shahnama-i Ismail, 146
shamans, 80
sharia (Islamic law), 120, 135
  imperial law and, 155
  ulama and, 98, 136
Shaybani Khan, Uzbek ruler, 145, 146
Shaybanids, 126n4, 193
Sher Shah of Sur, 156
Shi'ism, 189
  Abbas I and, 162
  occult sciences and, 157
  Twelver, 163
Siberia, 199, 251, 254
silk roads, 9, 28, 50, 85, 112, 121
  bands on, 212
  Chen Cheng and, 107
  ideational transmission via, 175
  Marco Polo and, 50
  seventeenth-century crises and, 210
  traversing times for, 210
slave trade, 193n93
Sneath, David, 26, 59, 74–6, 223
sociology, historical, 267
soft power, 117
Sokollu Mehmet Pasha, Ottoman
  vizier, 161, 168
Song Dynasty, 58, 64, 67
  conquest of, 70
sovereignty, 10, 221
  as territoriality, 12, 16
  centralisation of, 13–16, 24, 84
  Chinggisid model of, 18–22, 31, 54,
    59, 74, 80–2, 136, 137, 171, 217,
    225
  decentralised, 222n4
  external recognition of, 17–18
  hybrid legitimation of, 96
  interdependence, 12
  Islamic model of, 97, 135
  legitimation of, 81
  millennial, 99
  Ming notions of, 196
  models of, 13, 18
  modern, 11n33, 35
  post-Chinggisid model of, 90
  Roman model of, 175
  sacred kingship and, 178

Timurid model of, 20, 97, 127, 218
treatises on, 156
universal, 20, 32, 86, 140, 151, 213
Vattelian, 12
Westphalian model of, 25, 177
Spengler, Oswald, 260n64, 265
Stalinism, 262
stigmatisation, 231, 233, 236
Stoddard, T. Lothrop, 251, 262
Stoppard, Tom, 272
'strongmen', 238
Subrahmanyam, Sanjay, 132,
    168, 258
Suematsu, Kencho, 245, 246–50, 267
Sufism, 96
    Babur and, 142
    dervishes of, 204
    Iskandar and, 103
    Ismail and, 144
    kingshp and, 96n21
    occult sciences and, 157
    Timur and, 100
Süleyman I, Ottoman Sultan, 149–55,
    165
    as messiah of the End Time, 182
    as *sahibkıran*, 124, 183
    Charles V and, 150, 152, 154n151,
    176, 179–81
    Francis I and, 179–80
    golden helmet of, 180, 184
    millenarianism of, 154
    successors of, 161
Sunnism, 218
    Ottoman, 153, 189
Szapolyai, John, Hungarian king, 180

T'ajeong, Joseon ruler, 108
Tahmasp I, Safavid Shah, 153, 156–8
    Charles V and, 157
    Habsburg alliance with, 180
    occult sciences and, 157
Talas, battle of (751), 55
Talas Covenant, 69
Tamerlane. *See* Timur
Tang Dynasty, 55
Tanguts, 61, 62
tanistry, 24, 60, 81
    Ming Dynasty and, 103
    Muscovy and, 198
    primogeniture versus, 24, 147, 168

Tanzimat (Ottoman reform
    movement), 169
tarikat (religious-military
    brotherhood), 149
Tarmashirin Khan, Chagatai ruler, 72
Tatars, 59, 61, 251
'Tatar Yoke', 203
Temüjin. *See* Genghis Khan
Tengri (heaven), 68n91, 79, 80
Teutonic Knights, 255
Tezcan, Baki, 169
Thatcher, Margaret, 242
Third World, 257
Thirty Years War (1618–48), 208, 219
'Thucydides' Trap', 221
tianxia (all under Heaven), 8
Tibet, 55, 71
Timur, 23
    as *sahibkıran*, 97, 100, 165, 166, 219
    Babur and, 142
    death of, 94
    Genghis Khan and, 94
    Great House of, 29, 90, 115
    marriage of, 96
    rise of, 72
    Sufism and, 100
    Toqtamish Khan and, 204
    Zhu Yuanzhang and, 95–7
Timurid Empire, 227
    Chagatai Khanate and, 73
    decline of, 115–16
    IR studies of, 90
    sovereignty model of, 20, 97, 127,
    218
Timurid Renaissance, 3–4, 116
Toghan Temür, Yuan ruler, 71n108
Tokugawa Shogunate, 128
Tolui Khan, Chinggisid ruler, 69
Toluid Civil War (1260), 67, 69, 70, 86
Tönnies, Ferdinand, 250
Toqtamish Khan, Golden Horde ruler,
    72, 204
Toqto'a-Buqa, puppet Yuan ruler, 113
töre (customary law), 79
Töregene (Ögödei Khan's widow), 66
Toynbee, Arnold J., 224, 245, 258–61,
    266
    Lattimore and, 265
    Marx and, 258
Toyotomi Hideyoshi, 130

transhistoricity, 225
Transoxiana, 55, 63, 69, 193
  messianism in, 144
  Timurids and, 91
  Uzbeks of, 206
'tribal societies', 74
tributary system, Chinese, 8–9, 90, 218,
  271
Trubetskoi, Nikolai, 249, 254, 255
Trump, Donald, 239
Tudor Dynasty, 177
Tulunbay Khatun, Mongol princess, 84
Tumu incident (1449), 112, 113, 114,
  120, 121
Turan, 251, 253. *See also* pan-
  Turanism
Turcomans, 251
Turkestan Liberation Organisation
  (Basmachi), 251
Turkey
  as liminal country, 5
  Eurasianism in, 253
  Toynbee on, 259

Uighurs, 76
ulama (Islamic jurists), 58, 136
  as check on absolutism, 172
  sharia and, 97, 136
Ulugh Beg, Timurid ruler, 103, 115,
  117, 120
ulus, 68, 75n122, 77
Umayyad Caliphate, 136
United Mongol People (Khamag
  Monggol Ulus), 62
unity of history thesis, 260
universal empire, 24, 25, 213
  Braudel on, 184
  Charles V and, 176
  Chinggisid, 221
  conditions for, 93
  Habsburgs and, 179
  legitimacy claims of, 54, 86
  millennial sovereignty and, 164, 173,
    182, 186
  Mughals and, 159, 164
  Ottomans and, 139, 151, 175
  post-Chinggisid, 90, 93
  religious coversions and, 187
  Safavids and, 148
  sahibkıran and, 97, 127, 171

Timurid/Ming, 118
universal peace (*sulh-i kull*), 163
urban planning, 3
Uzbeks, 33, 72, 126n4, 193
  of Transoxiana, 206

Valois Dynasty, 179
Vambery, Arminius, 252
Vasily II, Russian tsar, 197
Vasily III, Russian tsar, 192, 197
Vattelian sovereignty, 12
Vernadsky, George, 245, 254–6
Vietnam War, 231
Vladimir, Grand Prince of Kiev, 198

Wallerstein, Immanuel, 269
Wanli Emperor (Zhu Yijun), 196
'War on Terror', 237
Weber, Max, 16
Western order, end of, 237–43
Westphalian ecumene, 229
Westphalian Peace
  IR origin myth of (1648), 32
Westphalian Peace (1648), 11, 213, 219
  Krasner on, 12
Westphalian sovereignty, 18, 25, 35,
  177
Westphalian System, 225
White Horde, 68
'white man's burden', 172
Wittfogel, Karl, 245, 261–3, 267
  Toynbee and, 259
world conquerors, 20, 26, 80, 165, 218
world history, 267
  macro-history and, 258
  Toynbee on, 258–61
world order, 22–7, 34–42, 217, 220
  builders of, 57
  Chinggisid, 71–3, 81, 82–5, 217, 271
  definitions of, 22, 26, 223
  demographics of, 174
  millenarianism and, 164–6
  of Great Houses, 126
  pluralist, 126
  post-Chinggisid, 90–3, 192
  post-Timurid, 124–7
  regional concerns versus, 214
  rise and fall of, 225–30
  United States and, 73
  universal, 10, 222

World War, the First, 259
World War, the Second, 257, 261, 264, 266

Xi Xia Dynasty, 58, 62
Xiognus, 76
Xuande Emperor, Zhu Zhanji, 110, 111

yam (postal system), 28, 50, 85, 91, 211n183
yasa (Genghis Khan's law), 21, 78, 120, 137
Yesügei (Genghis Khan's father), 60
Yin Qing, 105
Yongle Emperor. *See* Zhu Di
Yuan dynasty, 53, 70, 227
   legacy of, 30, 71, 91, 95

Zafarnama (Book of Conquest), 97
Zheng He, 106

Zhengtong Emperor, Zhu Qizhen, 112
Zhu Di, Yongle Emperor, 89, 103, 104–8, 110, 111
Zhu Hauzhao, Zhengde emperor, 114, 195
Zhu Houcoung, Jiajing emperor, 195
Zhu Qiyu, Jingtai emperor, 114
Zhu Qizhen, Zhengtong emperor, 112
Zhu Youcheng, Hongzhi emperor, 114
Zhu Yuanzhang, Hongwu emperor, 93, 115
   as khan, 101–4
   astronomy and, 102
   Kubilai Khan and, 101
   Timur and, 95–7
Zhu Zhanji, Xuande emperor, 110, 111
Zimbabwe, 122n147
Zoroastrianism, 99
Zuhab, Treaty of (1639), 4

CPSIA information can be obtained
at www.ICGtesting.com
Printed in the USA
LVHW020140010322
712298LV00009B/444